INSIDE MACINTOSH

Devices

Addison-Wesley Publishing Company

Reading, Massachusetts   Menlo Park, California   New York
Don Mills, Ontario   Wokingham, England   Amsterdam   Bonn
Sydney   Singapore   Tokyo   Madrid   San Juan
Paris   Seoul   Milan   Mexico City   Taipei

Every effort has been made to ensure that the information in this manual is accurate. Apple is not responsible for printing or clerical errors.

Apple Computer, Inc.
1 Infinite Loop
Cupertino, CA 95014
408-996-1010

Apple, the Apple logo, APDA, AppleLink, AppleTalk, A/UX, EtherTalk, LaserWriter, Macintosh, MPW, PowerBook, ProDOS, and TokenTalk are trademarks of Apple Computer, Inc., registered in the United States and other countries.

Apple Desktop Bus, Finder, Macintosh Quadra, PowerBook Duo, Power Macintosh, and QuickDraw, are trademarks of Apple Computer, Inc.

Adobe Illustrator, Adobe Photoshop, and PostScript are trademarks of Adobe Systems Incorporated, which may be registered in certain jurisdictions.

America Online is a registered service mark of America Online, Inc.

CompuServe is a registered service mark of CompuServe, Inc.

FrameMaker is a registered trademark of Frame Technology Corporation.

Helvetica and Palatino are registered trademarks of Linotype Company.

Internet is a trademark of Digital Equipment Corporation.

ITC Zapf Dingbats is a registered trademark of International Typeface Corporation.

Motorola is a registered trademark of Motorola Corporation.

NuBus is a trademark of Texas Instruments.

Optrotech is a trademark of Orbotech Corporation.

UNIX is a trademark of UNIX System Laboratories, Inc.

Simultaneously published in the United States and Canada.

ISBN 0-201-62271-8

2 3 4 5 6 7-CRW-9897969594
Second printing, November 1994

The paper used in this book meets the EPA standards for recycled fiber.

Library of Congress Cataloging-in-Publication Data

Inside Macintosh / [Apple Computer, Inc.].
        p.   cm.
    Includes index.
    ISBN 0-201-62271-8
    1. Macintosh (Computer)   2. Device drivers (Computer programs)
I. Apple Computer, Inc.
QA76.8.M3I43   1994
005.7′ 1265—dc20   94-18426
                                                     CIP

Contents

Chapter 2　　　　**Slot Manager**　　2-1

Chapter 4   **SCSI Manager 4.3**   4-1

Chapter 7   Serial Driver   7-1

Glossary

Index

Figures, Tables, and Listings

About This Book

This book, *Inside Macintosh: Devices,* describes the parts of the Macintosh Operating System that allow you to directly control, manage, and communicate with internal and external hardware devices. It contains information you need to know to write applications and device drivers that interface with the Device Manager, Slot Manager, SCSI Manager, SCSI Manager 4.3, ADB Manager, Power Manager, and Serial Driver.

If you are new to programming for Macintosh computers, you should read the book *Inside Macintosh: Overview* for an introduction to general concepts of Macintosh programming. You should also read other books in the *Inside Macintosh* series for specific information about other aspects of the Macintosh Toolbox and the Macintosh Operating System. In particular, to benefit most from this book, you should already be familiar with the run-time environment of Macintosh applications, as described in the two books *Inside Macintosh: Processes* and *Inside Macintosh: Memory.*

Format of a Typical Chapter

Most of the chapters in this book include the following four sections:

- "About the ... Manager." You should read this section for a general understanding of the manager and what tasks you can use it for.

- "Using the ... Manager." This section provides detailed instructions on using the manager. You should read this section if you need to use the services provided by that manager.

- "Reference." This section provides a complete reference to the constants, data structures, and routines provided by the manager. Each routine description also follows a standard format, which presents the routine declaration followed by a description of every parameter of the routine. Some routine descriptions also give additional information, such as circumstances under which you cannot call the routine.

- "Summary." This section provides the C, Pascal, and assembly-language interfaces for the constants, data structures, routines, and result codes associated with the manager.

In addition, most chapters contain additional sections that provide background information about a topic, or advanced information for specific types of programs.

Conventions Used in This Book

Inside Macintosh uses various conventions to present information. Words that require special treatment appear in specific fonts or font styles. Certain information, such as parameter blocks, appears in special formats so that you can scan it quickly.

Special Fonts

All code listings, reserved words, and the names of actual data structures, constants, fields, parameters, and routines are shown in Courier (`this is Courier`).

Words that appear in **boldface** are key terms or concepts and are defined in the glossary at the end of this book.

Types of Notes

There are several types of notes used in *Inside Macintosh*.

Note

A note like this contains information that is interesting but possibly not essential to an understanding of the main text. (An example appears on page 1-27 in the chapter "Device Manager.") ◆

IMPORTANT

A note like this contains information that is essential for an understanding of the main text. (An example appears on page 1-10 in the chapter "Device Manager.") ▲

▲ **WARNING**
Warnings like this indicate potential problems that you should be aware of as you design your application. Failure to heed these warnings could result in system crashes or loss of data. (An example appears on page 1-15 in the chapter "Device Manager.") ▲

Assembly-Language Information

Inside Macintosh provides information about the registers for specific routines like this:

Registers on entry

A0   Contents of register A0 on entry

Registers on exit

D0   Contents of register D0 on exit

In addition, *Inside Macintosh* presents information about the fields of a parameter block in this format:

Parameter block

↔	inAndOut	Handle	Input/output parameter.
←	output1	Ptr	Output parameter.
→	input1	Ptr	Input parameter.
✕	trashed	long	Affected field.

The arrow in the left column indicates whether the field is an input parameter, output parameter, or both. You must supply values for all input parameters and input/output parameters. The routine returns values in output parameters and input/output parameters.

The ✕ symbol designates fields that may be affected by the execution of the routine. Any value you store in one of these affected fields may be lost. Also, the meaning of these fields upon completion of the routine is undefined; your application should not depend on these values.

The second column shows the field name as defined in the MPW C or Pascal interface files; the third column indicates the C or Pascal data type of that field. The fourth column provides a brief description of the use of the field. For a complete description of each field, see the discussion that follows the parameter block or the description of the parameter block in the reference section of the chapter.

Development Environment

The system software routines described in this book are available using C, Pascal, or assembly-language interfaces. How you access these routines depends on the development environment you are using. This book shows the interface to system software routines provided by the Macintosh Programmer's Workshop (MPW).

Code listings in this book show methods of using various routines and illustrate techniques for accomplishing particular tasks. All code listings have been compiled and, in most cases, tested. However, Apple Computer does not intend that you use these code samples in your application.

For More Information

APDA is Apple's worldwide source for hundreds of development tools, technical resources, training products, and information for anyone interested in developing applications on Apple platforms. Customers receive the *APDA Tools Catalog* featuring all current versions of Apple development tools and the most popular third-party development tools. APDA offers convenient payment and shipping options, including site licensing.

To order products or to request a complimentary copy of the *APDA Tools Catalog*, contact

APDA
Apple Computer, Inc.
P.O. Box 319
Buffalo, NY 14207-0319

Telephone	1-800-282-2732 (United States)
	1-800-637-0029 (Canada)
	716-871-6555 (International)
Fax	716-871-6511
AppleLink	APDA
America Online	APDAorder
CompuServe	76666,2405
Internet	APDA@applelink.apple.com

If you provide commercial products and services, call 408-974-4897 for information on the developer support programs available from Apple.

For information on registering signatures, file types, Apple events, and other technical information, contact

Macintosh Developer Technical Support
Apple Computer, Inc.
1 Infinite Loop, M/S 303-2T
Cupertino, CA 95014

Device Manager

Contents

This chapter describes how your application can use the Device Manager to transfer information into and out of a Macintosh computer. The **Device Manager** controls the exchange of information between applications and hardware devices.

This chapter provides a brief introduction to devices and device drivers (the programs that control devices) and then explains how you can use the Device Manager functions to

- open, close, and exchange information with device drivers

- write your own device driver that can communicate with the Device Manager

- provide a user interface for your device driver by making it a Chooser extension or desk accessory.

You should read the sections "About the Device Manager" and "Using the Device Manager" if your application needs to use the Device Manager to communicate with a device driver. Applications often communicate with the Device Manager indirectly, by calling functions of other managers (for example, the File Manager) that use the Device Manager. However, sometimes applications must call Device Manager functions directly.

The sections "Writing a Device Driver," "Writing a Chooser-Compatible Device Driver," and "Writing a Desk Accessory," provide information you'll need if you are writing your own device driver.

If you writing a device driver, you should understand how memory is organized and allocated in Macintosh computers. See *Inside Macintosh: Memory*, for this information. You should also be familiar with resources and how the system searches resource files. You can find this information in the chapter "Resource Manager" in *Inside Macintosh: More Macintosh Toolbox*. If your device driver is to perform background tasks, you'll need to understand how processes are scheduled. *Inside Macintosh: Processes* covers these topics. If your driver will control a hardware device, you should read *Designing Cards and Drivers for the Macintosh Family*, third edition.

Introduction to Devices and Drivers

A **device** is a physical part of the Macintosh, or a piece of external equipment, that can exchange information with applications or with the Macintosh Operating System. Input devices transfer information into the Macintosh, while output devices receive information from the Macintosh. An I/O device can transfer information in either direction.

Devices transfer information in one of two ways. **Character devices** read or write a stream of characters, or bytes, one at a time. Character devices provide sequential access to data—they cannot skip over bytes in the data stream, and cannot go back to pick up bytes that have already passed. The keyboard and the serial ports are examples of character devices.

Block devices read and write blocks of bytes as a group. Disk drives, for example, can read and write blocks of 512 bytes or more. Block devices provide random access to data—they can read or write any block of data on demand.

Device Manager

Devices communicate with applications and with the Operating System through special programs called **device drivers**. A device driver typically controls a specific hardware device, such as a modem, hard disk, or printer. This type of device driver acts as a translator, converting software requests into hardware actions and hardware actions into software results. Figure 1-1 illustrates some of the hardware devices that communicate with the Macintosh through device drivers.

Figure 1-1   Devices and the Macintosh

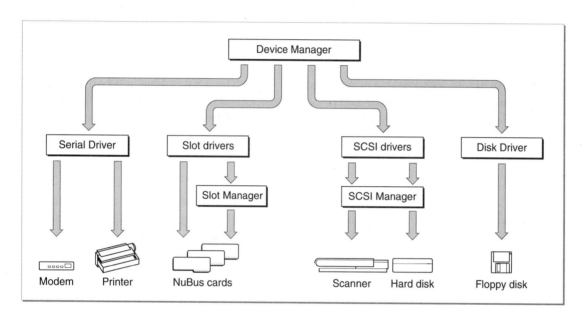

Macintosh device drivers may be either synchronous or asynchronous. A **synchronous device driver** completes a requested transaction before returning control to the Device Manager. An **asynchronous device driver** can initiate a transaction and return control to the Device Manager before the transaction is complete. This type of device driver usually relies on interrupts from a hardware device to regain control of the processor and complete the transaction.

The Macintosh ROM and system software contain device drivers for controlling the standard devices included with every Macintosh computer, such as the mouse, serial ports, and floppy disk drive. Before deciding to write your own device driver, you should consider whether your device can be accessed using one of the standard device drivers. The section "Writing a Device Driver," beginning on page 1-24, discusses the reasons why you may want to use a standard device driver rather than writing your own.

Although device drivers are often used to control hardware, they are not restricted to this function. For example, Macintosh desk accessories and Chooser extensions are small programs that are written as device drivers, even though they may have nothing to do with controlling hardware. In general, a device driver is a program that conforms to a standard interface and provides access to a service through a standard set of routines.

Your program can take advantage of this interface to perform tasks unrelated to actual physical devices.

About the Device Manager

The Device Manager provides a common programming interface for applications and other managers to use when communicating with device drivers. The Device Manager also includes support functions useful for writing your own device drivers.

Typically, your application won't communicate directly with device drivers; instead, it will call Device Manager functions or call the functions of another manager that calls the Device Manager. For example, your application can communicate with a disk driver by calling the Device Manager directly or by calling the File Manager, which calls the Device Manager. Figure 1-2 shows the relationship between applications, the Device Manager, other managers, device drivers, and devices.

Figure 1-2   Communication with devices

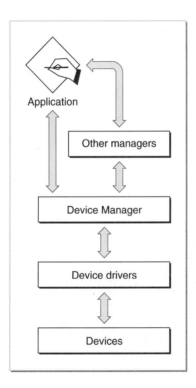

Before the Device Manager allows an application or another manager to communicate with a device driver, the driver must be open, which means the Device Manager has received a request to open the driver, has loaded the driver into memory, if necessary, and has successfully called the driver's open routine.

Your application opens a device driver using one of the Device Manager functions, `OpenDriver`, `OpenSlot`, or `PBOpen`. These functions return a **driver reference number** for the driver. You use the driver reference number to identify the driver in subsequent communication requests.

Your application communicates with a driver by calling Device Manager functions such as `FSRead` or `PBRead`, and supplying the driver reference number of the device. The Device Manager then invokes a corresponding routine in the device driver to perform the requested operation. The section "Driver Routines" on page 1-12 describes these routines and their relationship to the Device Manager functions.

The Device Manager uses several data structures to locate, manage, and communicate with device drivers. These structures are described in the following sections.

The Device Control Entry

The Device Manager maintains a data structure called a **device control entry** (DCE) for each open driver. The device control entry is a relocatable block in the system heap that contains a handle or pointer to the device driver code, and additional information about the driver. Typically, the Device Manager maintains one device control entry for each open device driver, but it is possible for multiple entries to refer to the same driver.

Figure 1-3 shows the device control entry structure. See "Device Manager Reference," beginning on page 1-53, for descriptions of the fields within the device control entry structure.

Figure 1-3   The device control entry

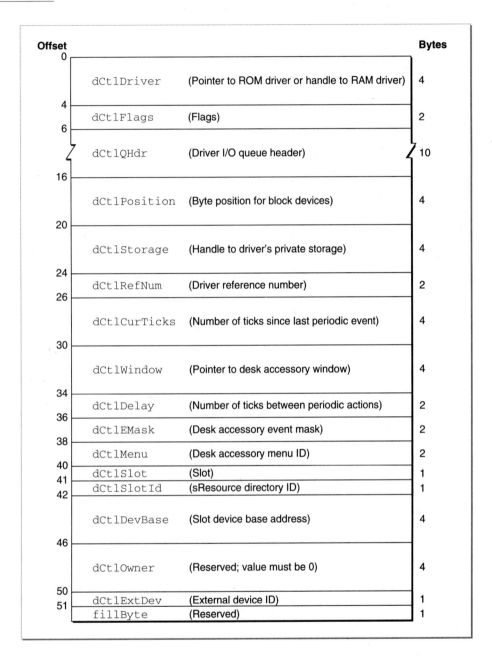

The Unit Table

The Device Manager uses a data structure called the **unit table** to organize and keep track of device control entries. The unit table is a nonrelocatable block in the system heap, containing an array of handles. Each handle points to the device control entry of an installed device driver. The location of a driver's device control entry handle in the unit table is called the driver's **unit number**. If the handle at a given unit number is nil, there is no device control entry installed in that position.

When you open a device driver, the Device Manager returns a driver reference number for the driver. The driver reference number is the one's complement (logical NOT) of the unit number.

The system global variable UTableBase points to the first entry of the unit table. The system global variable UnitNtryCnt contains the size of the unit table (that is, how many handles it can hold). Figure 1-4 shows the organization of the unit table, including the locations of some of the standard device drivers reserved by Apple Computer, Inc.

Figure 1-4   The unit table

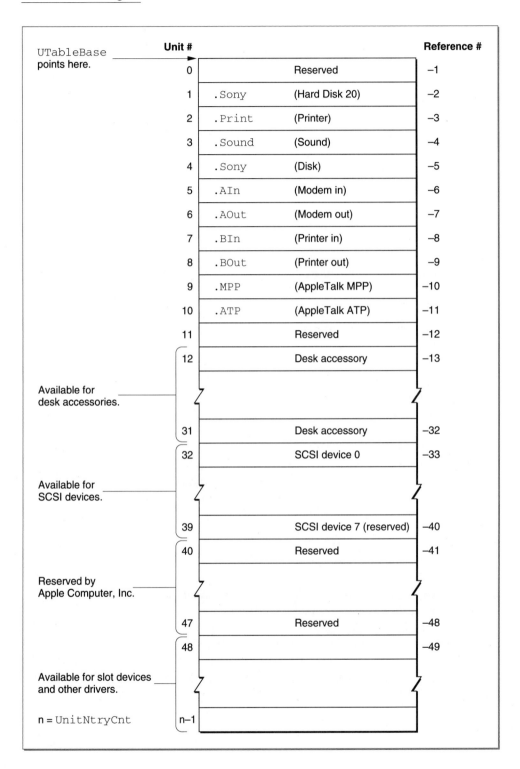

The Driver I/O Queue

The Device Manager maintains an I/O queue for each open device driver. An I/O queue is a standard Macintosh Operating System queue of type `ioQType`, as described in the chapter "Queue Utilities" in *Inside Macintosh: Operating System Utilities*.

At the head of a device driver's I/O queue is the request currently being processed by the driver. The rest of the queue contains pending I/O requests—those the Device Manager has received but not yet sent to the device driver. This queue allows your application to request a data transfer with a busy device and accomplish other tasks while the device processes previous requests.

With respect to the I/O queue, the Device Manager allows you to make three types of requests: asynchronous, synchronous, and immediate.

- **Asynchronous requests.** When you make an asynchronous request, the Device Manager places your request at the end of the driver I/O queue and returns control to your application—potentially before the request is processed. Your application is free to perform other tasks while the device driver processes the requests in its queue. The Device Manager provides mechanisms for your application to determine when the driver has processed the request.

- **Synchronous requests.** When you make a synchronous request, the Device Manager places your request at the end of the queue and waits until the device driver has handled every request in the queue, including the synchronous one, before returning control to your application. Notice there can never be more than one synchronous request in a driver I/O queue at any given time.

- **Immediate requests.** The Device Manager sends immediate requests directly to the device driver, bypassing the queue, and returns control to your application when the request is complete. Because the device driver might be in the middle of processing another request, you must make sure the driver is reentrant before making an immediate request. A **reentrant driver** is capable of handling multiple requests simultaneously. As some device drivers are not reentrant, you should always consult a driver's documentation to determine if it supports immediate requests.

IMPORTANT

The terms *synchronous* and *asynchronous* are used here to describe how the Device Manager queues your I/O requests. How a device driver processes these requests (synchronously or asynchronously) depends on the design of the driver. When you make a synchronous request to a device driver, the Device Manager waits for the driver to complete the request, regardless of whether the driver handles the request synchronously or asynchronously. ▲

Figure 1-5 shows the relationship of the unit table, device control entry, and I/O queue to a device driver.

Figure 1-5   Relationship of the Device Manager data structures

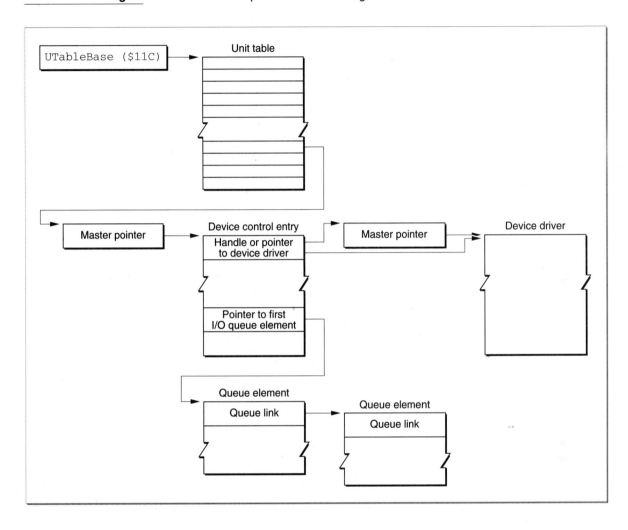

Driver Routines

Every device driver must provide a set of routines for handling requests from the Device Manager. When an application or another manager calls a Device Manager function, the Device Manager invokes one of the following routines in the designated device driver:

- The **open routine** allocates memory and initializes the device driver's data structures. It may also initialize a hardware device or perform any other tasks necessary to make the driver operational. All device drivers must implement an open routine.

- The **close routine** deactivates the device driver, releases any memory allocated by the driver, removes any patches installed by the driver, and performs any other tasks necessary to reverse the actions of the open routine. All drivers must implement a close routine.

- The **control routine** is usually used to send control information to the device driver. The function of this routine is driver-dependent. This routine is optional and need not be implemented.

- The **status routine** is usually used to return status information from the device driver. The function of this routine is driver-dependent. The status routine is optional and need not be implemented.

- The **prime routine** implements the input and output functions of the driver. This routine is optional. If the prime routine is implemented, it must support either read functions or write functions, or both.

Each driver routine is responsible for handling specific types of Device Manager requests. Table 1-1 shows the Device Manager I/O functions and the driver routines responsible for handling them. The Device Manager I/O functions are described in "Using the Device Manager," beginning on page 1-14. The section "Writing a Device Driver," beginning on page 1-24, describes the driver routines.

Table 1-1   Device Manager I/O functions and responsible driver routines

Device Manager function	Responsible driver routine
OpenDriver, PBOpen, OpenSlot	Open
FSRead, PBRead	Prime
FSWrite, PBWrite	Prime
Control, PBControl	Control
Status, PBStatus	Status
KillIO, PBKillIO	Control
CloseDriver, PBClose	Close

Driver Resources

Device drivers are usually stored in driver resources, which can be located in applications, system extension files, or the firmware of expansion cards. A driver resource consists of a header followed by the driver code. The header contains information about the driver such as which driver routines are implemented and where the routines are located within the driver code. The Device Manager copies the relevant information from the header into the device control entry when you open the driver. Figure 1-6 shows the structure of a driver resource. The section "Creating a Driver Resource," beginning on page 1-24, describes driver resources in detail.

Figure 1-6   Structure of a driver resource

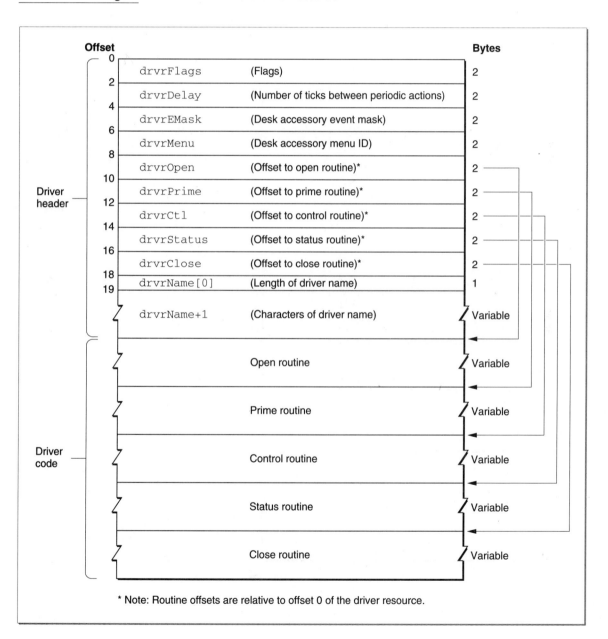

* Note: Routine offsets are relative to offset 0 of the driver resource.

Using the Device Manager

Your application can use Device Manager functions to communicate with devices through their device drivers. This section describes the Device Manager functions that allow you to open, close, and control device drivers, exchange information with them, and monitor their status. The Device Manager also provides support functions useful for writing and installing device drivers. The section "Writing a Device Driver," beginning on page 1-24, describes these support functions.

The Device Manager includes high-level and low-level versions of most of its functions. The high-level versions are somewhat easier to use, but they allow less control of how the Device Manager processes the I/O request (for example, they are always handled synchronously) and they return less information to your application. Conversely, the low-level functions require some additional setup, but they allow you greater control and return more information.

The high-level Device Manager functions call the low-level functions, which in turn call the appropriate driver routine. For example, the Device Manager converts the high-level `FSRead` function to a low-level `PBRead` function before calling the driver's prime routine. Figure 1-7 depicts this hierarchy.

Figure 1-7   Hierarchy of Device Manager functions

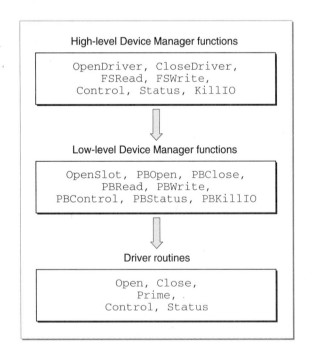

The high-level functions differ in form, but the low-level functions all have the form:

```
pascal OSErr PBRoutineName (ParmBlkPtr paramBlock, Boolean async);
```

The `paramBlock` parameter is a pointer to a structure of type `ParamBlockRec`. You use the fields of this structure to pass more complete information to the driver than you can with high-level functions, and the driver uses the same structure to pass information back. The `ParamBlockRec` is defined in C as a union of six structures, but only the `IOParam` and `CntrlParam` types are used by the Device Manager. Figure 1-8 shows the fields of the `ParamBlockRec` structure used by the Device Manager. These fields are described in detail later in this section and in "Data Structures" on page 1-53.

The `async` parameter specifies whether the Device Manager should process the function asynchronously. For synchronous requests you set this parameter to `false`; the Device Manager adds the parameter block to the driver I/O queue and waits until the driver completes the request (which means it has completed all previously queued requests) before returning control to your application.

▲ **WARNING**
Never call any Device Manager function synchronously at interrupt time. A synchronous request at interrupt time may block other pending I/O requests. Because the device driver cannot begin processing the synchronous request until it completes the other requests in its queue, this situation can cause the Device Manager to loop indefinitely while it waits for the device driver to complete the synchronous request. ▲

If you set the `async` parameter to `true`, the Device Manager adds the parameter block to the driver I/O queue and returns control to your application immediately. In this case, a `noErr` result code signifies that the request was successfully queued, not that the request was successfully completed. The Device Manager sets the `ioResult` field of the parameter block to 1 when the request is queued, and stores the actual result code there when the driver indicates the request is complete.

When you make an asynchronous request you can also provide a pointer to a completion routine in the `ioCompletion` field of the parameter block. The Device Manager executes this routine when the driver completes the asynchronous request. Your completion routine could, for example, set a flag to signal your application that the I/O operation is complete. See "Handling Asynchronous I/O," beginning on page 1-37, for more information about completion routines and asynchronous operation.

Assembly-Language Note
You can call a Device Manager function immediately, bypassing the I/O queue, by setting bit 9 of the trap word. You can set or test this bit using the global constant `noQueueBit`. However, remember that the device driver might be processing another request, especially if you make an immediate request during interrupt time. The driver must be reentrant to handle this situation properly. You should always check a driver's documentation to make sure the driver is reentrant before making immediate requests. ◆

Figure 1-8   Device Manager parameter blocks

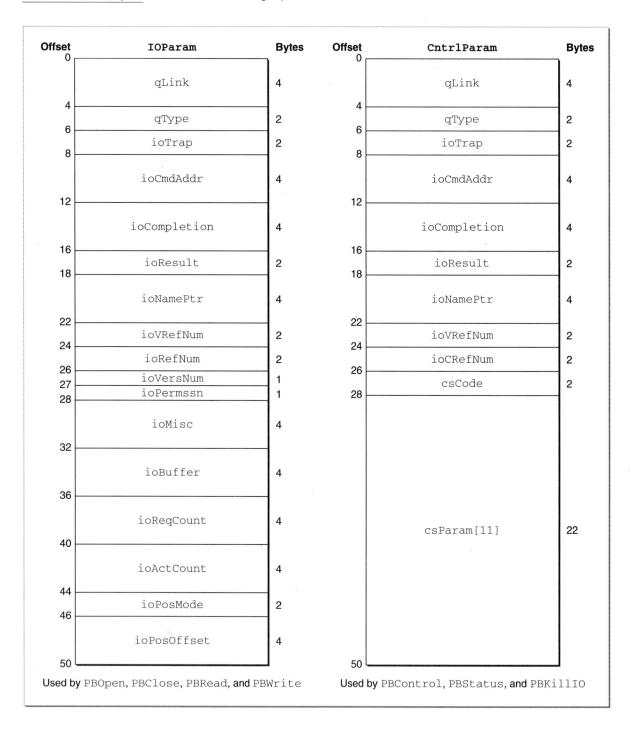

When you use a low-level Device Manager function, the Device Manager places the parameter block at the end of the driver I/O queue and then either waits for the driver to complete the request or returns control to your application, depending on the value of the `async` parameter. For the high-level functions, the Device Manager creates a parameter block for you, filling the required fields with the values you supplied. The Device Manager then inserts the parameter block at the end of the I/O queue as a synchronous request. As previously-queued requests are processed, the parameter block moves forward in the I/O queue. When the parameter block is at the beginning of the queue, the Device Manager calls the appropriate driver routine and passes it a pointer to the parameter block and a pointer to the driver's device control entry.

For read and write requests, the Device Manager calls the driver's prime routine. This routine can execute synchronously, completing the requested read or write transaction before returning control to the Device Manager, or asynchronously, beginning the requested transaction but returning control to the Device Manager before completing it. For information about reading and writing data to devices, see "Communicating With Device Drivers" on page 1-20.

If you are writing a device driver and your driver's prime routine can execute asynchronously, your driver must use some mechanism to regain control of the processor to complete asynchronous requests. Your driver would typically use an interrupt handler for this purpose, and notify the Device Manager when the transaction is complete. See "Writing a Prime Routine" on page 1-33 and "Handling Asynchronous I/O" on page 1-37 for more information about writing asynchronous routines.

The Device Manager handles control and status requests in the same way as read and write requests, except that for control requests it calls the control routine and for status requests it calls the status routine. See "Controlling and Monitoring Device Drivers" on page 1-22 for information about making these requests. For information about providing status and control routines for your own driver, see "Writing Control and Status Routines" on page 1-34.

The Device Manager responds to `KillIO` requests by calling the device driver's control routine with a value of `killCode` for the `csCode` parameter. If the driver returns `noErr`, the Device Manager removes all parameter blocks from the queue, calling their completion routines with the result code `abortErr`. For more information about canceling I/O requests, see the description of the `KillIO` function on page 1-80. For information on how your driver can handle `KillIO` requests, see "Writing Control and Status Routines" on page 1-34.

In response to a close request, the Device Manager waits until the driver is inactive, then calls the driver's close routine. When the driver indicates it has processed the close request, the Device Manager unlocks the driver resource if the `dRAMBased` flag is set, and unlocks the device control entry if the `dNeedLock` flag is not set. The Device Manager does not release the driver resource or dispose of the device control entry unless you call the `DriverRemove` function. The next section describes how to open and close a device driver. See "Writing Open and Close Routines" on page 1-31 for information about how your driver should respond to open and close requests.

Opening and Closing Device Drivers

You must open a driver before your application can communicate with it. The Device Manager provides three functions for opening device drivers: OpenDriver, OpenSlot, and PBOpen. Each of these functions requires a driver name and returns a driver reference number.

A driver name consists of a period (.) followed by any sequence of 1 to 254 printing characters; for example, .ATP is the name of one of the high-level AppleTalk drivers. The initial period in a driver name allows the Device Manager and the File Manager, which share the _Open trap, to distinguish between driver names and filenames. Refer to a device driver's documentation to determine the driver name.

The OpenDriver function, which is the high-level function for opening a device driver, takes the driver name as its first parameter and returns the driver reference number in its second parameter. When an application or another manager calls the OpenDriver function, the Device Manager first searches the unit table to see if a driver with the specified name is already installed. If the name does not match any installed driver, the Device Manager searches the current Resource Manager search path for a driver resource with the specified name.

To open a device driver from a resource, the Device Manager

- creates a device control entry for the driver, filling in the DCE with values from the header of the driver resource
- installs a handle to the device control entry in the unit table at a location determined by the driver resource ID
- calls the driver's open routine

Listing 1-1 shows an application-defined function that uses the OpenDriver function to open a driver.

Listing 1-1   Opening a device driver

```
short     gDrvrRefNum; /* global variable for storing
                          my driver reference number */


OSErr MyOpenDriver(void)
{
    Handle    drvrHdl;
    short     drvrID;
    short     tempDrvrID;
    ResType   drvrType;
    Str255    drvrName;
    OSErr     myErr;

    tempDrvrID = MyFindSpaceInUnitTable(); /* see Listing 1-14 */
```

```
    if (tempDrvrID > 0)
    {
        drvrHdl = GetNamedResource((ResType)'DRVR', "\p.MYDRIVER");
        GetResInfo(drvrHdl, &drvrID, &drvrType, drvrName);
        SetResInfo(drvrHdl, tempDrvrID, drvrName);

        myErr = OpenDriver("\p.MYDRIVER", &gDrvrRefNum);

        if (myErr == noErr)
            DetachResource(drvrHdl);

        drvrHdl = GetNamedResource((ResType)'DRVR', drvrName);
        SetResInfo(drvrHdl, drvrID, drvrName);

        return(myErr);
    }
    else
        return(openErr); /* no space in the unit table */
}
```

The OpenDriver function uses the resource ID of the driver resource as the unit
number for the device driver, which determines where the device control entry will be
stored in the unit table. Because the OpenDriver function does not check to see if
another device control entry is already located at that position in the unit table, the
MyOpenDriver function begins by searching for an available space in the unit table.
Listing 1-14 on page 1-39 shows the MyFindSpaceInUnitTable function.

If there is room in the unit table, the MyOpenDriver function calls GetNamedResource
to load the resource into memory, then changes the ID of the driver resource in the
resource map before calling the OpenDriver function.

After the driver is open, MyOpenDriver calls the DetachResource function to prevent
the driver resource from being released. Finally, MyOpenDriver restores the original
resource ID so that the driver's resource file remains unchanged.

You can use the PBOpen or OpenSlot functions instead of the OpenDriver function
when you want more control over how the Device Manager opens the device driver. For
example, you can set read and write permissions for the device with the ioPermssn
field of the parameter block. Use the OpenSlot function to open drivers that serve slot
devices, and the PBOpen function for all other drivers.

Because the Device Manager always opens device drivers synchronously, you must set
the async parameter to false when using the PBOpen or OpenSlot functions. If a
device driver is already open, the Device Manager simply returns the driver reference
number.

The remaining Device Manager functions require your application to use the driver
reference number, instead of the driver name, when referring to a device driver.

When you finish using a driver, you may want to close it. However, you do not normally close drivers that might be needed by the system or by other applications. Whether you should close a particular driver depends on the type of driver and how it is being used. Refer to the driver's documentation to determine if it should be closed. See the appropriate chapters in this book and other books in the *Inside Macintosh* series for information about standard Macintosh drivers.

If you do want to close a driver, you can use the high-level `CloseDriver` function or the low-level `PBClose` function. Listing 1-2 shows how to use the `PBClose` function to close the driver opened in Listing 1-1.

Listing 1-2   Closing a device driver

```
OSErr MyCloseDriver(short refNum)
{
    IOParam  paramBlock;

    paramBlock.ioRefNum = refNum;

    return(PBClose((ParmBlkPtr)&paramBlock, false));
}
```

The `MyCloseDriver` function specifies the driver to close by placing the driver reference number in the `ioRefNum` field of the parameter block and then calls the Device Manager `PBClose` function.

Communicating With Device Drivers

Once a device driver is open and you have its reference number, you can use Device Manager functions to exchange information with it. When you want to receive information from a device driver, you first allocate a data buffer to hold the information and then call the `FSRead` or `PBRead` function. To send information to a device driver, you first store the information in a data buffer and then call the `FSWrite` or `PBWrite` function. You must specify the number of bytes you want transferred when calling any of these functions.

The `PBRead` and `PBWrite` functions support asynchronous requests, and allow you to specify a completion routine. For block devices you specify the drive number, positioning mode, and positioning offset in the `ioVRefNum`, `ioPosMode`, and `ioPosOffset` fields of the parameter block. The Device Manager does not interpret these fields—they are used by the device driver to locate the desired data block.

The Macintosh Operating System defines three positioning modes for block devices:

■ At the current position. Transfer begins at the current position on the medium—typically where the last transfer ended.

■ Offset from the start. Transfer begins at the specified offset from the beginning of the medium.

■ Offset from the mark. Transfer begins at the specified offset from the current position.

You specify the positioning mode by setting the ioPosMode field to one of the defined constants, fsAtMark, fsFromStart, or fsFromMark. Be sure you specify a mode that is compatible with the device.

On completion, the PBRead and PBWrite functions return in the ioActCount field of the parameter block the total number of bytes actually transferred. For block devices, these functions also return a new positioning offset in the ioPosOffset field.

Certain device drivers provide additional abilities with the read and write functions. For example, the Disk Driver allows you to use the PBRead function to verify that data written to a block device matches the data in memory. To do this, you add the read-verify constant rdVerify to the value in the ioPosMode field of the parameter block, as explained in the description of the PBRead function on page 1-70.

Listing 1-3 shows an example of how to read from a device driver.

Listing 1-3   Reading from a device driver

```
OSErr MyReadFromDriver(short refNum)
{
    IOParam   paramBlock;
    char      buffer[256];

    paramBlock.ioRefNum = refNum;
    paramBlock.ioReqCount = 256;
    paramBlock.ioBuffer = (Ptr)buffer;

    return(PBRead((ParmBlkPtr)&paramBlock, false));
}
```

The MyReadFromDriver function uses a parameter block to specify the device driver (by its driver reference number), the number of bytes to read, and a pointer to a buffer to receive the data. When MyReadFromDriver calls the PBRead function, the Device Manager appends the parameter block to the end of the driver I/O queue. Because the async parameter is set to false, the Device Manager does not return control to MyReadFromDriver until the driver has completed every request in its queue.

Listing 1-4 shows an example of how to write to a device driver.

Listing 1-4   Writing to a device driver

```
OSErr MyWriteToDriver(short refNum)
{
    IOParam   paramBlock;
    char*     buffer;

    buffer = "Data to Write";

    paramBlock.ioCompletion = nil;
    paramBlock.ioRefNum = refNum;
    paramBlock.ioBuffer = (Ptr)buffer;
    paramBlock.ioReqCount = strlen(buffer);

    return(PBWrite((ParmBlkPtr)&paramBlock, false));
}
```

The MyWriteToDriver function also uses a parameter block to transfer information to the driver. After filling in the necessary fields, MyWriteToDriver sends the parameter block to the PBWrite function. Because the async parameter is false, the Device Manager appends the parameter block to the end of the I/O queue and does not return control to the MyWriteToDriver function until the driver has completed the request.

Controlling and Monitoring Device Drivers

In addition to the read and write functions, the Device Manager provides functions that allow your application to control and monitor device drivers in other ways.

The Control and PBControl functions send commands to a driver. Because the types of commands to which drivers respond varies, you need to consult a driver's documentation to determine what commands it accepts. As an example, you can send a command to the Disk Driver requesting that it eject a disk.

The Status and PBStatus functions return status information from a driver. Again, the type of information drivers provide varies widely. The Serial Driver, for example, can return a breakdown of the types of errors that have occurred recently.

The control and status functions use the CntrlParam structure of the ParamBlockRec union. This structure is defined in "Device Manager Parameter Block," beginning on page 1-53.

Because of the diversity of device drivers, the control and status functions have two general-purpose parameters: csCode and csParamPtr (or csParam for the low-level PBControl and PBStatus functions). You indicate the type of control or status information you are requesting by placing a driver-specific code in the csCode parameter. You send or receive information using the csParamPtr parameter.

Listing 1-5 shows an example of how to send control and status requests to a device driver using the PBControl and PBStatus functions.

Listing 1-5   Controlling and monitoring a device driver

```
OSErr MyIssueDriverControl(short refNum)
{
   CntrlParam  paramBlock;

   paramBlock.ioCRefNum = refNum;
   paramBlock.csCode = kClearAll;    /* driver-specific control request */

   return(PBControl((ParmBlkPtr)paramBlock, false));
}

OSErr MyGetDriverStatus(short refNum)
{
   CntrlParam  paramBlock;
   OSErr       myErr;
   short       count;

   paramBlock.ioCRefNum = refNum;
   paramBlock.csCode = kByteCount; /* driver-specific status request */

   myErr = PBStatus((ParmBlkPtr)&paramBlock, false);

   count = paramBlock.csParam[0]; /* value returned in csParam array */
   if (myErr == noErr)
      return(count);
   else
      return(myErr);
}
```

The `MyIssueDriverControl` and `MyGetDriverStatus` functions call the example device driver control and status routines shown in Listing 1-12 on page 1-35 and Listing 1-13 on page 1-36.

The `MyIssueDriverControl` function begins by setting up the fields of a parameter block. The `ioCRefNum` field specifies the driver reference number, and the `csCode` field specifies the type of control information being sent. The `MyDriverControl` function shown in Listing 1-12 interprets the driver-specific value `kClearAll` as a request for the device driver to clear the information in its private storage.

The `MyGetDriverStatus` function also begins by setting up the fields of a parameter block. The `ioCRefNum` field specifies the device driver reference number, and the `csCode` field specifies the type of status information being requested. The `MyDriverStatus` function shown in Listing 1-13 interprets a value of `kByteCount` as a request to return the number of bytes transferred by the last I/O operation. This information is returned in the `csParam` field of the parameter block.

Writing a Device Driver

This section shows you how to write a basic device driver—one that can respond to Device Manager requests. Although you will need to write some assembly-language interface code, you can write your device driver routines in a high-level language.

Before you decide to write your own device driver, you should consider whether your task can be more easily accomplished using one of the standard Macintosh drivers described in this book or other *Inside Macintosh* volumes. In general, you should consider writing a device driver only if your hardware device or system service needs to be accessed at unpredictable times or by more than one application.

For example, if you develop a new output device that you want to make available to any application, you might need to write a custom driver. On the other hand, if your product is a specialized device that can only be used by your application, it may be easier to control the device using private code within your application.

This section describes how to

- create a driver resource

- write the code in your driver resource so that it responds appropriately to Device Manager requests

- handle the special requirements of asynchronous I/O

- install and initialize your driver

Creating a Driver Resource

You will probably want to store your device driver in a driver resource, although if you are writing a driver for a slot device, you might want to store your driver in an sResource data structure in the declaration ROM of the expansion card. See the chapter "Slot Manager" in this book for information about sResource data structures.

Storing your driver in a driver resource allows the Device Manager to load your driver code into memory and install a device control entry for your driver in the unit table. Like all resources, your driver resource has a resource type, a resource ID, a resource name, and resource attributes.

- The resource type must be 'DRVR' if you plan to use the Device Manager to load your driver into memory. If you write your own routine to load the driver, you can choose a different resource type.

- The resource ID determines where in the unit table the Device Manager installs the driver's device control entry. Because you must choose the resource ID when creating your driver resource, you cannot know which unit numbers are available until you open your driver. Therefore, your driver-opening routine must find an empty location in the unit table and change the resource ID accordingly. "Installing a Device Driver" on page 1-38 discusses appropriate values for the resource ID.

■ The resource name should be the same as the driver name because the Device Manager calls `GetNamedResource` using this name if it can't find the driver in the unit table. A driver name consists of a period (.) followed by any sequence of 1 to 255 printing characters. The Device Manager ignores case (but not diacritical marks) when comparing names.

■ The resource attributes of your driver resource depend on your driver. A typical driver might have these attributes: locked, since most drivers contain code that is called at interrupt time; in the system heap, so that the driver exists over launches of applications; and preloaded, which makes resource loading slightly more efficient.

A driver resource has two parts:

■ a driver header that contains information about the driver

■ the routines that do the work of the driver

The driver header contains a few words of flags and other data, offsets to the driver's routines, and an optional driver name. Figure 1-9 shows the format of a driver header.

Figure 1-9   The driver header

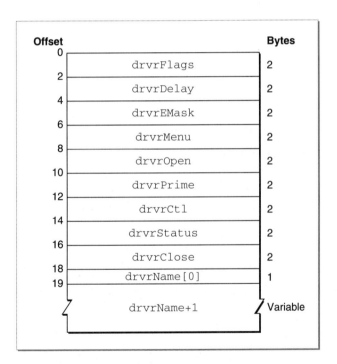

The elements of the driver header are:

Element	Description
`drvrFlags`	Flags in the high-order byte of this field specify certain characteristics of the driver. These flags are copied to the high-order byte of the `dCtlFlags` field of the device control entry when the

driver is opened. You can use the constants shown in Listing 1-6 to set or test the flags in this field.

Name	Bit	Meaning
dReadEnable	8	Set if the driver can respond to read requests.
dWritEnable	9	Set if the driver can respond to write requests.
dCtlEnable	10	Set if the driver can respond to control requests.
dStatEnable	11	Set if the driver can respond to status requests.
dNeedGoodbye	12	Set if the driver needs to be called before the application heap is reinitialized.
dNeedTime	13	Set if the driver needs time for performing periodic tasks.
dNeedLock	14	Set if the driver needs to be locked in memory as soon as it is opened.

drvrDelay	If the dNeedTime flag is set, this field contains the requested number of ticks between periodic actions. This value is approximate and should not be used as a timing reference.
drvrEMask	Used only by desk accessories, this field contains an event mask. See "Writing a Desk Accessory" on page 1-49 for information about this field.
drvrMenu	Used only by desk accessories, this field contains a menu ID. See "Writing a Desk Accessory" on page 1-49 for more information.
drvrOpen	The offset of the driver's open routine, relative to offset 0 of the driver header.
drvrPrime	The offset of the driver's prime routine.
drvrCtl	The offset of the driver's control routine.
drvrStatus	The offset of the driver's status routine.
drvrClose	The offset of the driver's close routine.
drvrName	A Pascal string containing the driver's name, up to 255 characters.

See the section "Entering and Exiting From Driver Routines" on page 1-29 for more information about the routine offsets.

Note

Your driver routines, which follow the driver header, must be aligned on a word boundary. ◆

Listing 1-6   Driver flag constants

```
enum {
    /* flags used in the driver header and device control entry */
    dNeedLockMask     = 0x4000, /* set if driver must be locked in memory as
                                   soon as it's opened */
    dNeedTimeMask     = 0x2000, /* set if driver needs time for performing
                                   periodic tasks */
    dNeedGoodByeMask  = 0x1000, /* set if driver needs to be called before the
                                   application heap is initialized */
    dStatEnableMask   = 0x0800, /* set if driver responds to status requests */
    dCtlEnableMask    = 0x0400, /* set if driver responds to control requests*/
    dWritEnableMask   = 0x0200, /* set if driver responds to write requests */
    dReadEnableMask   = 0x0100, /* set if driver responds to read requests */
};
```

The dReadEnable, dWritEnable, dCtlEnable, and dStatEnable flags indicate which Device Manager requests the device driver can respond to. The next section, "Responding to the Device Manager," describes these routines in detail.

Drivers in the application heap are lost when the heap is reinitialized. If you set the dNeedGoodbye flag, the Device Manager calls your driver before the heap is reinitialized so that you can perform any clean-up actions. See "Writing Control and Status Routines," beginning on page 1-34, for information about using this flag.

You set the dNeedTime flag if your device driver needs to perform some action periodically. For example, a network driver may want to poll its input buffer every 5 seconds to see if it has received any messages. The value of the drvrDelay field indicates how many ticks should pass between periodic actions. For example, a value of 0 in the drvrDelay field indicates that the action should happen as often as possible, a value of 1 means it should happen every sixtieth of a second, a value of 2 means at most every thirtieth of a second, and so on. Whether the action actually occurs this frequently depends on how often an application calls WaitNextEvent or SystemTask. See "Writing Control and Status Routines," beginning on page 1-34, for information about using this flag.

Note

If you do not want your driver to depend on applications to call WaitNextEvent or SystemTask, you can perform actions periodically by installing a VBL task, a Deferred Task Manager task, a Time Manager task, or a Notification Manager task. For more information, see *Inside Macintosh: Processes*. ◆

You need to set the dNeedLock flag if your device driver's code must be locked in memory. In particular, you need to set this flag in these two cases:

■ If any part of your driver's code can be called at interrupt time. Because the Operating System may perform memory management at interrupt time, your driver must be locked to prevent it from being moved.

■ If your driver provides the Operating System with a pointer to any part of its code. For example, if your driver uses the Device Manager to call another driver, you might provide the Device Manager with a pointer to a completion routine. If that completion routine is in your driver code, your driver code must be locked. Otherwise, that pointer might not be valid when the Device Manager calls the completion routine.

You can create your driver header in these ways:

■ You can use a resource compiler. See "Resources" on page 1-89 for the Rez format of the driver resource.

■ You can use the DC instruction, as shown in Listing 1-7, to position the header information directly in your assembly language code.

Listing 1-7   An assembly-language driver header

```
DHeader
DFlags    DC.W   0                        ;set by MyDriverOpen
DDelay    DC.W   0                        ;none
DEMask    DC.W   0                        ;DA event mask
DMenu     DC.W   0                        ;no menu
          DC.W   DOpen - DHeader    ;offset to Open
          DC.W   DPrime - DHeader   ;offset to Prime
          DC.W   DControl - DHeader ;offset to Control
          DC.W   DStatus - DHeader  ;offset to Status
          DC.W   DClose - DHeader   ;offset to Close
Name      DC.B   '.MYDRIVER'        ;driver name
          ALIGN 2                        ;word alignment
```

In this example, the drvrFlags word is cleared to 0 because the flags are set by the MyDriverOpen function, shown in Listing 1-9 on page 1-32. This is an implementation decision—you can set the flags in the driver header or in your driver's open routine. The drvrDelay field is set to 0 because this driver does not perform any periodic actions using the SystemTask function. The drvrEMask and drvrMenu fields are set to 0, as this driver is not a desk accessory. The next five fields contain offsets to the driver routines, defined in the next section, "Responding to the Device Manager." The header ends with the driver name and the word alignment directive.

Responding to the Device Manager

The Device Manager calls a driver routine by setting up registers and jumping to the address indicated by the routine's offset in the driver header.

■ Register A0 contains a pointer to the parameter block.

■ Register A1 contains a pointer to the driver's device control entry.

This interface requires you to use some assembly language when writing a driver. However, you can write your driver routines in a high-level language if you provide an assembly-language dispatching mechanism that acts as an interface between the Device Manager and your driver routines.

The next few sections discuss how you can provide a dispatching routine and how you can implement your driver routines in a high-level language.

Entering and Exiting From Driver Routines

Listing 1-8 shows an assembly-language dispatching routine that you can use as an interface between the Device Manager and your high-level language driver routines. This example properly handles synchronous, asynchronous, and immediate requests, as well as the special cases of open, close, and KillIO.

Listing 1-8   An assembly-language dispatching routine

```
DOpen
      MOVEM.L   A0-A1,-(SP)      ;save ParmBlkPtr, DCtlPtr across function call
      MOVEM.L   A0-A1,-(SP)      ;push ParmBlkPtr, DCtlPtr for C
      BSR       MyDriverOpen     ;call linked C function
      ADDQ      #8,SP            ;clean up the stack
      MOVEM.L   (SP)+,A0-A1      ;restore ParmBlkPtr, DCtlPtr
      RTS                        ;open is always immediate, must return via RTS


DPrime
      MOVEM.L   A0-A1,-(SP)      ;save ParmBlkPtr, DCtlPtr across function call
      MOVEM.L   A0-A1,-(SP)      ;push ParmBlkPtr, DCtlPtr for C
      BSR       MyDriverPrime    ;call linked C function
      ADDQ      #8,SP            ;clean up the stack
      MOVEM.L   (SP)+,A0-A1      ;restore ParmBlkPtr, DCtlPtr
      BRA.B     IOReturn


DControl
      MOVEM.L   A0-A1,-(SP)      ;save ParmBlkPtr, DCtlPtr across function call
      MOVEM.L   A0-A1,-(SP)      ;push ParmBlkPtr, DCtlPtr for C
      BSR       MyDriverControl  ;call linked C function
      ADDQ      #8,SP            ;clean up the stack
      MOVEM.L   (SP)+,A0-A1      ;restore ParmBlkPtr, DCtlPtr
      CMPI.W    #killCode,csCode(A0) ;test for KillIO call (special case)
      BNE.B     IOReturn
      RTS                        ;KillIO must always return via RTS


DStatus
      MOVEM.L   A0-A1,-(SP)      ;save ParmBlkPtr, DCtlPtr across function call
      MOVEM.L   A0-A1,-(SP)      ;push ParmBlkPtr, DCtlPtr for C
```

```
        BSR         MyDriverStatus  ;call linked C function
        ADDQ        #8,SP           ;clean up the stack
        MOVEM.L     (SP)+,A0-A1     ;restore ParmBlkPtr, DCtlPtr


IOReturn
        MOVE.W      ioTrap(A0),D1
        BTST        #noQueueBit,D1  ;immediate calls are not queued, and must RTS
        BEQ.B       @Queued         ;branch if queued


@NotQueued
        TST.W       D0              ;test asynchronous return result
        BLE.B       @ImmedRTS       ;result must be ≤0
        CLR.W       D0              ;"in progress" result (> 0) not passed back


@ImmedRTS
        MOVE.W      D0,ioResult(A0)   ;for immediate calls you must explicitly
                                      ; place the result in the ioResult field

        RTS


@Queued
        TST.W       D0              ;test asynchronous return result
        BLE.B       @MyIODone       ;I/O is complete if result ≤ 0
        CLR.W       D0              ;"in progress" result (> 0) not passed back
        RTS


@MyIODone
        MOVE.L      JIODone,-(SP)   ;push IODone jump vector onto stack
        RTS


DClose
        MOVEM.L     A0-A1,-(SP)     ;save ParmBlkPtr, DCtlPtr across function call
        MOVEM.L     A0-A1,-(SP)     ;push ParmBlkPtr, DCtlPtr for C
        BSR         MyDriverClose   ;call linked C function
        ADDQ        #8,SP           ;clean up the stack
        MOVEM.L     (SP)+,A0-A1     ;restore ParmBlkPtr, DCtlPtr
        RTS                         ;close is always immediate, must return via RTS
```

In this example, DOpen, DPrime, DControl, DStatus, and DClose are the five entry
points that the Device Manager locates using the offsets defined in the driver header.
These in turn call the actual driver routines, which are written in C. The C functions
return a result code if the I/O completed, or a positive value (usually 1) if the I/O is
being handled asynchronously.

When the driver routine returns, the dispatching routine removes the parameters from the stack, restores the A0 and A1 registers, and then returns control to the Device Manager in one of two ways:

■ Calling the IODone routine. This routine, described in detail on page 1-87, indicates to the Device Manager that the request is complete. The Device Manager removes the request from the I/O queue and calls the completion routine, if any. This is the normal method of returning from driver prime, control, and status routines.

■ Returning with an RTS instruction. Use this method when you do not want the Device Manager to remove the request from the I/O queue. There are three cases where the RTS instruction should be used:

  □ Returning from an asynchronous request that is not yet complete. After your device driver begins an asynchronous operation, it should return control to the Device Manager with an RTS instruction. The device driver can regain control of the processor using an interrupt handler, VBL task, or other method, and jump to IODone when the request is complete.

  □ Returning from an immediate request. Because the Device Manager does not queue immediate requests, they should always return with an RTS instruction.

  □ Returning from open, close, and KillIO requests. These requests are never queued and should always return with an RTS instruction.

To use this dispatching routine you would place it after the driver header in your assembly-language source file, and link it to your C-language driver routines. Listing 1-7 on page 1-28 shows the driver header. Sample driver routines are presented in the following sections.

Writing Open and Close Routines

You must provide both an open routine and a close routine for your device driver. The open routine should allocate any private storage your driver requires and place a handle to this storage in the dCtlStorage field of the device control entry. After allocating memory, the open routine should perform any other preparation required by your driver.

If your open routine installs an interrupt handler, you may want to store a pointer to the device control entry in private storage where it will be available for the interrupt handler. The section "Handling Asynchronous I/O" on page 1-37 discusses interrupt handling in more detail.

Listing 1-9 shows a sample open routine, MyDriverOpen. This function begins by checking whether the driver is already open (by examining the contents of the dCtlStorage field of the device control entry). If the driver is not already open, the MyDriverOpen function sets the appropriate flags in the device control entry and allocates memory in the system heap for private storage. The private storage of the driver in this example contains two fields, byteCount and lastErr, which store information about the last I/O function. The prime, control, and status routines described in the following sections use these fields.

If the MyDriverOpen function fails to allocate memory for private storage, it returns the openErr result code, which notifies the Device Manager that the driver did not open.

Device Manager

Listing 1-9   Example driver open routine

```
struct MyDriverGlobals {
    short      byteCount;
    short      lastErr;
};
typedef struct MyDriverGlobals MyDriverGlobals;
typedef struct MyDriverGlobals *MyDriverGlobalsPtr, **MyDriverGlobalsHdl;

OSErr MyDriverOpen(IOParamPtr pb, DCtlPtr dce)
{
    if (dce->dCtlStorage == nil)
    {
        /* set up flags in the device control entry */
        dce->dCtlFlags |= (dCtlEnableMask | dStatEnableMask | dWritEnableMask |
                           dReadEnableMask | dNeedLockMask | dRAMBasedMask );

        /* initialize dCtlStorage */
        dce->dCtlStorage = NewHandleSysClear(sizeof(MyDriverGlobals));
        if (dce->dCtlStorage == nil)
            return(openErr);
        else
            return(noErr);
    }
    else
    {
        /* the driver is already open */
        return(noErr);
    }
}
```

The close routine must reverse the effects of the open routine by releasing any memory allocated by the driver, removing interrupt handlers, removing any VBL or Time Manager tasks, and replacing changed interrupt vectors. If the close routine cannot complete the close request, it should return the `closErr` result code and the driver should continue to operate normally.

The Device Manager does not dispose of the device control entry when a driver is closed. If you want to save any information about the operational state of the driver until the next time the driver is opened, you can store a handle to the information in the `dCtlStorage` field of the device control entry.

Listing 1-10 shows a sample close routine, `MyDriverClose`. Because this device driver does not need to store any information until the next time it is opened, the `MyDriverClose` function disposes of the private storage allocated by `MyDriverOpen`.

Listing 1-10   Example driver close routine

```
OSErr MyDriverClose(IOParamPtr pb, DCtlPtr dce)
{
   if (dce->dCtlStorage != nil)
   {
      DisposeHandle(dce->dCtlStorage);
      dce->dCtlStorage = nil;
   }
   return(noErr);
}
```

Writing a Prime Routine

The prime routine implements I/O requests. You can write your prime routine to execute synchronously or asynchronously. While a synchronous prime routine completes an entire I/O request before returning to the Device Manager, an asynchronous prime routine can begin an I/O transaction but return to the Device Manager before the request is complete. In this case, the I/O request continues to be executed, typically when more data is available, by other routines such as interrupt handlers or completion routines. "Handling Asynchronous I/O" on page 1-37 discusses how to complete an asynchronous prime routine.

The Device Manager indicates whether it is requesting a read or a write operation by placing one of the following constants in the low-order byte of the `ioTrap` field of the parameter block:

```
enum {
   aRdCmd   = 2,   /* read operation requested */
   aWrCmd   = 3    /* write operation requested */
};
```

The Device Manager includes two routines, `Fetch` and `Stash`, that provide low-level support for reading and writing characters to and from data buffers. Use of these routines is optional. "Writing and Installing Device Drivers," beginning on page 1-82, describes these functions.

The `Fetch` and `Stash` routines update the `ioActCount` field of the parameter block. If you do not use these routines, you are responsible for updating this field.

If your driver serves a block device, you should update the `dCtlPosition` field of the device control entry.

Listing 1-11 shows a sample prime routine. This routine determines whether a read or write operation is being requested, then calls the appropriate function. The reading and writing functions, which are not shown here, would transfer the data to or from the hardware device.

Listing 1-11   Example driver prime routine

```
OSErr MyDriverPrime(IOParamPtr pb, DCtlPtr dce)
{
    MyDriverGlobalsHdl    dStore;
    short                 callType;
    long                  numBytes;
    short                 myErr;

    dStore = (MyDriverGlobalsHdl)dce->dCtlStorage;
    numBytes = pb->ioReqCount;
    callType = 0x00ff & pb->ioTrap; /* get the low byte */
    switch (callType)
    {
        case aRdCmd:
            myErr = MyReadBytes(pb->ioBuffer, numBytes);
            break;
        case aWrCmd:
            myErr = MyWriteBytes(pb->ioBuffer, numBytes);
            break;
    }
    (*dStore)->byteCount = numBytes; /* save in private storage */
    (*dStore)->lastErr = myErr;
    pb->ioActCount = numBytes; /* update parameter block field */
    return(myErr);
}
```

After obtaining a handle to the device driver's private storage from the dCtlStorage field of the device control entry, the MyDriverPrime function examines the low-order byte of the ioTrap field of the parameter block to determine whether the Device Manager is requesting a read operation or a write operation. MyDriverPrime then calls either the MyReadBytes or MyWriteBytes function to move the requested number of bytes to or from the buffer designated by the parameter block.

The MyDriverPrime function stores the result code and byte count in its private storage. These values will be used by the example control and status routines described in the next section. Finally, MyDriverPrime updates the ioActCount field of the parameter block and returns the result code.

Writing Control and Status Routines

Control and status routines are usually used to send and receive driver-specific information. However, you can use these routines for any kind of data transfer as long as you implement the minimum functionality described in this section. Like the prime routine, the control and status routines that you write can execute synchronously or asynchronously.

The Device Manager passes information to the control routine in the csCode and csParam fields of the parameter block. The csCode field specifies the type of control request and the csParam field contains any additional information. The csCode values -32767 through 127 are reserved by Apple Computer, Inc. Within this range, the following constant values are defined for use by all device drivers:

Constant name	Value	Meaning
killCode	1	KillIO requested
goodbye	–1	Heap being reinitialized
accRun	65	Time for periodic action

When the Device Manager receives a KillIO request, it removes every parameter block from the driver I/O queue. If your driver responds to any requests asynchronously, the part of your driver that completes asynchronous requests (for example, an interrupt handler) might expect the parameter block for the pending request to be at the head of the queue. The Device Manager notifies your driver of KillIO requests so that it can take the appropriate actions to stop work on the pending request. Your driver must return control to the Device Manager by means of an RTS instruction and not by jumping to the IODone routine.

If you set the dNeedGoodbye flag in the drvrFlags field of the driver header (or the dCtlFlags field of the device control entry), the Device Manager will call your control routine with the value goodbye in the csCode parameter before the heap is reinitialized. You driver can respond by performing any clean-up actions necessary before heap reinitialization.

If you set the dNeedTime flag in the drvrFlags field of the driver header (or the dCtlFlags field of the device control entry), the Event Manager will periodically call your control routine with the value accRun in the csCode parameter. Because these calls are immediate, your driver must be reentrant to handle them properly. For more information about the dNeedTime flag and periodic actions, see the description of the driver header, beginning on page 1-25.

Your control routine must return the controlErr result code for any csCode values that are not supported. You can define driver-specific csCode values if necessary, as long as they are outside the range reserved by Apple Computer, Inc.

Listing 1-12 shows a sample control routine, MyDriverControl. This function interprets the driver-specific csCode value of kClearAll as a command to clear the information saved in the driver's private storage by the MyDriverPrime routine.

Listing 1-12   Example driver control routine

```
OSErr MyDriverControl(CntrlParamPtr pb, DCtlPtr dce)
{
    MyDriverGlobalsHdl    dStore;

    dStore = (MyDriverGlobalsHdl)dce->dCtlStorage;
```

```
    switch (pb->csCode)
    {
       case kClearAll:
          (*dStore)->byteCount = 0;
          (*dStore)->lastErr = 0;
          return(noErr);
       default: /* always return controlErr for unknown csCode */
          return(controlErr);
    }
}
```

Your status routine should work in a similar manner. The Device Manager uses the csCode field to specify the type of status information requested. The status routine should respond to whatever requests are appropriate for your driver and return the error code statusErr for any unsupported csCode value.

The Device Manager interprets a status request with a csCode value of 1 as a special case. When the Device Manager receives such a status request, it returns a handle to the driver's device control entry. Your driver's status routine never sees this request.

Listing 1-13 shows a sample status routine, MyDriverStatus, that implements two driver-specific status requests, kByteCount and kLastErr. When MyDriverStatus receives one of these requests, it returns the byte count or error code values saved in private storage by the MyDriverPrime routine. MyDriverStatus returns this information in the csParam field.

Listing 1-13   Example driver status routine

```
OSErr MyDriverStatus(CntrlParamPtr pb, DCtlPtr dce)
{
    MyDriverGlobalsHdl    dStore;

    dStore = (MyDriverGlobalsHdl)dce->dCtlStorage;
    switch (pb->csCode)
    {
       case kByteCount:
          pb->csParam[0] = (*dStore)->byteCount;
          return(noErr);
       case kLastErr:
          pb->csParam[0] = (*dStore)->lastErr;
          return(noErr);
       default: /* always return statusErr for unknown csCode */
          return(statusErr);
    }
}
```

Handling Asynchronous I/O

If you design any of your driver routines to execute asynchronously, you must provide a mechanism for your driver to complete the requests. Some examples of routines that you might use are:

- Completion routines. Your driver routine could call another driver to start the data transfer. In this case, you can provide that driver with a completion routine. When the other driver completes the request, the Device Manager executes the completion routine. In the completion routine, you could call the other driver again to execute the next part of the I/O operation. When the entire operation is complete, the completion routine should return by calling the `IODone` routine.

- Interrupt handlers. If your driver serves a hardware device that generates interrupts, you can create an interrupt handler that responds to these interrupts. Your interrupt handler must clear the source of the interrupt and return as quickly as possible, while preserving all registers other than D0 through D3 and A0 through A3. For more information about interrupts and how to install an interrupt handler, see *Inside Macintosh: Processes* and *Designing Cards and Drivers for the Macintosh Family*, third edition.

- VBL, Time Manager, and Deferred Task Manager tasks. Installing any of these tasks ensures that your driver receives system time at some point in the future. During this time, you can check to see if the I/O operation is ready to continue.

If your driver serves a device on a NuBus™ expansion card, you might want to use slot interrupts to signal your driver. When a NuBus card device signals a slot interrupt, the CPU can quickly detect which card requested the interrupt service, but not which device on the card. To determine which device caused the interrupt, the system uses a polling procedure. Your driver should provide a polling routine that checks if the device it serves caused the current interrupt, and if so, calls the proper driver routine to handle the interrupt. The Slot Manager maintains a queue of these polling routines for each slot. Your driver can install an element in this queue using the Slot Manager function `SIntInstall`. You can remove a queue element with the `SIntRemove` function. See the chapter "Slot Manager" in this book for information about these functions.

You should observe these guidelines when writing or using asynchronous routines:

- Once you pass a parameter block to an asynchronous routine it is out of your control. You should not examine or change the parameter block until your completion routine is called because you have no way of knowing the state of the parameter block.

- Do not dispose of or reuse a parameter block until the asynchronous request is completed. For example, if you declare the parameter block as a local variable, your function cannot return until the request is complete because local variables are allocated on the stack and released when a function returns.

- Use a completion routine to determine when an asynchronous routine has completed, rather than polling the `ioResult` field of the parameter block. Polling the `ioResult` field is not efficient and defeats the purpose of asynchronous operation.

Installing a Device Driver

There are a variety of ways to install a device driver, depending on where the driver code is stored and how much control you want over the installation process.

- You can store the device driver in a resource within an application and have the application install the driver.

- You can store the device driver, and the code to install it, in a system extension file. See the chapter "Start Manager" in *Inside Macintosh: Operating System Utilities* for information about creating system extensions.

- You can store the device driver in the declaration ROM of an expansion card. Slot device drivers can be designed to load automatically at startup, or you can use the Slot Manager SGetDriver function to load the driver into memory. Refer to *Designing Cards and Drivers for the Macintosh Family*, third edition, for information about writing and installing slot device drivers.

If you store your driver in a resource of type 'DRVR' you can use the OpenDriver or PBOpen functions to install and open your driver. If you need more control over the installation process, you can use the DriverInstall function to create the device control entry and add it to the unit table, or you can create the device control entry yourself, install it in the unit table, and then use OpenDriver or PBOpen to open the driver. If the driver is already installed in the unit table, OpenDriver and PBOpen simply call the driver's open routine and return the driver reference number.

If you want to use the OpenDriver function to install your driver, you are responsible for examining the unit table and changing your driver resource ID so that the OpenDriver function installs your driver in an empty location in the unit table. If the handle at a given unit number is nil, there is no device control entry installed in that position. You can install your device control entry in any empty location in the unit table that is not listed as reserved by Apple Computer, Inc. Table 1-2 summarizes the unit numbers reserved for specific purposes.

Table 1-2   Reserved unit numbers

Unit number range	Reference number range	Purpose
0 through 11	–1 through –12	Reserved for serial, disk, AppleTalk, printer, and other drivers
12 through 31	–13 through –32	Available for desk accessories
32 through 38	–33 through –39	Available for SCSI devices
39 through 47	–40 through –48	Reserved
48 through 127	–49 through –128	Available for slot and other drivers

Listing 1-14 shows a method of searching the unit table for an appropriate location to install your driver. The MyOpenDriver function in Listing 1-1 on page 1-18 calls this function and then uses the OpenDriver function to install and open the device driver.

Listing 1-14   Finding space in the unit table

```c
short MyFindSpaceInUnitTable(void);
{
    Ptr        curUTableBase, newUTableBase;
    short      curUTableEntries, newUTableEntries;
    short      refNum, unitNum;

    /* get current unit table values from low memory globals */
    curUTableEntries = *(short*)UnitNtryCnt;
    curUTableBase = *(Ptr*)UTableBase;

    /* search for empty space in the current unit table */
    for ( unitNum = curUTableEntries - 1;
          unitNum >= 48; /* lowest available unit number */
          unitNum-- )
    {
        refNum = ~(unitNum);
        if (GetDCtlEntry(refNum) == nil)
            return(unitNum); /* found a space */
    }

    /* no space in the current table, so make a new one */

    /* increase the size of the table by 16 (an arbitrary value) */
    newUTableEntries = curUTableEntries + 16;

    /* allocate space for the new table */
    newUTableBase =
        NewPtrSysClear((long)newUTableEntries * sizeof(Handle));
    if (newUTableBase == nil)
        return(memErr);

    /* copy the old table to the new table */
    BlockMove(curUTableBase, newUTableBase,
              (long)curUTableEntries * sizeof(Handle));

    /* set the new unit table values in low memory */
    *(Ptr*)UTableBase = newUTableBase;
    *(short*)UnitNtryCnt = newUTableEntries;

    unitNum = newUTableEntries - 1;
    return(unitNum);
}
```

Although rare, it is possible for the unit table to become completely full. If the MyFindSpaceInUnitTable function does not find an empty unit table entry, it creates a larger unit table and copies the contents of the old unit table into the new one. To avoid the need for every driver to create a larger table, this function increases the size of the table by 16 entries—a reasonable amount in most cases.

The MyFindSpaceInUnitTable function does not need to disable interrupts when changing the values of the UTableBase and UnitNtryCnt system global variables because both unit tables are valid and drivers are not opened or closed at interrupt time.

Note that this function does not check for empty locations in the space reserved for desk accessories or SCSI drivers. You may wish to modify the function if you are installing one of these.

Writing a Chooser-Compatible Device Driver

The Chooser is a desk accessory that helps provide a standard user interface for networking and printing device drivers. The Chooser allows the user to make choices such as which serial port to use, which AppleTalk zone to communicate with, and which LaserWriter to use.

This section describes how the Chooser works, how to create a Chooser extension, and how to respond to actions from the user. You should read the previous section, "Writing a Device Driver," before you read this section.

How the Chooser Works

The Chooser allows users to select which devices they want to use. When the user opens the Chooser, it displays a window containing lists and buttons for making device-related choices. Typically, users select a type of device from the icon list, then select the particular device they want to use from the device list. For AppleTalk devices, the user must also select an AppleTalk zone from the zone list. The Chooser window can also display buttons, such as an OK button; and radio buttons, such as the background printing On and Off buttons. Figure 1-10 shows an example of the Chooser window.

Figure 1-10   The Chooser window

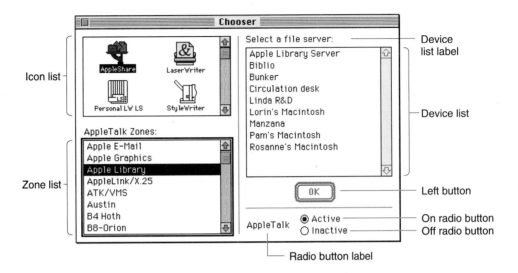

The Chooser relies on the List Manager for creating, displaying, and manipulating possible user selections in this window. You may want to read the chapter "List Manager" in *Inside Macintosh: More Macintosh Toolbox* for more information.

The Chooser does not communicate directly with device drivers; instead, it communicates with device packages. A **device package** is a resource similar to a driver resource, except a device package responds to Chooser messages instead of Device Manager requests. The device package is responsible for communicating the user's choices to the device driver.

Device packages are stored in Chooser extension files, which the Chooser looks for in the Extensions folder inside the System Folder of the startup disk. A Chooser extension file contains a number of resources in addition to the device package resource. These other resources contain information about the buttons, labels, and lists that the Chooser displays when the user selects the device icon from the icon list. You use these resources to define the following properties:

- The device list label. The Chooser displays this label over the device list.

- The buttons to use. The Chooser allows the device package to display up to four buttons, called the Left button, the Right button, the On radio button, and the Off radio button.

- The titles and positions of the buttons.

- The radio button label.

- The AppleTalk device type name. The Chooser searches the current AppleTalk zone for devices of this type.

- An AppleTalk Name-Binding Protocol (NBP) retry interval and a timeout count. The Chooser uses this information when searching for AppleTalk devices.

When a user selects the icon corresponding to a particular device package, the Chooser sends messages to that device package by calling the device package as if it were the following function:

```
pascal OSErr MyPackage (short message, short caller,
                        StringPtr objName, StringPtr zoneName,
                        long p1, long p2);
```

The Chooser passes the following parameters to the device package:

Parameter	Description
message	The operation to be performed; this parameter has one of the following values:

```
enum {
    /* Chooser messages */
    chooserInitMsg = 11,
    newSelMsg      = 12,
    fillListMsg    = 13,
    getSelMsg      = 14,
    selectMsg      = 15,
    deselectMsg    = 16,
    terminateMsg   = 17,
    buttonMsg      = 19
};
```

Table 1-4 on page 1-47 explains the meaning of these messages.

caller	A number that identifies the application calling your device package. The value chooserID indicates the Chooser. Values in the range 0–127 are reserved; values outside this range may be used by applications.
objName	Additional information whose meaning depends on the value of the message parameter. See Table 1-4 on page 1-47 for more information.
zoneName	The name of the AppleTalk zone containing the devices in the device list. If the Chooser is being used with the local zone and bit 24 of the flags field of the device package header is not set, the string value is "*", otherwise, it is the actual zone name. See "Creating a Device Package" on page 1-45 for more information about the package header.
p1	A handle to the List Manager list that contains the device choices displayed in the device list box.
p2	Additional information whose meaning depends on the value of the message parameter. See Table 1-4 on page 1-47 for more details.

When the user opens the Chooser, the Chooser searches the Extensions folder for Chooser extension files. For each one it finds, it opens the file, fetches the device icon, reads the flags field of the device package header, and closes the file. The Chooser then displays each device icon, and dims the icons for AppleTalk devices if AppleTalk is not connected.

When the user selects a device icon that is not dimmed, the Chooser reopens the corresponding Chooser extension file and performs the following actions:

1. The Chooser labels the device list with the device list label.

2. The Chooser sends the `chooserInitMsg` message to the device package.

3. If the selected device package represents a serial printer, the Chooser places the two icons that represent the printer port and the modem port serial drivers into the device list box. When the user makes a selection, the Chooser records the user's choice in low memory and parameter RAM.

4. If the selected device icon represents an AppleTalk device and the corresponding device package does not accept `fillListMsg` messages, the Chooser initiates an asynchronous routine that interrogates the current AppleTalk zone for all devices whose type matches the AppleTalk device type name specified in the Chooser extension file. The asynchronous routine uses the retry interval and the timeout count. As responses arrive, the Chooser updates the device list.

5. If the device package does accept `fillListMsg` messages, the Chooser sends the `fillListMsg` message to the device package. The device package responds by filling the device list with the appropriate device choices.

6. To determine which devices in the device list should be selected, the Chooser calls the device package with the `getSelMsg` message. The device package responds by inspecting the list and setting the selected or unselected state of each entry. The Chooser may send the `getSelMsg` message frequently; for example, each time a new response to the AppleTalk zone interrogation arrives. The Chooser does not send the `getSelMsg` message for serial printers; it highlights the icon corresponding to the currently selected serial port, as recorded in low memory.

7. If the device package allows multiple devices to be active at once, the Chooser sets the appropriate List Manager bits. When the user selects or deselects a device, the Chooser calls the device package with the appropriate message. For packages that do not accept multiple active devices, the Chooser sends the `selectMsg` or `deselectMsg` message; otherwise, it sends the `newSelMsg` message. The device package mounts or unmounts the device, if appropriate, and records the user's choice.

8. When the user selects a different device icon or closes the Chooser, the Chooser calls the current device package with the `terminateMsg` message, if the package accepts this kind of message. At this time, the package can clean up, if necessary. The Chooser then calls the `UpdateResFile` function, closes the device resource file, and flushes the system startup volume.

Creating a Chooser Extension File

The Chooser uses three file types to identify different kinds of devices supported by Chooser extension files:

File type	Device type
`'PRES'`	Serial printer
`'PRER'`	Non-serial printer
`'RDEV'`	Other device

You can specify the creator of your Chooser extension file, which allows you to give your device its own icon.

You can include the following resources in your Chooser extension file:

Resource type	Resource ID	Description
'PACK'	–4096	Device package. This resource contains the device package header and code.
'STR '	–4096	Type name for AppleTalk devices. The Chooser searches the current AppleTalk zone for devices of this type.
'GNRL'	–4096	AppleTalk information. The first byte of this resource contains the Name-Binding Protocol (NBP) retry interval, the second byte contains the timeout count.
'STR '	–4091	List box label. The Chooser labels the device list with this string after the user has selected the device's icon.
'STR '	–4087	Radio button label.
'STR '	–4088	Off radio button title.
'STR '	–4089	On radio button title.
'STR '	–4092	Right button title.
'STR '	–4093	Left button title.
'ncrt'	–4096	Button positions.
'LDEF'	–4096	Alternate list definition function. You can supply this function to modify the device list—to include pictures or icons, for example.
'STR '	–4090	Reserved for use by the Chooser.

You should also include a 'BNDL' resource (and appropriate icon family resources) to give your device type a distinctive icon because this may be the only way that devices are identified in the Chooser window. The chapter "Finder Interface" in *Inside Macintosh: Macintosh Toolbox Essentials* describes the 'BNDL' resource.

The Chooser allows your device package to display two buttons, called the Left button and the Right button because of their default positions. The Left button has a double border and is highlighted (the title string is dark) when one or more devices are selected in the device list. When this button is highlighted, pressing the Return or Enter key, or double-clicking in the device list, is equivalent to clicking the button. The Right button has a single border and is always highlighted. The user can activate it only by clicking it.

The Chooser also allows you to display two radio buttons and a radio button label. These buttons are called the On radio button and the Off radio button because those are the titles the LaserWriter uses, but you can name them anything you want.

You can position these buttons by including a resource of type 'ncrt' with an ID of –4096. The first word in this type of resource specifies the number of rectangles, and the rest of the resource contains the rectangle definitions. The first rectangle positions the Left button, the second positions the Right button, the third positions the On radio button, and the fourth positions the Off radio button. The fifth rectangle positions the radio button label.

Each rectangle definition is 8 bytes long and contains the rectangle coordinates in the order [*top*, *left*, *bottom*, *right*]. The default values are [112, 206, 132, 266] for the Left button and [112, 296, 132, 356] for the Right button. You could use the values [112, 251, 132, 331] to center a single button.

The Chooser uses the List Manager to produce and display the standard device list. You can supply a list definition function to modify this list. For example, you might want to include pictures or icons in your list. To do this, you must provide a resource of type 'LDEF' with an ID of –4096. For complete information about list construction and data structures, see the chapter "List Manager" in *Inside Macintosh: More Macintosh Toolbox*.

Creating a Device Package

Like a driver resource, a device package has two parts:

■ a header that contains flags and other information about the driver

■ the code that responds to Chooser messages

Figure 1-11 shows the structure of a device package.

Figure 1-11   Structure of a device package

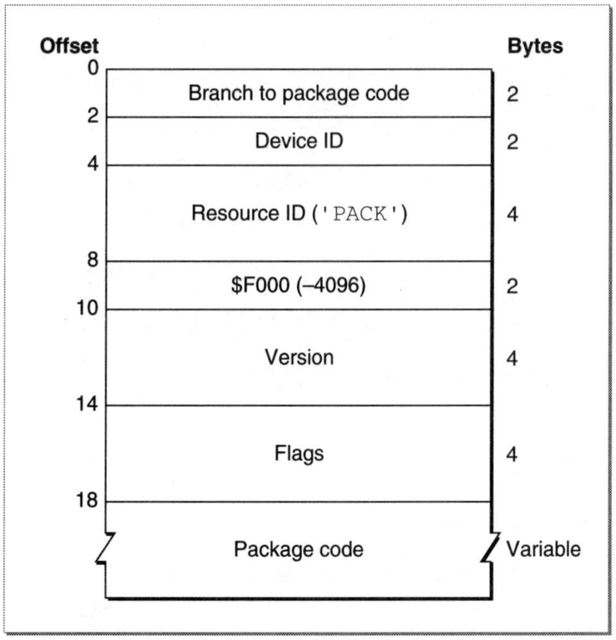

Since the Chooser expects the package code to be at the beginning of the device package, the first field of the package header should be a BRA.S instruction to the package code.

The device ID is an integer that identifies the device. The version field differentiates versions of the driver code.

The flags field contains information about the device package and the device it serves. Table 1-3 lists the meaning of each bit of the flags field.

The package code should implement the `MyPackage` function described on page 1-42. The following section, "Responding to the Chooser," discusses how to implement this function.

Table 1-3   Device package flags

Bit	Meaning
31	Set if an AppleTalk device
30–29	Reserved (clear to 0)
28	Set if the device package can have multiple instances selected at once
27	Set if the device package uses the Left button
26	Set if the device package uses the Right button
25	Set if no zone name has been saved
24	Set if the device package uses actual zone names
23–21	Reserved (clear to 0)
20	Set if the device uses the On and Off radio buttons and radio button label
19–17	Reserved (clear to 0)
17	Set if the device package accepts the `chooserInitMsg` message
16	Set if the device package accepts the `newSelMsg` message
15	Set if the device package accepts the `fillListMsg` message
14	Set if the device package accepts the `getSelMsg` message
13	Set if the device package accepts the `selectMsg` message
12	Set if the device package accepts the `deselectMsg` message
11	Set if the device package accepts the `terminateMsg` message
10–0	Reserved (clear to 0)

Responding to the Chooser

This section gives more details about how your device package should respond when it receives a message from the Chooser.

When the Chooser sends your device package a message, the Chooser extension file is the current resource file and the Chooser window is the current graphics port. The startup disk is the default volume and the System Folder of the startup disk is the default directory. Your device package must preserve all of these.

Table 1-4 lists the Chooser messages and how your device package should respond to them.

Table 1-4   Chooser messages and their meanings

Message	Meaning
chooserInitMsg	The Chooser sends this message to your device package when the user selects the icon representing your device in the icon list. The objName parameter contains a pointer to a data structure that contains a size word followed by four handles to structures of type ControlRecord. The size is at least 18 bytes (2 bytes for the size word and 4 bytes for each of the handles). The handles reference the Left and Right buttons and the On and Off radio buttons, in that order. Your device package can respond to this message by setting up the initial button configuration. To display any of the radio buttons, use the ShowControl function. To highlight them, use the SetControlValue function. The p2 parameter is not used. For more information about controls, see the chapter "Control Manager" in *Inside Macintosh: Macintosh Toolbox Essentials*.
newSelMsg	If your device package allows multiple selections, the Chooser sends this message to your package when the user changes or adds a selection. The objName and p2 parameters are not used.
fillListMsg	The Chooser sends this message when the user selects a device icon. The p1 parameter contains a handle to a List Manager list. Your device package should use the List Manager to fill this list with choices for the particular type of device. The objName and p2 parameters are not used.
getSelMsg	The Chooser sends this message to determine which devices in the device list should be selected. The p1 parameter contains a handle to a List Manager list. Your device package should respond by inspecting the list and setting the selected or unselected state of each entry, using the LSetSelect function. You should alter only the entries that require updating. The Chooser does not send this message for serial printers.
selectMsg	If your device package does not allow multiple selections, the Chooser sends this message to your package when the user selects a device in the device list. You should record the user's selection, preferably in your Chooser extension file. Your device package may not call the List Manager in response to this message.

If your device package accepts fillListMsg messages, the objName parameter is undefined and the p2 parameter contains the row number of the selected device.

If your device package does not accept fillListMsg messages, the objName parameter contains a pointer to a string containing the name of the device (up to 32 characters). If the device is an AppleTalk device, the p2 parameter contains the AddrBlock value for the address of the selected AppleTalk device. For more information about AppleTalk devices, refer to *Inside Macintosh: Networking*. |

continued

Table 1-4   Chooser messages and their meanings (continued)

Message	Meaning
deselectMsg	If your device package does not allow multiple selections, the Chooser sends this message to your package when the user deselects a device in the device list. Your device package may not call the List Manager in response to this message.
	If your device package accepts fillListMsg messages, the objName parameter is undefined and the p2 parameter contains the row number of the device that was deselected.
	If your device package does not accept fillListMsg messages, the objName parameter contains a pointer to a string containing the name of the device (up to 32 characters). If the device is an AppleTalk device, the p2 parameter contains the AddrBlock value for the address of the selected AppleTalk device. For more information about AppleTalk devices, refer to *Inside Macintosh: Networking*.
terminateMsg	The Chooser sends this message when the user selects a different device icon, closes the Chooser window, or changes zones. Your device package should perform any necessary cleanup tasks but should not dispose of the device list. The objName and p2 parameters are not used.
buttonMsg	The Chooser sends this message when the user clicks one of the buttons in the Chooser window. The low-order byte of the p2 parameter contains 1 if the user clicked the Left button, 2 if the user clicked the Right button, 3 if the user clicked the On radio button, and 4 if the user clicked the Off radio button. You must perform the appropriate highlighting for the radio buttons. The high-order word of the p2 parameter contains the modifier bits from the mouse-up event. See the chapters "Control Manager" and "Event Manager" in *Inside Macintosh: Macintosh Toolbox Essentials* for more information.

Allocating Private Storage

Device packages initially have no data space allocated. There are two ways your device package can acquire data space:

■ Use the List Manager to allocate extra memory in the device list.

■ Create a resource.

The Chooser uses column 0 of the device list structure to store the names displayed in the device list. For device packages that do not accept fillListMsg messages, the Chooser uses column 1 to store the 4-byte AppleTalk internet addresses of the devices in the list. Therefore, your device package can use column 1 and higher (if it accepts fillListMsg messages) or column 2 and higher to store private data. You can use standard List Manager functions to add these columns, store data in them, and retrieve the data stored there. Your device package can also use the refCon field of the device list for its own purposes.

Using the device list is limited by the fact that the Chooser disposes of the device list whenever the user changes device types or changes the current zone. However, the Chooser does call your device package with the terminateMsg message before it disposes of the list.

Also, if your device package does not accept `fillListMsg` messages, the Chooser disposes of the device list whenever a new response from the AppleTalk zone interrogation arrives. However, the Chooser does send the `getSelMsg` message immediately afterward.

The second way to obtain storage space is to create a resource in the device resource file. This file is always the current resource file when the Chooser sends a message to the package, so you can use the `GetResource` function to obtain a handle to the storage.

It is important for most device packages to record which devices the user has chosen. The recommended method for this is to create a resource in your driver resource file. This resource can be of any type; in fact, it's advantageous to provide your own resource type so that no other program will try to modify it. If you choose to use a standard resource type, you should use only resource IDs in the range –4080 through –4065.

Writing a Desk Accessory

Desk accessories are small applications designed like device drivers. Desk accessories typically provide a user interface with a window and a menu, perform some limited function, and are opened from the Apple menu. The Chooser is an example of a desk accessory.

Desk accessories were originally created for the Macintosh because they offered two distinct advantages over applications. They provided both a limited degree of multitasking and a primitive form of interapplication communication. However, modern Macintosh applications enjoy far more sophisticated versions of these capabilities. Users can even open applications from the Apple menu. For these reasons, you would be better served by writing a small application than by writing a desk accessory.

Control panels have largely replaced desk accessories as a user interface for device drivers. In addition to providing a more consistent and extensible interface, control panels can include an initialization (`'INIT'`) resource to load and execute your device driver at system startup. For more information about control panels, see the chapter "Control Panels" in *Inside Macintosh: More Macintosh Toolbox*.

If you're certain you need to write a desk accessory, you should read this section. You might also want to read the chapters "Event Manager," "Window Manager," "Dialog Manager," and "Menu Manager" in *Inside Macintosh: Macintosh Toolbox Essentials*.

How Desk Accessories Work

When the user opens a desk accessory (or when an application calls the `OpenDeskAcc` function), the system performs a major context switch, loads the desk accessory into the system heap, and calls the desk accessory driver open routine. The desk accessory can respond by creating its window and menu.

When events occur, the Event Manager directs them to the desk accessory by calling its driver control routine. The Event Manager handles switching between applications and desk accessories in the system heap.

When the user closes the desk accessory (by closing its window or choosing Quit from its menu) or an application closes the desk accessory (by calling the `CloseDeskAcc` function), the desk accessory disposes of its window and any other data structures associated with it.

In a single-application environment in System 6, and in a multiple-application environment in which the desk accessory is launched in the application's partition (for example, a desk accessory opened by the user from the Apple menu while holding down the Option key), the Event Manager handles events for desk accessories in a slightly different manner, although it still translates them into control requests. For details, see the chapter "Event Manager" in *Inside Macintosh: Macintosh Toolbox Essentials*.

Creating a Driver Resource for a Desk Accessory

You create a desk accessory by creating a driver resource and storing it in a resource file, as described in "Creating a Driver Resource," beginning on page 1-24. Typically, you store your desk accessory driver resource in a file of type `'dfil'`, which the user places in the Apple Menu Items folder.

Three fields of the driver resource header are of particular importance to desk accessories:

- The `drvrEMask` field. This field contains an event mask specifying which events your desk accessory can handle. If your desk accessory has a window, you should include keyboard, activate, update, and mouse-down events, but you should not include mouse-up events. When an event occurs, the Event Manager checks this field to determine whether the desk accessory can handle the type of event and, if so, calls the desk accessory driver control routine. See the chapter "Event Manager" in *Inside Macintosh: Macintosh Toolbox Essentials* for more information about events and event masks.

- The `drvrMenu` field. This field contains the menu ID of your desk accessory's menu, if it has one, or any one of its menus, if it has more than one. Otherwise, it contains 0. A desk accessory menu ID must be negative and must be different from the menu ID for other desk accessories.

- The `drvrDelay` field and the `dNeedTime` flag of the `drvrFlags` field. Desk accessories sometimes need to perform certain actions periodically. For example, a clock desk accessory might change the time it displays every second. If your desk accessory needs to perform a periodic action, set the `dNeedTime` flag and use the `drvrDelay` field to indicate how often the action should occur. "Creating a Driver Resource," beginning on page 1-24, describes these fields in more detail.

All desk accessories must implement open, close, and control routines. Your desk accessory can implement a prime and status routine if needed.

Opening and Closing a Desk Accessory

When the user chooses an item from the Apple menu, the foreground application calls the `OpenDeskAcc` function, which determines whether the item is a desk accessory, application, or document, and schedules it for execution. Applications call the `CloseDeskAcc` function if the user chooses the Close menu item from the File menu when the foreground window does not belong to the application. These functions are described in "Device Manager Reference," beginning on page 1-53.

Opening a desk accessory is similar to launching an application. In your desk accessory driver open routine, you should do the following:

- Create the desk accessory's window. You can do this with the Dialog Manager function `GetNewDialog` or `NewDialog`. You should specify that the window be invisible because the `OpenDeskAcc` function will display it. You should set the `windowKind` field of the `windowRecord` structure to the desk accessory's driver reference number, which you can find in the device control entry. You should also store a copy of the window pointer in the `dCtlWindow` field of the device control entry.

- Allocate private storage as you would for any device driver.

- Create any menus needed by your desk accessory. You are responsible for adding your menus to the menu bar. See the chapter "Menu Manager" in *Inside Macintosh: Macintosh Toolbox Essentials* for more details.

If your driver open routine is unable to complete its tasks (because of insufficient memory, for example), you should modify the code so it doesn't respond to events, and display an alert indicating failure.

As for all drivers, your close routine should undo the actions taken by the open routine, dispose of the desk accessory's window and private storage, clear the window pointer in the device control entry, and remove any menus that were added to the menu bar.

Responding to Events

When the Event Manager determines an event has occurred that your desk accessory should handle, it checks the `drvrEMask` field of the driver header and, if that field indicates your desk accessory handles the event type, it passes the event to your desk accessory by calling your driver control routine.

The Event Manager passes one of nine values in the `csCode` field to indicate the action to take:

Constant name	Value	Meaning
accEvent	64	Handle a given event
accRun	65	Time for periodic action
accCursor	66	Change cursor shape if appropriate
accMenu	67	Handle a given menu item
accUndo	68	Handle the Undo command

Constant name	Value	Meaning
accCut	70	Handle the Cut command
accCopy	71	Handle the Copy command
accPaste	72	Handle the Paste command
accClear	73	Handle the Clear command

Along with the accEvent message, the Event Manager sends a pointer to an event record in the csParam field. Your desk accessory can respond to the event in whatever way is appropriate. For example, when your desk accessory becomes active, it might install its menu in the menu bar.

Note

If your desk accessory window is a modeless dialog box and you are calling the Dialog Manager function IsDialogEvent in response to the event, you should set the windowKind field of your window record to 2 before you call IsDialogEvent. Setting this field to 2 allows the Dialog Manager to recognize and handle the event properly. You should restore the original value of the windowKind field before returning from your control routine. ◆

The Event Manager periodically sends the accRun message if your desk accessory has requested time for background processing. To request this service, you set the dNeedTime flag in the drvrFlags field of your desk accessory driver header. See "Writing Control and Status Routines," beginning on page 1-34, for more information.

The accCursor message makes it possible to change the shape of the cursor when it is inside your desk accessory window and your desk accessory window is active. Your control routine should check whether the mouse location is in your window and, if so, should set the cursor appropriately by calling the QuickDraw function InitCursor.

If your desk accessory window is a dialog box, you should respond to the accCursor message by generating a null event (storing the event code for a null event in an event record) and passing it to the Dialog Manager function DialogSelect. This allows the Dialog Manager to blink the insertion point in editText items.

When the Event Manager sends an accMenu message, it provides the menu ID followed by the menu item number in the csParam field. You should take the appropriate action and then call the Menu Manager function HiliteMenu with a value of 0 for the menuID parameter to remove the highlighting from the menu bar.

You should respond to the last five messages, accUndo through accClear, by processing the corresponding editing command in the desk accessory window, if appropriate. The chapter "Scrap Manager" in *Inside Macintosh: More Macintosh Toolbox* contains information about cutting and pasting.

Your desk accessory routines should restore the current resource file and graphics port if it changes either one.

Device Manager Reference

This section describes the data structures, functions, and resources that are specific to the Device Manager.

The "Data Structures" section shows the C declarations for the data structures that are used by the Device Manager. The "Device Manager Functions" section describes the functions you use to communicate with device drivers and the functions that provide support for writing your own device drivers. The "Resources" section describes the driver resource.

Data Structures

This section describes the parameter block structure, the device control entry structure, and the enumerated types you use to define values within them.

Device Manager Parameter Block

The Device Manager provides both a high-level and a low-level interface for communicating with device drivers. You pass information to the low-level functions in a parameter block structure, defined by the `ParamBlockRec` union.

```
typedef union ParamBlockRec {
    IOParam         ioParam;
    FileParam       fileParam;
    VolumeParam     volumeParam;
    CntrlParam      cntrlParam;
    SlotDevParam    slotDevParam;
    MultiDevParam   multiDevParam;
} ParamBlockRec;
typedef ParamBlockRec *ParmBlkPtr;
```

The Device Manager uses two forms of the parameter block: one for the open, close, read, and write functions (the `IOParam` structure) and another for the control and status functions (the `CntrlParam` structure). Other managers use other structures of the `ParamBlockRec` union.

```
typedef struct IOParam {
    QElemPtr   qLink;           /* next queue entry */
    short      qType;           /* queue type */
    short      ioTrap;          /* routine trap */
    Ptr        ioCmdAddr;       /* routine address */
    ProcPtr    ioCompletion;    /* completion routine address */
    OSErr      ioResult;        /* result code */
    StringPtr  ioNamePtr;       /* pointer to driver name */
```

CHAPTER 1

Device Manager

```
    short       ioVRefNum;      /* volume reference or drive number */
    short       ioRefNum;       /* driver reference number */
    char        ioVersNum;      /* not used by the Device Manager */
    char        ioPermssn;      /* read/write permission */
    Ptr         ioMisc;         /* not used by the Device Manager */
    Ptr         ioBuffer;       /* pointer to data buffer */
    long        ioReqCount;     /* requested number of bytes */
    long        ioActCount;     /* actual number of bytes completed */
    short       ioPosMode;      /* positioning mode */
    long        ioPosOffset;    /* positioning offset */
} IOParam;

typedef struct CntrlParam {
    QElemPtr    qLink;          /* next queue entry */
    short       qType;          /* queue type */
    short       ioTrap;         /* routine trap */
    Ptr         ioCmdAddr;      /* routine address */
    ProcPtr     ioCompletion;   /* completion routine address */
    OSErr       ioResult;       /* result code */
    StringPtr   ioNamePtr;      /* pointer to driver name */
    short       ioVRefNum;      /* volume reference or drive number */
    short       ioCRefNum;      /* driver reference number */
    short       csCode;         /* type of control or status request */
    short       csParam[11];    /* control or status information */
} CntrlParam;
```

The first eight fields are common to both structures. Each structure also includes its own unique fields.

Field descriptions for fields common to both structures

qLink
A pointer to the next entry in the driver I/O queue. (This field is used internally by the Device Manager to keep track of asynchronous calls awaiting execution.)

qType
The queue type. (This field is used internally by the Device Manager.)

ioTrap
The trap number of the routine that was called. (This field is used internally by the Device Manager.)

ioCmdAddr
The address of the routine that was called. (This field is used internally by the Device Manager.)

ioCompletion
A pointer to a completion routine. When making asynchronous requests, you must set this field to nil if you are not specifying a completion routine. The Device Manager automatically sets this field to nil when you make a synchronous request.

ioResult
A value indicating whether the routine completed successfully. The Device Manager sets this field to 1 when it queues an asynchronous request. When the driver completes the request, it places the actual

result code in this field. You can poll this field to detect when the driver has completed the request and to determine its result code. The Device Manager executes the completion routine after this field receives the result code.

ioNamePtr   A pointer to the name of the driver. You use this field only when opening a driver.

ioVRefNum   The drive number, if any. The meaning of this field depends on the device driver. The Disk Driver uses this field to identify disk devices.

Field descriptions for the `IOParam` structure

ioRefNum   The driver reference number.

ioVersNum   Not used.

ioPermssn   The read/write permission of the driver. When you open a driver, you must supply one of the following values in this field:

```
enum {
    /* access permissions */
    fsCurPerm   = 0, /* retain current permission */
    fsRdPerm    = 1, /* allow reads only */
    fsWrPerm    = 2, /* allow writes only */
    fsRdWrPerm  = 3  /* allow reads and writes */
};
```

The Device Manager compares subsequent read and write requests with the read/write permission of the driver. If the request type is not permitted, the Device Manager returns a result code indicating the error.

ioMisc   Not used.

ioBuffer   A pointer to the data buffer for the driver to use for reads or writes.

ioReqCount   The requested number of bytes for the driver to read or write.

ioActCount   The actual number of bytes the driver reads or writes.

ioPosMode   The positioning mode used by drivers of block devices. Bits 0 and 1 of this field indicate where an operation should begin relative to the physical beginning of the block-formatted medium. You can use the following constants to test or set the value of these bits:

```
enum {
    /* positioning modes */
    fsAtMark    = 0, /* at current position */
    fsFromStart = 1, /* offset from beginning */
    fsFromMark  = 3  /* offset from current
                           position  */
};
```

The Disk Driver allows you to add the following constant to this field to specify a read-verify operation:

```
enum {
    rdVerify = 64        /* read-verify mode */
};
```

See the description of the PBRead function on page 1-70.

ioPosOffset   The byte offset, relative to the position specified by the positioning mode, where the driver should perform the operation. If you specify the fsAtMark positioning mode, the Device Manager ignores this field.

Field descriptions for the CntrlParam structure

ioCRefNum   The driver reference number.

csCode   A value identifying the type of control or status request. Each driver may interpret this number differently.

csParam   The control or status information passed to or from the driver. This field is declared generically as an array of eleven integers. Each driver may interpret the contents of this field differently. Refer to the driver's documentation for specific information.

Device Control Entry

The device control entry structure, defined by the AuxDCE data type, stores information about each device driver in memory. The AuxDCE data type supersedes the original DCtlEntry data type, and provides additional fields for drivers that serve slot devices. See the chapter "Slot Manager" in this book for information about slot device drivers.

```
typedef struct AuxDCE {
    Ptr         dCtlDriver;     /* pointer or handle to driver */
    short       dCtlFlags;      /* flags */
    QHdr        dCtlQHdr;       /* I/O queue header */
    long        dCtlPosition;   /* current R/W byte position */
    Handle      dCtlStorage;    /* handle to private storage */
    short       dCtlRefNum;     /* driver reference number */
    long        dCtlCurTicks;   /* used internally */
    GrafPtr     dCtlWindow;     /* pointer to driver's window */
    short       dCtlDelay;      /* ticks between periodic actions */
    short       dCtlEMask;      /* desk accessory event mask */
    short       dCtlMenu;       /* desk accessory menu ID */
    char        dCtlSlot;       /* slot */
    char        dCtlSlotId;     /* sResource directory ID */
    long        dCtlDevBase;    /* slot device base address */
    Ptr         dCtlOwner;      /* reserved; must be 0 */
    char        dCtlExtDev;     /* external device ID */
```

```
    char          fillByte;       /* reserved */
} AuxDCE;
typedef AuxDCE *AuxDCEPtr, **AuxDCEHandle;
```

Field descriptions

dCtlDriver   A pointer or handle to the driver, as determined by the dRAMBased flag (bit 6) of the dCtlFlags field.

dCtlFlags   Flags describing the abilities and state of the driver. The high-order byte contains flags copied from the drvrFlags word of the driver resource. These flags are described in "Creating a Driver Resource," beginning on page 1-24.

The low-order byte of the dCtlFlags field contains the following run-time flags:

Name	Bit	Meaning
dOpened	5	Set by the Device Manager when the driver is opened, and cleared when it is closed.
dRAMBased	6	Set if the dCtlDriver field contains a handle.
drvrActive	7	Set by the Device Manager when the driver is executing a request, and cleared when the driver is inactive.

You can use the following constants to test or set the value of these flags:

```
enum {
    /* run-time flags in the device control entry */
    dOpenedMask    = 0x0020,
    dRAMBasedMask  = 0x0040,
    drvrActiveMask = 0x0080
};
```

dCtlQHdr   A pointer to the header of the driver I/O queue, which is a standard Operating System queue. See the chapter "Queue Utilities" in *Inside Macintosh: Operating System Utilities* for more information about the QHdr data type.

dCtlPosition   The current source or destination position for reading or writing. This field is used only by drivers of block devices. The value in this field is the number of bytes beyond the physical beginning of the medium used by the device, and must be a multiple of 512. For example, immediately after the Disk Driver reads the first block of data from a 3.5-inch disk, this field contains the value 512.

dCtlStorage   A handle to a driver's private storage. A driver may allocate a relocatable block of memory and keep a handle to it in this field.

dCtlRefNum   The driver reference number.

dCtlCurTicks	Used internally.
dCtlWindow	A pointer to the desk accessory window. See "Writing a Desk Accessory" on page 1-49 for more information.
dCtlDelay	The number of ticks to wait between periodic actions.
dCtlEMask	The desk accessory event mask. See "Writing a Desk Accessory" on page 1-49 for more information.
dCtlMenu	The menu ID of a desk accessory's menu, if any. See "Writing a Desk Accessory" on page 1-49 for more information.
dCtlSlot	The slot number of the slot device.
dCtlSlotId	The sResource directory ID of the slot device.
dCtlDevBase	The base address of the slot device. For a video card this field contains the address of the pixel map for the card's GDevice record.
dCtlOwner	Reserved. This field must be 0.
dCtlExtDev	The external device ID of the slot device.
fillByte	Reserved.

Device Manager Functions

This section describes the functions you use to

- open and close device drivers

- communicate with device drivers

- control and monitor device drivers

- write and install device drivers

The low-level Device Manager functions described in this section (those that use the parameter block structure to pass information) provide two advantages over the corresponding high-level functions:

- These functions can be executed asynchronously, returning control to your application before the operation is completed.

- In most cases, these functions provide more extensive information or perform advanced operations.

All of these functions exchange parameters with your application through a parameter block of type `ParamBlockRec`. When you call a low-level function, you pass the address of the parameter block to the function.

There are three versions of most low-level functions. The first takes two parameters: a pointer to the parameter block and a Boolean parameter that specifies whether the function is to execute asynchronously (`true`) or synchronously (`false`). For example, the first version of the low-level `PBRead` function has this declaration:

```
pascal OSErr PBRead(ParmBlkPtr paramBlock, Boolean async);
```

The second version does not take a second parameter; instead, it adds the suffix Sync to the name of the function.

```
pascal OSErr PBReadSync(ParmBlkPtr paramBlock);
```

Similarly, the third version of the function does not take a second parameter; instead, it adds the suffix Async to the name of the function.

```
pascal OSErr PBReadAsync(ParmBlkPtr paramBlock);
```

Only the first version of each function is documented in this section. Note, however, that the second and third versions of these functions do not use the glue code that the first version uses and are therefore more efficient. See "Summary of the Device Manager," beginning on page 1-91, for a listing of all three versions of these functions.

Assembly-Language Note
All Device Manager functions are synchronous by default. If you want a function to be executed asynchronously, set bit 10 of the trap word. To execute a function immediately, set bit 9 of the trap word. You can set these bits by appending the word ASYNC or IMMED as the second argument to the trap macro. For example:

```
_Read, ASYNC
_Control, IMMED
```

You can set or test bit 10 of a trap word using the global constant asyncTrpBit. You can set or test bit 9 of the trap word using the global constant noQueueBit. ◆

▲ **WARNING**
Never call any synchronous Device Manager function at interrupt time. This includes all of the high-level functions and the synchronous versions of the low-level functions.

A synchronous request at interrupt time may block other pending I/O requests. Because the device driver cannot begin processing the synchronous request until it completes the other requests in its queue, this situation can cause the Device Manager to loop indefinitely while it waits for the device driver to complete the synchronous request. ▲

Opening and Closing Device Drivers

A device driver must be open before your application can communicate with it. You can use the OpenDriver or PBOpen function to open closed drivers or to determine the driver reference number of a driver that is already open. You use the OpenSlot function to open drivers that serve slot devices. To open a desk accessory or other Apple menu item from within your application, use the OpenDeskAcc function.

When you finish communicating with a device driver, you can close it if you are sure no other application or part of the system needs to use it. You can use the `CloseDriver` or `PBClose` function to close a driver. You use the `CloseDeskAcc` function to close a desk accessory.

The `PBOpen` and `PBClose` functions use the `IOParam` union of the Device Manager parameter block. The `OpenSlot` function uses the `IOParam` union fields and some additional fields that apply only to slot devices.

IMPORTANT

Device drivers cannot be opened or closed asynchronously. The `PBOpen`, `PBClose`, and `OpenSlot` functions include an asynchronous option because they share code with the File Manager. The `async` parameter must be set to `false` when these functions are used to open or close a device driver. ▲

OpenDriver

You can use the `OpenDriver` function to open a closed device driver or to determine the driver reference number of an open device driver.

```
pascal OSErr OpenDriver(ConstStr255Param name, short *drvrRefNum);
```

name   The name of the driver to open. A driver name consists of a period (.) followed by any sequence of 1 to 255 printing characters. The Device Manager ignores case (but not diacritical marks) when comparing names.

drvrRefNum The driver reference number of the opened driver.

DESCRIPTION

The `OpenDriver` function opens the device driver specified by the name parameter and returns its driver reference number in the `drvrRefNum` parameter. To avoid replacing an open driver, the Device Manager searches the drivers that are already installed in the unit table before searching driver resources. If the specified driver is already open, this function simply returns the driver reference number.

If the driver is not already open, the Device Manager calls the `GetNamedResource` function using the specified name and the resource type `'DRVR'`. If the resource is found, the resource ID defines the unit number of the driver, which determines the location in the unit table where the Device Manager stores the handle to the driver's device control entry (DCE).

After loading the driver resource into memory, the Device Manager creates a DCE for the driver, copies the flags from the driver header to the `dCtlFlags` field, and places the driver reference number in the `dCtlRefNum` field.

The `OpenDriver` function is a high-level version of the low-level `PBOpen` function. Use the `PBOpen` function when you need to specify read/write permission for the driver. The next section describes the `PBOpen` function.

SPECIAL CONSIDERATIONS

Because another driver might already be installed in the unit table at the location determined by the driver's resource ID, you should first search for an unused location in the unit table and renumber the driver resource accordingly before calling this function. See Listing 1-1 on page 1-18 for an example.

The `OpenDriver` function may move memory; you should not call it at interrupt time.

RESULT CODES

noErr	0	No error
badUnitErr	–21	Driver reference number does not match unit table
unitEmptyErr	–22	Driver reference number specifies a `nil` handle in unit table
openErr	–23	Requested read/write permission does not match driver's open permission
dInstErr	–26	Driver resource not found

SEE ALSO

For information about the low-level functions for opening devices, see the next section, which describes the `PBOpen` function, and the description of the `OpenSlot` function on page 1-63. For an example of how to open a device driver using the `OpenDriver` function, see Listing 1-1 on page 1-18.

PBOpen

You can use the `PBOpen` function to open a closed device driver or to determine the driver reference number of an open device driver.

```
pascal OSErr PBOpen(ParmBlkPtr paramBlock, Boolean async);
```

paramBlock A pointer to an `IOParam` structure of the Device Manager parameter block.

async A Boolean value that indicates whether the request is asynchronous. You must set this field to `false` because device drivers cannot be opened asynchronously.

Parameter block

←	ioResult	OSErr	The device driver's result code.
→	ioNamePtr	StringPtr	A pointer to the driver name.
←	ioRefNum	short	The driver reference number.
→	ioPermssn	char	Read/write permission.

DESCRIPTION

The PBOpen function opens the device driver specified by the ioNamePtr field and returns its driver reference number in the ioRefNum field. To avoid replacing an open driver, the Device Manager searches the drivers that are already installed in the unit table before searching driver resources. If the specified driver is already open, this function simply returns the driver reference number.

If the driver is not already open, the Device Manager calls the GetNamedResource function using the specified name and the resource type 'DRVR'. If the resource is found, the resource ID defines the unit number of the driver, which determines the location in the unit table where the Device Manager stores the handle to the driver's device control entry (DCE).

After loading the driver resource into memory, the Device Manager creates a DCE for the driver, copies the flags from the driver header to the dCtlFlags field, and places the driver reference number in the dCtlRefNum field.

You specify the access permission for the device driver by placing one of the following constants in the ioPermssn field of the parameter block:

```
enum {
    /* access permissions */
    fsCurPerm        = 0,        /* retain current permission */
    fsRdPerm         = 1,        /* allow reads only */
    fsWrPerm         = 2,        /* allow writes only */
    fsRdWrPerm       = 3         /* allow reads and writes */
};
```

If the driver returns a negative result in register D0, the Device Manager returns the result code in the ioResult parameter and does not open the driver.

SPECIAL CONSIDERATIONS

Because another driver might already be installed in the unit table at the location determined by the driver's resource ID, you should first search for an unused location in the unit table and renumber the driver resource accordingly before calling this function. See Listing 1-1 on page 1-18 for an example.

The PBOpen function may move memory; you should not call it at interrupt time.

ASSEMBLY-LANGUAGE INFORMATION

The trap macro for the PBOpen function is _Open (0xA000). You must set up register A0 with the address of the parameter block. When _Open returns, register D0 contains the result code. Register D0 is the only register affected by this function.

Registers on entry

A0   Address of the parameter block

Registers on exit

D0   Result code

RESULT CODES

noErr	0	No error
badUnitErr	–21	Driver reference number does not match unit table
unitEmptyErr	–22	Driver reference number specifies a `nil` handle in unit table
openErr	–23	Requested read/write permission does not match driver's open permission
dInstErr	–26	Driver resource not found

SEE ALSO

For information about the high-level function for opening device drivers, see the description of the `OpenDriver` function on page 1-60. For information about the low-level function for opening device drivers that serve devices on expansion cards, see the next section, which describes the `OpenSlot` function. For an example of opening a device driver, see Listing 1-1 on page 1-18.

OpenSlot

You can use the `OpenSlot` function to open a device driver that serves a slot device.

```pascal
pascal OSErr OpenSlot(ParmBlkPtr paramBlock, Boolean async);
```

paramBlock   A pointer to a `SlotDevParam` or `MultiDevParam` structure of the `ParamBlockRec` union.

async   A Boolean value that indicates whether the request is asynchronous. You must set this field to `false` because device drivers cannot be opened asynchronously.

Parameter block

←	ioResult	OSErr	The device driver's result code.
→	ioNamePtr	StringPtr	A pointer to the driver name.
←	ioRefNum	short	The driver reference number.
→	ioPermssn	char	Read/write permission.

Additional fields for a single device

→	ioMix	Ptr	Reserved for use by the driver open routine.
→	ioFlags	short	Determines the number of additional fields.
→	ioSlot	char	The slot number.
→	ioId	char	The slot resource ID.

Additional fields for multiple devices

→	ioMMix	Ptr	Reserved for use by the driver open routine.
→	ioMFlags	short	The number of additional fields.
→	ioSEBlkPtr	Ptr	A pointer to an external parameter block.

DESCRIPTION

The OpenSlot function is equivalent to the PBOpen function, except that it sets bit 9 of the trap word, which signals the _Open routine that the parameter block includes additional fields.

If the sResource serves a single device, you should clear all the bits of the ioFlags field and include the slot number and slot resource ID in the ioSlot and ioID fields.

If the sResource serves multiple devices, you should set the fMulti bit (bit 0) of the ioFlags field (clearing all other bits to 0), and specify, in the ioSEBlkPtr field, an external parameter block that is customized for the devices installed in the slot.

SPECIAL CONSIDERATIONS

The OpenSlot function may move memory; you should not call it at interrupt time.

ASSEMBLY-LANGUAGE INFORMATION

The trap macro for the OpenSlot function is _Open (0xA200). Bit 9 of the trap word is set to signal that the parameter block contains additional fields for slot devices.

You must set up register A0 with the address of the parameter block. When _Open returns, register D0 contains the result code. Register D0 is the only register affected by this function.

Registers on entry

A0   Address of the parameter block

Registers on exit

D0   Result code

RESULT CODES

noErr	0	No error
badUnitErr	–21	Driver reference number does not match unit table
unitEmptyErr	–22	Driver reference number specifies a nil handle in unit table
openErr	–23	Requested read/write permission does not match driver's open permission
dInstErr	–26	Driver resource not found

SEE ALSO

For information about the low-level function for opening other device drivers, see the description of the PBOpen function on page 1-61. For an example of opening a device driver, see Listing 1-1 on page 1-18. Refer to the chapter "Slot Manager" in this book for more information about slot device drivers.

OpenDeskAcc

You can use the `OpenDeskAcc` function to open an item in the Apple menu.

```
pascal short OpenDeskAcc(ConstStr255Param deskAccName);
```

deskAccName   A Pascal string containing the name of the Apple menu item.

DESCRIPTION

The `OpenDeskAcc` function opens the Apple menu item specified by the `deskAccName` parameter. If the item is already open, the `OpenDeskAcc` function schedules it for execution and returns to your application. Otherwise, it prepares to open the item. In either case, your application receives a suspend event and the selected item is brought to the foreground.

You should ignore the value returned by `OpenDeskAcc`. If the menu item is a desk accessory and is successfully opened, the function result is a driver reference number for the desk accessory driver. Otherwise the function result is undefined. The desk accessory is responsible for informing the user of any errors.

Because some older desk accessories may not reset the current graphics port before returning, you should bracket your call to `OpenDeskAcc` with calls to the QuickDraw procedures `GetPort` and `SetPort`, to save and restore the current port.

SPECIAL CONSIDERATIONS

The `OpenDeskAcc` function may move memory; you should not call it at interrupt time.

SEE ALSO

For information about closing a desk accessory, see the description of the `CloseDeskAcc` function beginning on page 1-68.

CloseDriver

You can use the `CloseDriver` function to close an open device driver.

```
pascal OSErr CloseDriver(short refNum);
```

refNum   The driver reference number returned by the driver-opening function.

DESCRIPTION

The CloseDriver function closes the device driver indicated by the refNum parameter. The Device Manager waits until the driver is inactive before calling the driver's close routine. When the driver indicates it has processed the close request, the Device Manager unlocks the driver resource if the dRAMBased flag is set, and unlocks the device control entry if the dNeedLock flag is not set. The Device Manager does not dispose of the device control entry or remove it from the unit table.

This function is a high-level version of the low-level PBClose function. Use the PBClose function when you want to specify a completion routine.

▲ **WARNING**
You should not close drivers that other applications may be using, such as a disk driver, the AppleTalk drivers, and so on. ▲

SPECIAL CONSIDERATIONS

The Device Manager does not queue close requests.

▲ **WARNING**
Do not call the CloseDriver function at interrupt time because if the driver was processing a request when the interrupt occurred the Device Manager may loop indefinitely, waiting for the driver to complete the request. ▲

RESULT CODES

noErr	0	No error
badUnitErr	–21	Driver reference number does not match unit table
unitEmptyErr	–22	Driver reference number specifies a nil handle in unit table
closErr	–24	Driver unable to complete close request
dRemovErr	–25	Attempt to remove an open driver

SEE ALSO

For information about the low-level function for closing device drivers, see the next section, which describes the PBClose function.

PBClose

You can use the PBClose function to close an open device driver.

```pascal
pascal OSErr PBClose(ParmBlkPtr paramBlock, Boolean async);
```

paramBlock   A pointer to an IOParam structure of the Device Manager parameter block.

async   A Boolean value that indicates whether the request is asynchronous. You must set this field to `false` because device drivers cannot be closed asynchronously.

Parameter block

←	ioResult	OSErr	The device driver's result code.
→	ioRefNum	short	The driver reference number.

DESCRIPTION

The `PBClose` function closes the device driver specified by the `ioRefNum` field. The Device Manager waits until the driver is inactive before calling the driver's close routine. When the driver indicates it has processed the close request, the Device Manager unlocks the driver resource if the `dRAMBased` flag is set, and unlocks the device control entry if the `dNeedLock` flag is not set. The Device Manager does not dispose of the device control entry or remove it from the unit table.

If the driver returns a negative result in register D0, the Device Manager returns this result code in the `ioResult` field of the parameter block and does not close the driver.

▲ **WARNING**
You should not close drivers that other applications may be using, such as a disk driver, the AppleTalk drivers, and so on. ▲

SPECIAL CONSIDERATIONS

The Device Manager does not queue close requests.

▲ **WARNING**
Do not call the `PBClose` function at interrupt time because if the driver was processing a request when the interrupt occurred the Device Manager may loop indefinitely, waiting for the driver to complete the request. ▲

ASSEMBLY-LANGUAGE INFORMATION

The trap macro for the `PBClose` function is `_Close` (0xA001).

You must set up register A0 with the address of the parameter block. When `_Close` returns, register D0 contains the result code. Register D0 is the only register affected by this function.

Registers on entry

A0   Address of the parameter block

Registers on exit

D0   Result code

RESULT CODES

noErr	0	No error
badUnitErr	–21	Driver reference number does not match unit table
unitEmptyErr	–22	Driver reference number specifies a nil handle in unit table
closErr	–24	Driver unable to complete close request
dRemovErr	–25	Attempt to remove an open driver

SEE ALSO

For information about the high-level function for closing device drivers, see the description of the CloseDriver function on page 1-65. For an example of how to close a device driver using the PBClose function, see Listing 1-2 on page 1-20.

CloseDeskAcc

You can use the CloseDeskAcc function to close a desk accessory.

```
pascal void CloseDeskAcc(short refNum);
```

refNum   The driver reference number contained in the desk accessory's WindowRecord.

DESCRIPTION

The CloseDeskAcc function closes the desk accessory specified by the refNum parameter. Your application should call CloseDeskAcc only when the user selects the Close or Quit item from your File menu and the active window does not belong to your application.

You obtain the refNum parameter from the windowKind field of the desk accessory's WindowRecord. Do not use the driver reference number returned by OpenDeskAcc.

SPECIAL CONSIDERATIONS

The CloseDeskAcc function may move memory; you should not call it at interrupt time.

SEE ALSO

For information about opening a desk accessory or other Apple menu item, see the description of the OpenDeskAcc function on page 1-65.

Communicating With Device Drivers

You can use either the FSRead or PBRead function to read information from a device driver, and you can use the FSWrite or PBWrite function to write information to a device driver.

FSRead

You can use the FSRead function to read data from an open driver into a data buffer.

```
pascal OSErr FSRead(short refNum, long *count, void *buffPtr);
```

refNum   The driver reference number.

count   The number of bytes to read.

buffPtr   A pointer to a buffer to hold the data.

DESCRIPTION

Before calling the FSRead function, your application should allocate a data buffer large enough to hold the data to be read. The FSRead function attempts to read the number of bytes indicated by the count parameter and transfer them to the data buffer pointed to by the buffPtr parameter. The refNum parameter identifies the device driver. After the transfer is complete, the count parameter indicates the number of bytes actually read.

▲ **WARNING**
Be sure your buffer is large enough to hold the number of bytes specified by the count parameter, or this function may corrupt memory. ▲

The FSRead function is a high-level synchronous version of the low-level PBRead function. Use the PBRead function when you want to request asynchronous reading or need to specify a drive number or a positioning mode and offset. See the next section, which describes the PBRead function.

SPECIAL CONSIDERATIONS

Do not call the FSRead function at interrupt time. Synchronous requests at interrupt time may block other pending I/O requests and cause the Device Manager to loop indefinitely while it waits for the device driver to complete the interrupted requests.

RESULT CODES

noErr	0	No error
readErr	–19	Driver does not respond to read requests
badUnitErr	–21	Driver reference number does not match unit table
unitEmptyErr	–22	Driver reference number specifies a nil handle in unit table
abortErr	–27	Request aborted by KillIO
notOpenErr	–28	Driver not open

SEE ALSO

For information about the low-level function for reading from device drivers, see the next section, which describes the PBRead function.

PBRead

You can use the PBRead function to read data from an open driver into a data buffer.

```
pascal OSErr PBRead(ParmBlkPtr paramBlock, Boolean async);
```

paramBlock A pointer to an IOParam structure of the Device Manager parameter block.

async   A Boolean value that indicates whether the request is asynchronous.

Parameter block

→	ioCompletion	ProcPtr	A pointer to a completion routine.
←	ioResult	OSErr	The device driver's result code.
→	ioVRefNum	short	The drive number.
→	ioRefNum	short	The driver reference number.
→	ioBuffer	Ptr	A pointer to a data buffer.
→	ioReqCount	long	The requested number of bytes to read.
←	ioActCount	long	The actual number of bytes read.
→	ioPosMode	short	The positioning mode.
↔	ioPosOffset	long	The positioning offset.

DESCRIPTION

Before calling the PBRead function, your application should allocate a data buffer large enough to hold the data to be read. The PBRead function attempts to read the number of bytes indicated by the ioReqCount field and transfer them to the data buffer pointed to by the ioBuffer field. The ioRefNum field identifies the device driver. After the transfer is complete, the ioActCount field indicates the number of bytes actually read.

▲ **WARNING**
Be sure your buffer is large enough to hold the number of bytes specified by the count parameter, or this function may corrupt memory. ▲

For block devices such as disk drivers, the PBRead function allows you to specify a drive number in the ioVRefNum field and specify a positioning mode and offset in the ioPosMode and ioPosOffset fields. Bits 0 and 1 of the ioPosMode field indicate where an operation should begin relative to the physical beginning of the block-formatted medium. You can use the following constants to test or set the value of these bits:

```
enum {
    /* positioning modes */
    fsAtMark        = 0,    /* at current position */
    fsFromStart     = 1,    /* offset from beginning */
    fsFromMark      = 3     /* offset from current position */
};
```

The ioPosOffset field specifies the positive or negative byte offset where the data is to be read, relative to the positioning mode. The offset must be a multiple of 512. The ioPosOffset field is ignored when ioPosMode is set to fsAtMark.

After the transfer is complete, the ioPosOffset field indicates the current position of the block device.

The Disk Driver allows you to use the PBRead function to verify that data written to a block device matches the data in memory. To do this, call PBRead immediately after writing the data, and add the read-verify constant rdVerify to the ioPosMode field of the parameter block. The result code ioErr is returned if the data does not match.

SPECIAL CONSIDERATIONS

Do not call the PBRead function synchronously at interrupt time. Synchronous requests at interrupt time may block other pending I/O requests and cause the Device Manager to loop indefinitely while it waits for the device driver to complete the interrupted requests.

ASSEMBLY-LANGUAGE INFORMATION

The trap macro for the PBRead function is _Read (0xA002). Set bit 10 of the trap word to execute this function asynchronously. Set bit 9 to execute it immediately.

You must set up register A0 with the address of the parameter block. When _Read returns, register D0 contains the result code. Register D0 is the only register affected by this function.

Registers on entry

A0   Address of the parameter block

Registers on exit

D0   Result code

RESULT CODES

noErr	0	No error
readErr	–19	Driver does not respond to read requests
badUnitErr	–21	Driver reference number does not match unit table
unitEmptyErr	–22	Driver reference number specifies a nil handle in unit table
abortErr	–27	Request aborted by KillIO
notOpenErr	–28	Driver not open
ioErr	–36	Data does not match in read-verify mode

SEE ALSO

For information about the high-level function for reading from device drivers, see the description of the FSRead function beginning on page 1-69. For an example of how to read from a device driver using the PBRead function, see Listing 1-3 on page 1-21.

FSWrite

You can use the FSWrite function to write data from a data buffer to an open driver.

```
pascal OSErr FSWrite(short refNum, long *count,
                     const void *buffPtr);
```

refNum   The driver reference number.

count   The number of bytes to write.

buffPtr   A pointer to the buffer that holds the data.

DESCRIPTION

The FSWrite function attempts to write the number of bytes indicated by the count parameter from the data buffer pointed to by the buffPtr parameter to the device driver specified by the refNum parameter. After the transfer is complete, the count parameter indicates the number of bytes actually written.

The FSWrite function is a high-level synchronous version of the low-level PBWrite function. Use the PBWrite function when you want to request asynchronous writing or need to specify a drive number or a positioning mode and offset. See the next section, which describes the PBWrite function.

SPECIAL CONSIDERATIONS

Do not call the FSWrite function at interrupt time. Synchronous requests at interrupt time may block other pending I/O requests and cause the Device Manager to loop indefinitely while it waits for the device driver to complete the interrupted requests.

RESULT CODES

noErr	0	No error
writErr	–20	Driver does not respond to write requests
badUnitErr	–21	Driver reference number does not match unit table
unitEmptyErr	–22	Driver reference number specifies a nil handle in unit table
abortErr	–27	Request aborted by KillIO
notOpenErr	–28	Driver not open

SEE ALSO

For information about the low-level function for writing to device drivers, see the next section, which describes the PBWrite function.

PBWrite

You can use the PBWrite function to write data from a data buffer to an open driver.

```
pascal OSErr PBWrite(ParmBlkPtr paramBlock, Boolean async);
```

paramBlock   A pointer to an IOParam structure of the Device Manager parameter block.

async   A Boolean value that indicates whether the request is asynchronous.

Parameter block

→	ioCompletion	ProcPtr	A pointer to a completion routine.
←	ioResult	OSErr	The device driver's result code.
→	ioVRefNum	short	The drive number.
→	ioRefNum	short	The driver reference number.
→	ioBuffer	Ptr	A pointer to a data buffer.
→	ioReqCount	long	The requested number of bytes to write.
←	ioActCount	long	The actual number of bytes written.
→	ioPosMode	short	The positioning mode.
↔	ioPosOffset	long	The positioning offset.

DESCRIPTION

The PBWrite function attempts to write the number of bytes indicated by the ioReqCount field from the data buffer pointed to by the ioBuffer field to the device driver specified by the ioRefNum field. After the transfer is complete, the ioActCount field indicates the number of bytes actually written.

For block devices such as disk drivers, the PBWrite function allows you to specify a drive number in the ioVRefNum field and specify a positioning mode and offset in the ioPosMode and ioPosOffset fields. Bits 0 and 1 of the ioPosMode field indicate where an operation should begin relative to the physical beginning of the block-formatted medium. You can use the following constants to test or set the value of these bits:

```
enum {
    /* positioning modes */
    fsAtMark        = 0,      /* at current position */
    fsFromStart     = 1,      /* offset from beginning */
    fsFromMark      = 3       /* offset from current position */
};
```

The `ioPosOffset` field specifies the positive or negative byte offset where the data is to be written, relative to the positioning mode. The offset must be a multiple of 512. The `ioPosOffset` field is ignored when `ioPosMode` is set to `fsAtMark`.

After the transfer is complete, the `ioPosOffset` field indicates the new current position of a block device.

SPECIAL CONSIDERATIONS

Do not call the `PBWrite` function synchronously at interrupt time. Synchronous requests at interrupt time may block other pending I/O requests and cause the Device Manager to loop indefinitely while it waits for the device driver to complete the interrupted requests.

ASSEMBLY-LANGUAGE INFORMATION

The trap macro for the `PBWrite` function is `_Write` (0xA003). Set bit 10 of the trap word to execute this function asynchronously. Set bit 9 to execute it immediately.

You must set up register A0 with the address of the parameter block. When `_Write` returns, register D0 contains the result code. Register D0 is the only register affected by this function.

Registers on entry

A0   Address of the parameter block

Registers on exit

D0   Result code

RESULT CODES

noErr	0	No error
writErr	–20	Driver does not respond to write requests
badUnitErr	–21	Driver reference number does not match unit table
unitEmptyErr	–22	Driver reference number specifies a `nil` handle in unit table
abortErr	–27	Request aborted by `KillIO`
notOpenErr	–28	Driver not open

SEE ALSO

For information about the high-level function for writing to device drivers, see the description of the FSWrite function on page 1-72. For an example of how to write to a device driver using the PBWrite function, see Listing 1-4 on page 1-22.

Controlling and Monitoring Device Drivers

You can use either the Control or PBControl function to send control information to a device driver, and you can use the Status or PBStatus function to obtain status information from a device driver. The Device Manager also provides the KillIO and PBKillIO functions for terminating all requests in a driver I/O queue.

The PBControl, PBStatus, and PBKillIO functions use the CntrlParam structure, described on page 1-53.

Control

You can use the Control function to send control information to a device driver.

```
pascal OSErr Control(short refNum, short csCode,
                     const void *csParamPtr);
```

refNum   The driver reference number.

csCode   A driver-dependent code specifying the type of information sent.

csParamPtr A pointer to the control information.

DESCRIPTION

The Control function sends information to the device driver specified by the refNum parameter. The value you pass in the csCode parameter and the type of information pointed to by the csParamPtr parameter are defined by the driver you are calling. For more information, see the appropriate chapters for the standard device drivers in this book and other books in the *Inside Macintosh* series.

The Control function is a high-level synchronous version of the low-level PBControl function. Use the PBControl function if you need to specify a drive number or if you want the control request to be executed asynchronously.

SPECIAL CONSIDERATIONS

Do not call the Control function at interrupt time. Synchronous requests at interrupt time may block other pending I/O requests and cause the Device Manager to loop indefinitely while it waits for the device driver to complete the interrupted requests.

RESULT CODES

noErr	0	No error
controlErr	–17	Driver does not respond to this control request
badUnitErr	–21	Driver reference number does not match unit table
unitEmptyErr	–22	Driver reference number specifies a nil handle in unit table
abortErr	–27	Request aborted by KillIO
notOpenErr	–28	Driver not open

SEE ALSO

For information about the low-level function for controlling device drivers, see the next section, which describes the PBControl function.

PBControl

You can use the PBControl function to send control information to a device driver.

```
pascal OSErr PBControl(ParmBlkPtr paramBlock, Boolean async);
```

paramBlock A pointer to a CntrlParam structure of the Device Manager parameter block.

async A Boolean value that indicates whether the request is asynchronous.

Parameter block

→	ioCompletion	ProcPtr	A pointer to a completion routine.
←	ioResult	OSErr	The device driver's result code.
→	ioVRefNum	short	The drive number.
→	ioCRefNum	short	The driver reference number.
→	csCode	short	The type of control call.
→	csParam	short[11]	The control information.

DESCRIPTION

The PBControl function sends information to the device driver specified by the ioCRefNum field. The value you pass in the csCode field and the type of information in the csParam field are defined by the driver you are calling. For more information, see the appropriate chapters for the standard device drivers in this book and other books in the *Inside Macintosh* series.

SPECIAL CONSIDERATIONS

Do not call the PBControl function synchronously at interrupt time. Synchronous requests at interrupt time may block other pending I/O requests and cause the Device Manager to loop indefinitely while it waits for the device driver to complete the interrupted requests.

ASSEMBLY-LANGUAGE INFORMATION

The trap macro for the PBControl function is _Control (0xA004). Set bit 10 of the trap word to execute this routine asynchronously. Set bit 9 to execute it immediately.

You must set up register A0 with the address of the parameter block. When _Control returns, register D0 contains the result code. Register D0 is the only register affected by this routine.

Registers on entry

A0   Address of the parameter block

Registers on exit

D0   Result code

RESULT CODES

noErr	0	No error
controlErr	–17	Driver does not respond to this control request
badUnitErr	–21	Driver reference number does not match unit table
unitEmptyErr	–22	Driver reference number specifies a nil handle in unit table
abortErr	–27	Request aborted by KillIO
notOpenErr	–28	Driver not open

SEE ALSO

For information about the high-level function for controlling device drivers, see the description of the Control function on page 1-75. For an example of how to send control information to a device driver using the PBControl function, see Listing 1-5 on page 1-23.

Status

You can use the Status function to obtain status information from a device driver.

```
pascal OSErr Status(short refNum, short csCode,
                void *csParamPtr);
```

refNum   The driver reference number.

csCode   A driver-dependent code specifying the type of information requested.

csParamPtr A pointer to a csParam array where the status information will be returned.

DESCRIPTION

The Status function returns information about the device driver specified by the refNum parameter. The value you pass in the csCode parameter and the received information pointed to by the `csParamPtr` parameter are defined by the driver you are calling. For more information, see the appropriate chapters for the standard device drivers in this book and other books in the *Inside Macintosh* series.

The `Status` function is a high-level synchronous version of the low-level `PBStatus` function. Use the `PBStatus` function if you need to specify a drive number or if you want the status request to be asynchronous.

Note

The Device Manager interprets a `csCode` value of 1 as a special case. When the Device Manager receives a status request with a `csCode` value of 1, it returns a handle to the driver's device control entry. This type of status request is not passed to the device driver. ◆

SPECIAL CONSIDERATIONS

Do not call the `Status` function at interrupt time. Synchronous requests at interrupt time may block other pending I/O requests and cause the Device Manager to loop indefinitely while it waits for the device driver to complete the interrupted requests.

RESULT CODES

noErr	0	No error
statusErr	–18	Driver does not respond to this status request
badUnitErr	–21	Driver reference number does not match unit table
unitEmptyErr	–22	Driver reference number specifies a `nil` handle in unit table
abortErr	–27	Request aborted by `KillIO`
notOpenErr	–28	Driver not open

SEE ALSO

For information about the low-level function for monitoring device drivers, see the next section, which describes the `PBStatus` function.

PBStatus

You can use the `PBStatus` function to obtain status information from a device driver.

```
pascal OSErr PBStatus(ParmBlkPtr paramBlock, Boolean async);
```

paramBlock   A pointer to a `CntrlParam` structure of the Device Manager parameter block.

async   A Boolean value that indicates whether the request is asynchronous.

Parameter block

→	ioCompletion	ProcPtr	A pointer to a completion routine.
←	ioResult	OSErr	The device driver's result code.
→	ioVRefNum	short	The drive number.
→	ioCRefNum	short	The driver reference number.
→	csCode	short	The type of status call.
←	csParam	short[11]	The status information.

DESCRIPTION

The PBStatus function returns information about the device driver specified by the ioCRefNum field. The value you pass in the csCode field and the type of information received in the csParam field are defined by the driver you are calling. For more information, see the appropriate chapters for the standard device drivers in this book and other books in the *Inside Macintosh* series.

Note

The Device Manager interprets a csCode value of 1 as a special case. When the Device Manager receives a status request with a csCode value of 1, it returns a handle to the driver's device control entry. This type of status request is not passed to the device driver. ◆

SPECIAL CONSIDERATIONS

Do not call the PBStatus function synchronously at interrupt time. Synchronous requests at interrupt time may block other pending I/O requests and cause the Device Manager to loop indefinitely while it waits for the device driver to complete the interrupted requests.

ASSEMBLY-LANGUAGE INFORMATION

The trap macro for the PBStatus function is _Status (0xA005). Set bit 10 of the trap word to execute this function asynchronously. Set bit 9 to execute it immediately.

You must set up register A0 with the address of the parameter block. When _Status returns, register D0 contains the result code. Register D0 is the only register affected by this function.

Registers on entry

A0   Address of the parameter block

Registers on exit

D0   Result code

RESULT CODES

noErr	0	No error
statusErr	–18	Driver does not respond to this status request
badUnitErr	–21	Driver reference number does not match unit table
unitEmptyErr	–22	Driver reference number specifies a `nil` handle in unit table
abortErr	–27	Request aborted by `KillIO`
notOpenErr	–28	Driver not open

SEE ALSO

For information about the high-level function for monitoring device drivers, see the description of the `Status` function on page 1-77. For an example of how to request status information from a device driver using the `PBStatus` function, see Listing 1-5 on page 1-23.

KillIO

You can use the `KillIO` function to terminate all current and pending I/O requests for a device driver.

```
pascal OSErr KillIO(short refNum);
```

refNum   The driver reference number.

DESCRIPTION

The `KillIO` function stops any current I/O request being processed by the driver specified by the `RefNum` parameter, and removes all pending requests from the I/O queue for that driver. The Device Manager calls the completion routine, if any, for each pending request, and sets the `ioResult` field of each request equal to the result code `abortErr`.

The Device Manager passes `KillIO` requests to a driver only if the driver is open and enabled for control calls. If the driver returns an error, the I/O queue is left unchanged and no completion routines are called.

▲ **WARNING**
The `KillIO` function terminates all pending I/O requests for a driver, including requests initiated by other applications. ▲

SPECIAL CONSIDERATIONS

The Device Manager always executes the `KillIO` function immediately; that is, it never places a `KillIO` request in the I/O queue.

Although the Device Manager imposes no restrictions on calling `KillIO` at interrupt time, you should consult a device driver's documentation to determine if it supports this.

RESULT CODES

noErr	0	No error
controlErr	–17	Driver does not respond to this control request
badUnitErr	–21	Driver reference number does not match unit table
unitEmptyErr	–22	Driver reference number specifies a `nil` handle in unit table
notOpenErr	–28	Driver not open

SEE ALSO

For information about the low-level function for terminating current and pending I/O requests for a driver, see the next section, which describes the PBKillIO function.

PBKillIO

You can use the PBKillIO function to terminate all current and pending I/O requests for a device driver.

```
pascal OSErr PBKillIO(ParmBlkPtr paramBlock, Boolean async);
```

paramBlock   A pointer to a CntrlParam structure of the Device Manager parameter block.

async   A Boolean value that indicates whether the request is asynchronous. You must set this field to false because the PBKillIO function does not support asynchronous requests.

Parameter block

→	ioCompletion	ProcPtr	A pointer to a completion routine.
←	ioResult	OSErr	The device driver's result code.
→	ioCRefNum	short	The driver reference number.

DESCRIPTION

The PBKillIO function stops any current I/O request being processed by the driver specified by the ioCRefNum field, and removes all pending requests from the I/O queue for that driver. The Device Manager calls the completion routine, if any, for each pending request, and sets the ioResult field of each request equal to the result code abortErr.

The Device Manager passes PBKillIO requests to a device driver only if the driver is open and enabled for control calls. If the driver returns an error, the I/O queue is left unchanged and no completion routines are called.

▲ **WARNING**
The PBKillIO function terminates all pending I/O requests for a driver, including requests initiated by other applications. ▲

SPECIAL CONSIDERATIONS

The Device Manager always executes the PBKillIO function immediately; that is, it never places a PBKillIO request in the I/O queue. However, you should not call this function immediately—always call the PBKillIO function synchronously.

Although the Device Manager imposes no restrictions on calling PBKillIO at interrupt time, you should consult a device driver's documentation to determine if it supports this.

ASSEMBLY-LANGUAGE INFORMATION

The trap macro for the PBKillIO function is _KillIO (0xA006). You must set up register A0 with the address of the parameter block. When _KillIO returns, register D0 contains the result code. Register D0 is the only register affected by this function.

Registers on entry

A0   Address of the parameter block

Registers on exit

D0   Result code

RESULT CODES

noErr	0	No error
controlErr	–17	Driver does not respond to this control request
badUnitErr	–21	Driver reference number does not match unit table
unitEmptyErr	–22	Driver reference number specifies a nil handle in unit table
notOpenErr	–28	Driver not open

SEE ALSO

For information about the high-level function for terminating current and pending I/O requests for a driver, see the description of the KillIO function on page 1-80.

Writing and Installing Device Drivers

The Device Manager includes a number of functions that provide low-level support for device drivers.

The DriverInstall and DriverInstallReserveMem functions create a device control entry and install it in the unit table. The DriverInstallReserveMem function is preferred because it allocates the device control entry as low as possible in the system heap. The DriverRemove function removes an existing device control entry.

The GetDCtlEntry function returns a handle to a driver's device control entry.

The IODone routine notifies the Device Manager that an I/O operation is done. Driver routines call IODone when the current request is completed and ready to be removed from the I/O queue.

The Fetch and Stash routines can be used to move characters into and out of data buffers. You pass a pointer to the device control entry in the A1 register to each of these three routines. The Device Manager uses the device control entry to locate the active request. If no such request exists, these routines generate system error dsIOCoreErr.

In the interest of speed, you invoke the Fetch, Stash, and IODone routines with jump vectors, stored in the global variables JFetch, JStash, and JIODone, rather than macros. You can use a jump vector by moving its address onto the stack and executing an RTS instruction. An example is:

```
MOVE.L   JIODone,-(SP)
RTS
```

The Fetch and Stash routines do not return a result code; if an error occurs, the System Error Handler is invoked.

DriverInstall

You can use the DriverInstall function to create a device control entry and install it in the unit table.

```
pascal OSErr DriverInstall(Ptr drvrPtr, short refNum);
```

drvrPtr   A pointer to the device driver.
refNum   The driver reference number.

DESCRIPTION

The DriverInstall function allocates a device control entry (DCE) in the system heap and installs a handle to this DCE in the unit table location specified by the refNum parameter. You pass a pointer to the device driver in the drvrPtr parameter.

In addition, this function copies the refNum parameter to the dCtlRefNum field of the DCE, sets the dRAMBased flag in the dCtlFlags field, and clears all the other fields.

SPECIAL CONSIDERATIONS

The DriverInstall function does not load the driver resource into memory, copy the flags from the driver header to the dCtlFlags field, or open the driver. You can write code to perform these tasks, or use the OpenDriver, OpenSlot, or PBOpen functions instead.

The DriverInstall function allocates memory; you should not call it at interrupt time.

ASSEMBLY-LANGUAGE INFORMATION

The trap macro for the DriverInstall function is _DrvrInstall (0xA03D).

You place a pointer to the device driver in register A0, and the driver reference number in register D0. When _DrvrInstall returns, register D0 contains the result code.

Registers on entry

A0   A pointer to the device driver

D0   The driver reference number

Registers on exit

D0   Result code

RESULT CODES

noErr	0	No error
badUnitErr	–21	Driver reference number does not match unit table

SEE ALSO

For information about the DriverInstallReserveMem function, which installs a driver as low as possible in the system heap, see the next section.

DriverInstallReserveMem

You can use the DriverInstallReserveMem function to create a device control entry and install it in the unit table.

```
pascal OSErr DriverInstallReserveMem(Ptr drvrPtr, short refNum);
```

drvrPtr   A pointer to the device driver.

refNum   The driver reference number.

DESCRIPTION

The DriverInstallReserveMem function is equivalent to the DriverInstall function, except that it calls the Memory Manager ReserveMem function to compact the heap before allocating memory for the device control entry (DCE).

After calling the ReserveMem function, the DriverInstallReserveMem function allocates a DCE in the system heap and installs a handle to this DCE in the unit table location specified by the refNum parameter. You pass a pointer to the device driver in the drvrPtr parameter.

In addition, this function copies the refNum parameter to the dCtlRefNum field of the DCE, sets the dRAMBased flag in the dCtlFlags field, and clears all the other fields.

SPECIAL CONSIDERATIONS

The `DriverInstallReserveMem` function does not load the driver resource into memory, copy the flags from the driver header to the `dCtlFlags` field, or open the driver. You can write code to perform these tasks, or use the `OpenDriver`, `OpenSlot`, or `PBOpen` functions instead.

The `DriverInstallReserveMem` function allocates memory; you should not call it at interrupt time.

ASSEMBLY-LANGUAGE INFORMATION

The trap macro for the `DriverInstallReserveMem` function is `_DrvrInstall` (0xA03D). You must set bit 10 of the trap word to signal the Device Manager to call the `ReserveMem` function before allocating memory for the DCE.

You place a pointer to the device driver in register A0, and the driver reference number in register D0. When `_DrvrInstall` returns, register D0 contains the result code.

Registers on entry

A0   A pointer to the device driver

D0   The driver reference number

Registers on exit

D0   Result code

RESULT CODES

noErr	0	No error
badUnitErr	–21	Driver reference number does not match unit table

DriverRemove

You can use the `DriverRemove` function to remove a device driver's device control entry from the unit table and release the driver resource.

```pascal
pascal OSErr DriverRemove(short refNum);
```

refNum   The driver reference number.

DESCRIPTION

The `DriverRemove` function removes a device driver's device control entry from the unit table and releases the driver resource. You specify the device driver using the `refNum` parameter. You must close the device driver before calling `DriverRemove`.

If the driver is closed, `DriverRemove` calls the Memory Manager function `DisposeHandle` to release the device control entry, then sets the corresponding handle in the unit table to nil. If the driver's dRAMBased flag is set, DriverRemove calls the Resource Manager function ReleaseResource to release the driver resource.

SPECIAL CONSIDERATIONS

The DriverRemove function may move memory; you should not call it at interrupt time.

ASSEMBLY-LANGUAGE INFORMATION

The trap macro for the DriverRemove function is _DrvrRemove (0xA03E).

You place the driver reference number in register D0. When _DrvrRemove returns, register D0 contains the result code.

Registers on entry

D0   The driver reference number

Registers on exit

D0   Result code

RESULT CODES

noErr	0	No error
dRemovErr	–25	Attempt to remove an open driver

GetDCtlEntry

You can use the GetDCtlEntry function to obtain a handle to the device control entry of a device driver.

```
pascal DCtlHandle GetDCtlEntry (short refNum);
```

refNum   The reference number of the driver.

DESCRIPTION

The GetDCtlEntry function returns a handle to the device control entry of the device driver indicated by the refNum parameter.

SEE ALSO

For a description of the device control entry structure see page 1-56.

IODone

You use the IODone routine to notify the Device Manager that an I/O request has completed.

DESCRIPTION

The IODone routine sets the ioResult field of the parameter block with the value returned by the driver in register D0. It then removes the current request from the driver I/O queue and marks the driver inactive. If there are no pending requests, and the dNeedLock bit of the dCtlFlags word is not set, IODone unlocks the driver and its device control entry. Finally, IODone executes the completion routine, if any.

The section "Entering and Exiting From Driver Routines," beginning on page 1-29, explains when to use this routine.

ASSEMBLY-LANGUAGE INFORMATION

Registers on entry

A1   Pointer to DCE

D0   Result code

Jump vector

JIODone

SEE ALSO

For an example of how to call the IODone routine from an assembly-language dispatching routine, see Listing 1-8 on page 1-29.

Fetch

You can use the Fetch routine to get the next character from the data buffer.

DESCRIPTION

The Fetch routine gets the next character from the data buffer pointed to by the ioBuffer field of the parameter block of the pending request. It increments the ioActCount field by 1. If the ioActCount field equals the ioReqCount field, this routine sets bit 15 of register D0. After receiving the last byte request, the driver should jump to the IODone routine.

Registers on entry

A1   Pointer to the device control entry

Registers on exit

D0   Character fetched; bit 15 = 1 if this is the last character in the buffer

Jump vector

JFetch

Stash

You can use the Stash routine to store the next character from the data buffer.

DESCRIPTION

The Stash routine places the character in register D0 into the data buffer pointed to by the ioBuffer field of the parameter block of the pending request and increments the ioActCount field by 1. If the ioActCount field equals the ioReqCount field, this routine sets bit 15 of register D0. After stashing the last byte requested, the driver should jump to the IODone routine.

ASSEMBLY-LANGUAGE INFORMATION

Registers on entry

A1   Pointer to DCE

D0   Character to stash

Registers on exit

D0   Bit 15 = 1 if this is the last character in the buffer

Jump vector

JStash

Resources

This section describes the driver resource, which you can use to store your device drivers and desk accessories. If your device driver requires a user interface, you can create a Chooser extension and store your driver in a device package resource. For more information, see "Creating a Device Package" on page 1-45.

The Driver Resource

Listing 1-15 shows the Rez format of the 'DRVR' resource type.

Listing 1-15   'DRVR' resource format

```
type 'DRVR' {
    boolean = 0;
    boolean   dontNeedLock, needLock;          /* lock drvr in memory */
    boolean   dontNeedTime, needTime;          /* for periodic action */
    boolean   dontNeedGoodbye, needGoodbye;    /* call before heap reinit */
    boolean   noStatusEnable, statusEnable;    /* responds to Status */
    boolean   noCtlEnable, ctlEnable;          /* responds to Control */
    boolean   noWriteEnable, writeEnable;      /* responds to Write */
    boolean   noReadEnable, readEnable;        /* responds to Read */
    byte = 0;
    integer;                                   /* driver delay */
    unsigned hex integer;                      /* DA event mask */
    integer;                                   /* DA menu */
    unsigned hex integer;                      /* offset to Open */
    unsigned hex integer;                      /* offset to Prime */
    unsigned hex integer;                      /* offset to Control */
    unsigned hex integer;                      /* offset to Status */
    unsigned hex integer;                      /* offset to Close */
    pstring;                                   /* driver name */
    hex string;                                /* driver code */
};
```

The driver resource begins with seven flags that specify certain characteristics of the driver.

You need to set the dNeedLock flag if your driver's code should be locked in memory.

You set the dNeedTime flag of the drvrFlags word if your device driver needs to perform some action periodically.

You need to set the dNeedGoodbye flag if you want your application to receive a goodbye control request before the heap is reinitialized.

The last four flags indicate which Device Manager requests the driver's routines can respond to.

The next element of the resource specifies the time between periodic tasks.

The next two elements provide an event mask and menu ID for desk accessories. The section "Writing a Desk Accessory" on page 1-49 describes these fields.

Offsets to the driver routines follow the desk accessory fields. See "Entering and Exiting From Driver Routines" on page 1-29 for more information about the routine offsets.

The next element of the driver resource is the driver name. You can use uppercase and lowercase letters when naming your driver, but the first character should be a period—`.MyDriver`, for example.

Your driver routines, which follow the driver name, must be aligned on a word boundary.

The section "Creating a Driver Resource" on page 1-24 discusses this structure in detail.

Summary of the Device Manager

C Summary

Constants

```
enum {
    /* request codes passed by the Device Manager to a driver's
       prime routine */
    aRdCmd          = 2,      /* read operation requested */
    aWrCmd          = 3       /* write operation requested */
};

enum {
    /* flags used in the driver header and device control entry */
    dNeedLockMask     = 0x4000, /* set if driver must be locked in memory as
                                   soon as it is opened */
    dNeedTimeMask     = 0x2000, /* set if driver needs time for performing
                                   periodic tasks */
    dNeedGoodByeMask  = 0x1000, /* set if driver needs to be called before the
                                   application heap is initialized */
    dStatEnableMask   = 0x0800, /* set if driver responds to status requests */
    dCtlEnableMask    = 0x0400, /* set if driver responds to control requests */
    dWritEnableMask   = 0x0200, /* set if driver responds to write requests */
    dReadEnableMask   = 0x0100, /* set if driver responds to read requests */

    /* run-time flags used in the device control entry */
    drvrActiveMask    = 0x0080, /* driver is currently processing a request */
    dRAMBasedMask     = 0x0040, /* dCtlDriver is a handle (1) or pointer (0) */
    dOpenedMask       = 0x0020  /* driver is open */
};

enum {
    /* access permissions */
    fsCurPerm       = 0,      /* retain current permission */
    fsRdPerm        = 1,      /* allow reads only */
    fsWrPerm        = 2,      /* allow writes only */
    fsRdWrPerm      = 3,      /* allow reads and writes */
```

```
    /* positioning modes */
    fsAtMark            = 0,      /* at current position */
    fsFromStart         = 1,      /* offset from beginning */
    fsFromMark          = 3,      /* offset from current position */

    /* read modes */
    rdVerify            = 64      /* read-verify mode */
};

enum {
    /* control codes */
    goodbye             = -1,     /* heap being reinitialized */
    killCode            = 1,      /* KillIO requested */
    accEvent            = 64,     /* handle an event */
    accRun              = 65,     /* time for periodic action */
    accCursor           = 66,     /* change cursor shape */
    accMenu             = 67,     /* handle menu item */
    accUndo             = 68,     /* handle undo command */
    accCut              = 70,     /* handle cut command */
    accCopy             = 71,     /* handle copy command */
    accPaste            = 72,     /* handle paste command */
    accClear            = 73      /* handle clear command */
};

enum {
    /* Chooser messages */
    chooserInitMsg      = 11,     /* the user selected this device package */
    newSelMsg           = 12,     /* the user made new device selections */
    fillListMsg         = 13,     /* fill the device list with choices */
    getSelMsg           = 14,     /* mark one or more choices as selected */
    selectMsg           = 15,     /* the user made a selection */
    deselectMsg         = 16,     /* the user canceled a selection */
    terminateMsg        = 17,     /* allows device package to clean up */
    buttonMsg           = 19      /* the user selected a button */
};
```

Data Types

```
typedef union ParamBlockRec {
    IOParam             ioParam;
    FileParam           fileParam;
    VolumeParam         volumeParam;
    CntrlParam          cntrlParam;
```

```
    SlotDevParam     slotDevParam;
    MultiDevParam    multiDevParam;
} ParamBlockRec;
typedef ParamBlockRec *ParmBlkPtr;

typedef struct IOParam {
    QElemPtr    qLink;          /* next queue entry */
    short       qType;          /* queue type */
    short       ioTrap;         /* routine trap */
    Ptr         ioCmdAddr;      /* routine address */
    ProcPtr     ioCompletion;   /* completion routine address */
    OSErr       ioResult;       /* result code */
    StringPtr   ioNamePtr;      /* pointer to driver name */
    short       ioVRefNum;      /* volume reference or drive number */
    short       ioRefNum;       /* driver reference number */
    char        ioVersNum;      /* not used by the Device Manager */
    char        ioPermssn;      /* read/write permission */
    Ptr         ioMisc;         /* not used by the Device Manager */
    Ptr         ioBuffer;       /* pointer to data buffer */
    long        ioReqCount;     /* requested number of bytes */
    long        ioActCount;     /* actual number of bytes completed */
    short       ioPosMode;      /* positioning mode */
    long        ioPosOffset;    /* positioning offset */
} IOParam;

typedef struct CntrlParam {
    QElemPtr    qLink;          /* next queue entry */
    short       qType;          /* queue type */
    short       ioTrap;         /* routine trap */
    Ptr         ioCmdAddr;      /* routine address */
    ProcPtr     ioCompletion;   /* completion routine address */
    OSErr       ioResult;       /* result code */
    StringPtr   ioNamePtr;      /* pointer to driver name */
    short       ioVRefNum;      /* volume reference or drive number */
    short       ioCRefNum;      /* driver reference number */
    short       csCode;         /* type of control or status request */
    short       csParam[11];    /* control or status information */
} CntrlParam;

typedef struct AuxDCE {
    Ptr         dCtlDriver;     /* pointer or handle to driver */
    short       dCtlFlags;      /* flags */
    QHdr        dCtlQHdr;       /* I/O queue header */
    long        dCtlPosition;   /* current R/W byte position */
```

```
    Handle      dCtlStorage;    /* handle to private storage */
    short       dCtlRefNum;     /* driver reference number */
    long        dCtlCurTicks;   /* used internally */
    GrafPtr     dCtlWindow;     /* pointer to driver's window */
    short       dCtlDelay;      /* ticks between periodic actions */
    short       dCtlEMask;      /* desk accessory event mask */
    short       dCtlMenu;       /* desk accessory menu ID */
    char        dCtlSlot;       /* slot */
    char        dCtlSlotId;     /* sResource directory ID */
    long        dCtlDevBase;    /* slot device base address */
    Ptr         dCtlOwner;      /* reserved; must be 0 */
    char        dCtlExtDev;     /* external device ID */
    char        fillByte;       /* reserved */
} AuxDCE;
typedef AuxDCE *AuxDCEPtr, **AuxDCEHandle;
```

Functions

Opening and Closing Device Drivers

```
pascal OSErr OpenDriver      (ConstStr255Param name, short *drvrRefNum);
pascal OSErr PBOpen          (ParmBlkPtr paramBlock, Boolean async);
pascal OSErr PBOpenSync      (ParmBlkPtr paramBlock);
pascal OSErr OpenSlot        (ParmBlkPtr paramBlock, Boolean async);
pascal short OpenDeskAcc     (ConstStr255Param deskAccName);
pascal OSErr CloseDriver     (short refNum);
pascal OSErr PBClose         (ParmBlkPtr paramBlock, Boolean async);
pascal OSErr PBCloseSync     (ParmBlkPtr paramBlock);
pascal void  CloseDeskAcc    (short refNum);
```

Communicating With Device Drivers

```
pascal OSErr FSRead          (short refNum, long *count, void *buffPtr);
pascal OSErr PBRead          (ParmBlkPtr paramBlock, Boolean async);
pascal OSErr PBReadSync      (ParmBlkPtr paramBlock);
pascal OSErr PBReadAsync     (ParmBlkPtr paramBlock);
pascal OSErr FSWrite         (short refNum, long *count, const void *buffPtr);
pascal OSErr PBWrite         (ParmBlkPtr paramBlock, Boolean async);
pascal OSErr PBWriteSync     (ParmBlkPtr paramBlock);
pascal OSErr PBWriteAsync    (ParmBlkPtr paramBlock);
```

Controlling and Monitoring Device Drivers

```
pascal OSErr Control          (short refNum, short csCode, const void
                               *csParamPtr);

pascal OSErr PBControl        (ParmBlkPtr paramBlock, Boolean async);

pascal OSErr PBControlSync    (ParmBlkPtr paramBlock);

pascal OSErr PBControlAsync   (ParmBlkPtr paramBlock);

pascal OSErr Status           (short refNum, short csCode, void *csParamPtr);

pascal OSErr PBStatus         (ParmBlkPtr paramBlock, Boolean async);

pascal OSErr PBStatusSync     (ParmBlkPtr paramBlock);

pascal OSErr PBStatusAsync    (ParmBlkPtr paramBlock);

pascal OSErr KillIO           (short refNum);

pascal OSErr PBKillIO         (ParmBlkPtr paramBlock, Boolean async);

pascal OSErr PBKillIOSync     (ParmBlkPtr paramBlock);

pascal OSErr PBKillIOAsync    (ParmBlkPtr paramBlock);
```

Driver Support Functions

```
pascal OSErr DriverInstall  (Ptr drvrPtr, short refNum);

pascal OSErr DriverInstallReserveMem (Ptr drvrPtr, short refNum);

pascal OSErr DriverRemove   (short refNum);

pascal DCtlHandle GetDCtlEntry (short refNum);
```

Pascal Summary

Constants

```
CONST
    {request codes passed by the Device Manager to a driver's prime routine}
    aRdCmd          = 2;        {read operation requested}
    aWrCmd          = 3;        {write operation requested}

    {flags used in the driver header and device control entry}
    dNeedLockMask   = $4000;    {set if driver must be locked in memory as }
                                { soon as it is opened}

    dNeedTimeMask   = $2000;    {set if driver needs time for performing }
                                { periodic tasks}

    dNeedGoodByeMask = $1000;   {set if driver needs to be called before }
                                { the application heap is initialized}

    dStatEnableMask = $0800;    {set if driver responds to status requests}
```

```
dCtlEnableMask       = $0400;      {set if driver responds to control requests}
dWritEnableMask      = $0200;      {set if driver responds to write requests}
dReadEnableMask      = $0100;      {set if driver responds to read requests}

{run-time flags used in the device control entry}
drvrActiveMask       = $0080;      {driver is currently processing a request}
dRAMBasedMask        = $0040;      {dCtlDriver is a handle (1) or pointer (0)}
dOpenedMask          = $0020;      {driver is open}

{access permissions}
fsCurPerm            = 0;          {retain current permission}
fsRdPerm             = 1;          {allow reads only}
fsWrPerm             = 2;          {allow writes only}
fsRdWrPerm           = 3;          {allow reads and writes}

{positioning modes}
fsAtMark             = 0;          {at current position}
fsFromStart          = 1;          {offset from beginning}
fsFromMark           = 3;          {offset from current position}

{read modes}
rdVerify             = 64;         {read-verify mode}

{control codes}
goodbye              = -1;         {heap being reinitialized}
killCode             = 1;          {KillIO requested}
accEvent             = 64;         {handle an event}
accRun               = 65;         {time for periodic action}
accCursor            = 66;         {change cursor shape}
accMenu              = 67;         {handle menu item}
accUndo              = 68;         {handle undo command}
accCut               = 70;         {handle cut command}
accCopy              = 71;         {handle copy command}
accPaste             = 72;         {handle paste command}
accClear             = 73;         {handle clear command}

{Chooser messages}
chooserInitMsg       = 11;         {the user selected this device package}
newSelMsg            = 12;         {the user made new device selections}
fillListMsg          = 13;         {fill the device list with choices}
getSelMsg            = 14;         {mark one or more choices as selected}
selectMsg            = 15;         {the user made a selection}
```

```
   deselectMsg     = 16;        {the user canceled a selection}
   terminateMsg    = 17;        {allows device package to clean up}
   buttonMsg       = 19;        {the user selected a button}
```

Data Types

```
TYPE  ParamBlkType = (IOParam, FileParam, VolumeParam, CntrlParam,
                      SlotDevParam, MultiDevParam);

      ParamBlockRec =
      RECORD
          qLink:          QElemPtr;    {next queue entry}
          qType:          Integer;     {queue type}
          ioTrap:         Integer;     {routine trap}
          ioCmdAddr:      Ptr;         {routine address}
          ioCompletion:   ProcPtr;     {completion routine address}
          ioResult:       OSErr;       {result code}
          ioNamePtr:      StringPtr;   {pointer to driver name}
          ioVRefNum:      Integer;     {volume reference or drive number}
      CASE ParamBlkType OF
      IOParam:
          (ioRefNum:      Integer;     {driver reference number}
          ioVersNum:      SignedByte;  {not used}
          ioPermssn:      SignedByte;  {read/write permission}
          ioMisc:         Ptr;         {not used}
          ioBuffer:       Ptr;         {pointer to data buffer}
          ioReqCount:     LongInt;     {requested number of bytes}
          ioActCount:     LongInt;     {actual number of bytes}
          ioPosMode:      Integer;     {positioning mode}
          ioPosOffset:    LongInt);    {positioning offset}
      CntrlParam:
          (ioCRefNum:     Integer;     {driver reference number}
          csCode:         Integer;     {type of control or status request}
          csParam:        ARRAY[0..10] OF Integer);  {control or status info}
      END;
      ParmBlkPtr = ^ParamBlockRec;

      AuxDCE =
      RECORD
          dCtlDriver:     Ptr;         {pointer or handle to driver}
          dCtlFlags:      Integer;     {flags}
          dCtlQHdr:       QHdr;        {driver I/O queue header}
          dCtlPosition:   LongInt;     {byte position}
```

```
    dCtlStorage:      Handle;       {handle to private storage}
    dCtlRefNum:       Integer;      {driver reference number}
    dCtlCurTicks:     LongInt;      {used internally}
    dCtlWindow:       GrafPtr;      {pointer to driver's window}
    dCtlDelay:        Integer;      {ticks between periodic actions}
    dCtlEMask:        Integer;      {event mask for desk accessories}
    dCtlMenu:         Integer;      {menu ID for desk accessories}
    dCtlSlot:         Byte;         {slot}
    dCtlSlotId:       Byte;         {sResource directory ID}
    dCtlDevBase:      LongInt;      {slot device base address}
    dCtlOwner:        Ptr;          {reserved; must be 0}
    dCtlExtDev:       Byte;         {external device ID}
    fillByte:         Byte;         {reserved}
  END;
  AuxDCEPtr          = ^AuxDCE;
  AuxDCEHandle       = ^AuxDCEPtr;
```

Routines

Opening and Closing Device Drivers

```
FUNCTION OpenDriver        (name: Str255; VAR refNum: Integer): OSErr;
FUNCTION PBOpen            (paramBlock: ParmBlkPtr; async: Boolean): OSErr;
FUNCTION PBOpenSync        (paramBlock: ParmBlkPtr): OSErr;
FUNCTION OpenSlot          (paramBlock: ParmBlkPtr; async: Boolean): OSErr;
FUNCTION OpenDeskAcc       (deskAccName: Str255): INTEGER;
FUNCTION CloseDriver       (refNum: Integer): OSErr;
FUNCTION PBClose           (paramBlock: ParmBlkPtr; async: Boolean): OSErr;
FUNCTION PBCloseSync       (paramBlock: ParmBlkPtr): OSErr;
PROCEDURE CloseDeskAcc     (refNum: INTEGER);
```

Communicating With Device Drivers

```
FUNCTION FSRead            (refNum: Integer; VAR count: LongInt;
                            buffPtr: Ptr): OSErr;
FUNCTION PBRead            (paramBlock: ParmBlkPtr; async: Boolean): OSErr;
FUNCTION PBReadSync        (paramBlock: ParmBlkPtr): OSErr;
FUNCTION PBReadAsync       (paramBlock: ParmBlkPtr): OSErr;
FUNCTION FSWrite           (refNum: Integer: VAR count: LongInt;
                            buffPtr: Ptr): OSErr;
FUNCTION PBWrite           (paramBlock: ParmBlkPtr; async: Boolean): OSErr;
FUNCTION PBWriteSync       (paramBlock: ParmBlkPtr): OSErr;
```

```
FUNCTION PBWriteAsync        (paramBlock: ParmBlkPtr): OSErr;
```

Controlling and Monitoring Device Drivers

```
FUNCTION Control             (refNum: Integer; csCode: Integer;
                              csParamPtr: Ptr): OSErr;

FUNCTION PBControl           (paramBlock: ParmBlkPtr; async: Boolean): OSErr;

FUNCTION PBControlSync       (paramBlock: ParmBlkPtr): OSErr;

FUNCTION PBControlAsync      (paramBlock: ParmBlkPtr): OSErr;

FUNCTION Status              (refNum: Integer; csCode: Integer;
                              csParamPtr: Ptr): OSErr;

FUNCTION PBStatus            (paramBlock: ParmBlkPtr; async: Boolean): OSErr;

FUNCTION PBStatusSync        (paramBlock: ParmBlkPtr): OSErr;

FUNCTION PBStatusAsync       (paramBlock: ParmBlkPtr): OSErr;

FUNCTION KillIO              (refNum: Integer): OSErr;

FUNCTION PBKillIO            (paramBlock: ParmBlkPtr; async: Boolean): OSErr;

FUNCTION PBKillIOSync        (paramBlock: ParmBlkPtr): OSErr;

FUNCTION PBKillIOAsync       (paramBlock: ParmBlkPtr): OSErr;
```

Driver Support Routines

```
FUNCTION DriverInstall          (drvrPtr: Ptr; refNum: Integer): OSErr;

FUNCTION DriverInstallReserveMem (drvrPtr: Ptr; refNum: Integer): OSErr;

FUNCTION DriverRemove           (refNum: Integer): OSErr;

FUNCTION GetDCtlEntry           (refNum: Integer): DCtlHandle;
```

Assembly-Language Summary

Data Structures

Device Manager Parameter Block Header

0	qLink	long	used internally by the Device Manager
4	qType	word	used internally by the Device Manager
6	ioTrap	word	used internally by the Device Manager
8	ioCmdAddr	long	used internally by the Device Manager
12	ioCompletion	long	completion routine
16	ioResult	word	result code
18	ioNamePtr	long	driver name
22	ioVRefNum	word	drive number

I/O Parameter Structure

24	ioRefNum	word	driver reference number
26	ioVersNum	byte	not used
27	ioPermssn	byte	read/write permission
28	ioMisc	long	not used
32	ioBuffer	long	pointer to data buffer
36	ioReqCount	long	requested number of bytes
40	ioActCount	long	actual number of bytes
44	ioPosMode	word	positioning mode
46	ioPosOffset	long	positioning offset

Control Parameter Structure

24	ioCRefNum	word	driver reference number
26	csCode	word	type of control or status request
28	csParam	22 bytes	control or status information

Trap Macros

Trap Macro Names

C and Pascal name	Trap macro name
PBOpen	_Open
OpenSlot	_Open
PBClose	_Close
PBRead	_Read
PBWrite	_Write
PBControl	_Control
PBStatus	_Status
PBKillIO	_KillIO
DriverInstall	_DrvrInstall
DriverRemove	_DrvrRemove

Routines Requiring Jump Vectors

Routine	Jump vector
Fetch	JFetch
Stash	JStash
IODone	JIODone

Result Codes

noErr	0	No error
controlErr	–17	Driver does not respond to this control request
statusErr	–18	Driver does not respond to this status request
readErr	–19	Driver does not respond to read requests
writErr	–20	Driver does not respond to write requests
badUnitErr	–21	Driver reference number does not match unit table
unitEmptyErr	–22	Driver reference number specifies a nil handle in unit table
openErr	–23	Requested read/write permission does not match driver's open permission
closErr	–24	Driver unable to complete close request
dRemovErr	–25	Attempt to remove an open driver
dInstErr	–26	Driver resource not found
abortErr	–27	Request aborted by KillIO
notOpenErr	–28	Driver not open
ioErr	–36	Data does not match in read-verify mode

Slot Manager

Contents

This chapter describes how your application or device driver can use the Slot Manager to identify expansion cards and communicate with the firmware on a card.

You need to use the Slot Manager only if you are writing an application or a device driver that must address an expansion card directly. For example, you need to use the Slot Manager if you are writing a driver for a video card, but not if you only want to display information on a monitor for which a device driver already exists.

The **Slot Manager** provides functions to help you search through the data structures that expansion cards use to organize the information in their firmware. The meaning of the information in the data structures varies from card to card; you need to know the specifics of a card in order to interpret its data structures. To interpret these data structures, you need to know the information in *Designing Cards and Drivers for the Macintosh Family*, third edition, as well as information specific to the expansion card you're using.

This chapter begins with a brief introduction to Apple's implementation of the **NuBus expansion interface**. The NuBus interface provides a 32-bit-wide synchronous, multislot expansion bus for adding expansion cards to Macintosh computers. This introduction explains the firmware data structures of NuBus expansion cards, but does not provide much detail about the information these data structures contain. If you are designing an expansion card, you must read *Designing Cards and Drivers for the Macintosh Family*, third edition. If you are writing a driver for a device on a card, you should also read the chapter "Device Manager" in this book.

After introducing the NuBus architecture and expansion card design, this chapter discusses how you can

- enable and disable NuBus cards

- delete, restore, enable, disable, and find information in an expansion card's firmware

- install and remove slot interrupt handlers

Introduction to Slots and Cards

The Macintosh Operating System provides a standardized interface to expansion cards through the Slot Manager. The Slot Manager supports two types of expansion cards: NuBus and processor-direct slot (PDS). Most Macintosh computers include one or both of these expansion systems. Although the discussion and examples in this chapter use NuBus, the information also applies to PDS expansion cards.

Processor-direct slot expansion cards connect directly to the processor bus, giving them direct access to the microprocessor and therefore a speed advantage over NuBus cards. However, because the PDS expansion interface is an extension of the processor bus, the configuration of the slot depends on which microprocessor is used by the computer. Refer to *Designing Cards and Drivers for the Macintosh Family*, third edition, for information specific to PDS expansion cards.

Macintosh computers that include the NuBus expansion interface contain one or more identical NuBus slots. Each slot is identified by slot a number in the range $1 through $E. (Slot $0 corresponds to the main logic board, and slot $F is reserved for NuBus address translation.)

Note

For convenience, this chapter refers to a NuBus configuration with six slots numbered $9 through $E. Keep in mind that Macintosh computers may have more or fewer slots. Refer to the appropriate Macintosh Developer Note or *Guide to the Macintosh Family Hardware*, second edition, for information about specific models. ◆

In Macintosh computers, the processor bus (which connects the microprocessor to RAM, ROM, and the FPU) and the NuBus (which connects the NuBus slots) are connected by a **bus interface**, as shown in Figure 2-1.

Figure 2-1 Simplified processor-bus and NuBus architecture

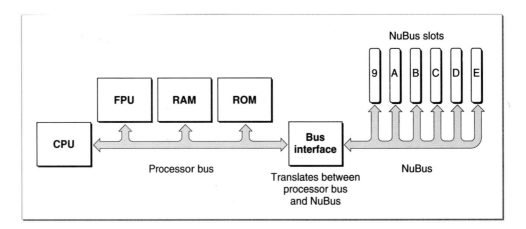

Both the processor bus and the NuBus are 4 bytes (32 bits) wide. The bus interface transfers data between the buses in byte lanes. A **byte lane** is any of the 4 bytes that make up the 32-bit bus. Because the processor bus and the NuBus interpret the significance of bytes within words differently, the bus interface must perform byte-lane swapping between the two buses.

The bus interface also performs some address translation between the two buses. It maps certain address ranges on each bus to different address ranges on the other bus. *Designing Cards and Drivers for the Macintosh Family*, third edition, discusses byte lanes and address translation in more detail.

The next section, "Slot Address Allocations," discusses the address ranges assigned by the Macintosh architecture to each NuBus slot.

The section "Firmware" on page 2-7 introduces the data structures that cards use to organize information in their firmware.

Slot Address Allocations

The Macintosh architecture assigns certain address ranges to each slot. The microprocessor communicates with an expansion card in a particular slot by reading or writing to memory in the slot's address range. Expansion cards can also communicate with each other in this manner.

The NuBus architecture supports 32-bit addressing, providing 4 gigabytes of address space. All Macintosh computers that use Motorola 68030, 68040, or PowerPC processors support 32-bit addressing under System 7. Macintosh computers that use Motorola 68000 or 68020 processors, and those running System 6, use 24-bit addressing. This section describes address space allocation in both the 32-bit and 24-bit modes.

In 32-bit mode, the Macintosh architecture assigns two address ranges to each NuBus slot: a 256-megabyte super slot space and a 16-megabyte standard slot space.

The 4 gigabytes of 32-bit address space contain 16 regions of 256 megabytes apiece. Each region constitutes the **super slot space** for one possible slot ID. Each super slot space spans an address range of $s000 0000 through $sFFF FFFF, where s is a hexadecimal digit $1 through $E, corresponding to the slot ID. For example, the address range $9000 0000 through $9FFF FFFF constitutes the super slot space for slot $9.

The **standard slot spaces** are 16 megabytes apiece and have address ranges of the form $Fs00 0000 through $FsFF FFFF, where s is the slot ID. The standard slot space for slot $9, for example, is $F900 0000 through $F9FF FFFF. Figure 2-2 shows the super slot and standard slot subdivisions of the 32-bit address space.

In 24-bit mode, software can address only a fraction of each card's allocated address range. In this mode, the Operating System assigns each slot a 1-megabyte **minor slot space**. The bus interface translates 24-bit addresses on the processor bus with the form $sx xxxx (where s is a slot ID and x is any hexadecimal digit) into 32-bit NuBus addresses of the form $Fs0x xxxx, which is the first megabyte of the slot's standard slot space.

For example, 24-bit addresses in the range $90 0000 through $9F FFFF constitute the minor slot space corresponding to slot $9. The hardware translates these addresses into the NuBus address range $F900 0000 through $F90F FFFF.

Figure 2-2   The NuBus 32-bit address space

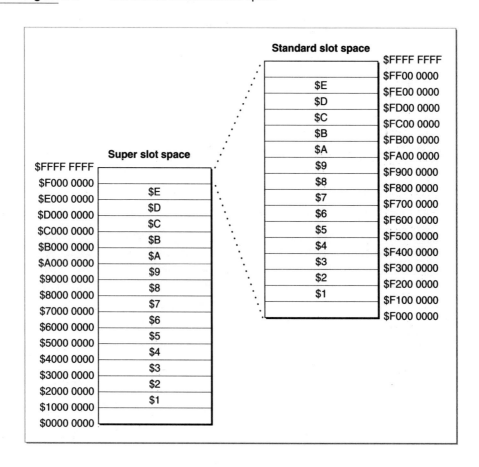

Table 2-1 shows the address allocations for each slot ID.

Table 2-1   Slot address allocations by slot ID

Slot ID	24-bit minor slot space (1 MB)	32-bit minor slot space (1 MB)	Standard slot space (16 MB)	Super slot space (256 MB)
$1	$1x xxxx	$F10x xxxx	$F1xx xxxx	$1xxx xxxx
$2	$2x xxxx	$F20x xxxx	$F2xx xxxx	$2xxx xxxx
$3	$3x xxxx	$F30x xxxx	$F3xx xxxx	$3xxx xxxx
$4	$4x xxxx	$F40x xxxx	$F4xx xxxx	$4xxx xxxx
$5	$5x xxxx	$F50x xxxx	$F5xx xxxx	$5xxx xxxx
$6	$6x xxxx	$F60x xxxx	$F6xx xxxx	$6xxx xxxx
$7	$7x xxxx	$F70x xxxx	$F7xx xxxx	$7xxx xxxx
$8	$8x xxxx	$F80x xxxx	$F8xx xxxx	$8xxx xxxx

continued

Table 2-1   Slot address allocations by slot ID (continued)

Slot ID	24-bit minor slot space (1 MB)	32-bit minor slot space (1 MB)	Standard slot space (16 MB)	Super slot space (256 MB)
$9	$9x xxxx	$F90x xxxx	$F9xx xxxx	$9xxx xxxx
$A	$Ax xxxx	$FA0x xxxx	$FAxx xxxx	$Axxx xxxx
$B	$Bx xxxx	$FB0x xxxx	$FBxx xxxx	$Bxxx xxxx
$C	$Cx xxxx	$FC0x xxxx	$FCxx xxxx	$Cxxx xxxx
$D	$Dx xxxx	$FD0x xxxx	$FDxx xxxx	$Dxxx xxxx
$E	$Ex xxxx	$FE0x xxxx	$FExx xxxx	$Exxx xxxx

Firmware

The firmware of a NuBus expansion card contains information that identifies the card and its functions. Your application uses the Slot Manager to communicate with this firmware. This firmware, called the **declaration ROM**, may also include other information, such as initialization code or code for drivers that communicate with devices on the card. The sole purpose of many Slot Manager routines is to provide access to the information in the declaration ROM.

This section discusses the data structures used to store information in the declaration ROM. You'll need to understand these structures in order to use the Slot Manager routines. To create firmware for an expansion card, you'll need to read *Designing Cards and Drivers for the Macintosh Family*, third edition.

The declaration ROM includes these elements:

- The **sResources**. An sResource is a data structure in the firmware of an expansion card's declaration ROM that defines a function or capability of the card. An sResource typically contains information about a single function or capability, although some sResources may contain other data—for example, device drivers, icons, fonts, code, or vendor-specific information.

- The **sResource directory**. The sResource directory is a special sResource that contains offsets to all of the other sResources in the declaration ROM.

- The **format block**. The format block is a data structure that allows the Slot Manager to find the declaration ROM and to validate it. It contains some identification information and an offset to the sResource directory.

The next few sections discuss these data structures in more detail.

The sResource

An sResource consists of a list of 4-byte entries. The first byte of each entry is an ID field that identifies the type of data contained in the entry. The next 3 bytes contain either data for the sResource or an offset to additional data such as icon definitions, code, or device drivers relating to the sResource.

Slot Manager

Note

An sResource is sometimes referred to as a *slot resource*. Note, however, that an sResource is a data structure in the firmware of a NuBus expansion card and not the type of Macintosh resource associated with the Resource Manager (which is described in *Inside Macintosh: More Macintosh Toolbox*). ◆

The last entry in an sResource must contain an end-of-list marker—a 4-byte series with the value $FF 00 00 00. Figure 2-3 shows the format of a typical sResource.

Figure 2-3   The structure of a typical sResource

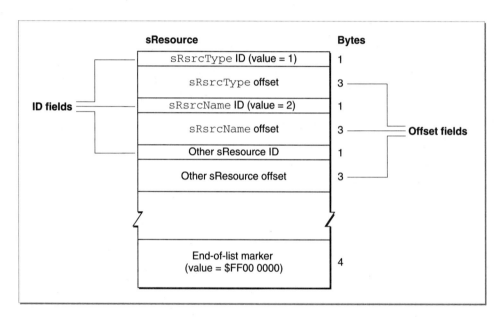

The ID field of each sResource entry indicates the type of information in the offset field of the entry. Apple reserves the range 0 through 127 for common sResource IDs. *Designing Cards and Drivers for the Macintosh Family*, third edition, includes a complete list of the Apple-defined sResource IDs and their meanings.

The offset field of each entry can contain a byte or word of data, or an offset to a larger block of data. This field takes one of three possible forms:

- two $00 bytes followed by an 8-bit byte of data
- a single $00 byte followed by a 16-bit word of data
- a signed 24-bit offset to a larger data structure; the offset is relative to the address of the preceding ID field

Table 2-2 lists the kinds of large data types commonly used in sResources.

Table 2-2   Large data types used in sResources

Data type	Description
Long	32 bits, signed or unsigned
Pointer	32 bits, signed or unsigned
cString	One-dimensional array of bytes, ending with 0
sBlock	A sized block of data (see Figure 2-4)
sExecBlock	A sized block of code (see Figure 2-4)

The **sBlock** and **sExecBlock** data structures begin with a **size** field, which contains the physical size of the block (including the **size** field). In the **sBlock** structure, the **size** field is followed by data. The **sExecBlock** structure includes additional fields and a code block. Figure 2-4 shows these structures.

Figure 2-4   The format of the **sBlock** and **sExecBlock** data structures

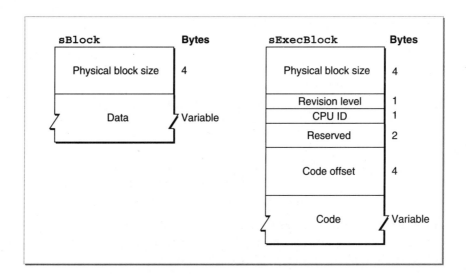

Type and Name Entries

As shown in Figure 2-3, the Slot Manager requires that each sResource contain an **sRsrcType** entry, which identifies the sResource type, and an **sRsrcName** entry, which provides the sResource name.

The **sRsrcType** entry contains an ID value of 1 and an offset to an **sRsrcType** entry. Figure 2-5 shows the format of an **sRsrcType** entry.

Figure 2-5 The sRsrcType entry format

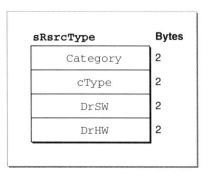

The fields of the sRsrcType entry are as follows:

Field	Description
Category	The most general classification of card functions. Examples of categories are catDisplay and catNetwork.
cType	The subclass of the category. For example, within the catDisplay category there is a typeVideo subcategory; within the catNetwork category, there is a typeEtherNet subcategory.
DrSW	The driver software interface to the card. (This provides the calling interface for applications and system software.) For example, under the catDisplay category and the typeVideo subcategory, there is a drSwApple software interface that indicates the Apple-defined interface to work with QuickDraw using Macintosh Operating System frame buffers.
DrHW	The identification of the specific hardware device associated with the driver software interface. Generally, only the driver interacts with the hardware specified here.

Every card has a unique sRsrcType entry that must be assigned by Apple Computer, Inc. If you are developing a card, refer to *Designing Cards and Drivers for the Macintosh Family*, third edition, for information on obtaining an sRsrcType entry.

The sRsrcName entry in an sResource contains an ID value of 2 and an offset to a cString data structure containing the sResource name. By convention, the sRsrcName field is derived by stripping the prefixes from the sRsrcType values and separating the fields by underscores. For example, the sRsrcName field for an sResource whose sRsrcType values are catDisplay, typeVideo, DrSwApple, and DrHwTFB becomes 'Display_Video_Apple_TFB'.

Designing Cards and Drivers for the Macintosh Family, third edition, provides information about these and other sResource entry types.

The Board sResource and Functional sResources

Every card must have a single **board sResource** that contains information about the card as a whole. An sResource relating to a specific function is called a **functional sResource**, and a card may have as many of them as necessary. For example, a video card may have separate functional sResources for every pixel depth it supports. (See Figure 2-8 on page 2-14 for an example of a functional sResources for a video card, and see *Designing Cards and Drivers for the Macintosh Family*, third edition, for additional examples that include code listings.)

The entries in the board sResource provide the Slot Manager with a card's identification number, vendor information, board flags, and initialization code. Like all sResources, the board sResource must include an `sRsrcType` entry and an `sRsrcName` entry. The board `sRsrcType` entry must contain the constants `CatBoard` ($0001), `TypBoard` ($0000), `DrSWBoard` ($0000), and `DrHWBoard` ($0000). The `sRsrcName` entry for the board sResource name does not follow the same convention as other sResources: the `sRsrcName` entry for the board sResource contains the name of the entire card (for example, `'Macintosh Display Card'`).

The board sResource must also contain a `BoardId` entry, a word that contains the card design identification number assigned by Apple Computer, Inc. *Designing Cards and Drivers for the Macintosh Family*, third edition, describes other Apple-defined entries specifically for board sResources.

Figure 2-6 shows a sample board sResource. It shows an `sRsrcType` entry and an `sRsrcName` entry and also includes three entry types, `BoardID`, `PRAMInitData`, and `PrimaryInit`, which are discussed in *Designing Cards and Drivers for the Macintosh Family*, third edition.

Figure 2-6   A sample board sResource

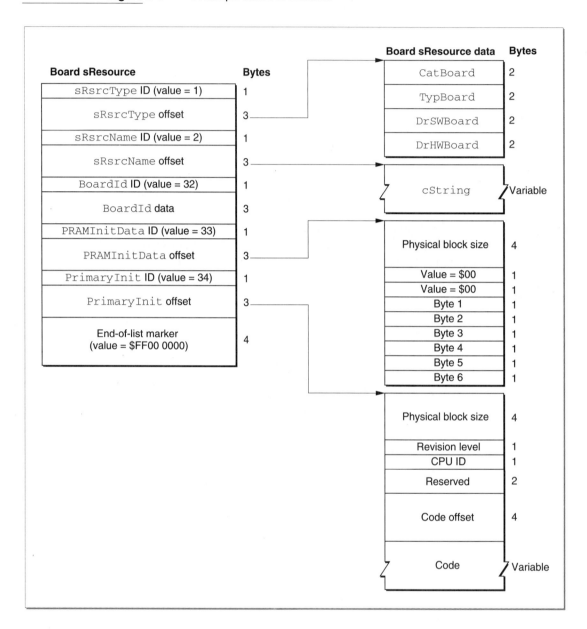

The sResource Directory

The sResource directory lists all the sResources in the declaration ROM and provides an offset to each one. The sResource directory has the same structure as an sResource—that is, an sResource directory consists of a series of 4-byte entries, where the first byte is an ID field and the next 3 bytes contain an offset to additional data. Figure 2-7 shows the format of the sResource directory.

Figure 2-7 The structure of the sResource directory

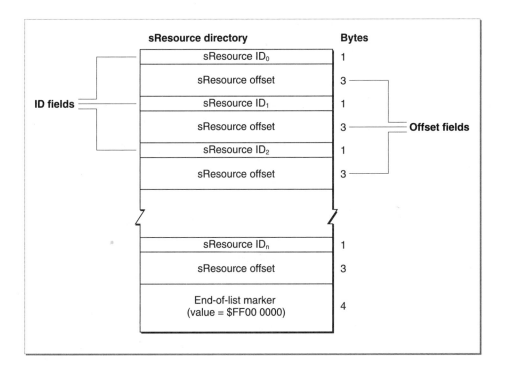

The sResource ID field of an entry in the sResource directory always identifies an sResource on the card. Each sResource in the card firmware requires a unique ID defined by the card designer, and the ID must be in the range 1 through 254. For example, an entry for the board sResource must appear first in a card's sResource directory, so card designers typically assign an sResource ID value of 1 to the board sResource. The sResource ID numbers must appear in the sResource directory in ascending order. An sResource directory must conclude with the end-of-list marker ($FF 00 00 00).

The offset field of each entry contains a signed 24-bit offset to the sResource corresponding to the sResource ID field. The offset value counts only those bytes accessible by valid byte lanes, and is relative to the address of the sResource ID field.

The Format Block

The format block always resides at the highest address in the standard slot space of a declaration ROM. At startup, the Slot Manager locates installed cards by searching each slot space for a valid format block. The format block contains information about the declaration ROM and an offset to the sResource directory. The Slot Manager uses the format block to validate the declaration ROM and locate the sResources.

The format block also contains a value that specifies which of the four byte lanes are occupied by the declaration ROM. These byte lanes are called the *valid byte lanes*. Some declaration ROMs do not appear on all four byte lanes, so software cannot read meaningful data at every memory location in the address space for the byte lanes.

Slot Manager

IMPORTANT

The format block defines which byte lanes are valid for the declaration ROM only. The valid byte lanes are determined by card design, and may be different for other memory-mapped devices on the card. ▲

Designing Cards and Drivers for the Macintosh Family, third edition, defines the structure of the format block and gives examples of how the valid byte lanes affect communication with a declaration ROM.

Figure 2-8 illustrates the relationship of the format block, the sResource directory, and the sResources for a sample video card. For every entry in the sResource directory and in the sResources, its ID number is shown on the left side of the entry. As shown in this figure, the board sResource is the first sResource listed in the sResource directory. Each functional sResource that follows in turns defines a display capability provided by the card. (To simplify this figure, only one complete functional sResource is shown.)

Figure 2-8   The format block and sResources for a sample video card

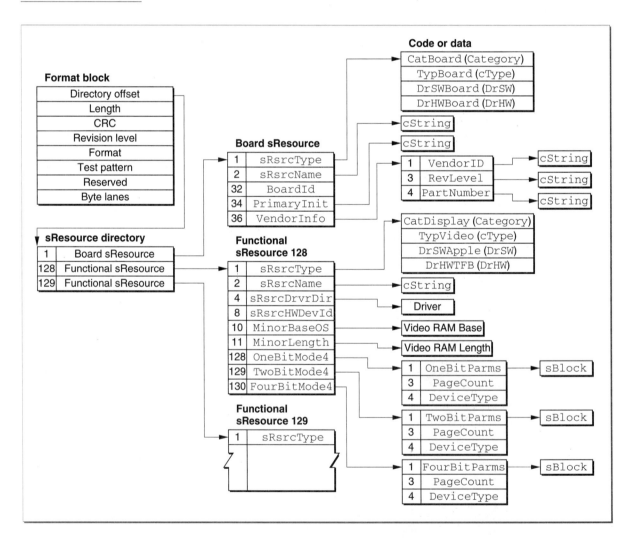

About the Slot Manager

The Slot Manager provides three basic services:

- On startup, it examines each slot and initializes any expansion cards it finds.

- It maintains data structures that contain information about each slot and every available sResource.

- It provides functions that allow you to get information about expansion cards and their sResources.

There are two variations of the System 7 Slot Manager: version 1 and version 2. Version 1 of the Slot Manager is RAM based and is installed by the user with the System 7 upgrade kit. Version 2 is included in the ROM of newer Macintosh computers.

At startup, the version of the Slot Manager in ROM searches each slot for a declaration ROM and creates a **slot information record** for each slot. See "Slot Information Record" on page 2-24 for the definition of the `SInfoRecord` data type.

As the Slot Manager searches the slots, it identifies all of the sResources in each declaration ROM and creates a table—the **slot resource table** (**SRT**)—that lists all of the sResources currently available to the system. The slot resource table is a private data structure maintained by the Slot Manager. Applications and device drivers use Slot Manager routines to get information from the slot resource table.

After building the slot resource table, the Slot Manager initializes the 6 bytes reserved for each slot in parameter RAM. If the slot has an expansion card with a `PRAMInitData` entry in its board sResource, the Slot Manager uses the values in that entry to initialize the parameter RAM; otherwise, it clears those bytes in parameter RAM.

Next, the Slot Manager disables interrupts and executes the code in the `PrimaryInit` entry of the board sResource for each card. Note that at this point in the startup, the keyboard and the mouse are not initialized and that a card's `PrimaryInit` code has only limited control over the functionality of the card itself.

If certain values (defined by the Start Manager) are set in a card's parameter RAM, a card with an `sRsrcBootRec` entry may take over the system startup process. The Start Manager passes control to the code in the `sRsrcBootRec` early in the startup sequence, before system patches are installed. Refer to the chapter "Start Manager" in *Inside Macintosh: Operating System Utilities* for more information about the startup process.

Designing Cards and Drivers for the Macintosh Family, third edition, describes the `PRAMInitData`, `PrimaryInit`, and `sRsrcBootRec` entry types.

If no card takes over, the normal system startup continues. After version 1 of the Slot Manager is loaded, it conducts a second search for declaration ROMs, this time in 32-bit mode. If the Slot Manager finds any additional NuBus cards, it adds their sResources to the slot resource table and executes the code in their `PrimaryInit` entries. (Version 2 of the Slot Manager, which resides in ROM, does not need to conduct a second search.)

Note

Some versions of the Slot Manager prior to System 7 address NuBus cards in 24-bit mode and may not be able to identify all cards. After version 1 of the Slot Manager is loaded, it locates these cards. ◆

After all system patches have been installed, version 1 or later of the Slot Manager executes the code in any `SecondaryInit` entries it finds in the declaration ROMs. It does not reexecute the code from `PrimaryInit` entries, reinitialize parameter RAM, or restore any sResources deleted by the `PrimaryInit` code.

Note

Most versions of the Slot Manager prior to System 7 do not execute code from `SecondaryInit` entries. ◆

After the Slot Manager executes `SecondaryInit` code, it searches for sResources that have an `sRsrcFlags` entry with the `fOpenAtStart` flag set. When the Slot Manager finds an sResource with this flag set, it loads the device driver from the `sRsrcDrvrDir` entry of the sResource, or calls the code in the sResource's `sRsrcLoadRec` entry, which loads the sResource's device driver.

Finally, the system executes initialization resources of type `'INIT'`.

See *Designing Cards and Drivers for the Macintosh Family*, third edition, for details about the `sRsrcFlags`, `sRsrcDrvrDir`, and `sRsrcLoadRec` entry types.

Using the Slot Manager

The Slot Manager allows you to enable and disable NuBus cards, manipulate the slot resource table, get information from slot information records, get status information, and read and change expansion cards' parameter RAM. However, the majority of Slot Manager routines search for sResources in the slot resource table or provide information from these structures.

The Slot Manager provides a variety of methods to find an sResource. These methods include searching for an sResource with a particular sResource ID, searching for an sResource with a particular sResource type, searching through all sResources, searching through only the enabled sResources, and so on.

The Slot Manager also provides a number of routines that return information from sResources. Some of these routines, like the `SReadByte` and `SGetCString` functions, return one particular type of data structure. Others, like the `SFindStruct` function, can return information about any data structure. Functions such as `SGetDriver` and `SExec` not only return information from an sResource, they also perform additional operations like loading the sResource's driver or executing the code of an `sExecBlock` data structure.

You can use the `SVersion` function, described on page 2-30, to determine if the Slot Manager is version 1, version 2, or a version that predates System 7.

Enabling and Disabling NuBus Cards

Version 1 and later of the Slot Manager allows you to temporarily disable your NuBus card. You might want to do this if, for example, you are designing a NuBus card that must be addressed in 32-bit mode or that requires RAM-based system software patches to be loaded into memory before the card is initialized. Your `PrimaryInit` code can disable the card temporarily and the `SecondaryInit` code can reenable it.

To disable a NuBus card temporarily, the initialization routine in your `PrimaryInit` record should return in the `seStatus` field of the `SEBlock` data structure (described in "Slot Execution Parameter Block" on page 2-27) an error code with a value in the range `svTempDisable` ($8000) through `svDisabled` ($8080). The Slot Manager places this code in the `siInitStatusV` field of the slot information record for the slot, and places the fatal error `smInitStatVErr` (–316) in the `siInitStatusA` field of the slot information record. The card and its sResources are then unavailable for use by the Operating System.

After the Operating System loads RAM patches, the Slot Manager checks the value of the `siInitStatusA` field of each slot information record. If this value is greater than or equal to 0, indicating no error, the Slot Manager executes the `SecondaryInit` code for the slot, if any. If the value in the `siInitStatusA` field is `smInitStatVErr`, the Slot Manager checks the `siInitStatusV` field. If the value of the `siInitStatusV` field is in the range `svTempDisable` through `svDisabled`, the Slot Manager sets the `siInitStatusA` field to 0 and runs the `SecondaryInit` code.

For examples of `PrimaryInit` and `SecondaryInit` code, see *Designing Cards and Drivers for the Macintosh Family*, third edition.

Deleting and Restoring sResources

Some NuBus cards have sResources to support a variety of system configurations or modes. The Slot Manager loads all of the sResources during system initialization, and then the card's `PrimaryInit` code can delete from the slot resource table any sResources that are not appropriate for the system as configured. If the user changes the system configuration or selects a different mode of operation, your card can reinstall a deleted sResource. The `SDeleteSRTRec` function deletes sResources; the `InsertSRTRec` function reinstalls them.

Because none of the Slot Manager functions can search for sResources that have been deleted from the slot resource table, you must keep a record of all sResources you delete so that you will have the appropriate parameter values when you want to reinstall one.

When you reinstall an sResource, it may be necessary to update the `dCtlSlotId` and `dCtlDevBase` fields in the slot device driver's device control entry. You need to update the `dCtlSlotId` field if you change the sResource ID. The `dCtlDevBase` field holds the base address of the slot device. For a video card this is the base address for the pixel map in the card's `GDevice` record (which is described in *Inside Macintosh: Imaging With QuickDraw*). The `InsertSRTRec` function updates the `dCtlDevBase` field automatically if you supply a valid driver reference number.

Enabling and Disabling sResources

Under certain circumstances, you might want to disable an sResource while it remains listed in the slot resource table. For example, a NuBus card might provide several modes of operation, only one of which can be active at a given time. Your application might want to disable the sResources associated with all but the active mode, but still list all available modes in a menu. When the user selects a new mode, your application can then disable the currently active sResource and enable the one the user selected.

You use the SetSRsrcState function to enable or disable an sResource. Listing 2-1 disables the sResource in slot $A with an sResource ID of 128 and enables the sResource in the same slot with an sResource ID of 131.

Listing 2-1   Disabling and enabling an sResource

```
PROCEDURE MyDisableAndEnableSResource;
VAR
    mySpBlk:     SpBlock;
    myErr:       OSErr;
BEGIN
    WITH mySpBlk DO        {set required values in parameter block}
    BEGIN
        spParamData := 1;        {disable}
        spSlot := $A;            {slot number}
        spID := 128;             {sResource ID}
        spExtDev := 0;           {ID of external device}
    END;
    myErr := SetSRsrcState(@mySpBlk);
    IF myErr = noErr THEN
    BEGIN
        WITH mySpBlk DO
        BEGIN
            spParamData := 0;        {enable}
            spSlot := $A;            {slot number}
            spID := 131;             {sResource ID}
            spExtDev := 0;           {ID of external device}
        END;
        myErr := SetSRsrcState(@mySpBlk);
    END;
END;
```

Searching for sResources

The Slot Manager provides several functions that search for sResources in the slot resource table. These functions allow you to specify which sResources to search, but each function provides slightly different options.

The SNextSRsrc and SNextTypeSRsrc functions allow you to search for enabled sResources by slot. The SGetSRsrc and SGetTypeSRsrc functions, available only with the System 7 Slot Manager (that is, version 1 and version 2 of the Slot Manager), allow you to search for disabled sResources as well as enabled ones. Table 2-3 summarizes the Slot Manager search routines and the options available for each.

Table 2-3   The Slot Manager search routines

Function	State of sResources for which it searches	Slots it searches	Which sResources it searches for	Type of sResource it searches for
SNextSRsrc	Enabled only	Specified slot and higher slots	Next sResource only	Any type
SGetSRsrc*	Your choice of enabled only or both enabled and disabled	Your choice of one slot only or specified slot and higher slots	Your choice of specified sResource or next sResource	Any type
SNextTypeSRsrc	Enabled only	Specified slot and higher slots	Next sResource only	Specified type only
SGetTypeSRsrc*	Your choice of enabled only or both enabled and disabled	Your choice of one slot only or specified slot and higher slots	Next sResource only	Specified type only

* Available only with the System 7 Slot Manager (that is, version 1 and version 2 of the Slot Manager)

Listing 2-2 shows how to use the SGetTypeSRsrc function to search all slots for both enabled and disabled sResources with an sResource type category of catDisplay and an sResource type subcategory of typeVideo.

Listing 2-2   Searching for a specified type of sResource

```
PROCEDURE MySResourceSearch;

VAR
    mySpBlk:      SpBlock;
    myErr:        OSErr;
```

```
BEGIN
   WITH mySpBlk DO                      {set required values in parameter block}
   BEGIN
      spParamData := fAll;              {fAll flag = 1: search all sResources}
      spCategory  := catDisplay;        {search for Category catDisplay}
      spCType     := typeVideo;         {search for cType typeVideo}
      spDrvrSW    := 0;                 {this field not being matched}
      spDrvrHW    := 0;                 {this field not being matched}
      spTBMask    := 3;                 {match only Category and cType fields}
      spSlot      := 1;                 {start search from slot 1}
      spID        := 1;                 {start search from sResource ID 1}
      spExtDev    := 0;                 {external device ID (card-specific)}
   END;
   myErr := noErr;
   WHILE myErr = noErr DO               {loop to search sResources}
   BEGIN
      myErr := SGetTypeSRsrc(@mySpBlk);
      MySRsrcProcess(mySpBlk);          {routine to process results}
   END;
   IF myErr <> smNoMoresRsrcs THEN      {all search functions return this value }
      MyHandleError(myErr);             { when search is complete}
END;
```

Obtaining Information From sResources

If you are writing a driver for a card device, you will most likely want access to the information in an sResource.

The Slot Manager provides many functions that return information from the entries of an sResource. The SOffsetData, SReadByte, and SReadWord functions return information from the offset field of an sResource entry. The SReadLong, SGetCString, and SGetBlock functions return copies of the standard data structures pointed to by the offset field of an sResource entry. The SFindStruct and SReadStruct functions allow access to other data structures pointed to by sResource entries.

Listing 2-3 shows an example of searching for a board sResource and obtaining its name. This example starts at a particular slot number and then searches for the board sResource in that slot or, if necessary, in higher slots. Once it finds the board sResource, Listing 2-3 calls the SGetCString function, which returns a pointer to a buffer containing the name string for the card.

Listing 2-3   Searching for the name of a board sResource

```
PROCEDURE FindBoardsResource  (VAR slotNumber: Integer;
                                VAR finished: Boolean);
VAR
    mySpBlk: SpBlock;
    myErr: OSErr;
BEGIN
    {First, get a pointer to the board sResource for the slot.}
    WITH mySpBlk DO BEGIN
        spSlot      := slotNumber;  {start searching in this slot, }
                                    { and continue until found}
        spID        := 0;
        spCategory  := 1;           {sRsrcType values for a board sResource}
        spCType     := 0;
        spDrvrSw    := 0;
        spDrvrHw    := 0;
    END;
    myErr := SNextTypeSRsrc(@mySpBlk);
    IF myErr <> noErr THEN
        MyHandleError(myErr)        {quit searching if no more sResources}
    ELSE
        gTheSlot := mySpBlk.spSlot; {the slot in which the sResource was found}

    {The spsPointer field of mySpBlock now contains a pointer to the }
    { board sResource list. The SGetCString function uses this field }
    { as one of two input fields.}
    mySpBlk.spID := 2;              {sRsrcName entry}
    myErr := SGetCString(@mySpBlk);
    IF myErr <> noErr THEN
        MyHandleError(myErr)
    ELSE BEGIN
        {The spResult field now points to a copy of the cString.}
        MyProcessCardName(gTheSlot, Ptr(mySpBlk.spResult));
        {Free memory allocated by SGetCString.}
        DisposePtr(Ptr(mySpBlk.spResult));
    END;
END;
```

Because the SGetCString function allocates memory for a buffer, your application
must dispose of the buffer afterward, using the Memory Manager procedure
DisposePtr (which is described in *Inside Macintosh: Memory*).

Installing and Removing Slot Interrupt Handlers

If your card generates hardware interrupts, you can install a slot interrupt handler to process interrupts from the card. The Slot Manager maintains an interrupt queue for each slot. You use the SIntInstall function, described on page 2-70, to install an interrupt handler in the slot interrupt queue. The SIntRemove function, described on page 2-71, removes an interrupt handler from the slot interrupt queue.

The SlotIntQElement data type, described on page 2-28, defines a slot interrupt queue element. The queue elements are ordered by priority and contain pointers to interrupt handlers. When a slot interrupt occurs, the Slot Manager calls the highest-priority interrupt handler in the slot's interrupt queue. If the interrupt handler returns without servicing the interrupt, the Slot Manager calls the next interrupt handler in the queue, in order of priority, until the interrupt is serviced. If the interrupt is not serviced by any interrupt handler, a system error dialog box is displayed.

Before returning to the Slot Manager, your interrupt handler should set a result code in register D0 to indicate whether the interrupt was serviced. If the interrupt was not serviced, your interrupt handler must return 0. Any value other than 0 indicates that the interrupt was serviced.

The Slot Manager returns to the interrupted task when your interrupt handler indicates that the interrupt was serviced; otherwise, it calls the next lower-priority interrupt handler for that slot. A system error is generated if the last interrupt handler returns to the Slot Manager without servicing the interrupt.

Slot Manager Reference

This section describes the data structures and routines you use to get information about the Slot Manager, expansion cards, and sResources.

Data Structures

This section describes the Slot Manager parameter block structure, the slot information record, the format header record, the slot parameter RAM record, the slot execution parameter block, and the slot interrupt queue element.

Many Slot Manager routines return information from data structures contained in the firmware of cards. See "Firmware," beginning on page 2-7, for a general discussion of these data structures, and see *Designing Cards and Drivers for the Macintosh Family*, third edition, for more detailed information.

Slot Manager Parameter Block

Every Slot Manager function requires a pointer to a Slot Manager parameter block as a parameter and returns an OSErr result code. Each routine uses only a subset of the fields of the parameter block. See the individual routine descriptions for a list of the fields used with each routine. The Slot Manager parameter block is defined by the SpBlock data type.

```
TYPE SpBlock =
PACKED RECORD                           {Slot Manager parameter block}
   spResult:        LongInt;            {result}
   spsPointer:      Ptr;                {structure pointer}
   spSize:          LongInt;            {size of structure}
   spOffsetData:    LongInt;            {offset or data}
   spIOFileName:    Ptr;                {reserved for Slot Manager}
   spsExecPBlk:     Ptr;                {pointer to SEBlock data structure}
   spParamData:     LongInt;            {flags}
   spMisc:          LongInt;            {reserved for Slot Manager}
   spReserved:      LongInt;            {reserved for Slot Manager}
   spIOReserved:    Integer;            {ioReserved field from SRT}
   spRefNum:        Integer;            {driver reference number}
   spCategory:      Integer;            {Category field of sRsrcType entry}
   spCType:         Integer;            {cType field of sRsrcType entry}
   spDrvrSW:        Integer;            {DrSW field of sRsrcType entry}
   spDrvrHW:        Integer;            {DrHW field of sRsrcType entry}
   spTBMask:        SignedByte;         {sRsrcType entry bit mask}
   spSlot:          SignedByte;         {slot number}
   spID:            SignedByte;         {sResource ID}
   spExtDev:        SignedByte;         {external device ID}
   spHwDev:         SignedByte;         {hardware device ID}
   spByteLanes:     SignedByte;         {valid byte lanes}
   spFlags:         SignedByte;         {flags used by Slot Manager}
   spKey:           SignedByte;         {reserved for Slot Manager}
END;
```

Field descriptions

spResult
: A general-purpose field used to contain the results returned by several different routines.

spsPointer
: A pointer to a data structure. The field can point to an sResource, a data block, or a declaration ROM, depending on the routine being executed.

spSize
: The size of the data pointed to in the spsPointer field.

spOffsetData
: The contents of the offset field of an sResource entry. Some routines use this field for other offsets or data.

spIOFileName
: Reserved for use by the Slot Manager.

spsExecPBlk	A pointer to an SEBlock data structure, which is described on page 2-27.
spParamData	On input, a long word containing flags that determine what sResources the Slot Manager searches. When set, bit 0 (the fAll flag) indicates that disabled sResources should be included. When set, bit 1 (the fOneSlot flag) restricts the search to sResources on a single card. Bit 2 (the fNext flag) indicates when set that the routine finds the next sResource. The rest of the bits must be cleared to 0.
	On output, this field indicates whether the sResource is enabled or disabled (if 0, the sResource is enabled; if 1, it is disabled).
spMisc	Reserved for use by the Slot Manager.
spReserved	Reserved for future use.
spIOReserved	The value of the ioReserved field from the sResource's entry in the slot resource table.
spRefNum	The driver reference number of the driver associated with an sResource, if there is one.
spCategory	The Category field of the sRsrcType entry (which is described on page 2-10).
spCType	The cType field of the sRsrcType entry.
spDrvrSW	The DrSW field of the sRsrcType entry.
spDrvrHW	The DrHW field of the sRsrcType entry.
spTBMask	A mask that determines which sRsrcType fields the Slot Manager examines when searching for sResources.
spSlot	The number of the slot with the NuBus card containing the requested, or returned, sResource.
spID	The sResource ID of the requested, or returned, sResource.
spExtDev	The external device identifier. This field allows you to distinguish between devices on a card.
spHwDev	The hardware device identifier from the sRsrcHWDevID field of the sResource.
spByteLanes	The byte lanes used by a declaration ROM.
spFlags	Flags typically used by the Slot Manager.
spKey	Reserved for use by the Slot Manager.

Listing 2-1 on page 2-18 illustrates how to set values in an SpBlock record to disable and enable an sResource. Listing 2-2 on page 2-19 illustrates how to use the values in an SpBlock record for searching for sResources.

Slot Information Record

The Slot Manager creates a slot information record for each slot. This structure is defined by the SInfoRecord data type.

```
TYPE SInfoRecord =                {slot information record}
PACKED RECORD
    siDirPtr:       Ptr;          {pointer to sResource directory}
    siInitStatusA:  Integer;      {initialization status}
    siInitStatusV:  Integer;      {status returned by vendor }
                                  { initialization routine}
    siState:        SignedByte;   {initialization state}
    siCPUByteLanes: SignedByte;   {byte lanes used}
    siTopOfROM:     SignedByte;   {highest valid address in ROM}
    siStatusFlags:  SignedByte;   {status flags}
    siTOConstant:   Integer;      {timeout constant for bus error}
    siReserved:     PACKED ARRAY [0..1] OF SignedByte;
                                  {reserved}
    siROMAddr:      Ptr;          {address of top of ROM}
    siSlot:         Char;         {slot number}
    siPadding:      PACKED ARRAY [0..2] OF SignedByte; {reserved}
END;
```

Field descriptions

siDirPtr
: A pointer to the sResource directory (described in "The sResource Directory" on page 2-12).

siInitStatusA
: The initialization status code set by the Slot Manager. A value of 0 indicates the card is installed and operational. Any other value is a Slot Manager error code indicating why the initialization failed.

siInitStatusV
: The initialization status code returned by the card's PrimaryInit routine in the seStatus field of the SEBlock parameter block (described on page 2-27). Negative values cause the card initialization to fail. Values in the range svTempDisable ($8000) through svDisabled ($8080) are used to temporarily disable a card. See "Enabling and Disabling NuBus Cards" on page 2-17 for more information.

siState
: Reserved for use by the Slot Manager.

siCPUByteLanes
: The byte lanes used by the declaration ROM.

siTopOfROM
: The least significant byte of the address stored in siROMAddr.

siStatusFlags
: Slot status flag field set by the Slot Manager. If the fCardIsChanged flag (bit 1) is set, the board ID of the installed card does not match the board ID stored in parameter RAM. Other flag bits are reserved.

siTOConstant
: The number of retries that will be performed when a bus error occurs while accessing the declaration ROM. The default is 100.

siReserved
: Reserved for use by the Slot Manager.

siROMAddr
: The highest address in the declaration ROM.

siSlot
: The slot number.

siPadding
: Reserved for use by the Slot Manager.

Format Header Record

The Slot Manager uses a format header record to describe the structure of a card's format block, which is located at the highest address in the slot's NuBus address space. By reading information from the format header record, the Slot Manager can locate and validate the card's declaration ROM. The format header record is defined by the FHeaderRec data type.

Note

For more information about the format block, see *Designing Cards and Drivers for the Macintosh Family*, third edition. ◆

```
TYPE FHeaderRec =                  {format header record}
PACKED RECORD
   fhDirOffset:   LongInt;         {offset to sResource directory}
   fhLength:      LongInt;         {length in bytes of declaration ROM}
   fhCRC:         LongInt;         {cyclic redundancy check}
   fhROMRev:      SignedByte;      {declaration ROM revision}
   fhFormat:      SignedByte;      {declaration ROM format}
   fhTstPat:      LongInt;         {test pattern}
   fhReserved:    SignedByte;      {reserved; must be 0}
   fhByteLanes:   SignedByte;      {byte lanes used by declaration ROM}
END;
```

Field descriptions

fhDirOffset	A self-relative signed offset to the sResource directory. This field specifies only bytes accessible by valid byte lanes; as a result, the value in this field might not be the absolute address difference.
fhLength	The number of valid bytes in the declaration ROM. The Slot Manager uses this value when computing the checksum.
fhCRC	A checksum that allows the Slot Manager to validate the entire declaration ROM.
fhROMRev	The current ROM revision level. This field should contain a value in the range 1–9; values greater than 9 cause the Slot Manager to generate the error smRevisionErr.
fhFormat	The format of the declaration ROM. A value of 1 designates the Apple format.
fhTstPat	A test pattern. This field must contain the value $5A932BC7.
fhReserved	Reserved. This field must be 0.
fhByteLanes	A signed byte that specifies which of the four byte lanes to use when communicating with the declaration ROM. Refer to *Designing Cards and Drivers for the Macintosh Family*, third edition, for a list of valid values.

Slot Parameter RAM Record

The Macintosh Operating System reserves eight bytes of parameter RAM for each slot. Six of these bytes are available for card designers to store information. The `SPRAMRecord` data type defines the organization of these bytes of data in parameter RAM. This data structure includes the Apple-defined `BoardID` and six bytes of vendor-specific information.

```
TYPE SPRAMRecord =                  {slot parameter RAM record}
PACKED RECORD
    boardID:        Integer;        {Apple-defined board ID}
    vendorUse1:     SignedByte;     {available for vendor use}
    vendorUse2:     SignedByte;     {available for vendor use}
    vendorUse3:     SignedByte;     {available for vendor use}
    vendorUse4:     SignedByte;     {available for vendor use}
    vendorUse5:     SignedByte;     {available for vendor use}
    vendorUse6:     SignedByte;     {available for vendor use}
END;
```

Field descriptions

`boardID`   The card identification number assigned by Apple Computer, Inc.

`vendorUse`   General-purpose fields that may be used by the card designer.

Slot Execution Parameter Block

The `SGetDriver` and `SExec` functions load and execute code from an sResource. These routines use the slot execution parameter block to exchange information with this code. The slot execution parameter block is defined by the `SEBlock` data type.

```
TYPE SEBlock =                      {slot execution parameter block}
PACKED RECORD
    seSlot:         SignedByte;     {slot number}
    sesRsrcID:      SignedByte;     {sResource ID}
    seStatus:       Integer;        {status of sExecBlock code}
    seFlags:        SignedByte;     {flags}
    seFiller0:      SignedByte;     {filler for word alignment}
    seFiller1:      SignedByte;     {filler}
    seFiller2:      SignedByte;     {filler}
    seResult:       LongInt;        {result of SLoadDriver}
    seIOFileName:   LongInt;        {pointer to driver name}
    seDevice:       SignedByte;     {device to read from}
    sePartition:    SignedByte;     {the partition}
    seOSType:       SignedByte;     {type of OS}
    seReserved:     SignedByte;     {reserved}
    seRefNum:       SignedByte;     {driver reference number}
```

```
    seNumDevices:  SignedByte;      {number of devices to load}
    seBootState:   SignedByte;      {state of StartBoot code}
END;
```

Field descriptions

seSlot   The slot number containing the code to be executed.

sesRsrcID   The sResource containing the code to be executed.

seStatus   The status returned by the executed code. A card's `PrimaryInit`
                    routine returns its initialization status in this field, and the value is
                    stored in the `siInitStatusV` field of the slot information record.

seFlags   Flags passed to or returned by the executed code.

Name	Bit	Meaning
fWarmStart	2	Set if a restart is being performed.
dRAMBased	6	Set if the `seResult` field contains a handle to a device driver.

seFiller0–2   Reserved.

seResult   A result value returned by the executed code. Normally used to
                    return a pointer or handle to a device driver.

seIOFileName   An optional pointer to a device driver name.

seDevice   The device number containing the code to be executed. This field is
                    used when loading code from a device attached to a card.

sePartition   The partition number containing the code to be executed. This field
                    is used when loading code from a device attached to a card.

seOSType   The operating system type identifier obtained from parameter RAM.
                    This field is used when loading code from a device attached to a card.

seReserved   Additional information from parameter RAM, used when loading
                    code from a device attached to a card.

seRefNum   The driver reference number returned by the loaded device driver.

seNumDevices   Unused.

seBootState   A value indicating the relative state of the boot process. During
                    initialization, the Slot Manager passes one of the following constant
                    values in this field:

Name	Value	Meaning
sbState0	0	State 0 of the boot process.
sbState1	1	State 1 the boot process.

Slot Interrupt Queue Element

The Slot Manager maintains a queue of interrupt handlers for each slot. You use the
`SIntInstall` and `SIntRemove` functions (described on page 2-70 and page 2-71,
respectively) to install and remove routines in the queue. The `SlotIntQElement`
data type defines a slot interrupt queue element.

```
TYPE SlotIntQElement =              {slot interrupt queue element}
RECORD
    sqLink:         Ptr;            {pointer to next queue element}
    sqType:         Integer;       {queue type ID; must be sIQType}
    sqPrio:         Integer;       {priority value in low byte}
    sqAddr:         ProcPtr;       {interrupt handler}
    sqParm:         LongInt;       {optional A1 parameter}
END;
```

Field descriptions

sqLink   A pointer to the next queue element. This field is maintained by the
                Slot Manager.

sqType   The queue type identifier, which you set to the defined type
                sIQType.

sqPrio   The relative priority level of the interrupt handler. Only the low-
                order byte of this field is used. The high-order byte must be set to 0.
                Valid priority levels are 0 through 199. Priority levels 200 through
                255 are reserved for Apple devices.

sqAddr   A pointer to the interrupt handler.

sqParm   An optional value that the Slot Manager places in register A1 before
                calling the interrupt handler. This field is typically used to store a
                handle to a driver's device control entry.

Slot Manager Routines

This section describes the routines provided by the Slot Manager. Most of the routines in
this section are used to locate sResources or read information from an entry in an
sResource. Some of the routines allow you to read and set information about expansion
cards, such as their parameter RAM values, and others allow you to manipulate Slot
Manager data structures, like the slot resource table.

Because the SGetCString, SGetBlock, SGetDriver, SExec, InitSDeclMgr,
SInitPRAMRecs, SInitSRsrcTable, and SPrimaryInit functions may allocate
memory, your application should not call them at interrupt time; however, your can call
any other Slot Manager function at interrupt time.

Because each routine uses a subset of the Slot Manager parameter block fields, each
routine reference section includes a list of pertinent fields and how they are used.

Parameter block

→	fieldName	FieldType	Input field.
←	fieldName	FieldType	Output field.
↔	fieldName	FieldType	Input/output field.
✕	fieldName	FieldType	Affected field.

The arrows show whether you provide a value in the field, the routine returns a value in
the field, or both. The ✕ symbol designates fields that may be affected by the execution

of the routine. Any value you store in one of these affected fields may be lost. Also, the meaning of these fields upon completion of the routine is undefined; your application should not depend on these values.

Assembly-Language Note

You can call Slot Manager routines using either the _SlotManager trap macro with a selector or an individual macro name consisting of the routine name preceded by an underscore. For example, you can call the SVersion function using the _SVersion macro. Because every routine name macro is equivalent to the _SlotManager trap macro that specifies the corresponding routine selector, you will need to know the routine selectors to trace your code in MacsBug. The _SlotManager trap macro selector for each routine is included in the routine description and summarized in "Trap Macros," beginning on page 2-99. ◆

Determining the Version of the Slot Manager

Unlike other system software managers, which use the Gestalt function to return version information, the Slot Manager includes its own function for providing this information.

SVersion

You can use the SVersion function to determine which version of the Slot Manager is in use by the Macintosh Operating System.

```
FUNCTION SVersion (spBlkPtr: SpBlockPtr): OSErr;
```

spBlkPtr   A pointer to a Slot Manager parameter block.

Parameter block

←	spResult	LongInt	The Slot Manager version number.
←	spsPointer	Ptr	A pointer to additional information.

DESCRIPTION

The SVersion function returns the version number of the Slot Manager in the spResult field of the Slot Manager parameter block that you point to in the spBlkPtr parameter. Version number 1 corresponds to the RAM-based Slot Manager and version number 2 corresponds to the ROM-based Slot Manager. Versions of the Slot Manager prior to System 7 do not recognize the SVersion function and return the result code smSelOOBErr. The spsPointer field is reserved for future use as a pointer to additional information.

ASSEMBLY-LANGUAGE INFORMATION

The trap macro and routine selector for the SVersion function are

Trap macro	Selector
_SlotManager	$0008

You must set up register D0 with the routine selector and register A0 with the address of the Slot Manager parameter block. When _SlotManager returns, register D0 contains the result code.

Registers on entry

A0   Address of the parameter block

D0 $0008

Registers on exit

D0   Result code

RESULT CODES

noErr	0	No error
smSelOOBErr	–338	Selector out of bounds or function not implemented

SEE ALSO

For more information on the different versions of the Slot Manager, see "About the Slot Manager" on page 2-15.

Finding sResources

The functions in this section locate sResources in the slot resource table and return pointers to them and additional information about them. The SRsrcInfo function is useful for finding the driver reference number of an SResource. The SGetSRsrc and SGetTypeSRsrc functions are the preferred routines for searching sResources. You can use these functions to step through the sResources and to find disabled as well as enabled sResources. Use the SNextSRsrc and SNextTypeSRsrc functions with System 6 and earlier versions of the Slot Manager.

SRsrcInfo

You can use the SRsrcInfo function to find an sResource. This function also provides additional information about the sResource, such as the driver reference number of the slot device driver.

```
FUNCTION SRsrcInfo (spBlkPtr: SpBlockPtr): OSErr;
```

spBlkPtr   A pointer to a Slot Manager parameter block.

Parameter block

←	spsPointer	Ptr	A pointer to an sResource (described in "The sResource," beginning on page 2-7).
←	spIOReserved	Integer	The value of the slot resource table ioReserved field.
←	spRefNum	Integer	The device driver reference number.
←	spCategory	Integer	The Category field of the sRsrcType entry (described on page 2-10).
←	spCType	Integer	The cType field of the sRsrcType entry.
←	spDrvrSW	Integer	The DrSW field of the sRsrcType entry.
←	spDrvrHW	Integer	The DrHW field of the sRsrcType entry.
→	spSlot	SignedByte	The slot number of the requested sResource.
→	spId	SignedByte	The sResource ID of the requested sResource.
→	spExtDev	SignedByte	The external device identifier.
←	spHwDev	SignedByte	The hardware device identifier.

DESCRIPTION

The SRsrcInfo function allows you to find an sResource from the slot resource table and provides additional information, including its driver reference number and the values contained in its sRsrcType entry.

You specify an sResource with the spSlot, spID, and spExtDev fields of the Slot Manager parameter block you point to in the spBlkPtr parameter.

The SRsrcInfo function returns a pointer to the sResource in the spsPointer field and returns information about the sResource type in the spRefNum, spCType, spDrvrSW, spDrvrHW fields. The function returns other information about the sResource in the spIOReserved, spRefNum, and spHwDev fields.

ASSEMBLY-LANGUAGE INFORMATION

The trap macro and routine selector for the SRsrcInfo function are

Trap macro   **Selector**

_SlotManager $0016

You must set up register D0 with the routine selector and register A0 with the address of the Slot Manager parameter block. When _SlotManager returns, register D0 contains the result code.

Registers on entry

A0   Address of the parameter block

D0 $0016

Registers on exit

D0   Result code

RESULT CODES

noErr	0	No error
smNoMoresRsrcs	–344	Requested sResource not found

SEE ALSO

For more control in finding sResources, you can use the SGetSRsrc function, described next, and the SGetTypeSRsrc function, described on page 2-35.

SGetSRsrc

You can use the SGetSRsrc function to find any sResource, even one that has been disabled.

```
FUNCTION SGetSRsrc (spBlkPtr: SpBlockPtr): OSErr;
```

spBlkPtr   A pointer to a Slot Manager parameter block.

Parameter block

←	spsPointer	Ptr	A pointer to an sResource (described in "The sResource," beginning on page 2-7).
↔	spParamData	LongInt	On input: parameter flags. On output: 0 if the sResource is enabled or 1 if disabled.
←	spRefNum	Integer	The slot resource table reference number.
←	spCategory	Integer	The Category field of the sRsrcType entry (described on page 2-10).
←	spCType	Integer	The cType field of the sRsrcType entry.
←	spDrvrSW	Integer	The DrSW field of the sRsrcType entry.
←	spDrvrHW	Integer	The DrHW field of the sRsrcType entry.
↔	spSlot	SignedByte	The slot number.
↔	spId	SignedByte	The sResource ID.
↔	spExtDev	SignedByte	The external device identifier.
←	spHWDev	SignedByte	The hardware device identifier.

DESCRIPTION

The SGetSRsrc function allows you to specify whether the function should include disabled sResources, whether it should continue looking for sResources in higher-numbered slots, and whether it should return information about the specified sResource or the one that follows it.

You specify an sResource with the spSlot, spID, and spExtDev fields of the Slot Manager parameter block you point to in the spBlkPtr parameter. You must also include flags in bits 0, 1, and 2 of the spParamData field as follows:

■ Set the fAll flag (bit 0) to search both enabled and disabled sResources. Clear this flag to search only enabled sResources.

■ Set the fOneSlot flag (bit 1) to search only the specified slot. Clear this flag to search all slots.

■ Set the fNext flag (bit 2) to return information about the sResource with the next higher sResource ID than the specified sResource (or the first one on the next card if the fAll flag is set). Clear this flag to return data about the specified sResource.

The SGetSRsrc function returns values in the spSlot, spID, and spExtDev fields corresponding to the sResource that it found. If you cleared the fNext flag, these fields retain the values you specified when calling the function. In addition, the function returns 0 in the spParamData field if the sResource is enabled or 1 if it is disabled. If you cleared the fAll bit, the spParamData field always returns the value 0.

The SGetSRsrc function also returns a pointer to the sResource in the spsPointer field and returns other information about the sResource in the spRefNum, spCategory, spCType, spDrvrSW, spDrvrHW, and spHwDev fields.

SPECIAL CONSIDERATIONS

The SGetSRsrc function is available only with version 1 or later of the Slot Manager. You can use the SVersion function, described on page 2-30, to determine whether the Slot Manager is version 1 or later.

ASSEMBLY-LANGUAGE INFORMATION

The trap macro and routine selector for the SGetSRsrc function are

Trap macro	Selector
_SlotManager	$000B

You must set up register D0 with the routine selector and register A0 with the address of the Slot Manager parameter block. When _SlotManager returns, register D0 contains the result code.

Registers on entry

A0   Address of the parameter block

D0 $000B

Registers on exit

D0   Result code

RESULT CODES

noErr	0	No error
smNoMoresRsrcs	–344	Requested sResource not found

SEE ALSO

For more control in finding sResources, you can also use the SGetTypeSRsrc function, described next.

SGetTypeSRsrc

You can use the `SGetTypeSRsrc` function to step through sResources of one type, including disabled ones.

```
FUNCTION SGetTypeSRsrc (spBlkPtr: SpBlockPtr): OSErr;
```

spBlkPtr   A pointer to a Slot Manager parameter block.

Parameter block

←	spsPointer	Ptr	A pointer to an sResource (described in "The sResource," beginning on page 2-7).
↔	spParamData	LongInt	On input: parameter flags. On output: 0 if the sResource is enabled or 1 if disabled.
←	spRefNum	Integer	The slot resource table reference number.
↔	spCategory	Integer	The Category field of the sRsrcType entry (described on page 2-10).
↔	spCType	Integer	The cType field of the sRsrcType entry.
↔	spDrvrSW	Integer	The DrSW field of the sRsrcType entry.
↔	spDrvrHW	Integer	The DrHW field of the sRsrcType entry.
→	spTBMask	SignedByte	The type bit mask for sRsrcType fields.
↔	spSlot	SignedByte	The slot number.
↔	spId	SignedByte	The sResource ID.
↔	spExtDev	SignedByte	The external device identifier.
←	spHWDev	SignedByte	The hardware device identifier.

DESCRIPTION

The `SGetTypeSRsrc` function allows you to find the next sResource of a certain type, as does the `SNextTypeSRsrc` function, but the `SGetTypeSRsrc` function also allows you to find disabled sResources and to limit searching to a single slot.

You specify an sResource with the `spSlot`, `spID`, and `spExtDev` fields of the Slot Manager parameter block you point to in the `spBlkPtr` parameter, and you specify the type of the sResource with the `spCategory`, `spCType`, `spDrvrSW`, and `spDrvrHW` fields. You must also use the `spTBMask` field to specify which of these `sRsrcType` fields should not be included in the search:

■ Set bit 0 to ignore the `DrHW` field.

■ Set bit 1 to ignore the `DrSW` field.

■ Set bit 2 to ignore the `cType` field.

■ Set bit 3 to ignore the `Category` field.

You must also set the `fAll` flag of the `spParamData` field (bit 0) to search both enabled and disabled sResources or clear this flag to search only enabled ones. Set the `fOneSlot` flag (bit 1) to search only the specified slot, or clear this flag to search all slots. The

SGetTypeSRsrc function does not use the fNext flag (bit 2) because it always searches for the next sResource of the given type.

The SGetTypeSRsrc function returns values in the spSlot, spID, and spExtDev fields corresponding to the sResource that it found, and it returns 0 in the spParamData field if that sResource is enabled or 1 if it is disabled.

The SGetTypeSRsrc function also returns a pointer to the sResource in the spsPointer field and returns other information about the sResource in the spRefNum, spCategory, spCType, spDrvrSW, spDrvrHW, and spHwDev fields.

SPECIAL CONSIDERATIONS

The SGetTypeSRsrc function is available only with version 1 or later of the Slot Manager. You can use the SVersion function, described on page 2-30, to determine whether the Slot Manager is version 1 or later.

ASSEMBLY-LANGUAGE INFORMATION

The trap macro and routine selector for the SGetTypeSRsrc function are

Trap macro	Selector
_SlotManager	$000C

You must set up register D0 with the routine selector and register A0 with the address of the Slot Manager parameter block. When _SlotManager returns, register D0 contains the result code.

Registers on entry

A0   Address of the parameter block

D0 $000C

Registers on exit

D0   Result code

RESULT CODES

noErr	0	No error
smNoMoresRsrcs	–344	Requested sResource not found

SEE ALSO

For information on enabling and disabling sResources, see "Enabling and Disabling sResources" on page 2-18 and the description of the SetSRsrcState function in the next section.

SNextSRsrc

You can use the SNextSRsrc function to step through the sResources on a card or from one card to the next.

```
FUNCTION SNextSRsrc (spBlkPtr: SpBlockPtr): OSErr;
```

spBlkPtr   A pointer to a Slot Manager parameter block.

Parameter block

←	spsPointer	Ptr	A pointer to an sResource (described in "The sResource," beginning on page 2-7).
←	spIOReserved	Integer	The value of the slot resource table ioReserved field.
←	spRefNum	Integer	The driver reference number.
←	spCategory	Integer	The Category field of the sRsrcType entry (described on page 2-10).
←	spCType	Integer	The cType field of the sRsrcType entry.
←	spDrvrSW	Integer	The DrSW field of the sRsrcType entry.
←	spDrvrHW	Integer	The DrHW field of the sRsrcType entry.
↔	spSlot	SignedByte	The slot number.
↔	spId	SignedByte	The sResource ID.
↔	spExtDev	SignedByte	The external device identifier.
←	spHWDev	SignedByte	The hardware device identifier.

DESCRIPTION

The SNextSRsrc function is similar to the SRsrcInfo function, except the SNextSRsrc function returns information about the sResource that follows the requested one—that is, the one with the next entry in the sResource directory or the first sResource on the next card. The SNextSRsrc function skips disabled sResources.

You specify a particular sResource with the spSlot, spID, and spExtDev fields of the Slot Manager parameter block you point to in the spBlkPtr parameter. The SNextSRsrc function finds the next sResource, returns a pointer to it in the spsPointer field, and updates the spSlot, spID, and spExtDev fields to correspond to the sResource it found. If there are no more sResources, the SNextSRsrc function returns the smNoMoresRsrcs result code.

The SNextSRsrc function returns other information about the sResource in the spRefNum, spCategory, spCType, spDrvrSW, and spDrvrHW fields.

ASSEMBLY-LANGUAGE INFORMATION

The trap macro and routine selector for the SNextSRsrc function are

Trap macro	Selector
_SlotManager	$0014

You must set up register D0 with the routine selector and register A0 with the address of the Slot Manager parameter block. When _SlotManager returns, register D0 contains the result code.

Registers on entry

A0   Address of the parameter block

D0 $0014

Registers on exit

D0   Result code

RESULT CODES

noErr	0	No error
smNoMoresRsrcs	–344	Requested sResource not found

SEE ALSO

For more control in finding sResources, you can use the SGetSRsrc function, described on page 2-33, and the SGetTypeSRsrc function, described on page 2-35.

SNextTypeSRsrc

You can use the SNextTypeSRsrc function to step through sResources of one type.

```
FUNCTION SNextTypeSRsrc (spBlkPtr: SpBlockPtr): OSErr;
```

spBlkPtr   A pointer to a Slot Manager parameter block.

Parameter block

←	spsPointer	Ptr	A pointer to an sResource (described in "The sResource," beginning on page 2-7).
←	spRefNum	Integer	The slot resource table reference number.
↔	spCategory	Integer	The Category field of the sRsrcType entry (described on page 2-10).
↔	spCType	Integer	The cType field of the sRsrcType entry.
↔	spDrvrSW	Integer	The DrSW field of the sRsrcType entry.
↔	spDrvrHW	Integer	The DrHW field of the sRsrcType entry.
→	spTBMask	SignedByte	The type bit mask for sRsrcType fields.
↔	spSlot	SignedByte	The slot number.
↔	spId	SignedByte	The sResource ID.
↔	spExtDev	SignedByte	The external device identifier.
←	spHWDev	SignedByte	The hardware device identifier.

DESCRIPTION

The `SNextTypeSRsrc` function allows you to find the next sResource, as does the `SNextSRsrc` function, but the `SNextTypeSRsrc` function skips disabled sResources.

You indicate the sResource you want returned by identifying the slot number, sResource ID, and device ID in the `spSlot`, `spID`, and `spExtDev` fields of the Slot Manager parameter block you point to in the `spBlkPtr` parameter. You specify the type of the sResource with the `spCategory`, `spCType`, `spDrvrSW`, and `spDrvrHW` fields. You must also use the `spTBMask` to specify which of these `sRsrcType` entry fields should not be included in the search:

- Set bit 0 to ignore the `DrHW` field.
- Set bit 1 to ignore the `DrSW` field.
- Set bit 2 to ignore the `cType` field.
- Set bit 3 to ignore the `Category` field.

The `SNextTypeSRsrc` function returns values in the `spSlot`, `spID`, and `spExtDev` fields corresponding to the sResource that it found.

The `SNextTypeSRsrc` function also returns a pointer to the sResource in the `spsPointer` field and returns other information about the sResource in the `spIOReserved`, `spRefNum`, `spCategory`, `spCType`, `spDrvrSW`, and `spDrvrHW` fields.

ASSEMBLY-LANGUAGE INFORMATION

The trap macro and routine selector for the `SNextTypeSRsrc` function are

Trap macro	Selector
`_SlotManager`	$0015

You must set up register D0 with the routine selector and register A0 with the address of the Slot Manager parameter block. When `_SlotManager` returns, register D0 contains the result code.

Registers on entry

A0   Address of the parameter block
D0 $0015

Registers on exit

D0   Result code

RESULT CODES

noErr	0	No error
smNoMoresRsrcs	–344	Requested sResource not found

SEE ALSO

For information on enabling and disabling sResources, see "Enabling and Disabling sResources" on page 2-18 and the description of the SetSRsrcState function on page 2-51.

Getting Information From sResources

The Slot Manager provides a number of routines that simplify access to the information in sResources. Most of these routines simply return the value of an sResource entry.

The SReadDrvrName function returns the name of an sResource, formatted as a Pascal string and prefixed with a period. You can pass this string to the Device Manager's OpenSlot function to open the driver.

The SReadByte, SReadWord, and SReadLong functions return byte, word, or long values from an sResource entry. The SGetCString, SGetBlock, SReadStruct, and SFindStruct functions return pointers to larger data types.

SReadDrvrName

You can use the SReadDrvrName function to read the name of an sResource in a format you can use to open the driver with Device Manager routines.

```
FUNCTION SReadDrvrName (spBlkPtr: SpBlockPtr): OSErr;
```

spBlkPtr   A pointer to a Slot Manager parameter block.

Parameter block

→	spSlot	SignedByte	The slot number.
→	spID	SignedByte	The sResource ID.
→	spResult	Ptr	A pointer to the driver name.
✕	spSize	LongInt	
✕	spsPointer	Ptr	

DESCRIPTION

The SReadDrvrName function reads the name of an sResource, prefixes a period to the value, and converts it to type Str255. The final driver name is compatible with the Device Manager's OpenDriver function.

You indicate an sResource by identifying the slot number and sResource ID in the spSlot and spID fields of the Slot Manager parameter block you point to in the spBlkPtr parameter. In your program, you should declare a Pascal string variable and pass a pointer to it in the spResult field.

The SReadDrvrName function returns the driver name by copying it into the string pointed to by the spResult field.

SPECIAL CONSIDERATIONS

This function may alter the values of the `spSize` and `spsPointer` fields of the parameter block. Your application should not depend on the values returned in these fields.

ASSEMBLY-LANGUAGE INFORMATION

The trap macro and routine selector for the `SReadDrvrName` function are

Trap macro	Selector
`_SlotManager`	$0019

You must set up register D0 with the routine selector and register A0 with the address of the Slot Manager parameter block. When `_SlotManager` returns, register D0 contains the result code.

Registers on entry

A0   Address of the parameter block

D0 $0019

Registers on exit

D0   Result code

RESULT CODES

noErr	0	No error
smNoMoresRsrcs	–344	Requested sResource not found

SEE ALSO

For more information about the device control entry and device driver reference numbers, see the chapter "Device Manager" in this book.

SReadByte

You can use the `SReadByte` function to determine the value of the low-order byte of an sResource entry.

```
FUNCTION SReadByte (spBlkPtr: SpBlockPtr): OSErr;
```

spBlkPtr   A pointer to a Slot Manager parameter block.

Parameter block

←	spResult	LongInt	The contents of the entry byte.
→	spsPointer	Ptr	A pointer to an sResource (described in "The sResource," beginning on page 2-7).
→	spID	SignedByte	The ID of the sResource entry.
X	spOffsetData	LongInt	
X	spByteLanes	SignedByte	

DESCRIPTION

The SReadByte function returns the low-order byte of the offset field of an entry in an sResource. You provide a pointer to the sResource in the spsPointer field and the ID of the entry in the spID field. The SReadByte function returns the value in the low-order byte of the spResult field.

SPECIAL CONSIDERATIONS

This function may alter the values of the spOffsetData and spByteLanes fields of the parameter block. Your application should not depend on the values returned in these fields.

ASSEMBLY-LANGUAGE INFORMATION

The trap macro and routine selector for the SReadByte function are

Trap macro	Selector
_SlotManager	$0000

You must set up register D0 with the routine selector and register A0 with the address of the Slot Manager parameter block. When _SlotManager returns, register D0 contains the result code.

Registers on entry

A0   Address of the parameter block

D0 $0000

Registers on exit

D0   Result code

RESULT CODES

noErr	0	No error
smNoMoresRsrcs	−344	Requested sResource not found

SReadWord

You can use the SReadWord function to determine the value of the low-order word of an sResource entry.

```
FUNCTION SReadWord (spBlkPtr: SpBlockPtr): OSErr;
```

spBlkPtr   A pointer to a Slot Manager parameter block.

Parameter block

←	spResult	LongInt	The contents of the entry word.
→	spsPointer	Ptr	A pointer to an sResource (described in "The sResource," beginning on page 2-7).
→	spID	SignedByte	The ID of the sResource entry.
X	spOffsetData	LongInt	
X	spByteLanes	SignedByte	

DESCRIPTION

The SReadWord function returns the low-order word of the offset field of an entry in an sResource. You provide a pointer to the sResource in the spsPointer field of the Slot Manager parameter block you point to in the spBlkPtr parameter, and you provide the ID of the entry in the spID field. The SReadWord function returns the value in the low-order word of the spResult field.

SPECIAL CONSIDERATIONS

This function may alter the values of the spOffsetData and spByteLanes fields of the parameter block. Your application should not depend on the values returned in these fields.

ASSEMBLY-LANGUAGE INFORMATION

The trap macro and routine selector for the SReadWord function are

Trap macro	Selector
_SlotManager	$0001

You must set up register D0 with the routine selector and register A0 with the address of the Slot Manager parameter block. When _SlotManager returns, register D0 contains the result code.

Registers on entry

A0   Address of the parameter block

D0 $0001

Registers on exit

D0   Result code

RESULT CODES

noErr	0	No error
smNoMoresRsrcs	–344	Requested sResource not found

SReadLong

You can use the SReadLong function to determine the value of a long word pointed to by the offset field of an sResource entry.

```
FUNCTION SReadLong (spBlkPtr: SpBlockPtr): OSErr;
```

spBlkPtr   A pointer to a Slot Manager parameter block.

Parameter block

←	spResult	LongInt	The contents of the long word.
→	spsPointer	Ptr	A pointer to an sResource (described in "The sResource," beginning on page 2-7).
→	spID	SignedByte	The ID of the sResource entry.
×	spSize	LongInt	
×	spOffsetData	LongInt	
×	spByteLanes	SignedByte	

DESCRIPTION

The SReadLong function returns the 32-bit value pointed to by the offset field of an sResource entry. In the Slot Manager parameter block you point to in the spBlkPtr parameter, you provide a pointer to the sResource in the spsPointer field and specify the ID of the entry in the spID field. The SReadLong function returns the long word value in the spResult field.

SPECIAL CONSIDERATIONS

This function may alter the values of the spSize, spOffsetData, and spByteLanes fields of the parameter block. Your application should not depend on the values returned in these fields.

ASSEMBLY-LANGUAGE INFORMATION

The trap macro and routine selector for the SReadLong function are

Trap macro	Selector
_SlotManager	$0002

You must set up register D0 with the routine selector and register A0 with the address of the Slot Manager parameter block. When _SlotManager returns, register D0 contains the result code.

Registers on entry

A0   Address of the parameter block

D0 $0002

Registers on exit

D0   Result code

RESULT CODES

noErr	0	No error
smNoMoresRsrcs	–344	Requested sResource not found

SGetCString

You can use the SGetCString function to determine the value of a string pointed to by the offset field of an sResource entry.

```
FUNCTION SGetCString (spBlkPtr: SpBlockPtr): OSErr;
```

spBlkPtr   A pointer to a Slot Manager parameter block.

Parameter block

←	spResult	Ptr	A pointer to a copy of the cString data structure.
→	spsPointer	Ptr	A pointer to an sResource (described in "The sResource," beginning on page 2-7).
→	spID	SignedByte	The ID of the sResource entry.
×	spSize	LongInt	
×	spOffsetData	LongInt	
×	spByteLanes	SignedByte	
×	spFlags	SignedByte	

DESCRIPTION

The SGetCString function returns a copy of the cString data structure pointed to by the offset field of an sResource entry.

You provide a pointer to the sResource in the spsPointer field and specify the ID of the entry in the spID field.

The SGetCString function allocates a memory buffer, copies the value of the cString data structure into it, and returns a pointer to it in the spResult field. You should dispose of this pointer by using the Memory Manager procedure DisposePtr.

SPECIAL CONSIDERATIONS

The SGetCString function may alter the values of the spSize, spOffsetData, spByteLanes, and spFlags fields of the parameter block. Your application should not depend on the values returned in these fields.

SPECIAL CONSIDERATIONS

The SGetCString function allocates memory; your application should not call this function at interrupt time.

ASSEMBLY-LANGUAGE INFORMATION

The trap macro and routine selector for the SGetCString function are

Trap macro	Selector
_SlotManager	$0003

You must set up register D0 with the routine selector and register A0 with the address of the Slot Manager parameter block. When _SlotManager returns, register D0 contains the result code.

Registers on entry

A0   Address of the parameter block

D0 $0003

Registers on exit

D0   Result code

RESULT CODES

noErr	0	No error
smNoMoresRsrcs	–344	Requested sResource not found

SEE ALSO

For more information about the cString data structure, see "Firmware," beginning on page 2-7.

SGetBlock

You can use the SGetBlock function to obtain a copy of an sBlock data structure pointed to by the offset field of an sResource entry.

```
FUNCTION SGetBlock (spBlkPtr: SpBlockPtr): OSErr;
```

spBlkPtr   A pointer to a Slot Manager parameter block.

Parameter block

←	spResult	Ptr	A pointer to a copy of an sBlock data structure (described on page 2-9).
→	spsPointer	Ptr	A pointer to an sResource (described in "The sResource," beginning on page 2-7).
→	spID	SignedByte	The ID of the sResource entry.
×	spSize	LongInt	
×	spOffsetData	LongInt	
×	spByteLanes	SignedByte	
×	spFlags	SignedByte	

DESCRIPTION

The SGetBlock function returns a copy of the sBlock data structure pointed to by the offset field of an sResource entry.

In the parameter block you point to in the spBlkPtr parameter, you provide a pointer to the sResource in the spsPointer field and specify the ID of the entry in the spID field.

The SGetBlock function allocates a memory buffer, copies the contents of the sBlock data structure into it, and returns a pointer to it in the spResult field. You should dispose of this pointer by using the Memory Manager procedure DisposePtr.

SPECIAL CONSIDERATIONS

The SGetBlock function may alter the values of the spSize, spOffsetData, spByteLanes, and spFlags fields of the parameter block. Your application should not depend on the values returned in these fields.

The SGetBlock function allocates memory; your application should not call this function at interrupt time.

ASSEMBLY-LANGUAGE INFORMATION

The trap macro and routine selector for the SGetBlock function are

Trap macro	Selector
_SlotManager	$0005

You must set up register D0 with the routine selector and register A0 with the address of the Slot Manager parameter block. When _SlotManager returns, register D0 contains the result code.

Registers on entry

A0   Address of the parameter block

D0 $0005

Registers on exit

D0   Result code

RESULT CODES

noErr	0	No error
smNoMoresRsrcs	−344	Requested sResource not found

SFindStruct

You can use the SFindStruct function to obtain a pointer to any data structure pointed to by the offset field of an sResource entry. You might want to use this function, for example, when the data structure type is defined by the card designer.

```
FUNCTION SFindStruct (spBlkPtr: SpBlockPtr): OSErr;
```

spBlkPtr   A pointer to a Slot Manager parameter block.

Parameter block

↔	spsPointer	Ptr	On input: a pointer to an sResource.
			On output: a pointer to a data structure.
→	spID	SignedByte	The ID of the sResource entry.
×	spByteLanes	SignedByte	

DESCRIPTION

You provide a pointer to the sResource in the spsPointer field, and the ID of the entry in the spID field. The SFindStruct function returns a pointer to the data structure in the spResult field.

SPECIAL CONSIDERATIONS

This function may alter the value of the spByteLanes field of the parameter block. Your application should not depend on the value returned in this field.

ASSEMBLY-LANGUAGE INFORMATION

The trap macro and routine selector for the SFindStruct function are

Trap macro	Selector
_SlotManager	$0006

You must set up register D0 with the routine selector and register A0 with the address of the Slot Manager parameter block. When _SlotManager returns, register D0 contains the result code.

Registers on entry

A0   Address of the parameter block

D0 $0006

Registers on exit

D0   Result code

RESULT CODES

noErr	0	No error
smNoMoresRsrcs	–344	Requested sResource not found

SEE ALSO

For information about obtaining a copy of a data structure pointed to by the offset field of an sResource entry, rather than a pointer to the data structure, see the next section, which describes the SReadStruct function.

SReadStruct

You can use the SReadStruct function to obtain a copy of any data structure pointed to by an sResource entry. You might want to use this function, for example, when the data structure type is defined by the card designer.

```
FUNCTION SReadStruct (spBlkPtr: SpBlockPtr): OSErr;
```

spBlkPtr   A pointer to a Slot Manager parameter block.

Parameter block

→	spResult	Ptr	A pointer to a memory block.
→	spsPointer	Ptr	A pointer to the structure.
→	spSize	LongInt	The length in bytes of the structure.
×	spByteLanes	SignedByte	

DESCRIPTION

The SReadStruct function copies any arbitrary data structure from the declaration ROM of an expansion card into memory.

You provide a pointer to the structure in the spsPointer field and specify the size of the structure in the spSize field. You must also allocate a memory block for the result and send a pointer to it in the spResult field.

The SReadStruct function copies the data structure into the memory block pointed to by the spResult field.

SPECIAL CONSIDERATIONS

This function may alter the value of the spByteLanes field of the parameter block. Your application should not depend on the value returned in this field.

ASSEMBLY-LANGUAGE INFORMATION

The trap macro and routine selector for the SReadStruct function are

Trap macro	Selector
_SlotManager	$0007

You must set up register D0 with the routine selector and register A0 with the address of the Slot Manager parameter block. When _SlotManager returns, register D0 contains the result code.

Registers on entry

A0   Address of the parameter block

D0 $0007

Registers on exit

D0   Result code

RESULT CODES

noErr	0	No error
smNoMoresRsrcs	−344	Requested sResource not found

SEE ALSO

For information about obtaining a pointer to a data structure pointed to by the offset field of an sResource entry, rather than a copy of the data structure, see the description of the SFindStruct function on page 2-48.

Enabling, Disabling, Deleting, and Restoring sResources

The functions in this section are primarily for use by device drivers. The SetSRsrcState function enables and disables sResources. The next two functions, SDeleteSRTRec and InsertSRTRec, delete sResources from and restore them to the slot resource table. The SUpdateSRT function updates the slot resource table record for an existing sResource.

SetSRsrcState

You can use the SetSRsrcState function to select which sResources are enabled.

```
FUNCTION SetSRsrcState (spBlkPtr: SpBlockPtr): OSErr;
```

spBlkPtr   A pointer to a Slot Manager parameter block.

Parameter block

→	spParamData	LongInt	Either a value of 0 to enable the sResource or a value of 1 to disable it.
→	spSlot	SignedByte	The slot number.
→	spId	SignedByte	The sResource ID.
→	spExtDev	SignedByte	The external device identifier.

DESCRIPTION

The SetSRsrcState function enables or disables an sResource. All of the Slot Manager functions recognize enabled sResources, while only the SGetSRsrc and SGetTypeSRsrc functions (described on page 2-33 and page 2-35, respectively) can recognize disabled ones.

You specify the sResource to enable or disable with the spSlot, spID, and spExtDev fields of the Slot Manager parameter block you point to in the spBlkPtr parameter, and you specify whether to enable or disable it in the spParamData field. The Slot Manager enables the sResource when the spParamData field has a value of 0 and disables it when the field has a value of 1.

SPECIAL CONSIDERATIONS

The SetSRsrcState function is available only with version 1 or later of the Slot Manager. You can use the SVersion function, described on page 2-30, to determine whether the Slot Manager is version 1 or later.

The trap macro and routine selector for the `SetSRsrcState` function are

Trap macro   **Selector**

`_SlotManager` $0009

You must set up register D0 with the routine selector and register A0 with the address of the Slot Manager parameter block. When `_SlotManager` returns, register D0 contains the result code.

Registers on entry

A0   Address of the parameter block

D0 $0009

Registers on exit

D0   Result code

noErr	0	No error
smNoMoresRsrcs	–344	Requested sResource not found

For more information on enabling and disabling sResources, see "Enabling and Disabling sResources" on page 2-18.

For information on finding disabled sResources, see the description of the `SGetSRsrc` function on page 2-33 and the description of the `SGetTypeSRsrc` function on page 2-35.

SDeleteSRTRec

You can use the `SDeleteSRTRec` function to remove an sResource from the slot resource table.

```
FUNCTION SDeleteSRTRec (spBlkPtr: SpBlockPtr): OSErr;
```

spBlkPtr   A pointer to a Slot Manager parameter block.

Parameter block

→	spSlot	SignedByte	The slot number.
→	spId	SignedByte	The sResource ID.
→	spExtDev	SignedByte	The external device identifier.

DESCRIPTION

The SDeleteSRTRec function deletes an sResource from the slot resource table. This routine is typically called by a card's PrimaryInit code to delete any sResources that are not appropriate for the system as configured.

SPECIAL CONSIDERATIONS

The SDeleteSRTRec function is available only with Manager. You can use the SVersion function, described on page 2-30, to determine whether the Slot Manager is version 1 or later.

ASSEMBLY-LANGUAGE INFORMATION

The trap macro and routine selector for the SDeleteSRTRec function are

Trap macro	Selector
_SlotManager	$0031

You must set up register D0 with the routine selector and register A0 with the address of the Slot Manager parameter block. When _SlotManager returns, register D0 contains the result code.

Registers on entry

A0   Address of the parameter block

D0 $0031

Registers on exit

D0   Result code

SEE ALSO

For more information about the slot resource table, see "About the Slot Manager" on page 2-15. For information about restoring an sResource to the slot resource table, see the InsertSRTRec function, described next. For more information on deleting and restoring sResources, see "Deleting and Restoring sResources" on page 2-17.

InsertSRTRec

You can use the `InsertSRTRec` function to add an sResource to the slot resource table.

```
FUNCTION InsertSRTRec (spBlkPtr: SpBlockPtr): OSErr;
```

spBlkPtr   A pointer to a Slot Manager parameter block.

Parameter block

→	spsPointer	Ptr	A NIL pointer.
→	spParamData	LongInt	Either a value of 0 to enable the sResource or a value of 1 to disable it.
→	spRefNum	Integer	The device driver reference number.
→	spSlot	SignedByte	The slot number.
→	spId	SignedByte	The sResource ID.
→	spExtDev	SignedByte	The external device identifier.

DESCRIPTION

The `InsertSRTRec` function installs an sResource from the firmware of a NuBus card into the slot resource table. For example, if the user makes a selection in the Monitors control panel that requires your video card to switch to a new sResource that was deleted by `PrimaryInit` code, you can use the `InsertSRTRec` function to restore that sResource.

You specify an sResource with the `spSlot`, `spID`, and `spExtDev` fields of the Slot Manager parameter block you point to in the `spBlkPtr` parameter. You must set the `spsPointer` field to NIL. Set the `spParamData` field to 1 to disable the restored sResource or to 0 to enable it.

If you place a valid device driver reference number in the `spRefNum` field, the Slot Manager updates the `dCtlDevBase` field in that device driver's device control entry (that is, in the device control entry that has that driver reference number in the `dCtlRefNum` field). The `dCtlDevBase` field contains the base address of the slot device. For a video card this is the base address for the pixel map in the card's `GDevice` record (which is described in *Inside Macintosh: Imaging With QuickDraw*). For other types of cards the base address is optional and defined by the card designer.

The base address consists of the card's slot address plus an optional offset that the card designer can specify using the `MinorBaseOS` or `MajorBaseOS` entries of the sResource. The Slot Manager calculates the base address by using bit 2 (the `f32BitMode` flag) of the `sRsrcFlags` entry of the sResource. As shown in Table 2-4, the Slot Manager first checks the value of bit 2 of the `sRsrcFlags` field, and then it checks for a `MinorBaseOS` entry. If it finds one, it uses this value to create a 32-bit value to store in the `dCtlDevBase` field. If it does not find a `MinorBaseOS` entry, it uses the value in the `MajorBaseOS` entry, if any.

Table 2-4 How the Slot Manager determines the base address of a slot device

sRsrcFlags	MinorBaseOS	MajorBaseOS	Address format
Field missing	$x xxxx	Any or none	$Fs0x xxxx
Field missing	None	$xx xxxx	$sxxx xxxx
Bit 2 is 0	$x xxxx	Any or none	$Fs0x xxxx
Bit 2 is 0	None	$xx xxxx	$sxxx xxxx
Bit 2 is 1	$x xxxx	Any or none	$Fsxx xxxx
Bit 2 is 1	None	$xx xxxx	$sxxx xxxx

Note

In this table, x represents any hexadecimal digit and s represents a slot number. ◆

SPECIAL CONSIDERATIONS

The `InsertSRTRec` function is available only with version 1 or later of the Slot Manager. You can use the `SVersion` function, described on page 2-30, to determine whether the Slot Manager is version 1 or later.

ASSEMBLY-LANGUAGE INFORMATION

The trap macro and routine selector for the `InsertSRTRec` function are

Trap macro	Selector
_SlotManager	$000A

You must set up register D0 with the routine selector and register A0 with the address of the Slot Manager parameter block. When `_SlotManager` returns, register D0 contains the result code.

Registers on entry

A0 Address of the parameter block

D0 $000A

Registers on exit

D0 Result code

RESULT CODES

noErr	0	No error
memFullErr	–108	Not enough room in heap
smUnExBusErr	–308	Bus error
smBadRefId	–330	Reference ID not found in list
smBadsList	–331	Bad sResource: Id1 < Id2 < Id3 ... format is not followed
smReservedErr	–332	Reserved field not zero
smSlotOOBErr	–337	Slot number out of bounds
smNoMoresRsrcs	–344	Specified sResource not found
smBadsPtrErr	–346	Bad pointer was passed to SCalcSPointer
smByteLanesErr	–347	ByteLanes field in card's format block was determined to be zero

SEE ALSO

For more information about the slot resource table, see "About the Slot Manager" on page 2-15.

For information about deleting an sResource from the slot resource table, see the SDeleteSRTRec function, described on page 2-52. For more information on deleting and restoring sResources, see "Deleting and Restoring sResources" on page 2-17.

For more information about the device control entry and device driver reference numbers, see the chapter "Device Manager" in this book.

SUpdateSRT

For system software versions earlier than System 7, you can use the SUpdateSRT function to update the slot resource table record for an existing sResource. A new record will be added if the sResource does not already exist in the slot resource table.

```
FUNCTION SUpdateSRT (spBlkPtr: SpBlockPtr): OSErr;
```

spBlkPtr   A pointer to a Slot Manager parameter block.

Parameter block

→	spIOReserved	Integer	The value to be stored in the IOReserved field of the slot resource table.
→	spRefNum	Integer	The device driver reference number.
→	spSlot	SignedByte	The slot number.
→	spId	SignedByte	The sResource ID.
→	spExtDev	SignedByte	The external device identifier.

DESCRIPTION

The SUpdateSRT function adds or updates an record in the slot resource table. You specify an sResource with the spSlot, spID, and spExtDev fields of the Slot Manager parameter block you point to in the spBlkPtr parameter. If a matching record is found in the slot resource table, the `RefNum` and `IOReserved` fields of the table are updated. If the record is not found, the sResource is added to the table by reading the appropriate declaration ROM. Updates may be made to enabled sResources only.

SPECIAL CONSIDERATIONS

In System 7, this function was replaced by the `InsertSRTRec` function (described on page 2-54). You should use the `SUpdateSRT` function only if version 1 or later of the Slot Manager is not available. You can use the `SVersion` function, described on page 2-30, to determine whether the Slot Manager is version 1 or later.

ASSEMBLY-LANGUAGE INFORMATION

The trap macro and routine selector for the `SUpdateSRT` function are

Trap macro	Selector
_SlotManager	$002B

You must set up register D0 with the routine selector and register A0 with the address of the Slot Manager parameter block. When `_SlotManager` returns, register D0 contains the result code.

Registers on entry

A0   Address of the parameter block

D0 $002B

Registers on exit

D0   Result code

RESULT CODES

noErr	0	No error
memFullErr	–108	Not enough room in heap
smEmptySlot	–300	No card in this slot
smUnExBusErr	–308	Bus error
smBadRefId	–330	Reference ID not found in list
smSlotOOBErr	–337	Slot number out of bounds
smNoMoresRsrcs	–344	Specified sResource not found

SEE ALSO

For more information about the slot resource table, see "About the Slot Manager" on page 2-15.

For information about the preferred routine for adding an sResource to the slot resource table, see the `InsertSRTRec` function, described on page 2-54. For information about deleting an sResource from the slot resource table, see the `SDeleteSRTRec` function, described on page 2-52.

Loading Drivers and Executing Code From sResources

The functions in this section allow you to load the device driver associated with an sResource or execute code from an `sExecBlock` data structure. Both of the functions in this section require you to provide extra information in a structure of type `SEBlock`. See "Slot Execution Parameter Block" on page 2-27 for information about the fields of this structure.

SGetDriver

You can use the `SGetDriver` function to load an sResource's device driver.

```
FUNCTION SGetDriver (spBlkPtr: SpBlockPtr): OSErr;
```

spBlkPtr   A pointer to a Slot Manager parameter block.

Parameter block

←	spResult	Handle	A handle to the device driver.
→	spsExecPBlk	Ptr	A pointer to the SEBlock.
→	spSlot	SignedByte	The slot number.
→	spID	SignedByte	The sResource ID.
→	spExtDev	SignedByte	The external device ID.
X	spSize	SignedByte	
X	spFlags	SignedByte	

DESCRIPTION

The `SGetDriver` function loads a device driver from an sResource into a relocatable block in the system heap.

You specify an sResource with the `spSlot`, `spID`, and `spExtDev` fields of the Slot Manager parameter block you point to in the `spBlkPtr` parameter, and provide a pointer to a slot execution parameter block in the `spsExecPBlk` field.

The `SGetDriver` function searches the sResource for an `sRsrcLoadRec` entry. If it finds one, it loads the `sLoadDriver` record and executes it. If no `sRsrcLoadRec` entry exists, the `SGetDriver` function looks for an `sRsrcDrvrDir` entry. If it finds one, it loads the driver into memory.

The `SGetDriver` function returns a handle to the driver in the `spResult` field of the parameter block.

SPECIAL CONSIDERATIONS

The `SGetDriver` function allocates memory; your application should not call this function at interrupt time.

ASSEMBLY-LANGUAGE INFORMATION

The trap macro and routine selector for the `SGetDriver` function are

Trap macro   **Selector**

`_SlotManager` $002D

You must set up register D0 with the routine selector and register A0 with the address of the Slot Manager parameter block. When `_SlotManager` returns, register A0 contains a handle to the loaded driver, and register D0 contains the result code.

Registers on entry

A0   Address of the parameter block

D0 $002D

Registers on exit

A0   Handle to loaded driver

D0   Result code

RESULT CODES

noErr	0	No error
smNoMoresRsrcs	−344	Requested sResource not found

SEE ALSO

For more information about sResources, including the `sRsrcDrvrDir` and `sRsrcLoadRec` entry types, see *Designing Cards and Drivers for the Macintosh Family,* third edition.

SExec

You can use the `SExec` function to execute code stored in an `sExecBlock` data structure.

`FUNCTION SExec (spBlkPtr: SpBlockPtr): OSErr;`

spBlkPtr   A pointer to a Slot Manager parameter block.

Parameter block

→	spsPointer	Ptr	A pointer to an sResource (described in "The sResource," beginning on page 2-7).
→	spsExecPBlk	Ptr	A pointer to the SEBlock.
→	spID	SignedByte	The ID of the sExecBlock entry in the sResource.
×	spResult	LongInt	

DESCRIPTION

The `SExec` function loads `sExecBlock` code from an sResource into the current heap zone, checks its revision level, and executes the code.

You specify the `sExecBlock` by providing a pointer to the sResource in the `spsPointer` field and the ID of the `sExecBlock` entry in the `spID` field. You must also provide in the `spsExecPBlk` field a pointer to a slot execution parameter block. The `SEBlock` structure allows you to provide information about the execution of the `sExecBlock` code.

The `SExec` function passes the `sExecBlock` code a pointer to the `SEBlock` structure in register A0.

SPECIAL CONSIDERATIONS

The `SExec` function allocates memory; your application should not call this function at interrupt time.

ASSEMBLY-LANGUAGE INFORMATION

The trap macro and routine selector for the `SExec` function are

Trap macro	Selector
`_SlotManager`	$0023

You must set up register D0 with the routine selector and register A0 with the address of the Slot Manager parameter block. When `_SlotManager` returns, register D0 contains the result code.

Registers on entry

A0   Address of the parameter block

D0 $0023

Registers on exit

D0   Result code

RESULT CODES

noErr	0	No error
smCodeRevErr	–333	The revision of the code to be executed by sExec was wrong
smCPUErr	–334	The CPU field of the code to be executed by sExec was wrong
smNoMoresRsrcs	–344	Requested sResource not found

SEE ALSO

For more information about the `sExecBlock` data structure, see page 2-9.

Getting Information About Expansion Cards and Declaration ROMs

The functions in this section return information about slot status or about entire declaration ROMs, instead of single sResources. The SReadInfo function returns information from the slot information record maintained by the Slot Manager for a particular slot. See "Slot Information Record," beginning on page 2-24 for a description of the slot information record.

The SReadFHeader functions returns a copy of the information in the format block of a card's declaration ROM. The SCkCardStat function returns a card's initialization status. The SCardChanged function reports whether the card in a particular slot has changed.

The SFindDevBase function returns the base address of a slot device.

SReadInfo

You can use the SReadInfo function to obtain a copy of the slot information record for a particular slot.

```
FUNCTION SReadInfo (spBlkPtr: SpBlockPtr): OSErr;
```

spBlkPtr   A pointer to a Slot Manager parameter block.

Parameter block

→	spResult	Pointer	A pointer to a slot information record.
→	spSlot	SignedByte	The slot number.
X	spSize	LongInt	

DESCRIPTION

The Slot Manager maintains a slot information record for each slot. The SReadInfo function copies the information from this data structure for the requested slot.

You specify the slot with the spSlot parameter. You must also allocate a slot information record, and provide a pointer to it in the spResult field. The SReadInfo function copies the information in the slot information record maintained by the Slot Manager into the data structure pointed to by the spResult field.

SPECIAL CONSIDERATIONS

This function may alter the contents of the spSize field. Your application should not depend on the value returned in this field.

ASSEMBLY-LANGUAGE INFORMATION

The trap macro and routine selector for the SReadInfo function are

Trap macro   **Selector**

_SlotManager $0010

You must set up register D0 with the routine selector and register A0 with the address of the Slot Manager parameter block. When _SlotManager returns, register D0 contains the result code.

Registers on entry

A0   Address of the parameter block

D0 $0010

Registers on exit

D0   Result code

RESULT CODES

noErr   0   No error
smEmptySlot   –300   No card in this slot

SEE ALSO

For general information about the slot information record, see "About the Slot Manager" on page 2-15. To obtain a pointer to the SInfoRecord data structure, instead of a copy of it, see the next section, which describes the SReadFHeader function.

SReadFHeader

You can use the SReadFHeader function to obtain a copy of the information in the format block of a declaration ROM.

```
FUNCTION SReadFHeader (spBlkPtr: SpBlockPtr): OSErr;
```

spBlkPtr   A pointer to a Slot Manager parameter block.

Parameter block

→	spResult	Pointer	A pointer to an FHeaderRec data structure (described on page 2-26).
→	spSlot	SignedByte	The slot number.
×	spsPointer	Ptr	
×	spSize	LongInt	
×	spOffsetData	LongInt	
×	spByteLanes	SignedByte	

DESCRIPTION

The `SReadFHeader` function copies the information from the format block of the expansion card in the requested slot to an `FHeaderRec` data structure you provide.

You specify the slot with the `spSlot` parameter. You must also allocate an `FHeaderRec` data structure and provide a pointer to it in the `spResult` field.

The `SReadInfo` function copies the information in the format block into the data structure pointed to by the `spResult` field.

SPECIAL CONSIDERATIONS

This function may alter the contents of the `spsPointer`, `spSize`, `spOffsetData`, and `spByteLanes` fields. Your application should not depend on the values returned in these fields.

ASSEMBLY-LANGUAGE INFORMATION

The trap macro and routine selector for the `SReadFHeader` function are

Trap macro	Selector
`_SlotManager`	$0013

You must set up register D0 with the routine selector and register A0 with the address of the Slot Manager parameter block. When `_SlotManager` returns, register D0 contains the result code.

Registers on entry

A0   Address of the parameter block

D0 $0013

Registers on exit

D0   Result code

RESULT CODES

noErr	0	No error
smEmptySlot	–300	No card in this slot

SEE ALSO

For general information about the format block, see "The Format Block," beginning on page 2-13. For information about the fields of the format block, see *Designing Cards and Drivers for the Macintosh Family*, third edition.

SCkCardStat

You can use the SCkCardStat function to check the initialization status of an expansion card.

```
FUNCTION SCkCardStat (spBlkPtr: SpBlockPtr): OSErr;
```

spBlkPtr   A pointer to a Slot Manager parameter block.

Parameter block

→	spSlot	SignedByte	The slot number.
X	spResult	LongInt	

DESCRIPTION

The SCkCardStat function checks the InitStatusA field of the slot information record for the expansion card in the designated slot. You specify the slot in the spSlot field of the Slot Manager parameter block you point to in the spBlkPtr parameter. The SCkCardStat function returns the noErr result code if the InitStatusA field contains a nonzero value.

SPECIAL CONSIDERATIONS

This function may alter the contents of the spResult field. Your application should not depend on the values returned in this field.

ASSEMBLY-LANGUAGE INFORMATION

The trap macro and routine selector for the SCkCardStat function are

Trap macro	Selector
_SlotManager	$0018

You must set up register D0 with the routine selector and register A0 with the address of the Slot Manager parameter block. When _SlotManager returns, register D0 contains the result code.

Registers on entry

A0   Address of the parameter block

D0 $0018

Registers on exit

D0   Result code

RESULT CODES

noErr	0	No error
smEmptySlot	–300	No card in this slot

SEE ALSO

For more information about card initialization, see "About the Slot Manager," beginning on page 2-15.

SCardChanged

You can use the SCardChanged function to determine if the card in a particular slot has been changed.

```
FUNCTION SCardChanged (spBlkPtr: SpBlockPtr): OSErr;
```

spBlkPtr   A pointer to a Slot Manager parameter block.

Parameter block

→	spSlot	SignedByte	The slot number.
←	spResult	LongInt	A Boolean signifying whether the card was changed.

DESCRIPTION

The SCardChanged function checks if the expansion card in a slot has been changed (that is, if the card's sPRAMInit record has been initialized). You specify the slot in the spSlot field of the Slot Manager parameter block you point to in the spBlkPtr parameter.

The SCardChanged function returns a value of TRUE in the spResult field of the parameter block if the card has been changed.

ASSEMBLY-LANGUAGE INFORMATION

The trap macro and routine selector for the SCardChanged function are

Trap macro	Selector
_SlotManager	$0022

You must set up register D0 with the routine selector and register A0 with the address of the Slot Manager parameter block. When _SlotManager returns, register D0 contains the result code.

Registers on entry

A0   Address of the parameter block

D0 $0022

Registers on exit

D0   Result code

RESULT CODES

noErr   0   No error
smEmptySlot   −300   No card in this slot

SFindDevBase

You can use the SFindDevBase function to determine the base address of a slot device.

FUNCTION SFindDevBase (spBlkPtr: SpBlockPtr): OSErr;

spBlkPtr   A pointer to a Slot Manager parameter block.

Parameter block

→	spSlot	SignedByte	The slot number.
→	spId	SignedByte	The sResource ID.
←	spResult	LongInt	The device base address.

DESCRIPTION

The SFindDevBase function returns the base address of a device, using information contained in the sResource. Use of the base address is optional (except for video cards) and device-specific. For a video card this must be the base address for the pixel map in the card's GDevice record (which is described in *Inside Macintosh: Imaging With QuickDraw*.) For other types of cards, the base address is defined by the card designer. The Slot Manager makes no use of this information.

The base address consists of the card's slot address plus an optional offset that the card designer can specify using the MinorBaseOS or MajorBaseOS entries of the sResource. See Table 2-4 on page 2-55 for a description of how the Slot Manager calculates the base address.

You specify the slot in the spSlot field of the Slot Manager parameter block you point to in the spBlkPtr parameter, and the sResource ID with the spId field. The SFindDevBase function returns the base address in the spResult field of the parameter block.

Note

The base address of a slot device is also stored in the dCtlDevBase field of the device control entry. The InsertSRTRec function automatically updates the dCtlDevBase field when a new record is added to the slot resource table. You need to call SFindDevBase only if you used the SUpdateSRTRec function to update the slot resource table. ◆

ASSEMBLY-LANGUAGE INFORMATION

The trap macro and routine selector for the SFindDevBase function are

Trap macro	Selector
_SlotManager	$001B

You must set up register D0 with the routine selector and register A0 with the address of the Slot Manager parameter block. When _SlotManager returns, register D0 contains the result code.

Registers on entry

A0   Address of the parameter block

D0 $001B

Registers on exit

D0   Result code

RESULT CODES

noErr	0	No error
smEmptySlot	–300	No card in this slot

SEE ALSO

For more information about how the device base address is calculated, see the description of the InsertSRTRec function on page 2-54.

Accessing Expansion Card Parameter RAM

The Macintosh Operating System reserves six bytes of parameter RAM per slot for any card-specific information that the card designer chooses to store. The functions in this section allow you to read or change the value of these bytes. Both of the functions in this section use the slot parameter RAM record to return the parameter RAM values.

SReadPRAMRec

You can use the SReadPRAMRec function to read the parameter RAM information for a particular slot.

```
FUNCTION SReadPRAMRec (spBlkPtr: SpBlockPtr): OSErr;
```

spBlkPtr   A pointer to a Slot Manager parameter block.

Parameter block

→	spSlot	SignedByte	The slot number.
→	spResult	Pointer	A pointer to an SPRAMRecord data structure (described on page 2-27).
✕	spSize	LongInt	

DESCRIPTION

The Macintosh Operating System allocates one SPRAMRecord data structure for each slot in the system parameter RAM. The Slot Manager initializes this structure with the data from the sPRAMInit record on the firmware of the expansion card. The SReadPRAMRec function provides a copy of this information to your application.

You specify the slot number in the spSlot field of the Slot Manager parameter block you point to in the spBlkPtr parameter. You must also allocate a SPRAMRecord data structure and store a pointer to it in the spResult field. The SReadPRAMRec function copies the appropriate parameter RAM information into this data structure.

ASSEMBLY-LANGUAGE INFORMATION

The trap macro and routine selector for the SReadPRAMRec function are

Trap macro	Selector
_SlotManager	$0011

You must set up register D0 with the routine selector and register A0 with the address of the Slot Manager parameter block. When _SlotManager returns, register D0 contains the result code.

Registers on entry

A0   Address of the parameter block

D0 $0011

Registers on exit

D0   Result code

RESULT CODES

noErr	0	No error
smEmptySlot	–300	No card in this slot

SEE ALSO

For more information about the sPRAMInit record, see *Designing Cards and Drivers for the Macintosh Family,* third edition.

SPutPRAMRec

You can use the SPutPRAMRec function to change the values stored in a slot's parameter RAM.

```
FUNCTION SPutPRAMRec (spBlkPtr: SpBlockPtr): OSErr;
```

spBlkPtr   A pointer to a Slot Manager parameter block.

Parameter block

→	spsPointer	Ptr	A pointer to an SPRAMRecord data structure (described on page 2-27).
→	spSlot	SignedByte	The slot number.

DESCRIPTION

The SPutPRAMRec function allows you to change the values stored in the parameter RAM of a slot.

In the parameter block you point to in the spBlkPtr parameter, you specify the slot number with the spSlot field and provide the new parameter RAM values in a SPRAMRecord data structure pointed to by the spsPointer field.

The SPutPRAMRec function copies the information from the six vendor-use fields into the parameter RAM for the slot. This function does not copy the boardID field, which is Apple-defined.

ASSEMBLY-LANGUAGE INFORMATION

The trap macro and routine selector for the SPutPRAMRec function are

Trap macro	Selector
_SlotManager	$0012

You must set up register D0 with the routine selector and register A0 with the address of the Slot Manager parameter block. When _SlotManager returns, register D0 contains the result code.

Registers on entry

A0   Address of the parameter block

D0 $0012

Registers on exit

D0   Result code

RESULT CODES

noErr	0	No error
smEmptySlot	–300	No card in this slot

Managing the Slot Interrupt Queue

The Slot Manager maintains an interrupt queue for each slot. If your card generates interrupts, you can install a slot interrupt handler to process the interrupts. You use the SIntInstall function to install an interrupt handler in the slot interrupt queue, and the SIntRemove function to remove an interrupt handler from the queue.

SIntInstall

You use the SIntInstall function to install an interrupt handler in the slot interrupt queue for a designated slot.

```
FUNCTION SIntInstall (sIntQElemPtr: SQElemPtr;
                        theSlot: Integer) : OsErr;
```

sIntQElemPtr
    A pointer to a slot interrupt queue element record, described on page 2-28.

theSlot The slot number.

DESCRIPTION

The SIntInstall function adds a new element to the interrupt queue for a slot. You provide a pointer to a slot interrupt queue element in the sIntQElemPtr parameter and specify the slot number in theSlot.

The Slot Manager calls your interrupt handler using a JSR instruction. Your routine must preserve the contents of all registers except A1 and D0, and return to the Slot Manager with an RTS instruction. Register D0 should be set to 0 if your routine did not service the interrupt, or any other value if the interrupt was serviced. Your routine should not set the processor priority below 2, and must return with the processor priority equal to 2.

ASSEMBLY-LANGUAGE INFORMATION

The trap macro for the SIntInstall function is _SIntInstall ($A075).

You must set up register D0 with the slot number and register A0 with the address of the slot queue element. When _SIntInstall returns, register D0 contains the result code.

Registers on entry

A0 address of the slot queue element

D0 slot number

Registers on exit

D0 Result code

RESULT CODES

noErr   0   No error

SIntRemove

You use the SIntRemove function to remove an interrupt handler from a slot's interrupt queue.

```
FUNCTION SIntRemove (sIntQElemPtr: SQElemPtr;
                          theSlot: Integer) : OsErr;
```

sIntQElemPtr
> A pointer to a slot interrupt queue element record, described on page 2-28.

theSlot   The slot number.

DESCRIPTION

The SIntRemove function removes an element from the interrupt queue for a slot. You provide a pointer to a slot interrupt queue element in the sIntQElemPtr parameter and specify the slot number in theSlot.

ASSEMBLY-LANGUAGE INFORMATION

The trap macro for the SIntRemove function is _SIntRemove ($A076).

You must set up register D0 with the slot number and register A0 with the address of the slot queue element. When _SIntRemove returns, register D0 contains the result code.

Registers on entry

A0   address of the slot queue element

D0   slot number

Registers on exit

D0   Result code

RESULT CODES

noErr   0   No error

SEE ALSO

For a description of the slot interrupt queue element record, see "Slot Interrupt Queue Element" on page 2-28.

Low-Level Routines

The routines in this section are used internally by the Macintosh Operating System during startup, and as needed by the Slot Manager. They are included here for reference only, and as an aid to debugging. These routines are not required or supported for application-level programming. Applications and device drivers should rely only on the high-level routines described in the previous section, "Slot Manager Routines."

▲ **WARNING**
The routines in this section are internal Macintosh Operating System functions that may be changed without notice by Apple Computer, Inc. These routines may not be supported by future versions of the Operating System. ▲

InitSDeclMgr

This function is used only by the Macintosh Operating System.

```
FUNCTION InitSDeclMgr (spBlkPtr: SpBlockPtr): OSErr;
```

spBlkPtr   A pointer to a Slot Manager parameter block.

DESCRIPTION

The InitSDeclMgr function initializes the Slot Manager. The contents of the parameter block are undefined. This function allocates the slot information record and checks each slot for a card. If a card is present, the Slot Manager validates the card's firmware and the resulting information is placed in the slot's sInfoRecord. For empty slots, or cards that fail to initialize, the Slot Manager stores the appropriate error code in the initStatusA field of the sInfoRecord for the slot.

SPECIAL CONSIDERATIONS

The InitSDeclMgr function allocates memory.

ASSEMBLY-LANGUAGE INFORMATION

The trap macro and routine selector for the InitSDeclMgr function are

Trap macro	Selector
_SlotManager	$0020

On entry, register D0 contains the routine selector and register A0 contains the address of the Slot Manager parameter block. When _SlotManager returns, register D0 contains the result code.

Registers on entry

A0   Address of the parameter block

D0 $0020

Registers on exit

D0   Result code

RESULT CODES

noErr	0	No error
smUnExBusErr	–308	A bus error occurred
smDisposePErr	–312	An error occurred during execution of DisposePtr
smBadsPtrErr	–346	Bad spsPointer value
smByteLanesErr	–347	Bad spByteLanes value

SEE ALSO

For more information about Slot Manager initialization, see "About the Slot Manager," beginning on page 2-15.

SCalcSPointer

This function is used only by the Macintosh Operating System.

```
FUNCTION SCalcSPointer (spBlkPtr: SpBlockPtr): OSErr;
```

spBlkPtr   A pointer to a Slot Manager parameter block.

Parameter block

↔	spsPointer	Ptr	A pointer to a byte in declaration ROM.
→	spOffsetData	LongInt	The offset in bytes to desired pointer.
→	spByteLanes	SignedByte	The byte lanes used.

DESCRIPTION

The SCalcSPointer function returns a pointer to a given byte in the declaration ROM of an expansion card.

ASSEMBLY-LANGUAGE INFORMATION

The trap macro and routine selector for the `SCalcSPointer` function are

Trap macro   **Selector**

`_SlotManager` $002C

On entry, register D0 contains the routine selector and register A0 contains the address of the Slot Manager parameter block. When `_SlotManager` returns, register D0 contains the result code.

Registers on entry

A0   Address of the parameter block

D0 $002C

Registers on exit

D0   Result code

RESULT CODES

noErr	0	No error
smNoMoresRsrcs	–344	Requested sResource not found

SCalcStep

This function is used only by the Macintosh Operating System.

```
FUNCTION SCalcStep (spBlkPtr: SpBlockPtr): OSErr;
```

spBlkPtr   A pointer to a Slot Manager parameter block.

Parameter block

←	spResult	LongInt	The function result.
→	spsPointer	Ptr	A pointer to a byte in declaration ROM.
→	spByteLanes	SignedByte	The byte lanes used.
→	spFlags	SignedByte	Flags.

DESCRIPTION

The `SCalcStep` function calculates the field sizes in the block pointed to by `spBlkPtr`. It is used for stepping through the card firmware one field at a time. If the `fConsecBytes` flag is set the function calculates the step value for consecutive bytes; otherwise it calculates it for consecutive IDs.

ASSEMBLY-LANGUAGE INFORMATION

The trap macro and routine selector for the `SCalcStep` function are

Trap macro	Selector
`_SlotManager`	$0028

On entry, register D0 contains the routine selector and register A0 contains the address of the Slot Manager parameter block. When `_SlotManager` returns, register D0 contains the result code.

Registers on entry

A0   Address of the parameter block

D0 $0028

Registers on exit

D0   Result code

RESULT CODES

noErr	0	No error
smNoMoresRsrcs	–344	Requested sResource not found

SFindBigDevBase

This function is obsolete.

```
FUNCTION SFindBigDevBase (spBlkPtr: SpBlockPtr): OSErr;
```

spBlkPtr   A pointer to a Slot Manager parameter block.

Parameter block

→	spSlot	SignedByte	The slot number.
→	spId	SignedByte	The sResource ID.
←	spResult	LongInt	The device base address.

DESCRIPTION

The `SFindBigDevBase` function has been superseded by the `SFindDevBase` function. Currently, both functions execute the same code and return the same result. However, for future compatibility you should use only the `SFindDevBase` function described on page 2-66.

ASSEMBLY-LANGUAGE INFORMATION

The trap macro and routine selector for the `SFindBigDevBase` function are

Trap macro	Selector
_SlotManager	$001C

On entry, register D0 contains the routine selector and register A0 contains the address of the Slot Manager parameter block. When `_SlotManager` returns, register D0 contains the result code.

Registers on entry

A0   Address of the parameter block

D0 $001C

Registers on exit

D0   Result code

RESULT CODES

noErr	0	No error
smEmptySlot	–300	No card in this slot

SEE ALSO

For information about the supported function for finding a device base address, see the description of the `SFindDevBase` function on page 2-66.

SFindSInfoRecPtr

This function is used only by the Macintosh Operating System.

```
FUNCTION SFindSInfoRecPtr (spBlkPtr: SpBlockPtr): OSErr;
```

spBlkPtr   A pointer to a Slot Manager parameter block.

Parameter block

←	spResult	LongInt	A pointer to the slot information record.
→	spSlot	SignedByte	The slot number.

DESCRIPTION

The `SFindSInfoRecPtr` function returns a pointer to the slot information record for a particular slot.

ASSEMBLY-LANGUAGE INFORMATION

The trap macro and routine selector for the SFindSInfoRecPtr function are

Trap macro   **Selector**

_SlotManager $002F

On entry, register D0 contains the routine selector and register A0 contains the address of the Slot Manager parameter block. When _SlotManager returns, register D0 contains the result code.

Registers on entry

A0   Address of the parameter block

D0 $002F

Registers on exit

D0   Result code

RESULT CODES

noErr   0   No error
smNoMoresRsrcs   −344   Requested sResource not found

SEE ALSO

For information about the high-level routine for reading the slot information record, see the description of the SReadInfo function on page 2-61.

SFindSRsrcPtr

This function is used only by the Macintosh Operating System.

```
FUNCTION SFindSRsrcPtr (spBlkPtr: SpBlockPtr): OSErr;
```

spBlkPtr   A pointer to a Slot Manager parameter block.

Parameter block

←	spsPointer	Ptr	A pointer to an sResource (described in "The sResource," beginning on page 2-7).
→	spSlot	SignedByte	The slot number of the requested sResource.
→	spId	SignedByte	The sResource ID of the requested sResource.
×	spResult	LongInt	

DESCRIPTION

The SFindSRsrcPtr function finds an sResource given its slot number and sResource ID. This function ignores disabled sResources.

ASSEMBLY-LANGUAGE INFORMATION

The trap macro and routine selector for the SFindSRsrcPtr function are

Trap macro   **Selector**

_SlotManager $0030

On entry, register D0 contains the routine selector and register A0 contains the address of the Slot Manager parameter block. When _SlotManager returns, register D0 contains the result code.

Registers on entry

A0   Address of the parameter block

D0 $0030

Registers on exit

D0   Result code

RESULT CODES

noErr   0   No error
smNoMoresRsrcs   –344   Requested sResource not found

SEE ALSO

For information about the high-level routines for locating sResources, see "Finding sResources," beginning on page 2-31.

SGetSRsrcPtr

This function is used only by the Macintosh Operating System.

```
FUNCTION SGetSRsrcPtr (spBlkPtr: SpBlockPtr): OSErr;
```

spBlkPtr   A pointer to a Slot Manager parameter block.

Parameter block

←	spsPointer	Ptr	A pointer to an sResource (described in "The sResource," beginning on page 2-7).
→	spParamData	LongInt	The parameter flags.
→	spSlot	SignedByte	The slot number of the requested sResource.
→	spID	SignedByte	The sResource ID of the requested sResource.
→	spExtDev	SignedByte	The external device identifier.

DESCRIPTION

The SGetSRsrcPtr function finds an sResource given its slot number and sResource ID. This function can search disabled sResources.

ASSEMBLY-LANGUAGE INFORMATION

The trap macro and routine selector for the `SGetSRsrcPtr` function are

Trap macro	Selector
_Slot Manager	$001D

On entry, register D0 contains the routine selector and register A0 contains the address of the Slot Manager parameter block. When `_SlotManager` returns, register D0 contains the result code.

Registers on entry

A0   Address of the parameter block

D0 $001D

Registers on exit

D0   Result code

RESULT CODES

noErr	0	No error
smNoMoresRsrcs	–344	Requested sResource not found

SEE ALSO

For information about the high-level routines for locating sResources, see "Finding sResources," beginning on page 2-31.

SInitPRAMRecs

This function is used only by the Macintosh Operating System.

```
FUNCTION SInitPRAMRecs (spBlkPtr: SpBlockPtr): OSErr;
```

spBlkPtr   A pointer to a Slot Manager parameter block.

DESCRIPTION

The `SInitPRAMRecs` function scans every slot and checks its `BoardId` value against the value stored in PRAM. If the values do not match, the `fCardIsChanged` flag is set and the board sResource is searched for a `PRAMInitData` entry. If one is found, the `sPRAMRecord` for the slot is initialized with the data from the card's `sPRAMInit` record; otherwise it is initialized to 0. The contents of the parameter block are undefined.

SPECIAL CONSIDERATIONS

The `SInitPRAMRecs` function may move memory.

ASSEMBLY-LANGUAGE INFORMATION

The trap macro and routine selector for the `SInitPRAMRecs` function are

Trap macro   **Selector**

`_SlotManager` $0025

On entry, register D0 contains the routine selector and register A0 contains the address of the Slot Manager parameter block. When `_SlotManager` returns, register D0 contains the result code.

Registers on entry

A0   Address of the parameter block

D0 $0025

Registers on exit

D0   Result code

RESULT CODES

noErr	0	No error
smUnExBusErr	–308	A bus error occurred
smDisposePErr	–312	An error occurred during execution of `DisposePtr`

SEE ALSO

For more information about Slot Manager initialization, see "About the Slot Manager," beginning on page 2-15.

SInitSRsrcTable

This function is used only by the Macintosh Operating System.

`FUNCTION SInitSRsrcTable (spBlkPtr: SpBlockPtr): OSErr;`

spBlkPtr   A pointer to a Slot Manager parameter block.

DESCRIPTION

The `SInitSRsrcTable` function initializes the slot resource table. The contents of the parameter block are undefined.

SPECIAL CONSIDERATIONS

The `SInitSRsrcTable` function allocates memory.

ASSEMBLY-LANGUAGE INFORMATION

The trap macro and routine selector for the `SInitSRsrcTable` function are

Trap macro	Selector
`_SlotManager`	$0029

On entry, register D0 contains the routine selector and register A0 contains the address of the Slot Manager parameter block. When `_SlotManager` returns, register D0 contains the result code.

Registers on entry

A0   Address of the parameter block

D0 $0029

Registers on exit

D0   Result code

RESULT CODES

noErr	0	No error
smUnExBusErr	–308	A bus error occurred
smDisposePErr	–312	An error occurred during execution of `DisposePtr`

SEE ALSO

For more information about Slot Manager initialization, see "About the Slot Manager," beginning on page 2-15.

SOffsetData

This function is used only by the Macintosh Operating System.

```
FUNCTION SOffsetData (spBlkPtr: SpBlockPtr): OSErr;
```

spBlkPtr   A pointer to a Slot Manager parameter block.

Parameter block

↔	spsPointer	Ptr	On output: A pointer to the sResource entry.
←	spOffsetData	LongInt	The contents of the `offset` field.
→	spID	SignedByte	The ID of the sResource entry.
←	spByteLanes	SignedByte	The byte lanes from the card's format block.

DESCRIPTION

The `SOffsetData` function returns the value of the offset field of an sResource entry.

ASSEMBLY-LANGUAGE INFORMATION

The trap macro and routine selector for the SOffsetData function are

Trap macro   **Selector**

_SlotManager $0024

On entry, register D0 contains the routine selector and register A0 contains the address of the Slot Manager parameter block. When _SlotManager returns, register D0 contains the result code.

Registers on entry

A0   Address of the parameter block

D0 $0024

Registers on exit

D0   Result code

RESULT CODES

noErr	0	No error
smNoMoresRsrcs	–344	Requested sResource not found

SEE ALSO

For information about high-level routines for getting information from sResources, see the descriptions of the SReadByte, SReadWord, SReadLong, SGetCString, SGetBlock, SReadStruct, and SFindStruct functions in "Getting Information From sResources," beginning on page 2-40.

SPrimaryInit

This function is used only by the Macintosh Operating System.

```
FUNCTION SPrimaryInit (spBlkPtr: SpBlockPtr): OSErr;
```

spBlkPtr   A pointer to a Slot Manager parameter block.

Parameter block

→	spFlags	SignedByte	Flags passed to the card's PrimaryInit code.

DESCRIPTION

Called by the Slot Manager during system startup, the SPrimaryInit function executes the code in the PrimaryInit entry of each card's board sResource. It passes the spFlags byte to the PrimaryInit code via the seFlags field of the SEBlock. The fWarmStart bit is set if a restart is being performed.

SPECIAL CONSIDERATIONS

The SPrimaryInit function may move memory.

ASSEMBLY-LANGUAGE INFORMATION

The trap macro and routine selector for the SPrimaryInit function are

Trap macro	Selector
_SlotManager	$0021

On entry, register D0 contains the routine selector and register A0 contains the address of the Slot Manager parameter block. When _SlotManager returns, register D0 contains the result code.

Registers on entry

A0   Address of the parameter block

D0 $0021

Registers on exit

D0   Result code

RESULT CODES

noErr	0	No error
smUnExBusErr	–308	A bus error occurred
smDisposePErr	–312	An error occurred during execution of DisposePtr
smBadsPtrErr	–346	Bad spsPointer value
smByteLanesErr	–347	Bad spByteLanes value

SEE ALSO

For more information about Slot Manager initialization, see "About the Slot Manager," beginning on page 2-15.

SPtrToSlot

This function is used only by the Macintosh Operating System.

```
FUNCTION SPtrToSlot (spBlkPtr: SpBlockPtr): OSErr;
```

spBlkPtr   A pointer to a Slot Manager parameter block.

Parameter block

→	spsPointer	Ptr	A pointer to a byte in declaration ROM.
←	spSlot	SignedByte	The slot number.

DESCRIPTION

The SPtrToSlot function returns the slot number of the card whose declaration ROM is pointed to by spsPointer. The value of spsPointer must have the form $Fsxx xxxx, where *s* is a slot number and *x* is a hexadecimal number.

ASSEMBLY-LANGUAGE INFORMATION

The trap macro and routine selector for the SPtrToSlot function are

Trap macro	Selector
_SlotManager	$002E

On entry, register D0 contains the routine selector and register A0 contains the address of the Slot Manager parameter block. When _SlotManager returns, register D0 contains the result code.

Registers on entry

A0   Address of the parameter block

D0 $002E

Registers on exit

D0   Result code

RESULT CODES

noErr	0	No error
smUnExBusErr	–308	A bus error occurred
smBadsPtrErr	–346	Bad spsPointer value

SReadPBSize

This function is used only by the Macintosh Operating System.

```
FUNCTION SReadPBSize (spBlkPtr: SpBlockPtr): OSErr;
```

spBlkPtr   A pointer to a Slot Manager parameter block.

Parameter block

↔	spsPointer	Ptr	A pointer to an sResource (described in "The sResource," beginning on page 2-7).
←	spSize	LongInt	The size of the sBlock data structure.
→	spID	SignedByte	The ID of the sBlock in the sResource.
←	spByteLanes	SignedByte	The byte lanes from the card's format block.
→	spFlags	SignedByte	Flags.

DESCRIPTION

The SReadPBSize function returns the size of an sBlock data structure.

ASSEMBLY-LANGUAGE INFORMATION

The trap macro and routine selector for the SReadPBSize function are

Trap macro	Selector
_SlotManager	$0026

On entry, register D0 contains the routine selector and register A0 contains the address of the Slot Manager parameter block. When _SlotManager returns, register D0 contains the result code.

Registers on entry

A0   Address of the parameter block

D0 $00026

Registers on exit

D0   Result code

RESULT CODES

noErr	0	No error
smNoMoresRsrcs	–344	Requested sResource not found

SEE ALSO

For more information about the high-level routine for obtaining information from an sBlock data structure, see the description of the SGetBlock function on page 2-47.

SSearchSRT

This function is used only by the Macintosh Operating System.

```
FUNCTION SSearchSRT (spBlkPtr: SpBlockPtr): OSErr;
```

spBlkPtr   A pointer to a Slot Manager parameter block.

Parameter block

←	spsPointer	Ptr	A pointer to a record in the slot resource table.
→	spID	SignedByte	The ID of the sResource entry.
→	spExtDev	SignedByte	The external device identifier.
→	spSlot	SignedByte	The slot.
→	spFlags	SignedByte	Flags.

DESCRIPTION

The SSearchSRT function searches the slot resource table for the record corresponding to the sResource in slot spSlot with list spId and external device identifier spExtDev, and returns a pointer to it in spsPointer. If the fCkForNext bit of spFlags is 0, the function searches for the specified record; if the flag is 1, it searches for the next record.

ASSEMBLY-LANGUAGE INFORMATION

The trap macro and routine selector for the SSearchSRT function are

Trap macro	Selector
_SlotManager	$002A

On entry, register D0 contains the routine selector and register A0 contains the address of the Slot Manager parameter block. When _SlotManager returns, register D0 contains the result code.

Registers on entry

A0   Address of the parameter block

D0 $002A

Registers on exit

D0   Result code

RESULT CODES

noErr	0	No error
smNoMoresRsrcs	–344	Requested sResource not found
smRecNotFnd	–351	Record not found in the slot resource table

Summary of the Slot Manager

Pascal Summary

Constants

```
CONST
    {siStatusFlags field of SInfoRecord}
    fCardIsChanged      = 1;                {card has changed}

    {flags for SSearchSRT}
    fCkForSame          = 0;                {check for same sResource in table}
    fCkForNext          = 1;                {check for next sResource in table}

    {flag passed to card by SPrimaryInit during startup or restart}
    fWarmStart          = 2;                {warm start if set; else cold start}

    {constants for siState field of sInfoRecord}
    stateNil            = 0;                {state}
    stateSDMInit        = 1;                {slot declaration manager init}
    statePRAMInit       = 2;                {sPRAM record init}
    statePInit          = 3;                {primary init}
    stateSInit          = 4;                {secondary init}

    {bit flags for spParamData field of SpBlock}
    fAll                = 0;                {if set, search all sResources}
    fOneSlot            = 1;                {if set, search in given slot only}
    fNext               = 2;                {if set, search for next sResource}
```

Data Types

```
TYPE SpBlock =                             {Slot Manager parameter block}
    PACKED RECORD
        spResult:       LongInt;           {function result}
        spsPointer:     Ptr;               {structure pointer}
        spSize:         LongInt;           {size of structure}
        spOffsetData:   LongInt;           {offset or data}
        spIOFileName:   Ptr;               {reserved for Slot Manager}
        spsExecPBlk:    Ptr;               {pointer to SEBlock data structure}
        spParamData:    LongInt;           {flags}
```

```
   spMisc:              LongInt;          {reserved for Slot Manager}
   spReserved:          LongInt;          {reserved for Slot Manager}
   spIOReserved:        Integer;          {ioReserved field from SRT}
   spRefNum:            Integer;          {driver reference number}
   spCategory:          Integer;          {Category field of sRsrcType entry}
   spCType:             Integer;          {cType field of sRsrcType entry}
   spDrvrSW:            Integer;          {DrSW field of sRsrcType entry}
   spDrvrHW:            Integer;          {DrHW field of sRsrcType entry}
   spTBMask:            SignedByte;       {sRsrcType entry bit mask}
   spSlot:              SignedByte;       {slot number}
   spID:                SignedByte;       {sResource ID}
   spExtDev:            SignedByte;       {external device ID}
   spHwDev:             SignedByte;       {hardware device ID}
   spByteLanes:         SignedByte;       {valid byte lanes}
   spFlags:             SignedByte;       {flags used by Slot Manager}
   spKey:               SignedByte;       {reserved for Slot Manager}
END;
SpBlockPtr = ^SpBlock;

SInfoRecord =                            {slot information record}
PACKED RECORD
   siDirPtr:            Ptr;              {pointer to sResource directory}
   siInitStatusA:       Integer;          {initialization error}
   siInitStatusV:       Integer;          {status returned by vendor }
                                          { initialization routine}
   siState:             SignedByte;       {initialization state}
   siCPUByteLanes:      SignedByte;       {byte lanes used}
   siTopOfROM:          SignedByte;       {highest valid address in ROM}
   siStatusFlags:       SignedByte;       {status flags}
   siTOConstant:        Integer;          {timeout constant for bus error}
   siReserved:          PACKED ARRAY [0..1] OF SignedByte;  {reserved}
   siROMAddr:           Ptr;              {address of top of ROM}
   siSlot:              Char;             {slot number}
   siPadding:           PACKED ARRAY [0..2] OF SignedByte;  {reserved}
END;
SInfoRecPtr = ^SInfoRecord;

FHeaderRec =                             {format header record}
PACKED RECORD
   fhDirOffset:         LongInt;          {offset to sResource directory}
   fhLength:            LongInt;          {length in bytes of declaration ROM}
   fhCRC:               LongInt;          {cyclic redundancy check}
   fhROMRev:            SignedByte;       {declaration ROM revision}
   fhFormat:            SignedByte;       {declaration ROM format}
```

```
    fhTstPat:          LongInt;        {test pattern}
    fhReserved:        SignedByte;     {reserved; must be 0}
    fhByteLanes:       SignedByte;     {byte lanes used by declaration ROM}
END;
FHeaderRecPtr = ^FHeaderRec;


SPRAMRecord =                          {slot parameter RAM record}
PACKED RECORD
    boardID:           Integer;        {Apple-defined card ID}
    vendorUse1:        SignedByte;     {reserved for vendor use}
    vendorUse2:        SignedByte;     {reserved for vendor use}
    vendorUse3:        SignedByte;     {reserved for vendor use}
    vendorUse4:        SignedByte;     {reserved for vendor use}
    vendorUse5:        SignedByte;     {reserved for vendor use}
    vendorUse6:        SignedByte;     {reserved for vendor use}
END;
SPRAMRecPtr = ^SPRAMRecord;


SEBlock =                              {slot execution parameter block}
PACKED RECORD
    seSlot:            SignedByte;     {slot number}
    sesRsrcId:         SignedByte;     {sResource ID}
    seStatus:          Integer;        {status of sExecBlock code}
    seFlags:           SignedByte;     {flags}
    seFiller0:         SignedByte;     {filler for word alignment}
    seFiller1:         SignedByte;     {filler}
    seFiller2:         SignedByte;     {filler}
    seResult:          LongInt;        {result of SLoadDriver}
    seIOFileName:      LongInt;        {pointer to driver name}
    seDevice:          SignedByte;     {device to read from}
    sePartition:       SignedByte;     {partition}
    seOSType:          SignedByte;     {type of OS}
    seReserved:        SignedByte;     {reserved}
    seRefNum:          SignedByte;     {driver reference number}
    seNumDevices:      SignedByte;     {number of devices to load}
    seBootState:       SignedByte;     {state of StartBoot code}
END;
```

```
SlotIntQElement =                              {slot interrupt queue element}
RECORD
   sqLink:              Ptr;                   {pointer to next queue element}
   sqType:              Integer;              {queue type ID; must be sIQType}
   sqPrio:              Integer;              {priority value in low byte}
   sqAddr:              ProcPtr;              {interrupt handler}
   sqParm:              LongInt;              {optional A1 parameter}
END;
SQElemPtr = ^SlotIntQElement;
```

Slot Manager Routines

Determining the Version of the Slot Manager

```
FUNCTION SVersion              (spBlkPtr: SpBlockPtr): OSErr;
```

Finding sResources

```
FUNCTION SRsrcInfo             (spBlkPtr: SpBlockPtr): OSErr;
FUNCTION SGetSRsrc             (spBlkPtr: SpBlockPtr): OSErr;
FUNCTION SGetTypeSRsrc         (spBlkPtr: SpBlockPtr): OSErr;
FUNCTION SNextSRsrc            (spBlkPtr: SpBlockPtr): OSErr;
FUNCTION SNextTypeSRsrc        (spBlkPtr: SpBlockPtr): OSErr;
```

Getting Information From sResources

```
FUNCTION SReadDrvrName         (spBlkPtr: SpBlockPtr): OSErr;
FUNCTION SReadByte             (spBlkPtr: SpBlockPtr): OSErr;
FUNCTION SReadWord             (spBlkPtr: SpBlockPtr): OSErr;
FUNCTION SReadLong             (spBlkPtr: SpBlockPtr): OSErr;
FUNCTION SGetCString           (spBlkPtr: SpBlockPtr): OSErr;
FUNCTION SGetBlock             (spBlkPtr: SpBlockPtr): OSErr;
FUNCTION SFindStruct           (spBlkPtr: SpBlockPtr): OSErr;
FUNCTION SReadStruct           (spBlkPtr: SpBlockPtr): OSErr;
```

Enabling, Disabling, Deleting, and Restoring sResources

```
FUNCTION SetSRsrcState         (spBlkPtr: SpBlockPtr): OSErr;
FUNCTION SDeleteSRTRec         (spBlkPtr: SpBlockPtr): OSErr;
FUNCTION InsertSRTRec          (spBlkPtr: SpBlockPtr): OSErr;
FUNCTION SUpdateSRT            (spBlkPtr: SpBlockPtr): OSErr;
```

Loading Drivers and Executing Code From sResources

```
FUNCTION SGetDriver        (spBlkPtr: SpBlockPtr): OSErr;
FUNCTION SExec             (spBlkPtr: SpBlockPtr): OSErr;
```

Getting Information About Expansion Cards and Declaration ROMs

```
FUNCTION SReadInfo         (spBlkPtr: SpBlockPtr): OSErr;
FUNCTION SReadFHeader      (spBlkPtr: SpBlockPtr): OSErr;
FUNCTION SCkCardStat       (spBlkPtr: SpBlockPtr): OSErr;
FUNCTION SCardChanged      (spBlkPtr: SpBlockPtr): OSErr;
FUNCTION SFindDevBase      (spBlkPtr: SpBlockPtr): OSErr;
```

Accessing Expansion Card Parameter RAM

```
FUNCTION SReadPRAMRec      (spBlkPtr: SpBlockPtr): OSErr;
FUNCTION SPutPRAMRec       (spBlkPtr: SpBlockPtr): OSErr;
```

Managing the Slot Interrupt Queue

```
FUNCTION SIntInstall       (sIntQElemPtr: SQElemPtr;
                            theSlot: Integer) : OsErr;
FUNCTION SIntRemove        (sIntQElemPtr: SQElemPtr;
                            theSlot: Integer) : OsErr;
```

Low-Level Routines

```
FUNCTION InitSDeclMgr      (spBlkPtr: SpBlockPtr): OSErr;
FUNCTION SCalcSPointer     (spBlkPtr: SpBlockPtr): OSErr;
FUNCTION SCalcStep         (spBlkPtr: SpBlockPtr): OSErr;
FUNCTION SFindBigDevBase   (spBlkPtr: SpBlockPtr): OSErr;
FUNCTION SFindSInfoRecPtr  (spBlkPtr: SpBlockPtr): OSErr;
FUNCTION SFindSRsrcPtr     (spBlkPtr: SpBlockPtr): OSErr;
FUNCTION SGetSRsrcPtr      (spBlkPtr: SpBlockPtr): OSErr;
FUNCTION SInitPRAMRecs     (spBlkPtr: SpBlockPtr): OSErr;
FUNCTION SInitSRsrcTable   (spBlkPtr: SpBlockPtr): OSErr;
FUNCTION SOffsetData       (spBlkPtr: SpBlockPtr): OSErr;
FUNCTION SPrimaryInit      (spBlkPtr: SpBlockPtr): OSErr;
FUNCTION SPtrToSlot        (spBlkPtr: SpBlockPtr): OSErr;
FUNCTION SReadPBSize       (spBlkPtr: SpBlockPtr): OSErr;
FUNCTION SSearchSRT        (spBlkPtr: SpBlockPtr): OSErr;
```

C Summary

Constants

```
enum {
    /* StatusFlags field of sInfoArray */
    fCardIsChanged = 1,                /* card has changed */

    /* flags for SearchSRT */
    fCkForSame     = 0,                /* check for same sResource in table */
    fCkForNext     = 1,                /* check for next sResource in table */

    /* flag passed to card by SPrimaryInit during startup or restart */
    fWarmStart     = 2,                /* warm start if set; else cold start */

    /* constants for siState field of sInfoRecord */
    stateNil       = 0,                /* state */
    stateSDMInit   = 1,                /* slot declaration manager init */
    statePRAMInit  = 2,                /* sPRAM record init */
    statePInit     = 3,                /* primary init */
    stateSInit     = 4,                /* secondary init */

    /* bit flags for spParamData field of SpBlock */
    fall           = 0,                /* if set, search all sResources */
    foneslot       = 1,                /* if set, search in given slot only */
    fnext          = 2                 /* if set, search for next sResource */
};
```

Data Types

```
typedef struct SpBlock {           /* Slot Manager parameter block */
    long    spResult;              /* function result */
    Ptr     spsPointer;            /* structure pointer */
    long    spSize;                /* size of structure */
    long    spOffsetData;          /* offset or data */
    Ptr     spIOFileName;          /* reserved for Slot Manager */
    Ptr     spsExecPBlk;           /* pointer to SEBlock structure */
    long    spParamData;           /* flags */
    long    spMisc;                /* reserved for Slot Manager */
    long    spReserved;            /* reserved for Slot Manager */
    short   spIOReserved;          /* ioReserved field from SRT */
    short   spRefNum;              /* driver reference number */
```

```
    short      spCategory;              /* Category field of sRsrcType entry */
    short      spCType;                 /* cType field of sRsrcType entry */
    short      spDrvrSW;                /* DrSW field of sRsrcType entry */
    short      spDrvrHW;                /* DrHW field of sRsrcType entry */
    char       spTBMask;                /* sRsrcType entry bit mask */
    char       spSlot;                  /* slot number */
    char       spID;                    /* sResource ID */
    char       spExtDev;                /* external device ID */
    char       spHwDev;                 /* hardware device ID */
    char       spByteLanes;             /* valid byte lanes */
    char       spFlags;                 /* flags used by Slot Manager */
    char       spKey;                   /* reserved for Slot Manager */
} SpBlock;
typedef SpBlock *SpBlockPtr;

typedef struct SInfoRecord {           /* slot information record */
    Ptr        siDirPtr;                /* pointer to sResource directory */
    short      siInitStatusA;           /* initialization error */
    short      siInitStatusV;           /* status returned by vendor
                                           initialization routine */
    char       siState;                 /* initialization state */
    char       siCPUByteLanes;          /* byte lanes used */
    char       siTopOfROM;              /* highest valid address in ROM */
    char       siStatusFlags;           /* status flags */
    short      siTOConst;               /* timeout constant for bus error */
    char       siReserved[2];           /* reserved */
    Ptr        siROMAddr;               /* address of top of ROM */
    char       siSlot;                  /* slot number */
    char       siPadding[3];            /* reserved */
} SInfoRecord;
typedef SInfoRecord *SInfoRecPtr;

typedef struct FHeaderRec {            /* format header record */
    long       fhDirOffset;             /* offset to sResource directory */
    long       fhLength;                /* length in bytes of declaration ROM */
    long       fhCRC;                   /* cyclic redundancy check */
    char       fhROMRev;                /* declaration ROM revision */
    char       fhFormat;                /* declaration ROM format */
    long       fhTstPat;                /* test pattern */
    char       fhReserved;              /* reserved; must be 0 */
    char       fhByteLanes;             /* byte lanes used by declaration ROM */
} FHeaderRec;
typedef FHeaderRec *FHeaderRecPtr;
```

```
typedef struct SPRAMRecord {        /* slot parameter RAM record */
    short      boardID;             /* Apple-defined card ID */
    char       vendorUse1;          /* reserved for vendor use */
    char       vendorUse2;          /* reserved for vendor use */
    char       vendorUse3;          /* reserved for vendor use */
    char       vendorUse4;          /* reserved for vendor use */
    char       vendorUse5;          /* reserved for vendor use */
    char       vendorUse6;          /* reserved for vendor use */
} SPRAMRecord;
typedef SPRAMRecord *SPRAMRecPtr;

typedef struct SEBlock {            /* slot execution parameter block */
    unsigned char      seSlot;      /* slot number */
    unsigned char      sesRsrcId;   /* sResource ID */
    short              seStatus;    /* status of sExecBlock code */
    unsigned char      seFlags;     /* flags */
    unsigned char      seFiller0;   /* filler for word alignment */
    unsigned char      seFiller1;   /* filler */
    unsigned char      seFiller2;   /* filler */
    long               seResult;    /* result of SLoadDriver */
    long               seIOFileName; /* pointer to driver name */
    unsigned char      seDevice     /* device to read from */
    unsigned char      sePartition; /* partition */
    unsigned char      seOSType;    /* type of OS */
    unsigned char      seReserved;  /* reserved */
    unsigned char      seRefNum;    /* driver reference number */
    unsigned char      seNumDevices; /* number of devices to load */
    unsigned char      seBootState; /* state of StartBoot code */
} SEBlock;

typedef struct SlotIntQElement {    /* slot interrupt queue element */
    Ptr       sqLink;               /* pointer to next queue element */
    short     sqType;               /* queue type ID; must be sIQType */
    short     sqPrio;               /* priority value in low byte */
    ProcPtr   sqAddr;               /* interrupt handler */
    long      sqParm;               /* optional A1 parameter */
} SlotIntQElement;
typedef SlotIntQElement *SQElemPtr;
```

Slot Manager Functions

Determining the Version of the Slot Manager

```
pascal OSErr SVersion          (SpBlockPtr spBlkPtr);
```

Finding sResources

```
pascal OSErr SRsrcInfo        (SpBlockPtr spBlkPtr);
pascal OSErr SGetSRsrc        (SpBlockPtr spBlkPtr);
pascal OSErr SGetTypeSRsrc    (SpBlockPtr spBlkPtr);
pascal OSErr SNextSRsrc       (SpBlockPtr spBlkPtr);
pascal OSErr SNextTypeSRsrc   (SpBlockPtr spBlkPtr);
```

Getting Information From sResources

```
pascal OSErr SReadDrvrName    (SpBlockPtr spBlkPtr);
pascal OSErr SReadByte        (SpBlockPtr spBlkPtr);
pascal OSErr SReadWord        (SpBlockPtr spBlkPtr);
pascal OSErr SReadLong        (SpBlockPtr spBlkPtr);
pascal OSErr SGetCString      (SpBlockPtr spBlkPtr);
pascal OSErr SGetBlock        (SpBlockPtr spBlkPtr);
pascal OSErr SFindStruct      (SpBlockPtr spBlkPtr);
pascal OSErr SReadStruct      (SpBlockPtr spBlkPtr);
```

Enabling, Disabling, Deleting, and Restoring sResources

```
pascal OSErr SetSRsrcState    (SpBlockPtr spBlkPtr);
pascal OSErr SDeleteSRTRec    (SpBlockPtr spBlkPtr);
pascal OSErr InsertSRTRec     (SpBlockPtr spBlkPtr);
pascal OSErr SUpdateSRT       (SpBlockPtr spBlkPtr);
```

Loading Drivers and Executing Code From sResources

```
pascal OSErr SGetDriver       (SpBlockPtr spBlkPtr);
pascal OSErr SExec            (SpBlockPtr spBlkPtr);
```

Getting Information About Expansion Cards and Declaration ROMs

```
pascal OSErr SReadInfo        (SpBlockPtr spBlkPtr);
pascal OSErr SReadFHeader     (SpBlockPtr spBlkPtr);
pascal OSErr SCkCardStat      (SpBlockPtr spBlkPtr);
pascal OSErr SCardChanged     (SpBlockPtr spBlkPtr);
pascal OSErr SFindDevBase     (SpBlockPtr spBlkPtr);
```

Accessing Expansion Card Parameter RAM

```
pascal OSErr SReadPRAMRec     (SpBlockPtr spBlkPtr);
pascal OSErr SPutPRAMRec      (SpBlockPtr spBlkPtr);
```

Managing the Slot Interrupt Queue

```
pascal OSErr SIntInstall      (SQElemPtr sIntQElemPtr, short theSlot);
pascal OSErr SIntRemove       (SQElemPtr sIntQElemPtr, short theSlot);
```

Low-Level Functions

```
pascal OSErr InitSDeclMgr     (SpBlockPtr spBlkPtr);
pascal OSErr SCalcSPointer    (SpBlockPtr spBlkPtr);
pascal OSErr SCalcStep        (SpBlockPtr spBlkPtr);
pascal OSErr SFindBigDevBase  (SpBlockPtr spBlkPtr);
pascal OSErr SFindSInfoRecPtr (SpBlockPtr spBlkPtr);
pascal OSErr SFindSRsrcPtr    (SpBlockPtr spBlkPtr);
pascal OSErr SGetSRsrcPtr     (SpBlockPtr spBlkPtr);
pascal OSErr SInitPRAMRecs    (SpBlockPtr spBlkPtr);
pascal OSErr SInitSRsrcTable  (SpBlockPtr spBlkPtr);
pascal OSErr SOffsetData      (SpBlockPtr spBlkPtr);
pascal OSErr SPrimaryInit     (SpBlockPtr spBlkPtr);
pascal OSErr SPtrToSlot       (SpBlockPtr spBlkPtr);
pascal OSErr SReadPBSize      (SpBlockPtr spBlkPtr);
pascal OSErr SSearchSRT       (SpBlockPtr spBlkPtr);
```

Assembly-Language Summary

Data Structures

Slot Manager Parameter Block

0	spResult	long	function result
4	spsPointer	long	structure pointer
8	spSize	long	size of structure
12	SpOffsetData	long	offset or data
16	spIOFileName	long	reserved for Slot Manager
20	spsExecPBlk	long	pointer to SEBlock data structure
24	spParamData	long	flags
28	spMisc	long	reserved for Slot Manager
32	spReserved	long	reserved for Slot Manager
36	spIOReserved	word	ioReserved field from SRT
38	spRefNum	word	driver reference number
40	spCategory	word	Category field of sRsrcType entry
42	spCType	word	cType field of sRsrcType entry
44	spDrvrSW	word	DrSW field of sRsrcType entry
46	spDrvrHW	word	DrHW field of sRsrcType entry
48	spTBMask	byte	sRsrcType entry bit mask
49	spSlot	byte	slot number
50	spID	byte	sResource ID
51	spExtDev	byte	external device ID
52	spHwDev	byte	hardware device ID
53	spByteLanes	byte	valid byte lanes
54	spFlags	byte	flags used by Slot Manager
55	spKey	byte	reserved for Slot Manager

Slot Information Record

0	siDirPtr	long	pointer to sResource directory
4	siInitStatusA	word	initialization error
6	siInitStatusV	word	status returned by vendor initialization routine
8	siState	byte	initialization state
9	siCPUByteLanes	byte	byte lanes used
10	siTopOfROM	byte	highest valid address in ROM
11	siStatusFlags	byte	status flags
12	siTOConst	word	timeout constant for bus error
14	siReserved	word	reserved
16	siROMAddr	long	address of top of ROM
20	siSlot	byte	slot number
21	siPadding	3 bytes	reserved

Format Header Record

0	fhDirOffset	long	offset to sResource directory
4	fhLength	long	length in bytes of declaration ROM
8	fhCRC	long	cyclic redundancy check
12	fhROMRev	byte	declaration ROM revision
13	fhFormat	byte	declaration ROM format
14	fhTstPat	long	test pattern
18	fhReserved	byte	reserved; must be 0
19	fhByteLanes	byte	byte lanes used by declaration ROM

Slot Parameter RAM Record

0	boardID	word	Apple-defined card ID
2	vendorUse1	byte	reserved for vendor use
3	vendorUse2	byte	reserved for vendor use
4	vendorUse3	byte	reserved for vendor use
5	vendorUse4	byte	reserved for vendor use
6	vendorUse5	byte	reserved for vendor use
7	vendorUse6	byte	reserved for vendor use

Slot Execution Parameter Block

0	seSlot	byte	slot number
1	sesRsrcId	byte	sResource ID
2	seStatus	word	status of sExecBlock code
4	seFlags	byte	flags
5	seFiller0	byte	filler for word alignment
6	seFiller1	byte	filler
7	seFiller2	byte	filler
8	seResult	long	result of SLoadDriver
12	seIOFileName	long	pointer to driver name
16	seDevice	byte	device to read from
17	sePartition	byte	partition
18	seOSType	byte	type of operating system
19	seReserved	byte	reserved
20	seRefNum	byte	driver reference number
21	seNumDevices	byte	number of devices to load
22	seBootState	byte	state of StartBoot code

Slot Interrupt Queue Element

0	sqLink	long	pointer to next queue element
4	sqType	word	queue type ID; must be sIQType
6	sqPrio	word	priority value in low byte
8	sqAddr	long	pointer to interrupt handler
12	sqParm	long	optional A1 parameter

Trap Macros

Trap Macros Requiring Routine Selectors

`_SlotManager`

Selector	Routine
$0000	SReadByte
$0001	SReadWord
$0002	SReadLong
$0003	SGetCString
$0005	SGetBlock
$0006	SFindStruct
$0007	SReadStruct
$0008	SVersion
$0009	SetSRsrcState
$000A	InsertSRTRec
$000B	SGetSRsrc
$000C	SGetTypeSRsrc
$0010	SReadInfo
$0011	SReadPRAMRec
$0012	SPutPRAMRec
$0013	SReadFHeader
$0014	SNextSRsrc
$0015	SNextTypeSRsrc
$0016	SRsrcInfo
$0018	SCkCardStat
$0019	SReadDrvrName
$001B	SFindDevBase
$001C	SFindBigDevBase
$001D	SGetSRsrcPtr
$0020	InitSDeclMgr
$0021	SPrimaryInit
$0022	SCardChanged
$0023	SExec
$0024	SOffsetData
$0025	SInitPRAMRecs
$0026	SReadPBSize
$0028	SCalcStep

Selector	Routine
$0029	SInitSRsrcTable
$002A	SSearchSRT
$002B	SUpdateSRT
$002C	SCalcSPointer
$002D	SGetDriver
$002E	SPtrToSlot
$002F	SFindSInfoRecPtr
$0030	SFindSRsrcPtr
$0031	SDeleteSRTRec

Result Codes

noErr	0	No error
memFullErr	−108	Not enough room in heap
smEmptySlot	−300	No card in this slot
smCRCFail	−301	CRC check failed
smFormatErr	−302	The format of the declaration ROM is wrong
smUnExBusErr	−308	A bus error occurred
smBLFieldBad	−309	A valid fhByteLanes field was not found
smDisposePErr	−312	An error occurred during execution of DisposePtr
smNoBoardsRsrc	−313	There is no board sResource
smNoBoardId	−315	There is no board ID
smInitStatVErr	−316	The InitStatusV field was negative after PrimaryInit
smBadRefId	−330	Reference ID was not found in the given list
smBadsList	−331	The IDs are not in ascending order
smReservedErr	−332	A reserved field was not zero
smCodeRevErr	−333	The revision of the code to be executed by sExec was wrong
smCPUErr	−334	The CPU field of the code to be executed by sExec was wrong
smsPointerNil	−335	The spsPointer value is NIL: no list is specified
smNilsBlockErr	−336	The physical block size of an sBlock was zero
smSlotOOBErr	−337	The given slot was out of bounds or does not exist
smSelOOBErr	−338	Selector out of bounds or function not implemented
smCkStatusErr	−341	Status of slot is bad
smGetDrvrNamErr	−342	An error occurred during execution of _sGetDrvrName
smNoMoresRsrcs	−344	Requested sResource not found
smBadsPtrErr	−346	Bad spsPointer value
smByteLanesErr	−347	Bad spByteLanes value
smRecNotFnd	−351	Record not found in the slot resource table

CHAPTER 3

✦

SCSI Manager

Contents

This chapter describes the original Macintosh SCSI Manager. The **SCSI Manager** is the part of the Macintosh Operating System that controls the transfer of data between a Macintosh computer and peripheral devices connected through the Small Computer System Interface (SCSI).

In 1993, Apple Computer introduced SCSI Manager 4.3, an enhanced version of the SCSI Manager that provides new features as well as compatibility with the original version. SCSI Manager 4.3 is described in the chapter "SCSI Manager 4.3" in this book.

SCSI Manager 4.3 Note
Throughout this chapter, notes like this one are used to point out areas where SCSI Manager 4.3 differs from the original SCSI Manager. ◆

You should read this chapter if you are writing a SCSI device driver or other program that needs to be compatible with the original SCSI Manager. To make best use of this chapter, you should understand the Device Manager and how device drivers are implemented in Macintosh computers. You should also be familiar with the SCSI-1 specification established by the American National Standards Institute (ANSI). The SCSI-1 specification appears in ANSI document X3.131-1986, entitled *Small Computer System Interface*. Unless otherwise noted, all mentions of a SCSI specification in this chapter refer to the SCSI-1 specification.

If you are designing a SCSI peripheral device for Macintosh computers, you should read *Designing Cards and Drivers for the Macintosh Family*, third edition, and *Guide to the Macintosh Family Hardware*, second edition.

This chapter provides a brief introduction to SCSI concepts and then explains

- how the SCSI standard is implemented on Macintosh computers

- how data is structured on SCSI disk drives and other block devices

- how you can use SCSI Manager routines and data structures to transfer data to and from SCSI peripheral devices

Introduction to SCSI Concepts

The **Small Computer System Interface (SCSI)** is a computer industry standard for connecting computers to peripheral devices such as hard disk drives, CD-ROM drives, printers, scanners, magnetic tape drives, and any other device that needs to transfer large amounts of data quickly.

The SCSI standard specifies the hardware and software interface at a level that minimizes dependencies on any specific hardware implementation. The specification allows a wide variety of peripheral devices to be connected to many types of computers.

A **SCSI bus** is a bus that conforms to the physical and electrical specifications of the SCSI standard. A **SCSI device** refers to any unit connected to the SCSI bus, either a peripheral device or a computer. Each SCSI device on the bus is assigned a **SCSI ID**, which is an integer value from 0 to 7 that uniquely identifies the device during SCSI transactions.

The Macintosh computer is always assigned the SCSI ID value of 7, and its internal hard disk drive is normally assigned the SCSI ID value of 0. In general, only one Macintosh computer can be connected to a SCSI bus at a given time, and most Macintosh models support only a single SCSI bus.

SCSI Manager 4.3 Note

Under the original SCSI Manager, the dual SCSI buses in high-performance computers such as the Macintosh Quadra 950 are treated as though they were a single physical bus. SCSI Manager 4.3 supports multiple SCSI buses and treats each bus separately. ◆

When two SCSI devices communicate, one device acts as the **initiator** and the other as the **target**. The initiator begins a transaction by selecting a target device. The target responds to the selection and requests a command. The initiator then sends a SCSI command, and the target carries out the action. After acknowledging the command, the target controls the remainder of the transaction. The role of initiator and target is fixed for each device, and does not usually change. Under the original SCSI Manager, the Macintosh computer always acts as initiator, and peripheral devices are always targets.

SCSI Manager 4.3 Note

SCSI Manager 4.3 allows multiple initiators, meaning that intelligent peripheral devices can initiate SCSI transactions without involving the computer. ◆

SCSI transactions involve interaction between bus signals, bus phases, SCSI commands, and SCSI messages. Although the SCSI Manager masks much of the underlying complexity of SCSI transactions, an understanding of these elements and how they interact will help you understand the role of the SCSI Manager.

The following sections briefly summarize the elements of a SCSI transaction.

SCSI Bus Signals

The SCSI specification defines 50 bus signals, half of which are tied to ground. Table 3-1 describes the 18 SCSI bus signals that are relevant to understanding SCSI transactions. Nine of these signals are used to initiate and control transactions, and nine are used for data transfer (8 data bits plus a parity bit).

Table 3-1   SCSI bus signals

Signal	Name	Description
/BSY	Busy	Indicates that the bus is in use.
/SEL	Select	The initiator uses this signal to select a target.
/C/D	Control/Data	The target uses this signal to indicate whether the information being transferred is control information (signal asserted) or data (signal negated).
/I/O	Input/Output	The target uses this signal to specify the direction of the data movement with respect to the initiator. When the signal is asserted, data flows to the initiator; when negated, data flows to the target.
/MSG	Message	This signal is used by the target during the message phase.
/REQ	Request	The target uses this signal to start a request/ acknowledge handshake.
/ACK	Acknowledge	This signal is used by the initiator to end a request/ acknowledge handshake.
/ATN	Attention	The initiator uses this signal to inform the target that the initiator has a message ready. The target retrieves the message, at its convenience, by transitioning to a message-out bus phase
/RST	Reset	This signal is used to clear all devices and operations from the bus, and force the bus into the bus free phase. The Macintosh computer asserts this signal at startup. SCSI peripheral devices should never assert this signal.
/DB0–/DB7, /DBP	Data	Eight data signals, numbered 0 to 7, and the parity signal. Macintosh computers generate proper SCSI parity, but the original SCSI Manager does not detect parity errors in SCSI transactions.

SCSI Bus Phases

A SCSI bus phase is an interval in time during which, by convention, certain control signals are allowed or expected, and others are not. The SCSI bus can never be in more than one phase at any given time.

For each of the bus phases, there is a set of allowable phases that can follow. For example, the bus free phase can only be followed by the arbitration phase, or by another bus free phase. A data phase can be followed by a command, status, message, or bus free phase.

Control signals direct the transition from one phase to another. For example, the reset signal invokes the bus free phase, while the attention signal invokes the message phase.

The SCSI standard specifies eight distinct phases for the SCSI bus:

- **Bus free**. This phase means that no SCSI devices are using the bus, and that the bus is available for another SCSI operation.

- **Arbitration**. This phase is preceded by the bus free phase and permits a SCSI device to gain control of the SCSI bus. During this phase, all devices wishing to use the bus assert the /BSY signal and put their SCSI ID onto the bus (using the data signals). The device with highest SCSI ID wins the arbitration.

- **Selection**. This phase follows the arbitration phase. The device that won arbitration uses this phase to select another device to communicate with.

- **Reselection**. This optional phase is used by systems that allow peripheral devices to disconnect and reconnect from the bus during lengthy operations. This phase is not supported by the original Macintosh SCSI Manager, but is by SCSI Manager 4.3.

- **Command**. During this phase, the target requests a command from the initiator.

- **Data**. The data phase occurs when the target requests a transfer of data to or from the initiator.

- **Status**. This phase occurs when the target requests that status information be sent to the initiator.

- **Message**. The message phase occurs when the target requests the transfer of a message. Messages are small blocks of data that carry information or requests between the initiator and a target. Multiple messages can be sent during this phase.

Together, the last four phases (command, data, status, and message) are known as the information transfer phases. Figure 3-1 shows the relationship of the SCSI bus phases.

Figure 3-1   SCSI bus phases and allowable transitions

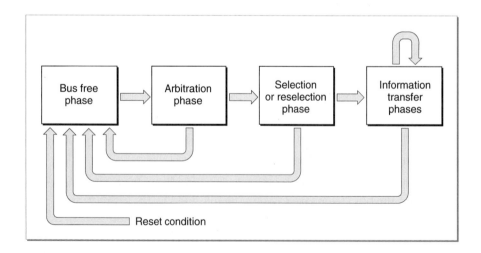

SCSI Commands

A **SCSI command** is an instruction from an initiator to a target to conduct an operation, such as reading or writing a block of data. Commands are read by the target when it is ready to do so, as opposed to being sent unrequested by the initiator.

SCSI commands are contained in a data structure called a **command descriptor block (CDB)**, which can be 6, 10, or 12 bytes in size. The first byte specifies the operation requested, and the remaining bytes are parameters used by that operation.

A single SCSI command may cause a peripheral device to undertake a relatively large amount of work, compared with other device interfaces. For example, the read command can specify multiple blocks of data rather than just one. The primary difference between the SCSI protocol and other interfaces typically used for storage devices is that SCSI commands address a device as a series of logical blocks rather than in terms of heads, tracks, and sectors. It is this abstraction from the physical characteristics of the device that allows the SCSI protocol to be used with a wide variety of devices.

SCSI Messages

The SCSI standard specifies a number of possible messages between initiator and target. **SCSI messages** are small blocks of data, often just one byte in size, that indicate the successful completion of an operation (the command complete message), or a variety of other events, requests, and status information. All messages are sent during the message phase.

The command complete message is required in all SCSI implementations. This message is sent from the target to the initiator and indicates that a command (or series of linked commands) has been completed, either successfully or unsuccessfully. Success or failure of the command is indicated by status information sent earlier during the status phase. The importance of the command complete message is more fully discussed in "Using the SCSIComplete Function," beginning on page 3-21.

Other SCSI messages are optional. During the selection phase, the initiator and target each specify their ability to handle messages other than the command complete message.

SCSI Handshaking

The SCSI standard defines the required sequence of transitions of the control and data signals to ensure reliable communication between SCSI devices. Because the request signal (/REQ) and the acknowledge signal (/ACK) both play a major role, this part of the SCSI protocol is often referred to as request/acknowledge handshaking (usually abbreviated as REQ/ACK handshaking).

The SCSI information transfer phases use REQ/ACK handshaking to transfer data or control information between the initiator and target, in either direction. The direction of the transfer depends on the particular bus phase. The handshaking occurs on every byte transferred, and constitutes the lowest level of the SCSI protocol.

For example, during the data phase, when a target sends data to the initiator, the target places the data on the SCSI bus data lines and then asserts the /REQ signal. The initiator senses the /REQ signal, reads the data lines, then asserts the /ACK signal. When the target senses the /ACK signal, it releases the data lines and negates the /REQ signal. The initiator then senses that the /REQ signal has been negated, and negates the /ACK signal. After the target senses that the /ACK signal has been negated, it can repeat the whole process again, to transfer another byte of data.

Unless you are designing a SCSI device, you do not need any special knowledge of SCSI handshaking to write software that uses the SCSI Manager. However, a general understanding of SCSI handshaking can be helpful when debugging. Refer to the SCSI specification for complete information about SCSI handshaking, bus phases, commands, and messages.

About the SCSI Manager

The SCSI Manager provides routines that allow Macintosh device drivers and other programs to communicate with SCSI peripheral devices using the SCSI protocol.

The SCSI Manager is a software layer that mediates between device drivers or applications and the SCSI controller hardware in the Macintosh computer. In some cases, the amount of mediation is small. For example, the SCSI Manager SCSIReset function does little except assert the reset signal on the SCSI bus. In other cases, a single SCSI Manager function may initiate a relatively complex series of actions.

Figure 3-2 shows the relationship of the SCSI Manager to the Macintosh system architecture. The architecture consists of multiple layers: the application layer, the system software layer (which is composed of several subordinate layers), and the hardware layer.

Figure 3-2   The role of the SCSI Manager

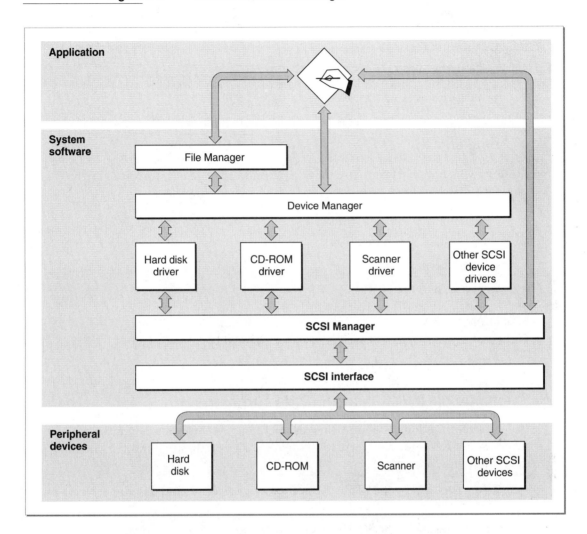

Application programs usually rely on high-level services such as those provided by the File Manager, but may also call low-level services directly. The File Manager calls the Device Manager, which calls the appropriate device driver. SCSI device drivers do not control SCSI hardware directly; they use the SCSI Manager to communicate with SCSI devices.

Conformance With the SCSI Specification

The SCSI specification has been revised considerably since the first Macintosh SCSI implementation. For information about the SCSI standard as originally defined, see ANSI document X3.131-1986, *Small Computer System Interface*. Many of the features described in the newer SCSI-2 specification are supported by SCSI Manager 4.3. However, the original SCSI Manager predates these extensions.

Due to hardware variations among Macintosh models, there are minor differences in the behavior of some SCSI Manager routines. These differences lie mostly outside the scope of the SCSI protocol. For information about these differences, see the description of the SCSIGet function on page 3-32.

All Macintosh computers support these aspects of the SCSI specification:

■ multiple targets

■ as many as eight devices on the bus (the computer and up to seven peripherals)

■ parity generation

The following optional features of the SCSI specification are not supported by the original SCSI Manager:

■ multiple SCSI buses

■ multiple initiators on a single bus

■ disconnect/reconnect

■ parity error detection

SCSI Manager 4.3 Note

These features and other enhancements are supported by SCSI Manager 4.3. ◆

Overview of SCSI Manager Data Structures

The SCSI specification and the Macintosh Operating System define a number of data structures for communicating with SCSI devices. These data structures fall into three categories:

■ structures defined by the SCSI specification, such as command descriptor blocks and SCSI messages

■ structures specific to the SCSI Manager, such as transfer instruction blocks and the 16-bit status word returned by the SCSIStat function

■ structures required for the proper operation of SCSI disk drives with the Start Manager and the File Manager; for example, the driver descriptor map and the partition map

The command descriptor block and other data structures defined by the SCSI specification are not discussed in detail in this chapter. Refer to the SCSI specification for complete information about these structures. See "Using CDB and TIB Structures," beginning on page 3-17, for an example of how to send a CDB to a SCSI device.

Although the driver descriptor map and the partition map are not used by the SCSI Manager, they must be present on all block devices compatible with the Macintosh Operating System. These structures are discussed in the following section.

A **transfer instruction block (TIB)** is a Macintosh-specific data structure that your program uses to pass instructions to the SCSI Manager. TIB structures are used to control data transfers, and for other purposes such as comparing data on a peripheral device with data in memory. TIB structures are passed as parameters to the SCSI Manager SCSIRead, SCSIRBlind, SCSIWrite, and SCSIWBlind functions. For read operations, the TIB specifies a memory location where the data should be stored. For write operations, the TIB specifies the location of the data to be written.

Although a transfer instruction block is data, not machine-executable code, it is analogous to code in that the data is interpreted and executed by the SCSI Manager in a manner similar to executing a program. The SCSIInstr data type defines a transfer instruction block.

```
TYPE SCSIInstr =              {transfer instruction block}
RECORD
    scOpcode:    Integer;     {operation code}
    scParam1:    LongInt;     {first parameter}
    scParam2:    LongInt;     {second parameter}
END;
```

The first field of the transfer instruction block contains a transfer operation code. This code is not a command in the SCSI protocol, but rather an instruction to the SCSI Manager that directs the transfer of data across the SCSI bus after a SCSI command has been sent. The instruction set consists of eight operation codes that allow you to transfer data, increment a counter, and form iterative loops. See "SCSI Manager TIB Instructions," beginning on page 3-27, for details of the TIB instruction set.

A sequence of TIB instructions is also known as a **TIB pseudoprogram**. Here is an example of a TIB pseudoprogram:

```
scInc    $67B50    512
scLoop   -10       6
scStop
```

This sample pseudoprogram consists of three TIB instructions that transfer six 512-byte blocks of data to or from address $67B50 (depending on whether these instructions are passed to a SCSIRead or a SCSIWrite function).

The first TIB instruction transfers a 512-byte block of data from a starting address and then increments that address by the amount of data transferred. The second TIB instruction branches back to the first (by branching back 10 bytes, which is the size of a TIB instruction), and forms a loop that is executed six times (as specified by the second parameter). The third and final TIB instruction terminates the execution sequence and returns to the calling routine.

See "Using CDB and TIB Structures," beginning on page 3-17, for an example of how to use TIB instructions.

The Structure of Block Devices

This section describes the low-level organization of data on random-access storage devices such as SCSI hard disk drives. Although this information is presented in the context of the SCSI Manager, it applies to any type of block device that can be used by the Macintosh Operating System, regardless of the hardware interface.

There are a number of ways to address data on block-structured storage devices such as disk drives. At the lowest level, a disk drive addresses a block by its cylinder, head, and sector number. The SCSI specification, however, conceals this level of detail. Instead, each block on a SCSI disk is assigned a number, beginning with 0 and extending to the last block on the disk. The SCSI specification describes these addresses as "logical" block numbers, but the SCSI Manager calls them physical block numbers because they correspond to a fixed location on the disk.

At an even higher level of abstraction, a device driver can define the mapping of physical addresses on a device to the logical addresses of a file system. This allows file systems to be independent of the characteristics of a particular device.

In the terminology of the SCSI Manager, a **physical block** refers to a specific, fixed location defined by the manufacturer of a SCSI device. A **logical block** refers to an abstract location defined by software. A **partition** is a series of contiguous logical blocks that have been allocated to a particular operating system, file system, or device driver. A disk can be divided into any number of partitions. Locations within these partitions are specified using logical block numbers, which are integer values ranging from 0 to the number of blocks in the partition.

The low-level organization of block devices is defined by two data structures: the driver descriptor record and the partition map. These structures are introduced in the following sections. See "Data Structures," beginning on page 3-23, for a complete description of the fields within these structures.

The Driver Descriptor Record

The driver descriptor record is a data structure that identifies the device drivers installed on a disk. To support multiple operating systems or other features, a disk can have more than one device driver installed, each in its own partition. The Start Manager reads the driver descriptor record during system startup and uses the information to locate and load the appropriate device driver.

The driver descriptor record is always located at physical block 0, the first block on the disk. The driver descriptor record is defined by the `Block0` data type.

```
TYPE Block0 =
PACKED RECORD
    sbSig:          Integer;      {device signature}
    sbBlkSize:      Integer;      {block size of the device}
    sbBlkCount:     LongInt;      {number of blocks on the device}
    sbDevType:      Integer;      {reserved}
    sbDevId:        Integer;      {reserved}
```

```
sbData:          LongInt;     {reserved}
sbDrvrCount:     Integer;     {number of driver descriptor entries}
ddBlock:         LongInt;     {first driver's starting block}
ddSize:          Integer;     {size of the driver, in 512-byte blocks}
ddType:          Integer;     {operating system type (MacOS = 1)}
ddPad:           ARRAY [0..242] OF Integer; {additional drivers, if any}
END;
```

The driver descriptor record consists of seven fixed fields, followed by a variable amount of driver-specific information. The first field in the driver descriptor record is a signature, which must be set to the value of the sbSIGWord constant to indicate that the record is valid (meaning that the disk has been formatted). The second field, sbBlkSize, specifies the size of the blocks on the device, in bytes. The sbBlkCount field specifies the total number of blocks on the device. The next three fields are reserved. The sbDrvrCount field specifies the number of drivers that are installed on the disk. The drivers can be located anywhere on the device and can be as large as necessary.

The ddBlock, ddSize, and ddType fields contain information about the first device driver on the disk. Information about any additional drivers is stored in the ddPad field, as an array of consecutive ddBlock, ddSize, and ddType fields.

To select a particular device driver for loading at system startup, you use the Start Manager SetOSDefault function and specify a value corresponding to the ddType field in the driver descriptor record.

The Partition Map

The partition map is a data structure that describes the partitions present on a block device. The Macintosh Operating System and all other operating systems from Apple use the same partitioning method. This allows a single device to support multiple operating systems.

The partition map always begins at physical block 1, the second block on the disk. With the exception of the driver descriptor record in block 0, every block on a disk must belong to a partition.

Each partition on a disk is described by an entry in the partition map. The partition map is itself a partition, and contains an entry describing itself. The partition map entry for the partition map is not necessarily the first entry in the map. Partition map entries can be in any order, and need not correspond to the physical organization of partitions on the disk.

The number of entries in the partition map is not restricted. However, because the partition map must begin at block 1 and must be contiguous, it cannot easily be expanded once other partitions are created. One way around this limitation is to create a large number of empty partition map entries when the disk is initialized.

To locate a partition, the Start Manager examines the pmMapBlkCnt field of the first partition map entry. This field contains the size of the partition map, in blocks. Then, using the block size value from the sbBlkSize field of the driver descriptor record, the

Start Manager reads each block in the partition map, looking for a valid signature in the pmSIG field of each partition map entry record.

The partition map entry record is defined by the Partition data type.

```
TYPE Partition =
RECORD
    pmSig:          Integer;        {partition signature}
    pmSigPad:       Integer;        {reserved}
    pmMapBlkCnt:    LongInt;        {number of blocks in partition map}
    pmPyPartStart:  LongInt;        {first physical block of partition}
    pmPartBlkCnt:   LongInt;        {number of blocks in partition}
    pmPartName:     PACKED ARRAY [0..31] OF Char; {partition name}
    pmParType:      PACKED ARRAY [0..31] OF Char; {partition type}
    pmLgDataStart:  LongInt;        {first logical block of data area}
    pmDataCnt:      LongInt;        {number of blocks in data area}
    pmPartStatus:   LongInt;        {partition status information}
    pmLgBootStart:  LongInt;        {first logical block of boot code}
    pmBootSize:     LongInt;        {size of boot code, in bytes}
    pmBootAddr:     LongInt;        {boot code load address}
    pmBootAddr2:    LongInt;        {reserved}
    pmBootEntry:    LongInt;        {boot code entry point}
    pmBootEntry2:   LongInt;        {reserved}
    pmBootCksum:    LongInt;        {boot code checksum}
    pmProcessor:    PACKED ARRAY [0..15] OF Char; {processor type}
    pmPad:          ARRAY [0..187] OF Integer;     {reserved}
END;
```

The first three fields in a partition map entry record are redundant, in that all entries in the partition map must contain the same values for these fields. The pmSig field contains the partition map signature, which is defined by the pMapSIG constant. The pmSigPad field is currently unused and must be set to 0. The pmMapBlkCnt field contains the size in blocks of the entire partition map. Because this value is duplicated in every entry, you can determine the size of the partition map from any entry in the map.

The remaining fields of the partition map entry record contain information about a particular disk partition. The pmPyPartStart field contains the physical block number of the first block of the partition. The pmPartBlkCnt field contains the number of blocks in the partition. The pmPartName field can contain an optional 32-character partition name. If this field contains a string beginning with Maci (for Macintosh), the Start Manager will perform checksum verification of the device driver's boot code. Otherwise, this field is ignored.

The pmParType field contains a string that identifies the partition type. Strings beginning with Apple_ are reserved for use by Apple Computer, Inc. The Start Manager uses this information to identify the type of device driver or file system in a partition.

A bootable system disk must contain both an `Apple_Driver` and an `Apple_HFS` partition. See page 3-26 for a list of the standard partition types defined by Apple.

For file systems that do not begin at logical block 0 of the partition, the `pmLgDataStart` field contains the logical block number of the first block of file system data. The `pmDataCnt` field specifies the size of the data area, in blocks. The `pmPartStatus` field is currently used only by the A/UX operating system.

For device driver partitions, the `pmLgBootStart` field specifies the logical block number of the first block containing boot code. The `pmBootSize` field contains the size in bytes of the boot code. The `pmBootAddr` field specifies the memory address where the boot code is to be loaded, while the `pmBootEntry` field specifies the address to which the Start Manager will transfer control after loading the boot code into memory. The `pmBootCksum` field holds the checksum of the boot code, which the Start Manager can compare against the calculated checksum after loading the code. The `pmProcessor` field is a string that identifies the type of processor that will execute the boot code.

For more information about the startup process and SCSI devices, see the chapter "Start Manager" in *Inside Macintosh: Operating System Utilities*.

Using the SCSI Manager

Your device driver or application can use the SCSI Manager routines to transfer data to and from SCSI peripheral devices. This section begins with a simple example that illustrates the basic steps necessary to read data from a SCSI device. Next, the details of using transfer instruction blocks and command descriptor blocks are presented, followed by a complete program that uses these concepts.

Reading Data From a SCSI Device

This section shows you how to use the SCSI Manager routines to read data from a SCSI peripheral device. Your application or device driver follows these steps for reading data from a SCSI device:

1. Create a command descriptor block (CDB) and a transfer instruction block (TIB).

2. Call the `SCSIGet` function to arbitrate for the SCSI bus.

3. Use the `SCSISelect` function to select the SCSI device to read from.

4. Use the `SCSICmd` function to send a command descriptor block (CDB) containing a SCSI read command to the device.

5. Call the `SCSIRead` function to transfer the data.

6. Call the `SCSIComplete` function to get the status and message bytes that mark the end of a transaction over the SCSI bus.

Listing 3-1 shows code illustrating these steps. The example is simplified, in that it excludes the details of setting up the CDB and TIB data structures prior to initiating the read operation. That information is presented in the next section.

Listing 3-1   Reading data from a SCSI device

```
FUNCTION MyReadSCSI : OSErr;
CONST
    kCompletionTimeout = 300;   {value passed to SCSIComplete }
                                { 300 ticks = 5 seconds}
VAR
    CDB:        PACKED ARRAY [0..5] OF Byte;     {command descriptor block}
    CDBLen:     Integer;                         {length of CDB}
    TIB:        PACKED ARRAY [0..1] OF SCSIInstr;{transfer instruction block}
    scsiID:     Integer;                         {SCSI ID of the target}
    compStat:   Integer;                         {status from SCSIComplete}
    compMsg:    Integer;                         {message from SCSIComplete}
    compErr:    OSErr;                           {result from SCSIComplete}
    myErr:      OSErr;                           {cumulative error result}
BEGIN
    {Note: This example assumes the CDB, CDBLen, TIB, and scsiID variables }
    { already contain appropriate values.}
    myErr := SCSIGet;                            {arbitrate for the bus}
    IF myErr = noErr THEN
    BEGIN
        myErr := SCSISelect(scsiID);             {select the target}
        IF myErr = noErr THEN
        BEGIN
            myErr := SCSICmd(@CDB, CDBLen);       {send read command}
            IF myErr = noErr THEN
                myErr := SCSIRead(@TIB);          {polled read}
            {complete the transaction and release the bus}
            compErr := SCSIComplete(compStat, compMsg, kCompletionTimeout);
            {return the most informative error result}
            IF myErr = noErr THEN                 {if no prior errors, then }
                myErr := compErr;                 { return SCSIComplete result}
        END;
    END;
    MyReadSCSI := myErr;                          {return result code}
END;
```

The `MyReadSCSI` function follows the steps presented earlier in this section, starting with calling the `SCSIGet` and `SCSISelect` functions to select the target device, sending a read command using the `SCSICmd` function, and reading the data with the `SCSIRead` function. Finally, the `SCSIComplete` function is called to obtain the status and message bytes from the device and restore the bus to the bus free phase.

The `MyReadSCSI` function assumes these variables have already been set up properly:

- a SCSI command descriptor block (the `CDB` variable)

- an integer specifying the length of the command descriptor block (the `CDBLen` variable)

- a transfer instruction block (the `TIB` variable)

- an integer specifying the SCSI ID of the target device (the `scsiID` variable)

Within its narrowed scope, the `MyReadSCSI` function is correct and complete. You can easily modify it to handle other operations, such as writing data, or conducting blind transfers.

The `MyReadSCSI` function shows one way of handling the error results returned by a series of SCSI Manager functions. The result codes returned by the SCSI Manager functions are put into the `myErr` local variable as each SCSI Manager function is called. Your code should likewise check the result codes and proceed only if there is no error. Calling the `SCSIComplete` function is the last step, and requires special handling. Your code should call the `SCSIComplete` function even if an earlier SCSI Manager routine has returned an error, because the `SCSIComplete` function takes whatever steps are necessary to restore the SCSI bus to the bus free phase. For more information, see "Using the SCSIComplete Function" on page 3-21.

Using CDB and TIB Structures

The command descriptor block (CDB) is a data structure defined by the SCSI specification for communicating commands to SCSI devices. The SCSI Manager does not interpret the commands in a CDB, it simply transfers them to the selected device.

You send a CDB to a SCSI device using the `SCSICmd` function. The size of the CDB structure can be 6, 10, or 12 bytes, depending on the number of parameters required by the command. The first byte specifies the command, and the remaining bytes contain parameters.

The SCSI specification includes a set of standard commands that all SCSI devices must implement, and a wide range of commands for specific device types. In addition, manufacturers can define proprietary command codes for their devices. You should refer to the manufacturer's documentation for information about the commands supported by a particular device.

You use the transfer instruction block (TIB) data structure to pass instructions to the SCSI Manager `SCSIRead`, `SCSIRBlind`, `SCSIWrite`, and `SCSIWBlind` functions. The TIB structure is defined by the `SCSIInstr` data type. The `scOpcode` field contains a transfer operation code, and the `scParam1` and `scParam2` fields contain parameters to the command. The instruction set consists of eight operation codes that allow you to transfer data, increment a counter, and form iterative loops. See "SCSI Manager TIB Instructions," beginning on page 3-27, for details of the TIB instruction set.

Listing 3-2 shows an example of how you can use CDB and TIB instructions to send a command and read information from a SCSI peripheral device. The `MySCSIInquiry` program uses the SCSI INQUIRY command to obtain a 256-byte record of information from a target device. This information includes the target's device type, vendor ID, product ID, revision data, and other vendor-specific information. The INQUIRY command is one of the standard commands that all SCSI devices must support.

Listing 3-2   Using TIB and CDB structures

```
PROGRAM MySCSIInquiry;
USES SCSI;

CONST
    kInquiryCmd = $12;           {SCSI command code for the INQUIRY command}
    kVendorIDSize = 8;           {size of the Vendor ID string}
    kProductIDSize = 16;         {size of the Product ID string}
    kRevisionSize = 4;           {size of the Revision string}
    kCompletionTimeout = 300;    {timeout value passed to SCSIComplete}
    kMySCSIID = 0;               {SCSI ID of the target device}

{This structure duplicates the format of the SCSI INQUIRY response record, }
{ as described in the SCSI-2 specification. The first 5 bytes are required }
{ for SCSI-1 devices. The first 36 bytes are required for SCSI-2 devices. }
{ The AdditionalLength field contains the length of the vendor-specific }
{ information, if any, beyond the 5 bytes required for all devices.}
TYPE MyInquiryRecord =
PACKED RECORD
    DeviceType:        Byte;     {SCSI device type code (disk, tape, etc.)}
    DeviceQualifier:   Byte;     {7-bit vendor-specific code}
    Version:           Byte;     {version of ANSI standard (SCSI-1 or SCSI-2)}
    ResponseFormat:    Byte;
    AdditionalLength:  Byte;     {length of vendor-specific information}
    VendorUse1:        Byte;
    Reserved1:         Integer;
    VendorID:          PACKED ARRAY [1..kVendorIDSize] OF Char;  {manufacturer}
    ProductID:         PACKED ARRAY [1..kProductIDSize] OF Char; {product code}
    Revision:          PACKED ARRAY [1..kRevisionSize] OF Char;  {firmware rev}
    VendorUse2:        PACKED ARRAY [1..20] OF Byte;
    Reserved2:         PACKED ARRAY [1..42] OF Byte;
    VendorUse3:        PACKED ARRAY [1..158] OF Byte;
END;                             {a total of 256 bytes of data may be returned}
```

```
VAR
   CDB:          PACKED ARRAY [0..5] OF Byte;       {command descriptor block}
   TIB:          PACKED ARRAY [0..1] OF SCSIInstr; {transfer instruction block}
   Response:     MyInquiryRecord; {holds target's response}
   compStat:     Integer;            {status information from SCSIComplete}
   compMsg:      Integer;            {message information from SCSIComplete}
   compErr:      OSErr;              {result from SCSIComplete}
   myErr:        OSErr;              {error result}
   i:            Integer;            {loop counter}
BEGIN
   {Set up the command buffer with the SCSI INQUIRY command.}
   CDB[0] := kInquiryCmd;       {SCSI command code for the INQUIRY command}
   CDB[1] := 0;                 {unused parameter}
   CDB[2] := 0;                 {unused parameter}
   CDB[3] := 0;                 {unused parameter}
   CDB[4] := 5;                 {maximum number of bytes target should return}
   CDB[5] := 0;                 {unused parameter}

   {Set up the two TIB structures; one to read, the other as terminator.}
   TIB[0].scOpcode := scNoInc;             {specify the scNoInc instruction}
   TIB[0].scParam1 := LongInt(@Response);  {pointer to buffer}
   TIB[0].scParam2 := 5;                   {number of bytes to move}
   TIB[1].scOpcode := scStop;              {specify the scStop instruction}
   TIB[1].scParam1 := LongInt(NIL);        {unused parameter}
   TIB[1].scParam2 := LongInt(NIL);        {unused parameter}

   WRITELN('SCSI inquiry example. Testing SCSI ID:', kMySCSIID);

   {Send the INQUIRY command twice. The first time to obtain the }
   { AdditionalLength value in the fifth byte of the INQUIRY response }
   { record and the second time to read that additional amount. Notice }
   { that SCSIComplete is always called if SCSISelect was successful.}
   FOR i := 1 to 2 DO
   BEGIN
      myErr := SCSIGet;                      {arbitrate for the bus}
      IF myErr = noErr THEN
         myErr := SCSISelect(kMySCSIID);   {select the target}
      IF myErr <> noErr THEN
      BEGIN
         WRITELN('Error result from SCSIGet or SCSISelect:', myErr);
         EXIT(MySCSIInquiry);
      END;
      myErr := SCSICmd(@CDB, 6);     {send INQUIRY command to the target}
```

```
    IF myErr = noErr THEN
    BEGIN
        myErr := SCSIRead(@TIB);    {read the INQUIRY response record}
        IF myErr = noErr THEN       {if there was no error, and }
            IF i = 1 THEN           { if this is the first time through }
            BEGIN                   { the loop, get the AdditionalLength}
                CDB[4] := CDB[4] + Response.AdditionalLength;
                TIB[0].scParam2 := TIB[0].scParam2 +
                                Response.AdditionalLength;
            END;
    END;

    {Call SCSIComplete to clean up. Results are ignored in this example.}
    compErr := SCSIComplete(compStat, compMsg, kCompletionTimeout);
    IF myErr <> noErr THEN
    BEGIN
        WRITELN('Error result from SCSICmd or SCSIRead:', myErr);
        EXIT(MySCSIInquiry);
    END;
END;   {FOR loop}

{Display the information.}
IF Response.AdditionalLength > 0 THEN
BEGIN
    WITH Response DO
    BEGIN
        WRITE('VendorID:');
        FOR i := 1 TO kVendorIDSize DO
            WRITE(VendorID[i]);
        WRITELN;
        WRITE('ProductID:');
        FOR i := 1 TO kProductIDSize DO
            WRITE(ProductID[i]);
        WRITELN;
        WRITE('Revision:');
        FOR i := 1 TO kRevisionSize DO
            WRITE(Revision[i]);
        WRITELN;
    END;
END;
END.
```

The `MySCSIInquiry` program first defines various constants, including the `kInquiryCmd` constant, which contains the operation code for the SCSI INQUIRY command. Next the `MyInquiryRecord` data type is declared, a 256-byte structure that holds the information returned by the target. The fields of this record are based on the SCSI-2 specification. The SCSI-1 specification requires that devices return at least the first 5 bytes of information (`DeviceType` through `AdditionalLength`), however, many SCSI-1 devices and all SCSI-2 devices return at least the first 36 bytes (`DeviceType` through `Revision`).

In the 6-byte CDB used by the SCSI INQUIRY command, the first byte contains the operation code and the fifth byte specifies the maximum number of bytes the target is allowed to send in response to the inquiry. Restricting the target's response to a specified number of bytes prevents it from overflowing the buffer the initiator has set aside to accept the data.

This program uses two transfer instruction blocks, both of which are relatively simple. The first TIB is an `scNoInc` instruction, whose parameters specify a data transfer into the `Response` record. The second TIB is an `scStop` instruction, which terminates the SCSI Manager processing that occurs inside the `SCSIRead` function.

The body of the `MySCSIInquiry` program consists of a loop that performs the arbitrate/select/command/transfer/complete sequence described in "Reading Data From a SCSI Device" on page 3-15. The loop executes this sequence of SCSI Manager functions twice. The first time sends the SCSI INQUIRY command to the target and requests only the standard 5 bytes of information supplied by all SCSI devices. The value of the fifth byte (returned in the `AdditionalLength` field of the `Response` record) indicates the amount of additional information the device is capable of returning. Before going through the loop a second time, both the CDB and the TIB are modified to reflect the additional size of the inquiry information.

The program checks for errors at each stage in the SCSI Manager calling sequence. If either the `SCSIGet` or `SCSISelect` function returns an error, the program exits. If the `SCSICmd` function returns an error, `SCSIRead` is not called. To complete the transaction and release the bus, the `SCSIComplete` function is always called if `SCSISelect` was successful.

Using the SCSIComplete Function

The `SCSIComplete` function completes a SCSI transaction and restores the bus to the bus free phase. You must call this function at the end of every transaction that proceeds past the selection phase, even if the transaction does not complete successfully.

The `SCSIComplete` function waits a specified number of ticks for the current transaction to complete, and then returns one byte of status information and one byte of message information from the target device. The function returns one of the following result codes:

- `noErr`. The `SCSIComplete` function was able to obtain both the status and message bytes successfully. This result code indicates that the information is valid.

- scComplPhaseErr. Upon entry, the SCSIComplete function detected that the target was ready to transfer information (that is, the /REQ signal was asserted) but the SCSI bus was not in the status phase. The SCSI Manager performed corrective action to bring the bus into the status phase. For example, accepting bytes from the target without passing them to your program ("bit-bucketing"), or sending an arbitrary number of bytes to the target. Once in status phase, the SCSIComplete function was able to transfer the status and message bytes successfully, and this information is valid.

- scPhaseErr. The SCSIComplete function could not force the SCSI bus into the status phase. The status and message bytes should be considered invalid. You may need to reset the bus to restore proper operation.

- scCommErr. This result code covers any other error conditions encountered by the SCSIComplete function, such as the timeout that occurs if the transaction does not complete within the specified number of ticks.

Choosing Polled or Blind Transfers

The SCSI Manager supports two data transfer methods: polled and blind. During a **polled transfer**, the SCSI Manager senses the state of the Macintosh SCSI controller hardware to determine when the controller is ready to transfer another byte. In a **blind transfer**, the SCSI Manager assumes that the SCSI controller (and the target device) can keep up with a specified transfer rate, and does not explicitly sense whether the hardware is ready.

Note

These transfer modes are specific to the Macintosh SCSI interface hardware implementation and are not part of the SCSI protocol. ◆

When the SCSI Manager retrieves data from the SCSI controller, it can explicitly verify that a byte was received by the controller and is ready for transfer. The SCSI Manager does this by polling a status register in the controller. Alternatively, the SCSI Manager can assume that a byte is available and can attempt to read it without checking first. As long as a SCSI device can supply data to the SCSI controller faster than the SCSI Manager can retrieve it, blind transfers work reliably. If the SCSI device cannot keep up, timeout errors and other problems can occur.

For example, in the Macintosh Plus (the first model to include a SCSI interface), if the SCSI Manager reads a byte from the SCSI controller chip before the chip receives a byte from the target, the read operation completes but the data is invalid. The SCSIComplete function does not always return an error result in this case.

Newer Macintosh models include hardware support for handshaking, allowing blind transfers to be both fast and reliable. This handshaking allows the SCSI controller to defer the CPU if no data is available to transfer. If the data doesn't arrive within a specified period, the SCSI Manager returns the scBusTOErr result. The timeout period varies for each Macintosh model. This type of timeout error does not occur when using polled transfers.

Polled transfers work reliably with all SCSI peripheral devices, and are a good choice for slow or unpredictable devices such as printers and scanners. You should also use polled transfers if you are unfamiliar with the characteristics of a particular device. You use the SCSIRead and SCSIWrite functions to initiate polled transfers.

For disk drives and other high-speed devices, blind transfers can significantly increase data throughput. As long as the device does not incur any delays during a transfer, or the delays occur at predictable times, blind transfers are a good choice. You use the SCSIRBlind and SCSIWBlind functions to initiate blind transfers.

Because the first byte transferred by each TIB instruction is always polled, even in blind mode, you can work around predictable delays using an appropriate sequence of TIB instructions. For example, if a peripheral device always pauses at a specific byte within a transfer, you can divide the transfer into blocks so that the delayed byte is located at the start of a TIB instruction. The SCSI Manager polls the controller before the first byte, then reads the remaining bytes using a blind transfer. For disk drives, predictable delays generally occur at sector boundaries, so you can compensate by dividing your transfers into sector-sized blocks.

SCSI Manager Reference

This section describes the data structures and routines that constitute the SCSI Manager, and also includes the data structures that describe the low-level structure of block devices.

The section "SCSI Manager TIB Instructions," beginning on page 3-27, contains descriptions of transfer instruction block (TIB) instructions. These structures are used to control data transfers conducted by the SCSI Manager. Although TIB instructions are data structures, not machine-executable code, they are analogous to code in that TIB instructions are interpreted and executed by the SCSI Manager. Because of this dual nature, TIB instructions are presented in their own section.

Data Structures

This section describes the driver descriptor record and the partition map entry record. These data structures are not used by the SCSI Manager, but represent the way data is structured on random access storage devices such as hard disk drives. The Start Manager uses this information to locate partitions and device drivers on SCSI disks.

Driver Descriptor Record

The driver descriptor record contains information about the device drivers resident on a SCSI peripheral device. The driver descriptor record is defined by the Block0 data type.

```
TYPE Block0 =
PACKED RECORD
    sbSig:          Integer;    {device signature}
```

```
    sbBlkSize:        Integer;          {block size of the device}
    sbBlkCount:       LongInt;          {number of blocks on the device}
    sbDevType:        Integer;          {reserved}
    sbDevId:          Integer;          {reserved}
    sbData:           LongInt;          {reserved}
    sbDrvrCount:      Integer;          {number of driver descriptor entries}
    ddBlock:          LongInt;          {first driver's starting block}
    ddSize:           Integer;          {size of the driver, in 512-byte blocks}
    ddType:           Integer;          {operating system type (MacOS = 1)}
    ddPad:            ARRAY [0..242] OF Integer; {additional drivers, if any}
END;
```

Field descriptions

sbSig
The device signature. This field should contain the value of the sbSIGWord constant ($4552) to indicate that the driver descriptor record is valid (meaning that the disk has been formatted).

sbBlkSize
The size of the blocks on the device, in bytes.

sbBlkCount
The number of blocks on the device.

sbDevType
Reserved.

sbDevId
Reserved.

sbData
Reserved.

sbDrvrCount
The number of drivers installed on the disk. More than one driver may be included when multiple operating systems or processors are supported. The drivers can be located anywhere on the device and can be as large as necessary.

ddBlock
The physical block number of the first block of the first device driver on the disk.

ddSize
The size of the device driver, in 512-byte blocks.

ddType
The operating system or processor supported by the driver. A value of 1 specifies the Macintosh Operating System. The values 0 through 15 are reserved for use by Apple Computer, Inc.

ddPad
Additional ddBlock, ddSize, and ddType entries for other device drivers on the disk.

If multiple device drivers exist on the device, you can use the Start Manager SetOSDefault function to control which operating system is loaded at startup by specifying a value that corresponds to the ddType field of the appropriate device driver. For more information on the startup process, see the chapter "Start Manager" in *Inside Macintosh: Operating System Utilities.*

See "The Structure of Block Devices," beginning on page 3-12, for more information about this data structure.

Partition Map Entry Record

The partition map entry record contains information about how data is stored on a block device, usually a SCSI disk drive. The partition map entry record is defined by the `Partition` data type.

```
TYPE Partition =
RECORD
    pmSig:          Integer;        {partition signature}
    pmSigPad:       Integer;        {reserved}
    pmMapBlkCnt:    LongInt;        {number of blocks in partition map}
    pmPyPartStart:  LongInt;        {first physical block of partition}
    pmPartBlkCnt:   LongInt;        {number of blocks in partition}
    pmPartName:     PACKED ARRAY [0..31] OF Char; {partition name}
    pmParType:      PACKED ARRAY [0..31] OF Char; {partition type}
    pmLgDataStart:  LongInt;        {first logical block of data area}
    pmDataCnt:      LongInt;        {number of blocks in data area}
    pmPartStatus:   LongInt;        {partition status information}
    pmLgBootStart:  LongInt;        {first logical block of boot code}
    pmBootSize:     LongInt;        {size of boot code, in bytes}
    pmBootAddr:     LongInt;        {boot code load address}
    pmBootAddr2:    LongInt;        {reserved}
    pmBootEntry:    LongInt;        {boot code entry point}
    pmBootEntry2:   LongInt;        {reserved}
    pmBootCksum:    LongInt;        {boot code checksum}
    pmProcessor:    PACKED ARRAY [0..15] OF Char; {processor type}
    pmPad:          ARRAY [0..187] OF Integer;    {reserved}
END;
```

Field descriptions

pmSig
: The partition signature. This field should contain the value of the `pMapSIG` constant ($504D). An earlier but still supported version uses the value $5453.

pmSigPad
: Reserved.

pmMapBlkCnt
: The size of the partition map, in blocks.

pmPyPartStart
: The physical block number of the first block of the partition.

pmPartBlkCnt
: The size of the partition, in blocks.

pmPartName
: An optional partition name, up to 32 bytes in length. If the string is less than 32 bytes, it must be terminated with the ASCII NUL character (a byte with a value of 0). If the partition name begins with `Maci` (for Macintosh), the Start Manager will perform checksum verification of the device driver's boot code. Otherwise, this field is ignored.

pmParType	A string that identifies the partition type. Names that begin with `Apple_` are reserved for use by Apple Computer, Inc. Names shorter than 32 characters must be terminated with the NUL character. The following standard partition types are defined for the `pmParType` field:

String	Meaning
Apple_partition_map	Partition contains a partition map
Apple_Driver	Partition contains a device driver
Apple_Driver43	Partition contains a SCSI Manager 4.3 device driver
Apple_MFS	Partition uses the original Macintosh File System (64K ROM version)
Apple_HFS	Partition uses the Hierarchical File System implemented in 128K and later ROM versions
Apple_Unix_SVR2	Partition uses the Unix file system
Apple_PRODOS	Partition uses the ProDOS file system
Apple_Free	Partition is unused
Apple_Scratch	Partition is empty

pmLgDataStart	The logical block number of the first block containing file system data. This is for use by operating systems, such as A/UX, in which the file system does not begin at logical block 0 of the partition.
pmDataCnt	The size of the file system data area, in blocks. This is used in conjunction with the `pmLgDataStart` field, for those operating systems in which the file system does not begin at logical block 0 of the partition.
pmPartStatus	Two words of status information about the partition. The low-order byte of the low-order word contains status information used only by the A/UX operating system:

Bit	Meaning
0	Set if a valid partition map entry
1	Set if partition is already allocated; clear if available
2	Set if partition is in use; may be cleared after a system reset
3	Set if partition contains valid boot information
4	Set if partition allows reading
5	Set if partition allows writing
6	Set if boot code is position-independent
7	Unused

	The remaining bytes of the `pmPartStatus` field are reserved.
pmLgBootStart	The logical block number of the first block containing boot code.
pmBootSize	The size of the boot code, in bytes.

pmBootAddr	The memory address where the boot code is to be loaded.
pmBootAddr2	Reserved.
pmBootEntry	The memory address to which the Start Manager will transfer control after loading the boot code into memory.
pmBootEntry2	Reserved.
pmBootCksum	The boot code checksum. The Start Manager can compare this value against the calculated checksum after loading the code.
pmProcessor	An optional string that identifies the type of processor that will execute the boot code. Strings shorter than 16 bytes must be terminated with the ASCII NUL character. The following processor types are defined: 68000, 68020, 68030, and 68040.
pmPad	Reserved.

See "The Structure of Block Devices," beginning on page 3-12, for more information about this data structure.

SCSI Manager TIB Instructions

The transfer instruction block (TIB) is a data structure that you use to control the data transfer process. TIB structures are passed as parameters to the SCSIRead, SCSIRBlind, SCSIWrite, and SCSIWBlind functions. The transfer instruction block is defined by the SCSIInstr data type.

```
TYPE SCSIInstr =
RECORD
    scOpcode:       Integer;      {operation code}
    scParam1:       LongInt;      {first parameter}
    scParam2:       LongInt;      {second parameter}
END;
```

The scOpcode field contains a value that specifies the operation to be performed. There are eight possible operations, known as TIB instructions, which carry out tasks such as moving data, looping, and address arithmetic. These instructions are described in this section. The operation codes for the TIB instructions are:

```
CONST
    scInc       = 1;      {transfer data, increment buffer pointer}
    scNoInc     = 2;      {transfer data, don't increment pointer}
    scAdd       = 3;      {add long to address}
    scMove      = 4;      {move long to address}
    scLoop      = 5;      {decrement counter and loop if > 0}
    scNop       = 6;      {no operation}
    scStop      = 7;      {stop TIB execution}
    scComp      = 8;      {compare SCSI data with memory}
```

To transfer data, you create a variable-length array of TIB instructions and pass a pointer to this array to any of the SCSI Manager data transfer functions (`SCSIRead`, `SCSIRBlind`, `SCSIWrite`, `SCSIWBlind`). These SCSI Manager functions interpret the TIB instructions and carry out the requested operations.

For an example of how to use TIB instructions, see "Using CDB and TIB Structures," beginning on page 3-17.

IMPORTANT

Before you call any of the SCSI Manager data transfer functions (`SCSIRead`, `SCSIRBlind`, `SCSIWrite`, or `SCSIWBlind`), you must first send a SCSI read or write command to the target using the `SCSICmd` function. ▲

scInc

You can use the `scInc` TIB instruction to transfer data and increment the buffer pointer.

Parameter block

→	scParam1	Ptr	A pointer to a data buffer.
→	scParam2	LongInt	The number of bytes to be transferred.

DESCRIPTION

The `scInc` instruction moves data to or from the buffer pointed to by `scParam1`. You specify the number of bytes to be transferred in `scParam2`. The buffer pointer in `scParam1` is incremented by the number of bytes transferred (for use by a subsequent iteration of this instruction).

scNoInc

You can use the `scNoInc` TIB instruction to transfer data without incrementing the buffer pointer.

Parameter block

→	scParam1	Ptr	A pointer to a data buffer.
→	scParam2	LongInt	The number of bytes to be transferred.

DESCRIPTION

The `scNoInc` instruction moves data to or from the buffer pointed to by `scParam1`. You specify the number of bytes to be transferred in `scParam2`. The buffer pointer in `scParam1` is unmodified by this instruction.

scAdd

You can use the scAdd TIB instruction to add a value to an address.

Parameter block

→	scParam1	Ptr	An address.
→	scParam2	LongInt	The number to add to the address.

DESCRIPTION

The scAdd instruction adds the long value in scParam2 to the address in scParam1.

scMove

You can use the scMove TIB instruction to copy a long value from one memory location to another.

Parameter block

→	scParam1	Ptr	The source address.
→	scParam2	Ptr	The destination address.

DESCRIPTION

The scMove TIB instruction copies the 32-bit value pointed to by the scParam1 parameter to the memory location specified by the scParam2 parameter.

scLoop

You can use the scLoop TIB instruction to repeat a sequence of TIB instructions a specified number of times.

Parameter block

→	scParam1	LongInt	The relative offset of the TIB instruction to branch to.
→	scParam2	LongInt	The number of times to loop.

DESCRIPTION

The scLoop TIB instruction decrements the value in scParam2 by 1. If the result is greater than 0, the flow of control branches to the TIB instruction whose relative offset is the current instruction plus the value in scParam1. If the result is 0, control passes to the instruction following the scLoop instruction. The offset in scParam1 is a signed value, and must be a multiple of 10 bytes (the size of the SCSIInstr data type). For example, to branch to the instruction immediately preceding the current one, you would specify a relative offset of –10. To jump ahead three instructions, you would specify a relative offset of 30.

scNop

The scNop TIB instruction does nothing.

DESCRIPTION

The scNop TIB instruction is analogous to an assembly-language NOP instruction. The two parameters are ignored.

scStop

You use the scStop TIB instruction to end a sequence of TIB instructions.

DESCRIPTION

The scStop TIB instruction stops execution of a sequence of TIB instructions and returns control to the calling SCSI Manager function. At least one scStop instruction is required in any TIB instruction sequence, usually at the end. The two parameters are ignored.

scComp

You can use the scComp TIB instruction to compare data on a SCSI device with data in memory.

Parameter block

→	scParam1	Ptr	A pointer to a data buffer.
→	scParam2	LongInt	The number of bytes to be compared.

DESCRIPTION

The scComp TIB instruction is used in conjunction with the SCSIRead function to compare data in memory with incoming data from a SCSI device. The SCSI Manager compares the result of the read command with the contents of the data buffer pointed to by scParam1. The scParam2 parameter specifies the number of bytes to read and compare. If all bytes do not compare, the SCSIRead function returns the result code scCompareErr.

SCSI Manager 4.3 Note

You should avoid using the scComp TIB instruction because it is not supported by SCSI Manager 4.3. ◆

SCSI Manager Routines

This section describes the SCSI Manager routines you use to

- reset the SCSI bus
- arbitrate for the SCSI bus
- select a SCSI device
- send SCSI commands and messages
- read or write data to SCSI devices
- obtain the status of the SCSI bus
- complete the processing of a SCSI transaction

SCSIReset

You can use the SCSIReset function to reset all devices on the SCSI bus.

```
FUNCTION SCSIReset: OSErr;
```

DESCRIPTION

The SCSIReset function directs the SCSI controller chip (or equivalent hardware) in the Macintosh computer to assert the SCSI bus reset signal. The reset signal causes all devices on the bus to clear pending I/O and forces the bus into the bus free phase.

▲ **WARNING**
The SCSIReset function interrupts SCSI communications and can cause data loss. Use this function only in exceptional circumstances. ▲

ASSEMBLY-LANGUAGE INFORMATION

The trap macro and routine selector for SCSIReset are

Trap macro	Selector
_SCSIDispatch	$0000

RESULT CODES

noErr	0	No error
scCommErr	2	Communications error, operation timeout

SEE ALSO

See "SCSI Bus Signals," beginning on page 3-4, and "SCSI Bus Phases," beginning on page 3-5, for more information about the reset signal and the bus free phase.

SCSIGet

You use the SCSIGet function to arbitrate for control of the SCSI bus.

```
FUNCTION SCSIGet: OSErr;
```

DESCRIPTION

The SCSIGet function prepares the SCSI Manager to initiate the arbitration sequence. If the SCSI Manager is busy with another operation, this function returns the scMgrBusyErr result. If arbitration failed because the bus was busy, the function returns the scArbNBErr result.

IMPORTANT

The operation of the SCSIGet function varies on different Macintosh models and does not necessarily initiate the SCSI bus arbitration phase. In some Macintosh models, the arbitration phase does not occur until your program calls the SCSISelect function. However, your program must always call the SCSIGet function before calling SCSISelect. ▲

ASSEMBLY-LANGUAGE INFORMATION

The trap macro and routine selector for SCSIGet are

Trap macro	Selector
_SCSIDispatch	$0001

RESULT CODES

noErr	0	No error
scCommErr	2	Communications error, operation timeout
scArbNBErr	3	Bus busy, arbitration timeout
scMgrBusyErr	7	SCSI Manager busy

SEE ALSO

See "SCSI Bus Phases," beginning on page 3-5, for a description of the arbitration phase.

SCSISelect

You use SCSISelect function to select a SCSI device for a subsequent operation.

```
FUNCTION SCSISelect (targetID: Integer): OSErr;
```

targetID   The SCSI ID of the target device, with a value from 0 to 7.

DESCRIPTION

The SCSISelect function selects the SCSI device identified by the targetID value.

IMPORTANT

You must call the SCSIGet function before calling SCSISelect. ▲

ASSEMBLY-LANGUAGE INFORMATION

The trap macro and routine selector for SCSISelect are

Trap macro	Selector
_SCSIDispatch	$0002

RESULT CODES

noErr	0	No error
scCommErr	2	Communications error, operation timeout
scArbNBErr	3	Bus busy, arbitration timeout
scSequenceErr	8	Attempted operation is out of sequence

SEE ALSO

See "SCSI Bus Phases," beginning on page 3-5, for a description of the selection phase.

SCSISelAtn

You can use the SCSISelAtn function to select a SCSI device and at the same time to assert the attention (/ATN) bus signal.

```
FUNCTION SCSISelAtn (targetID: Integer): OSErr;
```

targetID   The SCSI ID of the target device, with a value from 0 to 6.

DESCRIPTION

The SCSISelAtn function is identical to the SCSISelect function except that this function asserts the /ATN signal during selection. The /ATN signal informs the target that the initiator wants to send a message. The SCSISelAtn function must be followed by a call to the SCSIMsgOut function to send the message to the target device.

ASSEMBLY-LANGUAGE INFORMATION

The trap macro and routine selector for SCSISelAtn are

Trap macro	**Selector**
_SCSIDispatch	$000B

RESULT CODES

noErr	0	No error
scCommErr	2	Communications error, operation timeout

SEE ALSO

See "SCSI Bus Signals," beginning on page 3-4, and "SCSI Bus Phases," beginning on page 3-5, for more information about the attention signal and the selection phase.

SCSICmd

You use the SCSICmd function to send a SCSI command to a SCSI device.

```
FUNCTION SCSICmd (buffer: Ptr; count: Integer): OSErr;
```

buffer	A pointer to a buffer containing the SCSI command descriptor block.
count	The size of the command descriptor block, in bytes.

DESCRIPTION

The SCSICmd function sends a SCSI command to the previously selected target device. The command code and other parameters are contained in a command descriptor block (CDB) data structure pointed to by the buffer parameter. The count parameter specifies the size of the CDB structure, which can be 6, 10, or 12 bytes.

The SCSI specification describes the CDB data structure and lists the standard SCSI commands that all devices must support. Devices may support additional commands not defined by the SCSI specification.

ASSEMBLY-LANGUAGE INFORMATION

The trap macro and routine selector for SCSICmd are

Trap macro	**Selector**
_SCSIDispatch	$0003

RESULT CODES

noErr	0	No error
scCommErr	2	Communications error, operation timeout
scPhaseErr	5	Phase error on the SCSI bus

SEE ALSO

See "SCSI Commands," beginning on page 3-7, for an overview of SCSI commands. Refer to the SCSI specification for detailed information about SCSI commands.

SCSIMsgIn

You can use the SCSIMsgIn function to receive a message from a SCSI device.

```
FUNCTION SCSIMsgIn (VAR message: Integer): OSErr;
```

message   The low-order byte contains the message from the target device.

DESCRIPTION

The SCSIMsgIn function receives a SCSI message from the previously selected target device. The message is returned in the low-order byte of the message parameter. See the SCSI specification for information about the types of messages that can be sent from a target to an initiator.

The SCSIMsgIn function leaves the attention bus signal undisturbed if it is already asserted.

ASSEMBLY-LANGUAGE INFORMATION

The trap macro and routine selector for SCSIMsgIn are

Trap macro	Selector
_SCSIDispatch	$000C

RESULT CODES

noErr	0	No error
scCommErr	2	Communications error, operation timeout
scPhaseErr	5	Phase error on the SCSI bus

SEE ALSO

See "SCSI Messages," beginning on page 3-7, for an overview of SCSI messages. Refer to the SCSI specification for detailed information about SCSI messages.

SCSIMsgOut

You can use the SCSIMsgOut function to send a message to a SCSI device.

```
FUNCTION SCSIMsgOut (message: Integer): OSErr;
```

message   The low-order byte contains the message to be sent to the target device.

DESCRIPTION

The SCSIMsgOut function sends a SCSI message to the previously selected target device. The message is contained in the low-order byte of the message parameter. See the SCSI specification for information about the types of messages that can be sent from an initiator to a target.

ASSEMBLY-LANGUAGE INFORMATION

The trap macro and routine selector for SCSIMsgOut are

Trap macro	Selector
_SCSIDispatch	$000D

RESULT CODES

noErr	0	No error
scCommErr	2	Communications error, operation timeout
scPhaseErr	5	Phase error on the SCSI bus

SEE ALSO

See "SCSI Messages," beginning on page 3-7, for an overview of SCSI messages. Refer to the SCSI specification for detailed information about SCSI messages.

SCSIRead

You can use the SCSIRead function to read data from a SCSI device using a polled transfer.

```
FUNCTION SCSIRead (tibPtr: Ptr): OSErr;
```

tibPtr   A pointer to an array of TIB instructions.

DESCRIPTION

The SCSIRead function reads data from the previously selected target device. The data transfer instructions are specified by the TIB array pointed to by the tibPtr parameter.

ASSEMBLY-LANGUAGE INFORMATION

The trap macro and routine selector for SCSIRead are

Trap macro	Selector
_SCSIDispatch	$0005

RESULT CODES

noErr	0	No error
scCommErr	2	Communications error, operation timeout
scBadParmsErr	4	Unrecognized TIB instruction
scPhaseErr	5	Phase error on the SCSI bus
scCompareErr	6	Comparison error from scComp instruction

SEE ALSO

See "Using CDB and TIB Structures," beginning on page 3-17, for information about
using TIB instructions. See "SCSI Manager TIB Instructions," beginning on page 3-27, for
details of the TIB instruction set.

SCSIRBlind

You can use the SCSIRBlind function to read data from a SCSI device using a blind
transfer.

```
FUNCTION SCSIRBlind (tibPtr: Ptr): OSErr;
```

tibPtr   A pointer to an array of TIB instructions.

DESCRIPTION

The SCSIRBlind function is identical to the SCSIRead function but does not poll the
SCSI controller before transferring each byte of data. The SCSI controller is polled only
for the first byte transferred by each scInc, scNoInc, or scComp TIB instruction.

SPECIAL CONSIDERATIONS

You should use this function only if the device you are reading from is capable of
transferring data fast enough to avoid timeout errors from the SCSI controller.

ASSEMBLY-LANGUAGE INFORMATION

The trap macro and routine selector for SCSIRBlind are

Trap macro	Selector
_SCSIDispatch	$0008

RESULT CODES

noErr	0	No error
scCommErr	2	Communications error, operation timeout
scBadParmsErr	4	Unrecognized TIB instruction
scPhaseErr	5	Phase error on the SCSI bus
scCompareErr	6	Comparison error from scComp instruction
scBusTOErr	9	Bus timeout during blind transfer

SEE ALSO

See the description of the SCSIRead function on page 3-36 for information about performing a polled transfer. See "Choosing Polled or Blind Transfers," beginning on page 3-22, for additional information.

SCSIWrite

You can use the SCSIWrite function to write to a SCSI device using a polled transfer.

```
FUNCTION SCSIWrite (tibPtr: Ptr): OSErr;
```

tibPtr   A pointer to an array of TIB instructions.

DESCRIPTION

The SCSIWrite function transfers data to the previously selected target device. The data transfer instructions are specified by the TIB array pointed to by the tibPtr parameter.

ASSEMBLY-LANGUAGE INFORMATION

The trap macro and routine selector for SCSIWrite are

Trap macro	Selector
_SCSIDispatch	$0006

RESULT CODES

noErr	0	No error
scCommErr	2	Communications error, operation timeout
scBadParmsErr	4	Unrecognized TIB instruction
scPhaseErr	5	Phase error on the SCSI bus

SEE ALSO

See "Using CDB and TIB Structures," beginning on page 3-17, for information about using TIB instructions. See "SCSI Manager TIB Instructions," beginning on page 3-27, for details of the TIB instruction set.

SCSIWBlind

You can use the `SCSIWBlind` function to write to a SCSI device using a blind transfer.

```
FUNCTION SCSIWBlind (tibPtr: Ptr): OSErr;
```

tibPtr   A pointer to an array of TIB instructions.

DESCRIPTION

The `SCSIWBlind` function is identical to the `SCSIWrite` function but does not poll the SCSI controller before transferring each byte of data. The SCSI controller is polled only for the first byte transferred by each `scInc`, `scNoInc`, or `scComp` TIB instruction.

SPECIAL CONSIDERATIONS

You should use this function only if the device you are writing to is capable of accepting data fast enough to avoid timeout errors from the SCSI controller.

ASSEMBLY-LANGUAGE INFORMATION

The trap macro and routine selector for `SCSIWBlind` are

Trap macro	Selector
_SCSIDispatch	$0009

RESULT CODES

noErr	0	No error
scCommErr	2	Communications error, operation timeout
scBadParmsErr	4	Unrecognized TIB instruction
scPhaseErr	5	Phase error on the SCSI bus
scBusTOErr	9	Bus timeout during blind transfer

SEE ALSO

See the description of the `SCSIWrite` function on page 3-38 for information about performing a polled transfer. See "Choosing Polled or Blind Transfers," beginning on page 3-22, for additional information.

SCSIComplete

You use the SCSIComplete function to complete a SCSI transaction.

```
FUNCTION SCSIComplete(VAR stat: Integer; VAR message: Integer;
                      wait: LongInt): OSErr;
```

stat   The low-order byte contains the status byte from the target device.

message   The low-order byte contains the message byte from the target device.

wait   The number of ticks to wait for the command to complete.

DESCRIPTION

The SCSIComplete function performs the tasks necessary to properly complete the current SCSI transaction and leave the bus in the bus free phase. This function must be called at the end of each SCSI transaction, even if the transaction does not complete successfully.

The SCSIComplete function waits for the transaction to complete, and then returns one byte of status information and one byte of message information. If the transaction fails to complete within the number of ticks specified by the wait parameter, the scCommErr result is returned.

The SCSIComplete function uses a number of strategies to correct anomalous conditions on the SCSI bus and restore the bus into a known state. These include accepting arbitrary amounts of data sent by the target (and throwing this data away), and sending arbitrary data (bytes with the value of $EE) as requested by the target. The function returns the scComplPhaseErr result if either of these steps were necessary.

ASSEMBLY-LANGUAGE INFORMATION

The trap macro and routine selector for SCSIComplete are

Trap macro	Selector
_SCSIDispatch	$0004

RESULT CODES

noErr	0	No error
scCommErr	2	Communications error, operation timeout
scPhaseErr	5	Phase error on the SCSI bus
scComplPhaseErr	10	SCSI bus was not in status phase on entry to SCSIComplete

SEE ALSO

See "Using the SCSIComplete Function," beginning on page 3-21, for more information about this function.

SCSIStat

You can use the SCSIStat function to obtain status information from the SCSI Manager.

```
FUNCTION SCSIStat: Integer;
```

DESCRIPTION

The SCSIStat function returns a 16-bit value containing status information. This information includes the state of all SCSI bus control signals as well as the status of the NCR 5380 SCSI controller chip (or equivalent hardware). In Macintosh models that use other SCSI controller hardware, the status information conforms to the 5380 format, but may not represent the actual state of the hardware.

IMPORTANT

Because hardware differences make it difficult to accurately interpret the status information, use of this function is not recommended. ▲

Bits 0 through 9 represent the state of the SCSI bus signals, and bits 10 through 15 report status information from the SCSI controller hardware. The status bits have these meanings:

Bit	Name	Meaning
0	DBP	Data parity signal
1	/SEL	Select signal
2	/I/O	I/O signal
3	/C/D	Command/Data signal
4	/MSG	Message signal
5	/REQ	Request signal
6	/BSY	Busy signal
7	/RST	Reset signal
8	/ACK	Acknowledge signal
9	/ATN	Attention signal
10	BSY ERR	Busy error
11	PHS MAT	Phase match
12	INT REQ	Interrupt request
13	PTY ERR	Parity error
14	DMA REQ	Direct memory access request
15	END DMA	Direct memory access complete

Note

The SCSI bus control signals are active low; therefore, the status bits represent the complement of the bus signals. ◆

ASSEMBLY-LANGUAGE INFORMATION

The trap macro and routine selector for SCSIStat are

Trap macro	Selector
_SCSIDispatch	$000A

RESULT CODES

noErr	0	No error
scCommErr	2	Communications error, operation timeout
scPhaseErr	5	Phase error on the SCSI bus

SEE ALSO

See "SCSI Bus Signals," beginning on page 3-4, for an overview of SCSI bus signals. Refer to the SCSI specification for detailed information about SCSI bus signals. Refer to the NCR 5380 SCSI controller specification for information about that device.

Summary of the SCSI Manager

Pascal Summary

Constants

```
CONST
    scInc       = 1;        {transfer data, increment buffer pointer}
    scNoInc     = 2;        {transfer data, don't increment pointer}
    scAdd       = 3;        {add long to address}
    scMove      = 4;        {move long to address}
    scLoop      = 5;        {decrement counter and loop if > 0}
    scNop       = 6;        {no operation}
    scStop      = 7;        {stop TIB execution}
    scComp      = 8;        {compare SCSI data with memory}

    {signature values}
    sbSIGWord   = $4552;    {driver descriptor map signature}
    pMapSIG     = $504D;    {partition map signature}
```

Data Types

```
TYPE SCSIInstr =
    RECORD
        scOpcode:       Integer;    {operation code}
        scParam1:       LongInt;    {first parameter}
        scParam2:       LongInt;    {second parameter}
    END;

    Block0 =
    PACKED RECORD
        sbSig:          Integer;    {device signature}
        sbBlkSize:      Integer;    {block size of the device}
        sbBlkCount:     LongInt;    {number of blocks on the device}
        sbDevType:      Integer;    {reserved}
        sbDevId:        Integer;    {reserved}
        sbData:         LongInt;    {reserved}
        sbDrvrCount:    Integer;    {number of driver descriptor entries}
        ddBlock:        LongInt;    {first driver's starting block}
        ddSize:         Integer;    {size of the driver, in 512-byte blocks}
```

```
    ddType:          Integer;     {operating system type (MacOS = 1)}
    ddPad:           ARRAY [0..242] OF Integer; {additional drivers, if any}
END;

Partition =
RECORD
    pmSig:           Integer;     {partition signature}
    pmSigPad:        Integer;     {reserved}
    pmMapBlkCnt:     LongInt;     {number of blocks in partition map}
    pmPyPartStart:   LongInt;     {first physical block of partition}
    pmPartBlkCnt:    LongInt;     {number of blocks in partition}
    pmPartName:      PACKED ARRAY [0..31] OF Char; {partition name}
    pmParType:       PACKED ARRAY [0..31] OF Char; {partition type}
    pmLgDataStart:   LongInt;     {first logical block of data area}
    pmDataCnt:       LongInt;     {number of blocks in data area}
    pmPartStatus:    LongInt;     {partition status information}
    pmLgBootStart:   LongInt;     {first logical block of boot code}
    pmBootSize:      LongInt;     {size of boot code, in bytes}
    pmBootAddr:      LongInt;     {boot code load address}
    pmBootAddr2:     LongInt;     {reserved}
    pmBootEntry:     LongInt;     {boot code entry point}
    pmBootEntry2:    LongInt;     {reserved}
    pmBootCksum:     LongInt;     {boot code checksum}
    pmProcessor:     PACKED ARRAY [0..15] OF Char; {processor type}
    pmPad:           ARRAY [0..187] OF Integer;    {reserved}
END;
```

Routines

```
FUNCTION SCSIReset          : OSErr;
FUNCTION SCSIGet            : OSErr;
FUNCTION SCSISelect        (targetID: Integer): OSErr;
FUNCTION SCSISelAtn        (targetID: Integer): OSErr;
FUNCTION SCSICmd           (buffer: Ptr; count: Integer): OSErr;
FUNCTION SCSIMsgIn         (VAR message: Integer): OSErr;
FUNCTION SCSIMsgOut        (message: Integer): OSErr;
FUNCTION SCSIRead          (tibPtr: Ptr): OSErr;
FUNCTION SCSIRBlind        (tibPtr: Ptr): OSErr;
FUNCTION SCSIWrite         (tibPtr: Ptr): OSErr;
FUNCTION SCSIWBlind        (tibPtr: Ptr): OSErr;
FUNCTION SCSIComplete      (VAR stat: Integer; VAR message: Integer;
                            wait: LongInt): OSErr;
```

```
FUNCTION SCSIStat            : Integer;
```

C Summary

Constants

```
enum {
    /* TIB instruction opcodes */
    scInc       = 1,        /* transfer data, increment buffer pointer */
    scNoInc     = 2,        /* transfer data, don't increment pointer */
    scAdd       = 3,        /* add long to address */
    scMove      = 4,        /* move long to address */
    scLoop      = 5,        /* decrement counter and loop if > 0 */
    scNop       = 6,        /* no operation */
    scStop      = 7,        /* stop TIB execution */
    scComp      = 8,        /* compare SCSI data with memory */

    /* signature values */
    sbSIGWord   = 0x4552,   /* driver descriptor map signature */
    pMapSIG     = 0x504D    /* partition map signature */
};
```

Data Types

```
struct SCSIInstr {
    unsigned short      scOpcode;       /* operation code */
    unsigned long       scParam1;       /* first parameter */
    unsigned long       scParam2;       /* second parameter */
};
typedef struct SCSIInstr SCSIInstr;

struct Block0 {
    unsigned short      sbSig;          /* device signature */
    unsigned short      sbBlkSize;      /* block size of the device*/
    unsigned long       sbBlkCount;     /* number of blocks on the device*/
    unsigned short      sbDevType;      /* reserved */
    unsigned short      sbDevId;        /* reserved */
    unsigned long       sbData;         /* reserved */
    unsigned short      sbDrvrCount;    /* number of driver descriptor entries */
    unsigned long       ddBlock;        /* first driver's starting block */
    unsigned short      ddSize;         /* driver's size, in 512-byte blocks */
```

```
    unsigned short    ddType;          /* operating system type (MacOS = 1) */
    unsigned short    ddPad[243];      /* additional drivers, if any */
};
typedef struct Block0 Block0;

Partition {
    unsigned short    pmSig;           /* partition signature */
    unsigned short    pmSigPad;        /* reserved */
    unsigned long     pmMapBlkCnt;     /* number of blocks in partition map */
    unsigned long     pmPyPartStart;   /* first physical block of partition */
    unsigned long     pmPartBlkCnt;    /* number of blocks in partition */
    unsigned char     pmPartName[32];  /* partition name */
    unsigned char     pmParType[32];   /* partition type */
    unsigned long     pmLgDataStart;   /* first logical block of data area */
    unsigned long     pmDataCnt;       /* number of blocks in data area */
    unsigned long     pmPartStatus;    /* partition status information */
    unsigned long     pmLgBootStart;   /* first logical block of boot code */
    unsigned long     pmBootSize;      /* size of boot code, in bytes */
    unsigned long     pmBootAddr;      /* boot code load address */
    unsigned long     pmBootAddr2;     /* reserved */
    unsigned long     pmBootEntry;     /* boot code entry point */
    unsigned long     pmBootEntry2;    /* reserved */
    unsigned long     pmBootCksum;     /* boot code checksum */
    unsigned char     pmProcessor[16]; /* processor type */
    unsigned short    pmPad[188];      /* reserved */
};
typedef struct Partition Partition;
```

Functions

```
pascal OSErr SCSIReset      (void);
pascal OSErr SCSIGet        (void);
pascal OSErr SCSISelect     (short targetID);
pascal OSErr SCSISelAtn     (short targetID);
pascal OSErr SCSICmd        (Ptr buffer, short count);
pascal OSErr SCSIMsgIn      (short *message);
pascal OSErr SCSIMsgOut     (short message);
pascal OSErr SCSIRead       (Ptr tibPtr);
pascal OSErr SCSIRBlind     (Ptr tibPtr);
pascal OSErr SCSIWrite      (Ptr tibPtr);
pascal OSErr SCSIWBlind     (Ptr tibPtr);
```

```
pascal OSErr SCSIComplete    (short *stat, short *message,
                              unsigned long wait);

pascal short SCSIStat        (void);
```

Assembly-Language Summary

Data Structures

Transfer Instruction Block

0	scOpcode	word	operation code
2	scParam1	long	first parameter
6	scParam2	long	second parameter

Driver Descriptor Record

0	sbSig	word	device signature
2	sbBlkSize	word	block size of the device
4	sbBlkCount	long	number of blocks on the device
8	sbDevType	word	reserved
10	sbDevId	word	reserved
12	sbData	long	reserved
16	sbDrvrCount	word	number of driver descriptor entries
18	ddBlock	long	first driver's starting block
22	ddSize	word	driver's size, in 512-byte blocks
24	ddType	word	operating system type (MacOS = 1)
26	ddPad	486 bytes	additional drivers, if any

Partition Map Entry Record

0	pmSig	word	partition signature
2	pmSigPad	word	reserved
4	pmMapBlkCnt	long	number of blocks in partition map
8	pmPyPartStart	long	first physical block of partition
12	pmPartBlkCnt	long	number of blocks in partition
16	pmPartName	32 bytes	partition name
48	PmParType	32 bytes	partition type
80	pmLgDataStart	long	first logical block of data area
84	pmDataCnt	long	number of blocks in data area
88	pmPartStatus	long	partition status information
92	pmLgBootStart	long	first logical block of boot code
96	pmBootSize	long	size of boot code, in bytes
100	pmBootAddr	long	boot code load address
104	pmBootAddr2	long	reserved
108	pmBootEntry	long	boot code entry point
112	pmBootEntry2	long	reserved

116	pmBootCksum	long	boot code checksum
120	pmProcessor	16 bytes	processor type
136	pmPad	376 bytes	reserved

Trap Macros

Trap Macros Requiring Routine Selectors

_SCSIDispatch

Selector	Routine
$00	SCSIReset
$01	SCSIGet
$02	SCSISelect
$03	SCSICmd
$04	SCSIComplete
$05	SCSIRead
$06	SCSIWrite
$08	SCSIRBlind
$09	SCSIWBlind
$0A	SCSIStat
$0B	SCSISelAtn
$0C	SCSIMsgIn
$0D	SCSIMsgOut

Result Codes

noErr	0	No error
scCommErr	2	Communications error, operation timeout
scArbNBErr	3	Bus busy, arbitration timeout
scBadParmsErr	4	Bad parameter or unrecognized TIB instruction
scPhaseErr	5	Phase error on the SCSI bus
scCompareErr	6	Comparison error from scComp instruction
scMgrBusyErr	7	SCSI Manager busy
scSequenceErr	8	Attempted operation is out of sequence
scBusTOErr	9	Bus timeout during blind transfer
scComplPhaseErr	10	SCSI bus was not in status phase on entry to SCSIComplete

SCSI Manager 4.3

Contents

SCSI Manager 4.3 is an enhanced version of the SCSI Manager that provides new features as well as compatibility with the original version. SCSI Manager 4.3 is contained in the ROM of high-performance computers such as the Macintosh Quadra 840AV and the Power Macintosh 8100/80. Beginning with system software version 7.5, SCSI Manager 4.3 is also available as a system extension that can be installed in any Macintosh computer that uses the NCR 53C96 SCSI controller chip.

In addition to the capabilities of the original SCSI Manager, SCSI Manager 4.3 provides

- support for asynchronous SCSI I/O
- support for optional SCSI features such as disconnect/reconnect
- a hardware-independent programming interface that minimizes the SCSI-specific tasks a device driver must perform

You should read this chapter if you are writing a SCSI device driver or other software for Macintosh computers that use SCSI Manager 4.3. To make best use of this chapter, you should understand the Device Manager and the implementation of device drivers in Macintosh computers. If you are designing a SCSI peripheral device for the Macintosh, you should read *Designing Cards and Drivers for the Macintosh Family*, third edition, and *Guide to the Macintosh Family Hardware*, second edition.

This chapter assumes you are familiar with the following SCSI specifications established by the American National Standards Institute (ANSI):

- X3.131-1986, *Small Computer System Interface*
- X3.131-1994, *Small Computer System Interface–2*
- X3.232 (draft), *SCSI-2 Common Access Method*

If you are writing a device driver for a block-structured storage device such as hard disk, you should also read the chapter "SCSI Manager" in this book for information about the structure of block devices used by the Macintosh Operating System. Because many Macintosh models continue to use the original SCSI Manager, you may want to design your software to operate with both SCSI Manager 4.3 and the original SCSI Manager.

About SCSI Manager 4.3

The SCSI Manager 4.3 application program interface (API) is modeled on the Common Access Method (CAM) software interface being developed by ANSI committee X3T9. The SCSI Manager 4.3 interface, however, includes Apple-specific differences required for compatibility with the original SCSI Manager and the Macintosh Operating System.

The CAM specification defines the operation of three functional units—the transport (XPT), the SCSI interface module (SIM), and the host bus adapter (HBA). The XPT is the entry point to SCSI Manager 4.3 and is responsible for passing requests to the appropriate SIM. Each SIM is responsible for managing the HBA for a particular bus.

In addition to the XPT, SCSI Manager 4.3 includes a SIM for managing the NCR 53C96 SCSI controller used in high-performance Macintosh computers. Other SIM modules and HBA hardware can be added at any time by Apple or third-party developers. For example, a NuBus or PDS expansion card can provide an additional SCSI bus, which device drivers can access through SCSI Manager 4.3 in exactly the same way as the internal bus. Figure 4-1 shows the relationship between device drivers, SCSI Manager 4.3, and the SCSI controller hardware.

Figure 4-1   The SCSI Manager 4.3 architecture

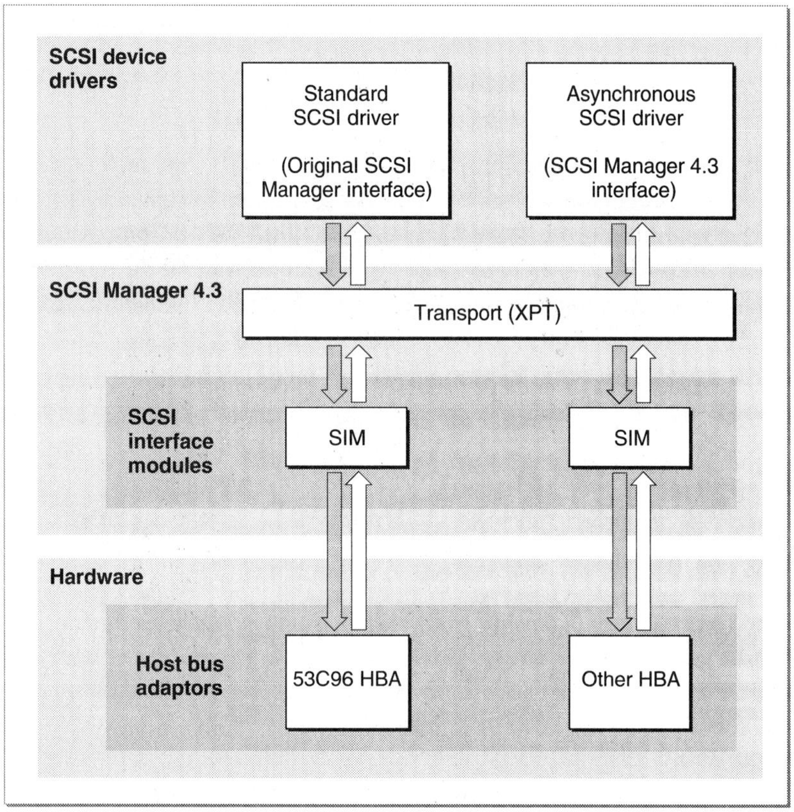

The features and capabilities of SCSI Manager 4.3 include

- **SCSI-2 compliance.** All mandatory SCSI-2 messages and protocol actions are supported as defined for an initiator. Optional SCSI-2 hardware features, such as fast and wide transfers, are anticipated by the SCSI Manager 4.3 architecture and supported by the interface.

- **Concurrent asynchronous I/O.** SCSI Manager 4.3 handles both synchronous and asynchronous I/O requests. In addition, it allows multiple device drivers to issue multiple requests and attempts to overlap the operations as much as possible.

- **Hardware-independent programming interface.** A new hardware-independent interface allows device drivers to work with any SCSI Manager 4.3-compatible host bus adapter (HBA), including those from third-party developers.

- **Direct memory access (DMA).** SCSI Manager 4.3 automatically takes advantage of the DMA capabilities available in high-performance Macintosh models. Direct memory access allows the computer to perform other functions while data bytes are transferred to or from the SCSI bus.

- **Support for multiple buses.** SCSI Manager 4.3 supports any number of SCSI buses, each with a full complement of devices. For example, on Macintosh computers with dual SCSI buses (such as the Power Macintosh 8100/80), up to 14 SCSI devices can be attached. In addition, developers can design NuBus or PDS expansion cards that offer enhanced SCSI bus capabilities.

- **Support for multiple logical units on each target.** SCSI Manager 4.3 allows access to all logical units on a target device. Logical units are treated as separate entities, and I/O requests are queued according to logical unit number (LUN).

- **Disconnect/reconnect.** This capability helps maximize SCSI bus utilization by allowing a device to disconnect and release control of the SCSI bus while it processes a command, then reconnect when it is ready to complete the transaction. This allows a device driver to submit requests to multiple targets so that those requests are executed in parallel. For example, the driver for a disk array can issue a request to one disk, which disconnects, then issue another request to a different disk. The two disks can perform their seek operations simultaneously, reducing the effective seek time.

- **Parity detection.** SCSI Manager 4.3 detects and handles parity errors in data received from a target. For compatibility reasons, this feature can be disabled on a per-transaction basis. (All Macintosh computers generate parity for write operations, but the original SCSI Manager does not detect parity errors in incoming data.)

- **Autosense.** SCSI Manager 4.3 automatically sends a `REQUEST SENSE` command in response to a `CHECK CONDITION` status and retrieves the sense data. This feature can be disabled.

- **Compatibility.** SCSI Manager 4.3 supports all original SCSI Manager functions and TIB instructions, except for `scComp` (compare).

Transport

The SCSI Manager 4.3 transport (XPT) provides the software interface to applications and device drivers, and is responsible for

- providing the means to register host bus adapters, their characteristics, and their respective SCSI interface modules

- routing requests to the proper SCSI interface module

- notifying the caller when a request is complete

- providing the high-level facilities for emulating the original SCSI Manager interface. This consists of maintaining a translation table of SCSI ID numbers and their corresponding host bus adapters, and directing original SCSI Manager requests accordingly

- isolating SCSI interface modules from certain operating system requirements, such as those imposed by the Virtual Memory Manager

SCSI Interface Modules

A SCSI interface module (SIM) provides the software interface between the transport (XPT) and a host bus adapter (HBA) in SCSI Manager 4.3. The SIM processes and executes SCSI requests directed to it by the XPT and is responsible for handling all aspects of a SCSI transaction, including

- maintaining the request queue, including freezing and unfreezing for error handling as necessary, and queuing multiple operations for all logical units on all target devices

- managing the selection, disconnection, reconnection, and data pointers of the SCSI protocol

- assigning tags for tag queuing, if supported

- managing the HBA hardware

- identifying abnormal conditions on the SCSI bus and performing error recovery

- providing a time-out mechanism for tracking SCSI command execution

- emulating original SCSI Manager functions, if supported

System Performance

In terms of maximum data transfer (bytes-per-second) over the internal SCSI bus, SCSI Manager 4.3 performs similarly to the original SCSI Manager. This aspect of performance is limited by the capability of the SCSI controller hardware and can be improved by adding a faster HBA.

In terms of overall system performance, the asynchronous capability of SCSI Manager 4.3 can provide significant benefits by allowing application code to regain control of the system while a SCSI transaction is in progress. This concurrency is a key benefit of asynchronous operation. In addition, support for disconnect/reconnect allows applications to initiate multiple I/O requests on multiple targets simultaneously, allowing further increases in throughput.

Multiple bus systems offer the added benefit of concurrency between buses. If DMA is used for both buses, their data transfer periods can be overlapped as well.

Compatibility

All the functions provided by the original SCSI Manager are emulated by the SCSI Manager 4.3 XPT and SIM for the internal SCSI bus. This level of compatibility is optional for third-party SIM/HBA developers. When a SIM registers its HBA with the SCSI Manager 4.3 XPT, the SIM specifies whether or not it is able to emulate the original SCSI Manager functions by setting the `oldCallCapable` field of the SIM initialization record.

When an application or device driver calls the original SCSI Manager function `SCSIGet`, the XPT sets a flag preventing any additional `SCSIGet` function calls but performs no other action. Upon receipt of a `SCSISelect` function call, the XPT issues a `SCSIOldCall` request to the appropriate SIM, which places the request in its queue.

Once the `SCSIOldCall` request begins execution, the SIM emulates subsequent original SCSI Manager function calls passed to it by the XPT. During this emulation, no new requests are processed until the entire transaction is completed and the `SCSIComplete` function returns. Any `SCSIGet` or `SCSISelect` requests received after the start of a `SCSIOldCall` request are rejected and return the `scMgrBusyErr` code.

While the original SCSI Manager emulation is in progress, asynchronous requests made by other applications or device drivers (using SCSI Manager 4.3 functions) are queued but do not execute until the emulation is complete. Requests to other SIMs are not affected and continue to execute normally.

The `SCSIReset` function resets only those buses that are capable of handling original SCSI Manager functions. The `SCSIStat` function returns results as accurate as possible for the SIM/HBA handling the request.

The `scComp` (compare) TIB instruction is not supported by SCSI Manager 4.3 because DMA transfers do not permit this type of compare operation. This should pose few compatibility problems because this instruction is rarely used. You can, of course, write your own code to compare data on a SCSI device with data in memory.

▲ **WARNING**
Applications or device drivers that bypass the SCSI Manager for any part of a transaction are not supported and will interfere with the operation of SCSI Manager 4.3. ▲

Using SCSI Manager 4.3

A fundamental difference between SCSI Manager 4.3 and the original SCSI Manager is that a single function, `SCSIAction`, handles an entire SCSI transaction. You do not need to explicitly arbitrate for the bus, select a device, or send a SCSI command. In most cases, your program does not need to be aware of SCSI bus phases.

The `SCSIAction` function is the entry point for all SCSI Manager 4.3 client functions. These functions provide the services that clients (applications and device drivers) need to communicate with SCSI devices. The only parameter to `SCSIAction` is a pointer to a SCSI Manager parameter block data structure. You use the `scsiFunctionCode` field of the parameter block to specify which function to perform. Most functions use specialized versions of the parameter block to carry the input parameters and return the results. For example, the `SCSIBusInquiry` function requires a SCSI bus inquiry parameter block (`SCSIBusInquiryPB`).

Perhaps the most important `SCSIAction` function is `SCSIExecIO`, which you use to request a SCSI I/O transaction. This function uses the SCSI I/O parameter block (`SCSIExecIOPB`), which specifies the destination of the request (the bus, target, and logical unit), the command descriptor block (CDB), the data buffers that either contain or receive the data, and a variety of other fields and flags required to fulfill the transaction.

You can call the `SCSIExecIO` function either synchronously or asynchronously. If the `scsiCompletion` field of the parameter block contains a pointer to a completion routine, the SCSI Manager executes the function asynchronously. If you set the `scsiCompletion` field to `nil`, the request is executed synchronously.

Because of interrupt handling considerations, device drivers must issue synchronous `SCSIExecIO` requests as such, rather than issuing them asynchronously and creating a synchronous wait loop inside the device driver. See "Writing a SCSI Device Driver," beginning on page 4-11, for more information about the proper handling of synchronous and asynchronous requests by device drivers. Applications are not subject to the same restrictions as device drivers and may create synchronous wait loops if desired.

Different SIM implementations may require additional fields beyond the standard fields of the SCSI I/O parameter block. Some of these may be input or output fields providing access to special capabilities of a SIM; others may be private fields required during the processing of the request. You can use the `SCSIBusInquiry` function to determine the size of the SCSI I/O parameter block for a particular SIM, as well as the largest parameter block required by any registered SIM.

You can also use the `SCSIBusInquiry` function to get information about various hardware and software characteristics of a SIM and its HBA. You can use this information to form a request that takes advantage of all the capabilities of a SIM.

Parameter blocks are queued separately for each logical unit (LUN) on a target device. When an error occurs during a `SCSIExecIO` request, the SIM freezes the queue for the LUN on which the error occurred, to allow you to perform any necessary error recovery. After correcting the error condition, you must use the `SCSIReleaseQ` function to enable normal handling of I/O requests to that LUN. See "Error Recovery Techniques" on page 4-10 for more information.

Locating SCSI Devices

SCSI Manager 4.3 supports multiple buses, allowing a client to specify a device based on its bus number as well as its target ID and LUN. To emulate original SCSI Manager functions that understand only a target ID, the technique first used in the Macintosh Quadra 900 has been expanded to include not only built-in SCSI buses but any compatible HBA installed in a NuBus or PDS expansion slot.

When multiple buses are registered with the XPT, emulated original SCSI Manager transactions are directed to the first bus that responds to a selection for the requested target ID. The target ID specified in a `SCSISelect` function is called the **virtual ID** because it designates a device on the single **virtual bus** (which encompasses all original SCSI Manager-compatible buses).

When you make a `SCSISelect` request, the XPT first attempts to select a device on the built-in internal bus. If there is no response on that bus, the XPT tries the built-in external bus (on models that include two SCSI buses), or the first registered add-on bus. Additional buses are searched in the order they were registered.

When the XPT finds a device that responds to the selection, all subsequent `SCSISelect` requests are directed to the bus on which that selection occurred. Until a successful selection occurs on one of the buses, the virtual ID is not assigned to any physical bus.

Once established, the mapping of virtual ID to physical bus is not changed until restart. You can use the `SCSIGetVirtualIDInfo` function to determine which physical bus a device is attached to.

It is possible for devices to be available through the original SCSI Manager interface but not through the SCSI Manager 4.3 interface. For example, a third-party SIM may install its own XPT if SCSI Manager 4.3 is not available. This creates a functional SCSI Manager 4.3 interface that does not include the built-in SCSI bus. Another possibility is the presence of a third-party SCSI adapter that does not comply with SCSI Manager 4.3 but patches the original SCSI Manager interface to create its own virtual bus. To locate all SCSI devices in these environments you must use the SCSI Manager 4.3 functions to scan for devices on all SIMs and then use the original SCSI Manager functions to scan for devices that are not accessible through the SCSI Manager 4.3 interface.

Describing Data Buffers

SCSI Manager 4.3 recognizes three data types for describing the source and destination memory buffers for a SCSI data transfer. The most familiar is a simple buffer, consisting of a single contiguous block of memory. An extension of this is the **scatter/gather list**, which consists of one or more elements, each of which describes the location and size of one buffer. Scatter/gather lists allow you to group multiple buffers of any size into a single virtual buffer for an I/O transaction.

In addition to these, SCSI Manager 4.3 supports the transfer instruction block (TIB) data type used by the original SCSI Manager interface. This structure is used only for emulating original SCSI Manager functions. During the execution of a `SCSIRead`, `SCSIWrite`, `SCSIRBlind`, or `SCSIWBlind` function, TIB instructions are interpreted by the SCSI Manager to determine the source and destination of the data. See the chapter "SCSI Manager" in this book for more information about TIB instructions.

Handshaking Instructions

In the original SCSI Manager interface, you use TIB instructions to show the SCSI Manager where long delays (greater than 16 microseconds) may occur in a blind transfer. Without these instructions, the SCSI Manager can lose data or crash the system if delays occur at unexpected times in a data transfer.

You use the `scsiHandshake` field of the SCSI I/O parameter block to specify handshaking instructions to SCSI Manager 4.3. This field contains a series of word values, each of which specifies the number of bytes between potential delays in the SCSI data transfer. You terminate the instructions with a value of 0.

For example, a "1, 511" TIB is a common TIB structure used with disk drives that have a 512-byte block size and sometimes experience a delay between the first and second bytes in the block, as well as a delay between the last byte of a block and the first byte of the following block. This TIB structure translates to a `scsiHandshake` field of "1, 511, 0", which indicates a request to synchronize and transfer 1 byte, synchronize and transfer 511 bytes, synchronize and transfer 1 byte, and so on.

Like the original SCSI Manager, SCSI Manager 4.3 always synchronizes on the first byte of a data phase. In addition, the handshaking cycle is reset whenever a device disconnects. That is, the cycle starts over from the beginning when a device reconnects. The scsiHandshake field should also indicate where a device may disconnect.

The handshaking cycle continues across scatter/gather list elements. For example, if the handshake array contains "2048, 0" and the scatter/gather list specifies a transfer of 512 bytes and then 8192 bytes, a handshake synchronization will occur 1536 bytes into the second scatter/gather element.

You should use polled transfers for devices that may experience unpredictable delays during the data phase or can disconnect at unpredictable times.

Error Recovery Techniques

SCSI Manager 4.3 provides a feature called queue freezing that you can use to recover from I/O errors. When a SCSIExecIO request returns an error, the SIM freezes the I/O queue for the LUN that caused the error. You can then issue additional requests with the scsiSIMQHead flag set so that they will be inserted in front of any requests that were already in the queue. You can use this method to perform retries, block remapping, or other error recovery techniques. After inserting your error handling requests, you call the SCSIReleaseQ function to allow the request at the head of the queue to be dispatched. If necessary, multiple requests can be single-stepped by setting the scsiSIMQFreeze flag as well as the scsiSIMQHead flag on each of the requests and following each with a SCSIReleaseQ call.

Note
You can disable queue freezing for a single transaction by setting the scsiSIMQNoFreeze flag. ◆

Optional Features

The following optional features may not be supported by all SIMs. You should use the SCSIBusInquiry function to determine which features are supported by a particular bus.

■ synchronous data transfer

■ target command queuing

■ HBA engine support

■ target mode

■ asynchronous event notification

Writing a SCSI Device Driver

This section provides additional information you need to write a device driver that is compatible with both SCSI Manager 4.3 and the original SCSI Manager.

Loading and Initializing a Driver

During system startup of Macintosh models that do not include SCSI Manager 4.3 in ROM, the Start Manager scans the SCSI bus from SCSI ID 6 to SCSI ID 0, looking for devices that have both an `Apple_HFS` and `Apple_Driver` partition. For each device found, the driver is loaded and executed, and installs itself into the unit table. The driver then places an element in the drive queue for any HFS partitions that are on the drive.

When SCSI Manager 4.3 is present in ROM, the Start Manager loads all SCSI Manager 4.3 drivers from all devices on all registered buses. Drivers that support SCSI Manager 4.3 are identified by the string `Apple_Driver43` in the `pmParType` field of the partition map. Traditional (`Apple_Driver`) drivers are then loaded for any devices on the virtual bus that do not contain a SCSI Manager 4.3 driver.

If SCSI Manager 4.3 is not present in ROM, the Start Manager treats SCSI Manager 4.3 drivers exactly like traditional drivers. Because the Start Manager in earlier Macintosh computers checks only the first 12 characters of the `pmParType` field before loading and executing a driver, both SCSI Manager 4.3 drivers and traditional drivers will load on these models. To initialize the driver, the Start Manager jumps to the first byte of the driver's code (using a `JSR` instruction), with register D5 set to the SCSI ID of the device the driver was loaded from.

SCSI Manager 4.3 drivers contain a second entry point at an offset of 8 bytes from the standard entry. Use of this entry point means that SCSI Manager 4.3 is present and that register D5 contains a device identification record. No other registers are used.

There are seven unit table entries (32 through 38) reserved for SCSI drivers controlling devices at SCSI ID 0 through SCSI ID 6 on the virtual SCSI bus. For compatibility with existing SCSI utility software, drivers serving devices on the virtual bus should continue to install themselves in the unit table locations reserved for traditional SCSI drivers. Drivers for devices that are not on the virtual bus should choose a unit number outside the range reserved for traditional SCSI drivers. See the chapter "Device Manager" in this book for information about installing device drivers in the unit table.

To allow clients to determine whether a driver has been loaded for a particular SCSI device, the XPT maintains a driver registration table. This table cross-references device identification records with driver reference numbers. The device identification record is a SCSI Manager 4.3 data structure that specifies a device by its bus, SCSI ID, and logical unit number. The device identification record is defined by the `DeviceIdent` data type, which is described on page 4-19.

A device identification record can have only one driver reference number associated with it, but a single driver reference number may be registered to multiple devices. You can use the `SCSICreateRefNumXref`, `SCSILookupRefNumXref`, and `SCSIRemoveRefNumXref` functions to access the driver registration table. Drivers loaded through the SCSI Manager 4.3 entry point must use the `SCSICreateRefNumXref` function to register with the XPT. This is done automatically by SCSI Manager 4.3 for traditional drivers.

Selecting a Startup Device

After all device drivers are loaded and initialized, the Start Manager searches for the default startup device in the drive queue. If the device is found, it is mounted and the boot process begins. Macintosh models that do not include SCSI Manager 4.3 in ROM identify the boot drive by a driver reference number stored in PRAM. This works well when drivers retain the same reference number between startups, but SCSI Manager 4.3 drivers allocate unit table entries dynamically if the device they are controlling is not on the virtual bus.

Macintosh models that include SCSI Manager 4.3 in ROM designate the startup device using Slot Manager values in PRAM. Slot number 0 is used for devices on the built-in bus or buses. The `dCtlSlot` and `dCtlSlotId` fields of the driver's device control entry must contain the slot number and sResource ID number, respectively. These are available in the bus inquiry data from the SIM. The `dCtlExtDev` field should contain both the SCSI ID and LUN of the device that the driver is controlling. The high-order 5 bits contain the SCSI ID (up to 31 for a 32-bit wide SCSI bus) and the low-order 3 bits contain the LUN.

Transitions Between SCSI Environments

Because SCSI Manager 4.3 can be installed as a system extension in older Macintosh models, your device driver may be loaded before SCSI Manager 4.3 is active. This can also occur if a NuBus or PDS expansion card loads SCSI Manager 4.3 or an equivalent XPT from the card's ROM. In this case, the expansion card will load a subset of the SCSI Manager 4.3 XPT and a SIM responsible for the card's HBA, but it will not load a SIM for the built-in bus. This creates a situation in which SCSI Manager 4.3 is loaded but some buses may be accessible only through the original interface.

To determine whether to use the SCSI Manager 4.3 interface, your driver should first check for the presence of the `_SCSIAtomic` trap (0xA089). If the trap exists, the driver can pass the SCSI ID of its device to the `SCSIGetVirtualIDInfo` function to get the device identification record of its device. If the `scsiExists` field of the parameter block returns `true`, the device is available through the SCSI Manager 4.3 interface. If the `scsiExists` field returns `false`, the device is on a bus that is not available through SCSI Manager 4.3.

The best time for your driver to perform this check is at the first `accRun` tick, which occurs after all system patches are in place. The Event Manager calls your driver at this time if you set the `dNeedTime` flag in the device control entry. If your driver can access its device through SCSI Manager 4.3, it should allocate and initialize a SCSI I/O parameter block at this time.

Even if your driver is loaded and initialized by a ROM-based SCSI Manager 4.3, you can use the first `accRun` tick to check for new features that may have been installed by a system patch.

Handling Asynchronous Requests

When a client makes a read or write request to a device driver, the Device Manager places the request in the driver's I/O queue. When the driver is ready to accept the request, the Device Manager passes it to the driver's prime routine. The prime routine should fill in a SCSI I/O parameter block with the appropriate values and call the SCSIExecIO function. The XPT passes the parameter block to the proper SIM, which then adds the request to its queue and possibly starts processing it before returning back to the driver.

If the SCSIExecIO function returns noErr, the request was accepted and the contents of the parameter block cannot be reliably viewed by the driver. At this point, virtually nothing can be assumed about the request. It may only have been queued, or it may have proceeded all the way to completion.

IMPORTANT

Once a parameter block is accepted by XPT, do not attempt to examine the parameter block until the completion routine is called. ▲

If SCSIExecIO returns an error result, the request was rejected and the completion routine will not be called. This is usually due to an input parameter error.

Completion routines can execute before the XPT returns to your driver. Because the completion routine may initiate a new request to the driver, it is possible that by the time control returns to the calling function, the parameter block is being used for a completely different transaction.

Asynchronous I/O requests from a client to a device driver can occur at interrupt time. Because you cannot allocate memory at interrupt time, you must reserve memory for parameter blocks, scatter/gather lists, and any other structures you need when the driver is initialized. You cannot use the stack for this purpose (as you can for synchronous requests) because parameters on the stack are discarded when the device driver returns from its prime routine.

Asynchronous requests may start at any time and may end at any time. There is no implied ordering of requests with respect to when they were issued. An earlier request may start later, or a later request may complete earlier. However, a series of requests to the same device (bus number, target ID, and LUN) is issued to that device in the order received (unless the scsiSIMQHead flag is set in the scsiFlags field of the SCSI I/O parameter block, in which case the request is inserted at the head of the queue).

Handling Immediate Requests

If your device driver supports immediate requests, it must be reentrant. The Device Manager neither sets nor checks the drvrActive flag in the dCtlFlags field of the device control entry before making an immediate request. Asynchronous operation makes it even more likely that an immediate request will happen when your driver is busy because the immediate request may have been made from application time while your driver was asynchronous. When this happens you need to be careful not to reuse parameter blocks or other variables that might be busy.

Virtual Memory Compatibility

Because page faults can occur while interrupts are disabled, SCSI device drivers can receive synchronous I/O requests from the Virtual Memory Manager when the processor interrupt level is not 0. The SCSI Manager handles the resulting SCSI transaction without the benefit of interrupts. This requires that all synchronous wait loops be performed either in the SCSI Manager or in the Device Manager, where code is provided to poll the SCSI interrupt sources.

When your driver receives a synchronous I/O request, it can issue the subsequent SCSI I/O request synchronously as well, or it can issue the SCSI request asynchronously and return to the Device Manager. This second option is generally preferred because it simplifies driver design. The Device Manager waits for the synchronous request to complete, allowing your driver to handle it asynchronously. The driver should jump to IODone after it receives the SCSI completion callback. If a single driver request translates to multiple SCSI requests, and your driver handles them asynchronously, the driver should not call IODone until after the callbacks for all of the SCSI requests have been received.

IMPORTANT

Because SCSI completion routines must not cause a page fault, all code and data used by SCSI completion routines must be held in real memory. This is automatic for device drivers loaded in the system heap. Applications (or drivers within applications) must use the HoldMemory function to ensure their completion routine code and data is held. See the chapter "Virtual Memory Manager" in *Inside Macintosh: Memory* for more information. ▲

Writing a SCSI Interface Module

This section provides additional information that HBA developers need to write a SCSI interface module.

SIM Initialization and Operation

When SCSI Manager 4.3 is present in ROM, the Start Manager loads any SIM drivers it finds in the declaration ROM of all installed expansion cards. A SIM driver may contain the actual SIM, or it may contain code to load the SIM from some other location (such as a device attached to the expansion card). The Start Manager searches for SIM drivers using the Slot Manager `SNextTypeSRsrc` function, and loads all drivers matching the following criteria:

sResource type	Constant	Value
spCatagory	CatIntBus	12
spCType	TypSIM	12
spDrvrSW	DrvrSwScsi43	1

After loading a SIM driver, the Start Manager calls the driver's open routine. If the SIM is contained in the driver, it should register itself with the XPT at this time. If the registration is successful, the open routine should return `noErr`. If the open routine returns an error result, the Start Manager removes the driver from the unit table and releases it from memory. A SIM loader can use this technique to remove itself after loading and registering the actual SIM. Because no other driver entry points are used, you do not need to implement the close, prime, status, or control routines, but they should return appropriate errors.

For Macintosh models that do not include SCSI Manager 4.3 in ROM, your SIM can either provide its own temporary XPT or wait until SCSI Manager 4.3 is installed by the system before registering with the XPT. If you wait for SCSI Manager 4.3 to load, devices on your bus cannot be used as the boot device or as the paging device for virtual memory but can be mounted after SCSI Manager 4.3 is running and your bus is registered.

If your SIM supplies its own XPT, your SIM and XPT must be prepared for the possibility that a system patch will install a new XPT later. To provide a consistent environment for driver clients of your SIM when the XPT is replaced, your XPT must maintain information about any virtual ID numbers it assigns (including a driver registration table) and correctly fill in the XPT fields of the bus inquiry record. When the SCSI Manager4.3 XPT loads, it uses the `SCSIGetVirtualIDInfo`, `SCSILookupRefNumXref`, and `SCSIBusInquiry` functions to query your XPT, then calls the `SetTrapAddress` function to install itself. Next, it uses your XPT to send a `SCSIRegisterWithNewXPT` command to each registered SIM. A SIM must respond by using the `SCSIReregisterBus` function to export its assigned bus number, entry points, and static data storage pointer to the new XPT. Finally, the SCSI Manager 4.3 XPT calls your XPT with a `SCSIKillXPT` command. Your XPT should then release any memory it has allocated and remove or disable any patches it may have installed.

Your XPT must reserve bus number 0 for the built-in SCSI bus. For Macintosh computers with dual SCSI buses, you must reserve bus numbers 0 and 1. If the SCSI Manager 4.3 XPT is installed after your XPT, it will assign these bus numbers to the built-in buses.

After determining the presence of the XPT, a SIM should register itself using the `SCSIRegisterBus` function. The SIM initialization record for this request contains the SIM's function entry points, required static data storage size, and the `oldCallCapable` status of the SIM. The SIM initialization record, defined by the `SIMInitInfo` data type, is shown on page 4-36. The XPT allocates the requested number of bytes for the SIM's static storage, fills in the appropriate fields of the SIM initialization record, and then calls the SIM's `SIMInit` function. If the `SIMInit` function returns `noErr`, the XPT completes the registration process, making the SIM available to the system. If `SIMInit` returns an error, the registration request fails.

Once the registration is complete, the XPT makes calls to the `SIMAction` entry point whenever a `SCSIAction` request is received that is destined for this bus. The XPT passes a pointer to the parameter block and a pointer to the SIM's static storage to the `SIMAction` function. The SIM should parse the parameter block for illegal or unsupported parameters and return an error result if necessary. After queuing the request, the `SIMAction` function should return to the XPT. When the request completes, the SIM calls the XPT's `MakeCallback` function with the appropriate parameter block. The XPT then calls the client's completion routine.

Other types of requests should be implemented to conform to the function descriptions provided in this chapter. Functions or features not implemented by the SIM should return appropriate errors (for example, `scsiFunctionNotAvailable` or `scsiProvideFail`).

The `SIMInteruptPoll` function is called during the Device Manager's synchronous wait loop to give time to the SIM when interrupts are masked. The sole parameter is a pointer to the SIM's static data, which is passed on the stack. Because this call does not imply the presence of an interrupt, the SIM should check for interrupts before proceeding.

The `EnteringSIM` and `ExitingSIM` functions provide compatibility with the Virtual Memory Manager and should be called every time the SIM is entered and exited, respectively. In other words, these two function calls should surround all SIM entry and exit points, including interrupt handlers and callbacks to client code made through the `MakeCallback` function.

Parameter blocks must appear to the client to be queued on a per-LUN basis, because queue freezing and unfreezing are performed one LUN at a time. The actual implementation may vary as long as this appearance is maintained.

Supporting the Original SCSI Manager

If your SIM indicates that it is capable of supporting original SCSI Manager functions, the XPT adds it to the list of buses that are searched when a `SCSISelect` request is received.

The XPT is responsible for converting original SCSI Manager functions into the proper format and submitting them to the SIM. It also receives the results for each of the functions from the SIM and returns them to the client.

When it receives a SCSIGet request, the XPT simply notes that the call was made by setting an internal flag, then returns to the caller. In response to a SCSISelect request, the XPT generates a SCSIOldCall request and submits it to the SIM's SIMAction entry point. The scsiDevice field of the parameter block contains the bus number of the SIM, the target ID specified in the SCSISelect request, and a LUN of 0. This parameter block should be queued like any other.

When your SIM receives a SCSIOldCall request, it should attempt to select the device and return a result code to the XPT in the scsiOldCallResult field of the parameter block (scsiRequestComplete if successful and scsiSelectTimeout if not). Intermediate function results are not communicated through the scsiResult field because this would be interpreted as completion of the entire transaction rather than only the portion of the transaction resulting from a single original function. As subsequent original function calls are made, the XPT fills in the appropriate fields of the parameter block and calls the SIM's NewOldCall entry point. Table 4-1 shows the original function parameters and the fields that are filled in by the XPT.

Table 4-1   Original SCSI Manager parameter conversion

Function	Parameter	Direction	Parameter block field	Notes
SCSIGet				XPT handles internally.
SCSISelect	targetID	→	scsiDevice	bus set by XPT, LUN = 0.
SCSICmd	buffer	→	scsiCDB	Field is a pointer.
	count	→	scsiCDBLength	
SCSIRead, SCSIWrite, SCSIRBlind, SCSIWBlind	tibPtr	→	scsiDataPtr	Field is a pointer.
SCSIComplete	stat	←	scsiSCSIstatus	Field contains status.
	message	←	scsiSCSImessage	Field contains message.
	wait	→	scsiTimeout	Time in Time Manager format.
SCSIMsgIn	message	←	scsiSCSImessage	Field contains message.
SCSIMsgOut	message	→	scsiSCSImessage	Field contains message.
SCSIReset				Translated to SCSIResetBus.
SCSIStat				XPT handles internally.

To provide the highest level of compatibility with the original SCSI Manager, a SIM should be able to perform a SCSI arbitration and select process independently of a SCSI message-out or command phase. A SIM that requires the CDB or message-out bytes in order to perform a select operation will be unable to execute the SCSISelect function properly, and must always return `noErr` to a `SCSISelect` request. This can create a false indication of the presence of a device at a SCSI ID, causing all future `SCSISelect` requests to that SCSI ID to be directed only to that bus. Devices installed on buses that registered after that bus would not be accessible through the original interface.

Handshaking of Blind Transfers

Handshaking instructions are used to prevent bus errors when a target fails to deliver the next byte within the processor bus error timeout period. This timeout is 250 milliseconds for the Macintosh SE and 16 microseconds for all Macintosh models since the Macintosh II.

The SCSI Manager 4.3 SIM requires this handshaking information for blind transfers when DMA is not available. Your SIM does not need to pay attention to the `scsiHandshake` field unless your hardware requires it.

Supporting DMA

DMA typically requires that the data buffer affected by the transfer be locked (so that the physical address does not change) and that it be non-cacheable. SCSI Manager 4.3 provides an improved version of the `LockMemory` function, which you can call at interrupt time as long as the affected pages are already held in real memory. You can also call the `GetPhysical` function at interrupt time, but only on pages that are locked.

Loading Drivers

The Start Manager is normally responsible for loading SCSI drivers. However, if the startup device specified in PRAM is on a third-party HBA and the SIM is a Slot Manager device, the Start Manager will call the boot record of the card's declaration ROM. The boot record code should examine the `dCtlExtDev` field to determine which SCSI device is the startup device and then load a driver from that device (and only that device).

All other drivers are loaded by the Start Manager, but SIMs are given the opportunity to override this if necessary. Before the Start Manager attempts to load a driver from a device, it calls the SIM with a `SCSILoadDriver` request. If the function succeeds, the Start Manager does nothing further with that device. If the function fails (the normal case), the Start Manager reads the partition map on the device and loads a driver from it. If this fails, the Start Manager calls the SIM again with a `SCSILoadDriver` request, this time with the `scsiDiskLoadFailed` parameter set to indicate that no driver was available on the media.

This facility allows a SIM to provide a default driver to be used instead of any driver that may be on the device. For example, if a SIM does support the original SCSI Manager, it can use the second `SCSILoadDriver` request to load a SCSI Manager 4.3-compatible driver if none is present on the device.

SCSI Manager 4.3 Reference

This section describes the data structures, functions, and constants that are specific to SCSI Manager 4.3.

The "Data Structures" section shows the C declarations for the data structures defined by SCSI Manager 4.3.

The "SCSI Manager 4.3 Functions" section describes the functions you use to communicate with SCSI devices, the functions that a SIM uses to communicate with the XPT, and the functions a SIM must include in order to be compatible with SCSI Manager 4.3.

Data Structures

This section describes the parameter blocks you use to communicate with the SCSI Manager and the data structures you use to define values within them.

IMPORTANT

Always set unused or reserved fields to 0 before passing a parameter block to any of the SCSI Manager 4.3 functions. ▲

Simple Data Types

SCSI Manager 4.3 uses these simple data types:

```
typedef char     SInt8;
typedef short    SInt16;
typedef long     SInt32;
typedef unsigned char   UInt8;
typedef unsigned short  UInt16;
typedef unsigned long   UInt32;
```

Device Identification Record

You use the device identification record to specify a target device by its bus, SCSI ID, and logical unit number (LUN). The device identification record is defined by the `DeviceIdent` data type.

```
struct DeviceIdent
{
    UInt8    diReserved;
    UInt8    bus;
    UInt8    targetID;
    UInt8    LUN;
};
typedef struct DeviceIdent DeviceIdent;
```

Field descriptions

bus	The bus number of the SIM/HBA for the target device.
targetID	The SCSI ID number of the target device.
LUN	The target LUN, or 0 if the device does not support logical units.

Command Descriptor Block Record

You use the command descriptor block record to pass SCSI commands to the SCSIAction function. The SCSI commands can be stored within this structure, or you can provide a pointer to them. You set the scsiCDBIsPointer flag in the SCSI parameter block if this record contains a pointer.

The command descriptor block record is defined by the CDB data type.

```
union CDB
{
    UInt8     *cdbPtr;
    UInt8     cdbBytes[maxCDBLength];
};
typedef union CDB CDB, *CDBPtr;
```

Field descriptions

cdbPtr	A pointer to a buffer containing a CDB.
cdbBytes	A buffer in which you can place a CDB.

Scatter/Gather List Element

You use scatter/gather lists to specify the data buffers to be used for a transfer. A scatter/gather list consists of one or more elements, each of which describes the location and size of one buffer.

The scatter/gather list element is defined by the SGRecord data type.

```
struct SGRecord
{
    Ptr       SGAddr;
    SInt32    SGCount;
};
typedef struct SGRecord SGRecord;
```

Field descriptions

SGAddr	A pointer to a data buffer.
SGCount	The size of the data buffer, in bytes.

SCSI Manager Parameter Block Header

You use the SCSI Manager parameter block to pass information to the `SCSIAction` function. Because many of the functions that you access through `SCSIAction` require additional information, the parameter block consists of a common header (`SCSIPBHdr`) followed by function-specific fields, if any. This section describes the parameter block header common to all `SCSIAction` functions. The function-specific extensions are described in the following sections.

The SCSI Manager parameter block header is defined by the `SCSI_PB` data type.

```
#define SCSIPBHdr                       \
    struct    SCSIHdr *qLink;          \
    SInt16    scsiReserved1;           \
    UInt16    scsiPBLength;            \
    UInt8     scsiFunctionCode;        \
    UInt8     scsiReserved2;           \
    OSErr     scsiResult;              \
    DeviceIdent scsiDevice;            \
    CallbackProc scsiCompletion;\
    UInt32    scsiFlags;               \
    UInt8     *scsiDriverStorage;\
    Ptr       scsiXPTprivate;          \
    SInt32    scsiReserved3;

struct SCSI_PB
{
    SCSIPBHdr
};
typedef struct SCSI_PB SCSI_PB;
```

Field descriptions

qLink   A pointer to the next entry in the request queue. This field is used internally by the SCSI Manager and must be set to 0 when the parameter block is initialized. The SCSI Manager functions always set this field to 0 before returning, so you do not need to set it to 0 again before reusing a parameter block.

scsiPBLength   The size of the parameter block, in bytes, including the parameter block header.

scsiFunctionCode
                      A function selector code that specifies the service being requested. Table 4-2 on page 4-39 lists these codes.

scsiResult   The result code returned by the XPT or SIM when the function completes. The value `scsiRequestInProgress` indicates that the request is still in progress or queued.

scsiDevice | A 4-byte value that uniquely identifies the target device for a request. The DeviceIdent data type designates the bus number, target SCSI ID, and logical unit number (LUN).

scsiCompletion | A pointer to a completion routine.

scsiFlags | Flags indicating the transfer direction and any special handling required for this request.

scsiDirectionMask

A bit field that specifies transfer direction, using these constants:

scsiDirectionIn | Data in
scsiDirectionOut | Data out
scsiDirectionNone | No data phase expected

scsiDisableAutosense

Disable the automatic REQUEST SENSE feature.

scsiCDBLinked

The parameter block contains a linked CDB. This option may not be supported by all SIMs.

scsiQEnable | Enable target queue actions. This option may not be supported by all SIMs.

scsiCDBIsPointer

Set if the scsiCDB field of a SCSI I/O parameter block contains a pointer. If clear, the scsiCDB field contains the actual CDB. In either case, the scsiCDBLength field contains the number of bytes in the SCSI command descriptor block.

scsiInitiateSyncData

Set if the SIM should attempt to initiate a synchronous data transfer by sending the SDTR message. If successful, the device normally remains in the synchronous transfer mode until it is reset or until you specify asynchronous mode by setting the scsiDisableSyncData flag. Because SDTR negotiation occurs every time this flag is set, you should set it only when negotiation is actually needed.

scsiDisableSyncData

Disable synchronous data transfer. The SIM sends an SDTR message with a REQ/ACK offset of 0 to indicate asynchronous data transfer mode. You should set this flag only when negotiation is actually needed.

scsiSIMQHead | Place the parameter block at the head of the SIM queue. This can be used to insert error handling at the head of a frozen queue.

scsiSIMQFreeze

Freeze the SIM queue after completing this transaction. See "Error Recovery Techniques" on page 4-10 for information about using this flag.

scsiSIMQNoFreeze
    Disable SIM queue freezing for this transaction.

scsiDoDisconnect
    Explicitly allow device to disconnect.

scsiDontDisconnect
    Explicitly prohibit device disconnection. If this flag
    and the scsiDoDisconnect flag are both 0, the
    SIM determines whether to allow or prohibit
    disconnection, based on performance criteria.

scsiDataReadyForDMA
    Data buffer is locked and non-cacheable.

scsiDataPhysical
    Data buffer address is physical.

scsiSensePhysical
    Autosense data pointer is physical.

scsiDriverStorage
    A pointer to the device driver's private storage. This field is not
    affected or used by the SCSI Manager.

SCSI I/O Parameter Block

You use the SCSI I/O parameter block to pass information to the SCSIExecIO function.
The SCSI I/O parameter block is defined by the SCSIExecIOPB data type.

```
#define SCSI_IO_Macro \
    SCSIPBHdr                                          \
    UInt16          scsiResultFlags;                   \
    UInt16          scsiReserved12;                    \
    UInt8           *scsiDataPtr;                      \
    SInt32          scsiDataLength;                    \
    UInt8           *scsiSensePtr;                     \
    SInt8           scsiSenseLength;                   \
    UInt8           scsiCDBLength;                     \
    UInt16          scsiSGListCount;                   \
    UInt32          scsiReserved4;                     \
    UInt8           scsiSCSIstatus;                    \
    SInt8           scsiSenseResidual;                 \
    UInt16          scsiReserved5;                     \
    SInt32          scsiDataResidual;                  \
    CDB             scsiCDB;                           \
    SInt32          scsiTimeout;                       \
    UInt8           *scsiReserved13;                   \
    UInt16          scsiReserved14;                    \
    UInt16          scsiIOFlags;                       \
    UInt8           scsiTagAction;                     \
```

```
        UInt8           scsiReserved6;              \
        UInt16          scsiReserved7;              \
        UInt16          scsiSelectTimeout;          \
        UInt8           scsiDataType;               \
        UInt8           scsiTransferType;           \
        UInt32          scsiReserved8;              \
        UInt32          scsiReserved9;              \
        UInt16          scsiHandshake[8];           \
        UInt32          scsiReserved10;             \
        UInt32          scsiReserved11;             \
        struct SCSI_IO  *scsiCommandLink;           \
        UInt8           scsiSIMpublics[8];          \
        UInt8           scsiAppleReserved6[8];      \
        UInt16          scsiCurrentPhase;           \
        SInt16          scsiSelector;               \
        OSErr           scsiOldCallResult;          \
        UInt8           scsiSCSImessage;            \
        UInt8           XPTprivateFlags;            \
        UInt8           XPTextras[12];

struct SCSI_IO
{
    SCSI_IO_Macro
};
typedef struct SCSI_IO SCSI_IO;
typedef SCSI_IO SCSIExecIOPB;
```

Field descriptions

SCSIPBHdr   A macro that includes the SCSI Manager parameter block header, described on page 4-21.

scsiResultFlags

Output flags that modify the scsiResult field.

scsiSIMQFrozen

The SIM queue for this LUN is frozen because of an error. You must call the SCSIReleaseQ function to release the queue and resume processing requests.

scsiAutosenseValid

An automatic REQUEST SENSE was performed after this I/O because of a CHECK CONDITION status message from the device. The data contained in the scsiSensePtr buffer is valid.

scsiBusNotFree

The SCSI Manager was unable to clear the bus after an error. You may need to call the SCSIResetBus function to restore operation.

scsiDataPtr   A pointer to a data buffer or scatter/gather list. You specify the data type using the `scsiDataType` field.

scsiDataLength   The amount of data to be transferred, in bytes.

scsiSensePtr   A pointer to the autosense data buffer. If autosense is enabled (the `scsiDisableAutosense` flag is not set), the SCSI Manager returns REQUEST SENSE information in this buffer.

scsiSenseLength   The size of the autosense data buffer, in bytes.

scsiCDBLength   The length of the SCSI command descriptor block, in bytes.

scsiSGListCount   The number of elements in the scatter/gather list.

scsiSCSIstatus   The status returned by the SCSI device.

scsiSenseResidual

                  The automatic REQUEST SENSE residual length (that is, the number of bytes that were expected but not transferred). This number is negative if extra bytes had to be transferred to force the target off of the bus.

scsiDataResidual

                  The data transfer residual length (that is, the number of bytes that were expected but not transferred). This number is negative if extra bytes had to be transferred to force the target off the bus.

scsiCDB   This field can contain either the actual CDB or a pointer to the CDB. You set the `scsiCDBIsPointer` flag if this field contains a pointer.

scsiTimeout   The length of time the SIM should allow before reporting a timeout of the SCSI bus. The time value is represented in Time Manager format (positive values for milliseconds, negative values for microseconds). The timer is started when the I/O request is sent to the target. If the request does not complete within the specified time, the SIM attempts to issue an ABORT message, either by reselecting the device or by asserting the attention (/ATN) signal. A value of 0 specifies the default timeout for the SIM. The default timeout for the SCSI Manager 4.3 SIM is infinite (that is, no timeout).

scsiIOFlags   Additional I/O flags describing the data transfer.

                  scsiNoParityCheck
                                    Disable parity error detection for this transaction.

                  scsiDisableSelectWAtn
                                    Do not send the IDENTIFY message for LUN selection. The LUN is still required in the `scsiDevice` field so that the request can be placed in the proper queue. The LUN field in the CDB is untouched. The purpose is to provide compatibility with older devices that do not support this aspect of the SCSI-2 specification.

                  scsiSavePtrOnDisconnect
                                    Perform a SAVE DATA POINTER operation automatically in response to a DISCONNECT message from the target. The purpose of this flag is to provide compatibility with devices that do not properly implement this aspect of the SCSI-2 specification.

scsiNoBucketIn

> Prohibit bit-bucketing during the data-in phase of the transaction. **Bit-bucketing** is the practice of throwing away excess data bytes when a target tries to supply more data than the initiator expects. For example, if the CDB requests more data than you specified in the scsiDataLength field, the SCSI Manager normally throws away the excess and returns the scsiDataRunError result code. If this flag is set, the SCSI Manager refuses any extra data, terminates the I/O request, and leaves the bus in the data-in phase. You must reset the bus to restore operation. This flag is intended only for debugging purposes.

scsiNoBucketOut

> Prohibit bit-bucketing during the data-out phase of the transaction. If a target requests more data than you specified in the scsiDataLength field, the SCSI Manager normally sends an arbitrary number of meaningless bytes (0xEE) until the target releases the bus. If this flag is set, the SCSI Manager terminates the I/O request when the last byte is sent and leaves the bus in the data-out phase. You must reset the bus to restore operation. This flag is intended only for debugging purposes.

scsiDisableWide

> Disable wide data transfer negotiation for this transaction if it had been previously enabled. This option may not be supported by all SIMs.

scsiInitiateWide

> Attempt wide data transfer negotiation for this transaction if it is not already enabled. This option may not be supported by all SIMs.

scsiRenegotiateSense

> Attempt to renegotiate synchronous or wide transfers before issuing a REQUEST SENSE. This is necessary when the error was caused by problems operating in synchronous or wide transfer mode. It is optional because some devices flush sense data after performing negotiation.

scsiTagAction   Reserved.

scsiSelectTimeout

> An optional SELECT timeout value, in milliseconds. The default is 250 ms, as specified by SCSI-2. The accuracy of this period is dependent on the HBA. A value of 0 specifies the default timeout. Some SIMs ignore this parameter and always use a value of 250 ms.

scsiDataType   The data type pointed to by the `scsiDataPtr` field. You specify the type using one of the following constants:

> **scsiDataBuffer**
>> The `scsiDataPtr` field contains a pointer to a contiguous data buffer, and the `scsiDataLength` field contains the length of the buffer, in bytes.
>
> **scsiDataSG**   The `scsiDataPtr` field contains a pointer to a scatter/gather list. The `scsiDataLength` field contains the total number of bytes to be transferred, and the `scsiSGListCount` field contains the number of elements in the scatter/gather list.
>
> **scsiDataTIB**   The `scsiDataPtr` field contains a pointer to a transfer instruction block. This is used by the XPT during original SCSI Manager emulation, when communicating with a SIM that supports this.

scsiTransferType

> The type of transfer mode to use during the data phase. You specify the type using one of the following constants:
>
> **scsiTransferBlind**
>> Use DMA, if available; otherwise, perform a blind transfer using the handshaking information contained in the `scsiHandshake` field.
>
> **scsiTransferPolled**
>> Use polled transfer mode. The `scsiHandshake` field is not required for this mode.

scsiHandshake[8]

> Handshaking instructions for blind transfers, consisting of an array of word values, terminated by 0. The SIM polls for data ready after transferring the amount of data specified in each successive `scsiHandshake` entry. When it encounters a 0 value, the SIM starts over at the beginning of the list. Handshaking always starts from the beginning of the list every time a device transitions to data phase. See "Handshaking Instructions," beginning on page 4-9, for more information.

scsiCommandLink

> A pointer to a linked parameter block. This field provides support for SCSI linked commands. This optional feature ensures that a set of commands sent to a device are executed in sequential order without interference from other applications. You create a list of commands using this pointer to link additional parameter blocks. Each parameter block except the last should have the `scsiCDBLinked` flag set in the `scsiFlags` field. A `CHECK CONDITION` status from the device will abort linked command execution. Linked commands may not be supported by all SIMs.

scsiSIMpublics[8]

> An additional input field available for use by SIM developers.

scsiCurrentPhase

> The current SCSI bus phase reported by the SIM after handling an original SCSI Manager function. This field is used only by the XPT and SIM during original SCSI Manager emulation. The phases are defined by the following constant values:

```
enum {
    kDataOutPhase,
    kDataInPhase,
    kCommandPhase,
    kStatusPhase,
    kPhaseIllegal0,
    kPhaseIllegal1,
    kMessageOutPhase,
    kMessageInPhase,
    kBusFreePhase,
    kArbitratePhase,
    kSelectPhase
};
```

scsiSelector

> The function selector code that was passed to the _SCSIDispatch trap during original SCSI Manager emulation. The SIM uses this field to determine which original SCSI Manager function to perform.

scsiOldCallResult

> The result code from an emulated original SCSI Manager function. The SIM returns results to all original SCSI Manager functions in this field, except for the SCSIComplete result, which it returns in scsiResult.

scsiSCSIMessage The message byte returned by an emulated SCSIComplete function. This field is only used by the XPT and SIM during original SCSI Manager emulation.

XPTprivateFlags Reserved.

XPTextras[12]   Reserved.

SCSI Bus Inquiry Parameter Block

You use the SCSI bus inquiry parameter block with the SCSIBusInquiry function to get information about a bus. The SCSI bus inquiry parameter block is defined by the SCSIBusInquiryPB data type.

```
struct SCSIBusInquiryPB
{
    SCSIPBHdr
    UInt16    scsiEngineCount;
    UInt16    scsiMaxTransferType;
    UInt32    scsiDataTypes;
```

```
    UInt16    scsiIOpbSize;
    UInt16    scsiMaxIOpbSize;
    UInt32    scsiFeatureFlags;
    UInt8     scsiVersionNumber;
    UInt8     scsiHBAInquiry;
    UInt8     scsiTargetModeFlags;
    UInt8     scsiScanFlags;
    UInt32    scsiSIMPrivatesPtr;
    UInt32    scsiSIMPrivatesSize;
    UInt32    scsiAsyncFlags;
    UInt8     scsiHiBusID;
    UInt8     scsiInitiatorID;
    UInt16    scsiBIReserved0;
    UInt32    scsiBIReserved1;
    UInt32    scsiFlagsSupported;
    UInt16    scsiIOFlagsSupported;
    UInt16    scsiWeirdStuff;
    UInt16    scsiMaxTarget;
    UInt16    scsiMaxLUN;
    SInt8     scsiSIMVendor[16];
    SInt8     scsiHBAVendor[16];
    SInt8     scsiControllerFamily[16];
    SInt8     scsiControllerType[16];
    SInt8     scsiXPTversion[4];
    SInt8     scsiSIMversion[4];
    SInt8     scsiHBAversion[4];
    UInt8     scsiHBAslotType;
    UInt8     scsiHBAslotNumber;
    UInt16    scsiSIMsRsrcID;
    UInt16    scsiBIReserved3;
    UInt16    scsiAdditionalLength;
};
typedef struct SCSIBusInquiryPB SCSIBusInquiryPB;
```

Field descriptions

SCSIPBHdr   A macro that includes the SCSI Manager parameter block header,
                   described on page 4-21.

scsiEngineCount
                   The number of engines on the HBA. This value is 0 for a built-in
                   SCSI bus. See the CAM specification for information about HBA
                   engines.

scsiMaxTransferType
                   The number of data transfer types available on the HBA.

scsiDataTypes   A bit mask describing the data types supported by the SIM/HBA.
Bits 3 through 15 and bit 31 are reserved by Apple Computer, Inc.
Bits 16 through 30 are available for use by SIM developers. The
following bits are currently defined. These types correspond to the
scsiDataType field of the SCSI I/O parameter block.

```
enum {
    scsiBusDataBuffer    = 0x00000001,
    scsiBusDataTIB       = 0x00000002,
    scsiBusDataSG        = 0x00000004,
    /* bits 3 to 15 are reserved by Apple */
    /* bits 16 to 30 are available for 3rd parties */
    scsiBusDataReserved  = 0x80000000
};
```

scsiIOpbSize   The minimum size of a SCSI I/O parameter block for this SIM.

scsiMaxIOpbSize The minimum size of a SCSI I/O parameter block for all currently
registered SIMs. That is, the largest registered scsiIOpbSize.

scsiFeatureFlags
These flags describe various physical characteristics of the SCSI bus.

scsiBusInternal
                 The bus is at least partly internal to the computer.

scsiBusExternal
                 The bus extends outside of the computer.

scsiBusInternalExternal
                 The bus is both internal and external.

scsiBusInternalExternalUnknown
                 The internal/external state of the bus is unknown.

scsiBusCacheCoherentDMA
                 DMA is cache coherent.

scsiBusOldCallCapable
                 The SIM supports the original SCSI Manager
                 interface.

scsiBusDifferential
                 The bus uses a differential SCSI interface.

scsiBusFastSCSI
                 The bus supports SCSI-2 fast data transfers.

scsiBusDMAavailable
                 DMA is available.

scsiVersionNumber
                 The version number of the SIM/HBA.

scsiHBAInquiry   Flags describing the capabilities of the bus.

> scsiBusMDP   Supports the MODIFY DATA POINTER message.
>
> scsiBusWide32   Supports 32-bit wide transfers.
>
> scsiBusWide16   Supports 16-bit wide transfers.
>
> scsiBusSDTR   Supports synchronous transfers.
>
> scsiBusLinkedCDB
> Supports linked commands.
>
> scsiBusTagQ   Supports tagged queuing.
>
> scsiBusSoftReset
> Supports soft reset.

scsiTargetModeFlags
Reserved.

scsiScanFlags   Reserved.

scsiSIMPrivatesPtr
A pointer to the SIM's private storage.

scsiSIMPrivatesSize
The size of the SIM's private storage, in bytes.

scsiAsyncFlags   Reserved.

scsiHiBusID   The highest bus number currently registered with the XPT. If no buses are registered, this field contains 0xFF (the ID of the XPT).

scsiInitiatorID
The SCSI ID of the HBA. This value is 7 for a built-in SCSI bus.

scsiFlagsSupported
A bit mask that defines which scsiFlags bits are supported.

scsiIOFlagsSupported
A bit mask that defines which scsiIOFlags bits are supported.

scsiWeirdStuff   Flags that identify unusual aspects of a SIM's operation.

> scsiOddDisconnectUnsafeRead1
> Indicates that a disconnect or other phase change on a odd byte boundary during a read operation will result in inaccurate residual counts or data loss. If your device can disconnect on odd bytes, use polled transfers instead of blind.
>
> scsiOddDisconnectUnsafeWrite1
> Indicates that a disconnect or other phase change on a odd byte boundary during a write operation will result in inaccurate residual counts or data loss. If your device can disconnect on odd bytes, use polled transfers instead of blind.
>
> scsiBusErrorsUnsafe
> Indicates that a delay of more than 16 microseconds or a phase change during a blind transfer on a non-handshaked boundary may cause a system crash. If you cannot predict where delays or disconnects will occur, use polled transfers.

scsiRequiresHandshake
Indicates that a delay of more than 16 microseconds or a phase change during a blind transfer on a non-handshaked boundary may result in inaccurate residual counts or data loss. If you cannot predict where delays or disconnects will occur, use polled transfers.

scsiTargetDrivenSDTRSafe
Indicates that the SIM supports target-initiated synchronous data transfer negotiation. If your device supports this feature and this bit is not set, you must set the scsiDisableSelectWAtn flag in the scsiIOFlags field.

scsiMaxTarget   The highest SCSI ID value supported by the HBA.

scsiMaxLUN   The highest logical unit number supported by the HBA.

scsiSIMVendor[16]
An ASCII text string that identifies the SIM vendor. This field returns 'Apple Computer' for a built-in SCSI bus.

scsiHBAVendor[16]
An ASCII text string that identifies the HBA vendor. This field returns 'Apple Computer' for a built-in SCSI bus.

scsiControllerFamily[16]
An optional ASCII text string that identifies the family of parts to which the SCSI controller chip belongs. This information is provided at the discretion of the HBA vendor.

scsiControllerType[16]
An optional ASCII text string that identifies the specific type of SCSI controller chip. This information is provided at the discretion of the HBA vendor.

scsiXPTversion[4]
An ASCII text string that identifies the version number of the XPT. You should use the other fields of this parameter block to check for specific features, rather than relying on this value.

scsiSIMversion[4]
An ASCII text string that identifies the version number of the SIM. You should use the other fields of this parameter block to check for specific features, rather than relying on this value.

scsiHBAversion[4]
An ASCII text string that identifies the version number of the HBA. You should use the other fields of this parameter block to check for specific features, rather than relying on this value.

scsiHBAslotType   The slot type, if any, used by this HBA. You specify the type using one of the following constants:

scsiMotherboardBus
A built-in SCSI bus.

scsiNuBus   A NuBus slot.

scsiPDSBus   A processor-direct slot.

scsiHBAslotNumber

The slot number for the SIM. Device drivers should copy this value into the dCtlSlot field of the device control entry. This value is 0 for a built-in SCSI bus.

scsiSIMsRsrcID   The sResource ID for the SIM. Device drivers should copy this value into the dCtlSlotID field of the device control entry. This value is 0 for a built-in SCSI bus.

scsiAdditionalLength

The additional size of this parameter block, in bytes. If this structure includes extra fields to return additional information, this field contains the number of additional bytes.

SCSI Abort Command Parameter Block

You use the SCSI abort command parameter block to identify the SCSI I/O parameter block to be canceled by the SCSIAbortCommand function. The SCSI abort command parameter block is defined by the SCSIAbortCommandPB data type.

```
struct SCSIAbortCommandPB
{
    SCSIPBHdr
    SCSI_IO * scsiIOptr;
};
typedef struct SCSIAbortCommandPB SCSIAbortCommandPB;
```

Field descriptions

SCSIPBHdr   A macro that includes the SCSI Manager parameter block header, described on page 4-21.

scsiIOptr   A pointer to the parameter block to be canceled.

SCSI Terminate I/O Parameter Block

You use the SCSI terminate I/O parameter block to identify the SCSI I/O parameter block to be canceled by the SCSITerminateIO function. The SCSI terminate I/O parameter block is defined by the SCSITerminateIOPB data type.

```
struct SCSITerminateIOPB
{
    SCSIPBHdr
    SCSI_IO * scsiIOptr;
};
typedef struct SCSITerminateIOPB SCSITerminateIOPB;
```

Field descriptions

SCSIPBHdr   A macro that includes the SCSI Manager parameter block header, described on page 4-21.

scsiIOptr   A pointer to the parameter block to be canceled.

SCSI Virtual ID Information Parameter Block

You use the SCSI virtual ID information parameter block with the
SCSIGetVirtualIDInfo function to get the device identification record for a device
on the virtual bus. The SCSI virtual ID information parameter block is defined by
the SCSIGetVirtualIDInfoPB data type.

```
struct SCSIGetVirtualIDInfoPB
{
    SCSIPBHdr
    UInt16    scsiOldCallID;
    Boolean   scsiExists;
};
typedef struct SCSIGetVirtualIDInfoPB SCSIGetVirtualIDInfoPB;
```

Field descriptions

SCSIPBHdr   A macro that includes the SCSI Manager parameter block header,
                   described on page 4-21. The device information record is returned
                   in the scsiDevice field of the parameter block header.

scsiOldCallID   The virtual SCSI ID of the device you are searching for.

scsiExists   The XPT returns true in this field if the scsiDevice field contains
                   a valid device identification record.

SCSI Load Driver Parameter Block

The Start Manager uses this parameter block with the SCSILoadDriver function to
load a driver for a SCSI device. The SCSI load driver parameter block is defined by
the SCSILoadDriverPB data type.

```
struct SCSILoadDriverPB
{
    SCSIPBHdr
    SInt16    scsiLoadedRefNum;
    Boolean   scsiDiskLoadFailed;
};
typedef struct SCSILoadDriverPB SCSILoadDriverPB;
```

Field descriptions

SCSIPBHdr   A macro that includes the SCSI Manager parameter block header,
                   described on page 4-21.

scsiLoadedRefNum
                   If the driver is successfully loaded, this field contains the driver
                   reference number returned by the SIM.

`scsiDiskLoadFailed`

> If this field is set to `true`, the SIM should attempt to load its own driver regardless of whether there is one on the device. If this field is set to `false`, the SIM has the option of loading a driver from the device or using one of its own.

SCSI Driver Identification Parameter Block

You use the SCSI driver identification parameter block with the `SCSICreateRefNumXref`, `SCSILookupRefNumXref`, and `SCSIRemoveRefNumXref` functions to exchange device driver registration information. The SCSI driver identification parameter block is defined by the `SCSIDriverPB` data type.

```
struct SCSIDriverPB
{
    SCSIPBHdr
    SInt16      scsiDriver;
    UInt16      scsiDriverFlags;
    DeviceIdent scsiNextDevice;
};
typedef struct SCSIDriverPB SCSIDriverPB;
```

Field descriptions

`SCSIPBHdr`   A macro that includes the SCSI Manager parameter block header, described on page 4-21.

`scsiDriver`   The driver reference number of the device driver associated with this device identification record.

`scsiDriverFlags`
                  Driver information flags. These flags are not interpreted by the XPT but can be used to provide information about the driver to other clients. The following flags are defined:

  `scsiDeviceSensitive`
                  Only the device driver should access this device. SCSI utilities and other applications that bypass drivers should check this flag before accessing a device.

  `scsiDeviceNoOldCallAccess`
                  This driver or device does not accept original SCSI Manager requests.

`scsiNextDevice` The device identification record of the next device in the driver registration list.

SIM Initialization Record

You use the SIM initialization record to provide information about your SIM when you register it with the XPT using the SCSIRegisterBus function. The SIM initialization record is defined by the SIMInitInfo data type.

```
struct SIMInitInfo {
    UInt8              *SIMstaticPtr;
    SInt32              staticSize;
    SIMInitProc         SIMInit;
    SIMActionProc       SIMAction;
    SCSIProc            SIM_ISR;
    InterruptPollProc   SIMInterruptPoll;
    SIMActionProc       NewOldCall;
    UInt16              ioPBSize;
    Boolean             oldCallCapable;
    UInt8               simInfoUnused1;
    SInt32              simInternalUse;
    SCSIProc            XPT_ISR;
    SCSIProc            EnteringSIM;
    SCSIProc            ExitingSIM;
    MakeCallbackProc    MakeCallback;
    UInt16              busID;
    UInt16              simInfoUnused3;
    SInt32              simInfoUnused4;
};
typedef struct SIMInitInfo SIMInitInfo;
```

Field descriptions

SIMstaticPtr   A pointer to the storage allocated by the XPT for the SIM's static variables.

staticSize   The amount of memory requested by the SIM for storing its static variables.

SIMInit   A pointer to the SIM's initialization function. See the description of the SIMInit function on page 4-60 for more information.

SIMAction   A pointer to the SIM function that handles SCSIAction requests. See the description of the SIMAction function on page 4-61 for more information.

SIM_ISR   Reserved.

SIMInterruptPoll
                  A pointer to the SIM's interrupt polling function. The Device Manager periodically calls this routine while waiting for a synchronous request to complete if the processor's interrupt priority level is not 0. This allows the Virtual Memory Manager to initiate SCSI transactions when interrupts are disabled. See the description of the SIMInterruptPoll function on page 4-61 for more information.

NewOldCall	If the oldCallCapable field is set to true, this field contains a pointer to the SIM function that handles original SCSI Manager requests. See the description of the NewOldCall function beginning on page 4-63 for more information.
ioPBSize	The minimum size that a SCSI I/O parameter block must be for use with this SIM.
oldCallCapable	A Boolean value that indicates whether the SIM emulates original SCSI Manager functions.
simInfoUnused1	Reserved.
simInternalUse	A long word available for use by the SIM. This field is not affected or used by the SCSI Manager.
XPT_ISR	Reserved.
EnteringSIM	A pointer to the XPT EnteringSIM function. This function provides support for virtual memory. Your SIM must call this function prior to executing any other SIM code. See the description of the EnteringSIM function on page 4-58 for more information.
ExitingSIM	A pointer to the XPT ExitingSIM function. Your SIM must call this function before passing control to any code that could cause a page fault, including completion routines. See the description of the ExitingSIM function on page 4-59 for more information.
MakeCallback	A pointer to the XPT MakeCallback function. Your SIM must call this function after completing a transaction. The XPT then calls the completion routine specified in the scsiCompletion field of the parameter block header. See the description of the MakeCallback function on page 4-59 for more information.
busID	The bus number assigned by the XPT to this SIM/HBA.

SCSI Manager 4.3 Functions

This section describes the functions you use to communicate with SCSI devices and with the XPT and SIM components of SCSI Manager 4.3.

- "Client Functions" describes the functions that applications and device drivers use to communicate with SCSI devices and the XPT.

- "SIM Support Functions" describes the functions a SIM uses to register its bus and communicate with the XPT.

- "SIM Internal Functions" describes the functions that a SIM must provide in order to be compatible with SCSI Manager 4.3 and the functions that a SIM must include if it supports original SCSI Manager emulation.

Client Functions

This section describes the functions that clients (applications and device drivers) use to communicate with SCSI devices and the XPT.

SCSIAction

You use the SCSIAction function to initiate a SCSI transaction or request a service from the XPT or SIM.

```
OSErr SCSIAction(SCSI_PB *scsiPB);
```

scsiPB   A pointer to a SCSI Manager parameter block.

Parameter block

→	scsiPBLength	UInt16	The size of the parameter block.
→	scsiFunctionCode	UInt8	The function selector code.
←	scsiResult	OSErr	The returned result code.
→	scsiDevice	DeviceIdent	A 4-byte value that uniquely identifies the target device.
→	scsiCompletion	CallbackProc	A pointer to a completion routine. If this field is set to nil, the function is executed synchronously.
→	scsiFlags	UInt32	Flags indicating the transfer direction and any special handling required for the request. See page 4-22 for descriptions of these flags.
→	scsiDriverStorage	UInt8 *	Optional pointer to the device driver's private storage.

DESCRIPTION

The SCSIAction function initiates the request specified by the scsiFunctionCode field of the parameter block. Certain types of requests are handled by the XPT, but most are handled by the SIM. Table 4-2 lists the function selector codes. See the following sections for descriptions of the functions you access through SCSIAction.

When called asynchronously, SCSIAction normally returns the NoErr result code, indicating that the request was queued successfully. The result of the SCSI transaction is returned in the scsiResult field upon completion. If the SCSIAction function returns an error code, the request was not queued and the completion routine will not be called.

When the completion routine is called, it receives the A5 world that existed when the SCSIAction request was received. If A5 was invalid when the request was made, it is also invalid in the completion routine.

Your completion routine should use the following function prototype:

```
pascal void (*CallbackProc) (void * scsiPB);
```

There is no implied ordering of asynchronous requests made to different devices. An earlier request may be started later, and a later request may complete earlier. However, a series of requests to the same device is issued to that device in the order received, except when the scsiSIMQHead flag is set in the scsiFlags field of the parameter block.

When called synchronously, the SCSIAction function returns the actual result of the operation. It also places this result in the scsiResult field.

Table 4-2 SCSIAction function selector codes

Code	Function	Operation
00	SCSINop	No operation.
01	SCSIExecIO	Execute a SCSI I/O transaction.
02	Reserved	
03	SCSIBusInquiry	Bus inquiry.
04	SCSIReleaseQ	Release a frozen SIM queue.
05–0F	Reserved	
10	SCSIAbortCommand	Abort a SCSI command.
11	SCSIResetBus	Reset the SCSI bus.
12	SCSIResetDevice	Reset a SCSI device.
13	SCSITerminateIO	Terminate I/O transaction.
14–7F	Reserved	
80	SCSIGetVirtualIDInfo	Return DeviceIdent of a virtual SCSI ID.
81	Reserved	
82	SCSILoadDriver	Load a driver from a SCSI device.
83	Reserved	
84	SCSIOldCall	SIM support function for original SCSI Manager emulation.
85	SCSICreateRefNumXref	Register a device driver.
86	SCSILookupRefNumXref	Find a driver reference number.
87	SCSIRemoveRefNumXref	Deregister a device driver.
88	SCSIRegisterWthNewXPT	XPT was replaced; SIM needs to reregister.
89–BF	Reserved	
C0–FF	Vendor unique	Requests in this range are passed directly to the SIM without evaluation by the XPT.

RESULT CODES

noErr   0   Asynchronous request successfully queued, or synchronous request successfully completed

Note

Result codes for specific SCSIAction function requests are listed in the following sections. See page 4-90 for a list of all result codes. ◆

SCSINop

The SCSINop function does nothing.

```
OSErr SCSIAction(SCSI_PB *scsiPB);
```

scsiPB   A pointer to a SCSI Manager parameter block.

Parameter block

→	scsiFunctionCode	UInt8	The SCSINop function selector code (0x00).

DESCRIPTION

The SCSINop function performs no action, returns no values in the parameter block, and does not call a completion routine. It is provided for compatibility with the CAM specification, and may be useful for debugging.

RESULT CODES

noErr   0   No error

SCSIExecIO

You use the SCSIExecIO function to perform SCSI I/O operations.

```
OSErr SCSIAction(SCSIExecIOPB *scsiPB);
```

scsiPB   A pointer to a SCSI I/O parameter block, which is described on page 4-23.

Parameter block

→	scsiPBLength	UInt16	The size of the parameter block. This value must be equal to or greater than the scsiIOpbSize for the SIM.
→	scsiFunctionCode	UInt8	The SCSIExecIO function selector code (0x01).
←	scsiResult	OSErr	The returned result code.
→	scsiDevice	DeviceIdent	The device identification record.
→	scsiCompletion	CallbackProc	A pointer to a completion routine. If this field is set to nil, the function is executed synchronously.
→	scsiFlags	UInt32	Flags indicating the transfer direction and any special handling required for the request. See page 4-22 for descriptions of these flags.
→	scsiDriverStorage	UInt8 *	Optional pointer to the device driver's private storage.

←	scsiResultFlags	UInt16	Output flags that modify the scsiResult field. See page 4-24.
→	scsiDataPtr	UInt8 *	A pointer to a data buffer or scatter/gather list.
→	scsiDataLength	UInt32	The amount of data to be transferred.
→	scsiSensePtr	UInt8 *	A pointer to the autosense buffer.
→	scsiSenseLength	UInt8	The size of the autosense buffer.
→	scsiCDBLength	UInt8	The size of the CDB.
→	scsiSGListCount	UInt16	The number of elements in the scatter/gather list.
←	scsiSCSIstatus	UInt8	Status returned by the SCSI device.
←	scsiSenseResidual	SInt8	The autosense residual length.
←	scsiDataResidual	SInt32	The data transfer residual length.
→	scsiCDB	CDB	The CDB, or a pointer to the CDB, depending on the setting of the scsiCDBIsPointer flag.
→	scsiTimeout	SInt32	The SCSI bus timeout period.
→	scsiIOFlags	UInt16	Additional I/O flags. See page 4-25.
→	scsiSelectTimeout	UInt16	Optional SELECT timeout value.
→	scsiDataType	UInt8	The data type pointed to by the scsiDataPtr field. See page 4-27.
→	scsiTransferType	UInt8	The transfer mode (polled or blind). See page 4-27.
→	scsiHandshake[8]	UInt16	Handshaking instructions.
→	scsiCommandLink	SCSI_IO *	Optional pointer to a linked CDB.

DESCRIPTION

The SCSIExecIO function sends a request to a SIM to carry out a SCSI transaction. The SIM performs all the actions necessary to fulfill the request, including arbitrating for the bus, selecting the device, sending the CDB, receiving or sending data, performing disconnect operations, and so on. The parameter block contains all the information required for the SIM to complete the SCSI request, including issuing a REQUEST SENSE command if necessary.

RESULT CODES

noErr	0	No error
scsiRequestInProgress	1	Parameter block request is in progress
scsiCDBLengthInvalid	-7863	The CDB length supplied is not supported by this SIM; typically this means it was too big
scsiTransferTypeInvalid	-7864	The scsiTransferType requested is not supported by this SIM
scsiDataTypeInvalid	-7865	SIM does not support the requested scsiDataType
scsiIDInvalid	-7866	The initiator ID is invalid
scsiLUNInvalid	-7867	The logical unit number is invalid
scsiTIDInvalid	-7868	The target ID is invalid
scsiBusInvalid	-7869	The bus ID is invalid
scsiRequestInvalid	-7870	The parameter block request is invalid

scsiFunctionNotAvailable	-7871	The requested function is not supported by this SIM
scsiPBLengthError	-7872	The parameter block length supplied was too small for this SIM
scsiQLinkInvalid	-7881	The qLink field was not 0
scsiNoSuchXref	-7882	No driver has been cross-referenced with this device
scsiDeviceConflict	-7883	Attempt to register more than one driver to a device
scsiNoHBA	-7884	No HBA detected
scsiDeviceNotThere	-7885	SCSI device not installed or available
scsiProvideFail	-7886	Unable to provide the requested service
scsiBusy	-7887	SCSI subsystem is busy
scsiTooManyBuses	-7888	SIM registration failed because the XPT registry is full
scsiCDBReceived	-7910	The SCSI CDB was received
scsiNoNexus	-7911	Nexus is not established
scsiTerminated	-7912	Parameter block request terminated by the host
scsiBDRsent	-7913	A SCSI bus device reset (BDR) message was sent to the target
scsiWrongDirection	-7915	Data phase was in an unexpected direction
scsiSequenceFail	-7916	Target bus phase sequence failure
scsiUnexpectedBusFree	-7917	Unexpected bus free phase
scsiDataRunError	-7918	Data overrun/underrun error
scsiAutosenseFailed	-7920	Automatic REQUEST SENSE command failed
scsiParityError	-7921	An uncorrectable parity error occurred
scsiSCSIBusReset	-7922	Execution of this parameter block was halted because of a SCSI bus reset
scsiMessageRejectReceived	-7923	REJECT message received
scsiIdentifyMessageRejected	-7924	The target issued a REJECT message in response to the IDENTIFY message; the LUN probably does not exist
scsiCommandTimeout	-7925	The timeout value for this parameter block was exceeded and the parameter block was aborted
scsiSelectTimeout	-7926	Target selection timeout
scsiUnableToTerminate	-7927	Unable to terminate I/O parameter block request
scsiNonZeroStatus	-7932	The target returned non-zero status upon completion of the request
scsiUnableToAbort	-7933	Unable to abort parameter block request
scsiRequestAborted	-7934	Parameter block request aborted by the host

SCSIBusInquiry

You use the SCSIBusInquiry function to get information about a SCSI bus.

```
OSErr SCSIAction(SCSIBusInquiryPB *scsiPB);
```

scsiPB   A pointer to a SCSI bus inquiry parameter block, which is described on page 4-28.

Parameter block

→	scsiPBLength	UInt16	The size of the parameter block.
→	scsiFunctionCode	UInt8	The SCSIBusInquiry function selector code (0x03).
←	scsiResult	OSErr	The returned result code.
→	scsiDevice	DeviceIdent	The device identification record. Only the bus number is required.
→	scsiCompletion	CallbackProc	Unused. Must be nil.
←	scsiEngineCount	UInt16	The number of HBA engines.
←	scsiMaxTransferType	UInt16	The number of data transfer types available on the HBA.
←	scsiDataTypes	UInt32	The data types supported.
←	scsiIOpbSize	UInt16	The minimum parameter block size for this SIM.
←	scsiMaxIOpbSize	UInt16	The largest parameter block size currently registered.
←	scsiFeatureFlags	UInt32	Features of the SIM/HBA.
←	scsiVersionNumber	UInt8	The version of the SIM/HBA
←	scsiHBAInquiry	UInt8	Features of the SIM/HBA.
←	scsiSIMPrivatesPtr	UInt32	A pointer to the SIM's storage.
←	scsiSIMPrivatesSize	UInt32	The size of the SIM's storage.
←	scsiHiBusID	UInt8	The highest registered bus number.
←	scsiInitiatorID	UInt8	SCSI ID of the HBA.
←	scsiFlagsSupported	UInt32	Bit mask of supported scsiFlags.
←	scsiIOFlagsSupported	UInt16	Bit mask of supported scsiIOFlags.
←	scsiWeirdStuff	UInt16	Additional flags.
←	scsiMaxTarget	UInt16	The highest SCSI ID value supported by the HBA.
←	scsiMaxLUN	UInt16	The highest logical unit number supported by the HBA.
←	scsiSIMVendor	SInt8[16]	SIM vendor string.
←	scsiHBAVendor	SInt8[16]	HBA vendor string.
←	scsiControllerFamily	SInt8[16]	Controller family string.
←	scsiControllerType	SInt8[16]	Controller type string.
←	scsiXPTversion	SInt8[4]	XPT version string.
←	scsiSIMversion	SInt8[4]	SIM version string.
←	scsiHBAversion	SInt8[4]	HBA version string.
←	scsiHBAslotType	UInt8	The slot type of the HBA.

←	scsiHBAslotNumber	UInt8	The slot number of the HBA.
←	scsiSIMsRsrcID	UInt16	The sResource ID of the SIM.
←	scsiAdditionalLength	UInt16	The additional size of this parameter block, if any.

DESCRIPTION

The SCSIBusInquiry function returns information about the SIM and HBA for a bus. This function is typically used to find the minimum size of the SCSI I/O parameter block for a particular SIM. You can also use this function to determine whether a bus supports various optional features such as synchronous or wide transfer modes. Because this function is always executed synchronously, the scsiCompletion field must be set to nil.

To find all buses, first request information about the XPT by setting the bus number in the scsiDevice field to 0xFF, then use the value returned in the scsiHiBusID field to set the limits of the search.

RESULT CODES

noErr	0	No error
scsiBusInvalid	-7869	The bus ID is invalid
scsiRequestInvalid	-7870	The parameter block request is invalid
scsiPBLengthError	-7872	The parameter block is too small for this SIM
scsiQLinkInvalid	-7881	The qLink field was not 0
scsiNoHBA	-7884	No HBA detected
scsiBusy	-7887	SCSI subsystem is busy

SCSIReleaseQ

You use the SCSIReleaseQ function to release a frozen queue for a LUN.

```
OSErr SCSIAction(SCSI_PB *scsiPB);
```

scsiPB   A pointer to a SCSI Manager parameter block.

Parameter block

→	scsiPBLength	UInt16	The size of the parameter block.
→	scsiFunctionCode	UInt8	The SCSIReleaseQ function selector code (0x04).
←	scsiResult	OSErr	The returned result code.
→	scsiDevice	DeviceIdent	The device identification record.
→	scsiCompletion	CallbackProc	Unused. Must be set to nil.

DESCRIPTION

The SCSIReleaseQ function releases a frozen I/O queue for the logical unit number specified in the scsiDevice field. If an I/O request returns with the scsiSIMQFrozen flag set in the scsiResultFlags field, you must call this function to restore normal operation.

Queue freezing provides the opportunity to insert error-handling requests at the beginning of the queue using the scsiSIMQHead flag. You then release the queue using this function. Subsequent errors will continue to freeze the queue, allowing you to step through the queue one request at a time without aborting any other pending requests.

Because this function is always executed synchronously, the scsiCompletion field must be set to nil. Unlike other synchronous functions, however, you can call SCSIReleaseQ from a completion routine.

RESULT CODES

noErr	0	No error
scsiIDInvalid	-7866	The initiator ID is invalid
scsiLUNInvalid	-7867	The logical unit number is invalid
scsiTIDInvalid	-7868	The target ID is invalid
scsiBusInvalid	-7869	The bus ID is invalid
scsiRequestInvalid	-7870	The parameter block request is invalid
scsiPBLengthError	-7872	The parameter block is too small for this SIM
scsiQLinkInvalid	-7881	The qLink field was not 0

SEE ALSO

See "Error Recovery Techniques" on page 4-10 for more information about queue freezing.

SCSIAbortCommand

You can use the SCSIAbortCommand function to cancel an I/O request.

```
OSErr SCSIAction(SCSIAbortCommandPB *scsiPB);
```

scsiPB   A pointer to a SCSI abort command parameter block, which is described on page 4-33.

Parameter block

→	scsiPBLength	UInt16	The size of the parameter block.
→	scsiFunctionCode	UInt8	The SCSIAbortCommand function selector code (0x10).
←	scsiResult	OSErr	The returned result code.
→	scsiDevice	DeviceIdent	The device identification record.
→	scsiCompletion	CallbackProc	A pointer to a completion routine. If this field is set to nil, the function is executed synchronously.
→	scsiDriverStorage	UInt8 *	Optional pointer to the device driver's private storage.
→	scsiIOptr	SCSI_IO *	A pointer to the SCSI I/O parameter block to be canceled.

DESCRIPTION

The SCSIAbortCommand function cancels the SCSIExecIO request identified by the scsiIOptr field. If the request has not yet been delivered to the device, it is removed from the queue and its completion routine is called with a result code of scsiRequestAborted. If the request has already been started, the SIM attempts to send an ABORT message to the device, either by asserting the /ATN signal or by reselecting the device. The function returns the scsiUnableToAbort result code if the specified request has already been completed.

SPECIAL CONSIDERATIONS

Because the interrupt that calls the completion routine can pre-empt the SCSIAbortCommand request, this function can produce unexpected results if the completion routine for the canceled request reuses the parameter block.

RESULT CODES

noErr	0	No error
scsiBusInvalid	-7869	The bus ID is invalid
scsiRequestInvalid	-7870	The parameter block request is invalid
scsiPBLengthError	-7872	The parameter block is too small for this SIM
scsiQLinkInvalid	-7881	The qLink field was not 0
scsiUnableToAbort	-7933	Unable to abort parameter block request

SEE ALSO

See the description of the SCSITerminateIO function on page 4-48 for information about another method of canceling a request.

SCSIResetBus

You use the SCSIResetBus function to reset a SCSI bus.

```
OSErr SCSIAction(SCSI_PB *scsiPB);
```

scsiPB   A pointer to a SCSI Manager parameter block.

Parameter block

→	scsiPBLength	UInt16	The size of the parameter block.
→	scsiFunctionCode	UInt8	The SCSIResetBus function selector code (0x11).
←	scsiResult	OSErr	The returned result code.
→	scsiDevice	DeviceIdent	The device identification record. Only the bus number is required.
→	scsiCompletion	CallbackProc	A pointer to a completion routine. If set to nil, the function is executed synchronously.

→   scsiDriverStorage   UInt8 *   Optional pointer to the device
                                            driver's private storage.

DESCRIPTION

The SCSIResetBus function directs the HBA to assert the SCSI bus reset signal, causing all devices on the bus to clear pending I/O and forcing the bus into the bus free phase. In addition, the SIM calls the completion routines for all requests that were already delivered to devices. The appropriate LUN queue is frozen for each of the requests that were reset, unless the scsiSIMQNoFreeze flag is set.

SPECIAL CONSIDERATIONS

The SCSIResetBus function interrupts SCSI communications and can cause data loss. You should use this function only to restore operation in the event that a device refuses to release the bus. You can use the SCSIResetDevice function to reset a single device when the SCSI bus is operational and the device is still responding to selection.

RESULT CODES

noErr	0	No error
scsiBusInvalid	-7869	The bus ID is invalid
scsiRequestInvalid	-7870	The parameter block request is invalid
scsiPBLengthError	-7872	The parameter block is too small for this SIM
scsiQLinkInvalid	-7881	The qLink field was not 0

SCSIResetDevice

You use the SCSIResetDevice function to reset a SCSI device.

```
OSErr SCSIAction(SCSI_PB *scsiPB);
```

scsiPB   A pointer to a SCSI Manager parameter block.

Parameter block

→	scsiPBLength	UInt16	The size of the parameter block.
→	scsiFunctionCode	UInt8	The SCSIResetDevice function selector code (0x12).
←	scsiResult	OSErr	The returned result code.
→	scsiDevice	DeviceIdent	The device identification record.
→	scsiCompletion	CallbackProc	A pointer to a completion routine. If set to nil, the function is executed synchronously.
→	scsiDriverStorage	UInt8 *	Optional pointer to the device driver's private storage.

DESCRIPTION

The SCSIResetDevice function attempts to send a BUS DEVICE RESET message to the target. If the device is currently on the bus, the SIM asserts the /ATN signal and sends the message at the next message-out phase. If the target is not on the bus, the SIM selects it and sends an IDENTIFY message followed by a BUS DEVICE RESET message.

SPECIAL CONSIDERATIONS

The BUS DEVICE RESET message clears all I/O transactions for all logical units of the target device. This function may result in data loss and should be used only to restore operation in the event that a device fails to respond to other messages.

RESULT CODES

noErr	0	No error
scsiBusInvalid	-7869	The bus ID is invalid
scsiRequestInvalid	-7870	The parameter block request is invalid
scsiPBLengthError	-7872	The parameter block is too small for this SIM
scsiQLinkInvalid	-7881	The qLink field was not 0
scsiMessageRejectReceived	-7923	REJECT message received

SCSITerminateIO

You can use the SCSITerminateIO function to cancel an I/O request.

```
OSErr SCSIAction(SCSITerminateIOPB *scsiPB);
```

scsiPB   A pointer to a SCSI terminate I/O parameter block, which is described on page 4-33.

Parameter block

→	scsiPBLength	UInt16	The size of the parameter block.
→	scsiFunctionCode	UInt8	The SCSITerminateIO function selector code (0x13).
←	scsiResult	OSErr	The returned result code.
→	scsiDevice	DeviceIdent	The device identification record.
→	scsiCompletion	CallbackProc	A pointer to a completion routine. If this field is set to nil, the function is executed synchronously.
→	scsiDriverStorage	UInt8 *	Optional pointer to the device driver's private storage.
→	scsiIOptr	SCSI_IO *	A pointer to the SCSI I/O parameter block to be canceled.

DESCRIPTION

The SCSITerminateIO function cancels the SCSIExecIO request identified by the scsiIOptr field. If the request has not yet been delivered to the device, it is removed from the queue and its completion routine is called with a result code of scsiTerminated. If the request has already been started, the SIM attempts to send a TERMINATE IO PROCESS message to the device, either by asserting the /ATN signal or by reselecting the device. The function returns the scsiUnableToTerminate result code if the specified request has already been completed.

The SCSITerminateIO function differs from the SCSIAbortCommand function (described on page 4-45) only in the message it sends over the SCSI bus. TERMINATE IO PROCESS is an optional SCSI-2 message that instructs the device to complete a request normally although prematurely, while attempting to maintain media integrity.

SPECIAL CONSIDERATIONS

Because the interrupt that calls the completion routine can pre-empt the SCSITerminateIO request, this function can produce unexpected results if the completion routine for the canceled request reuses the parameter block.

RESULT CODES

noErr	0	No error
scsiBusInvalid	-7869	The bus ID is invalid
scsiRequestInvalid	-7870	The parameter block request is invalid
scsiPBLengthError	-7872	The parameter block is too small for this SIM
scsiQLinkInvalid	-7881	The qLink field was not 0
scsiUnableToTerminate	-7927	Unable to terminate I/O parameter block request

SCSIGetVirtualIDInfo

You can use the SCSIGetVirtualIDInfo funtion to get the device identification record for a virtual SCSI ID.

```
OSErr SCSIAction(SCSIGetVirtualInfoPB *scsiPB);
```

scsiPB   A pointer to a SCSI virtual ID information parameter block, which is described on page 4-34.

Parameter block

→	scsiPBLength	UInt16	The size of the parameter block.
→	scsiFunctionCode	UInt8	The SCSIGetVirtualIDInfo function selector code (0x80).
←	scsiResult	OSErr	The returned result code.
←	scsiDevice	DeviceIdent	The device identification record.
→	scsiCompletion	CallbackProc	Unused. Must be set to nil.
→	scsiOldCallID	UInt16	The virtual SCSI ID to search for.

←	scsiExists	Boolean	Returns true if the scsiDevice field contains a valid device identification record.

DESCRIPTION

The SCSIGetVirtualIDInfo function returns the device identification record of a device on the virtual bus. This function is typically used by a device driver during the transition from a ROM-based original SCSI Manager to SCSI Manager 4.3. If a device with the specified SCSI ID is not found on the virtual bus, or the device exists but is not accessible through the SCSI Manager 4.3 interface, the scsiExists field returns false and the scsiDevice field should be ignored.

Because this function is always executed synchronously, the scsiCompletion field must be nil.

RESULT CODES

noErr	0	No error
scsiTIDInvalid	-7868	The target ID is invalid
scsiPBLengthError	-7872	The parameter block is too small for this SIM
scsiQLinkInvalid	-7881	The qLink field was not 0

SCSILoadDriver

The Start Manager uses the SCSILoadDriver function to provide an opportunity for a SIM to load a driver other than one found on the media.

```
OSErr SCSIAction(SCSILoadDriverPB *scsiPB);
```

scsiPB   A pointer to a SCSI load driver parameter block, which is described on page 4-34.

Parameter block

→	scsiPBLength	UInt16	The size of the parameter block.
→	scsiFunctionCode	UInt8	The SCSILoadDriver function selector code (0x82).
←	scsiResult	OSErr	The returned result code.
→	scsiDevice	DeviceIdent	The device identification record.
→	scsiCompletion	CallbackProc	A pointer to a completion routine. If this field is set to nil, the function is executed synchronously.
→	scsiDriverStorage	UInt8 *	Optional pointer to the device driver's private storage.
←	scsiLoadedRefNum	UInt16	The driver reference number returned by the SIM.
→	scsiDiskLoadFailed	Boolean	Set to true if a driver could not be loaded from the media.

DESCRIPTION

The `SCSILoadDriver` function is called by the Start Manager to load device drivers for SCSI devices. You can use this function to load a driver for a device that was not available at system startup.

The Start Manager can call this function both before and after attempting to load a driver from the media. On the first attempt, the `scsiDiskLoadFailed` field is set to `false`, indicating to the SIM that it can choose to load a driver from the media or install another (typically newer) driver of its own choosing.

If the first attempt to load a driver fails, the Start Manager calls the `SCSILoadDriver` function a second time, with the `scsiDiskLoadFailed` field set to `true` to indicate that a driver could not be loaded from the media. The SIM then loads its own driver, if possible, or returns an error result.

SPECIAL CONSIDERATIONS

The `SCSILoadDriver` function may move memory; you should not call it at interrupt time.

RESULT CODES

noErr	0	No error
scsiFunctionNotAvailable	-7871	The requested function is not supported by this SIM

SCSICreateRefNumXref

You use the `SCSICreateRefNumXref` function to register a device driver with the XPT.

```
OSErr SCSIAction(SCSIDriverPB *scsiPB);
```

scsiPB   A pointer to a SCSI driver identification parameter block, which is described on page 4-35.

Parameter block

→	scsiPBLength	UInt16	The size of the parameter block.
→	scsiFunctionCode	UInt8	The `SCSICreateRefNumXref` function selector code (0x85).
←	scsiResult	OSErr	The returned result code.
→	scsiDevice	DeviceIdent	The device identification record.
→	scsiCompletion	CallbackProc	Unused. Must be set to `nil`.
→	scsiDriver	SInt16	The driver reference number.
→	scsiDriverFlags	UInt16	Optional driver flags.

DESCRIPTION

The SCSICreateRefNumXref function adds an element to the XPT's driver registration table. You specify a device identification record in the scsiDevice field and a driver reference number in the scsiDriver field. The scsiDriverFlags field provides information about the driver that other clients can access using the SCSILookupRefNumXref function. The XPT does not interpret these flags.

A device identification record can have only one driver reference number associated with it, but a driver reference number may be registered to multiple devices. This function returns the scsiDeviceConflict result code if a driver is already registered to the specified device identification record.

Because this function is always executed synchronously, the scsiCompletion field must be set to nil.

SPECIAL CONSIDERATIONS

The SCSICreateRefNumXref function is executed synchronously and may move memory; you should not call it at interrupt time.

RESULT CODES

noErr	0	No error
scsiQLinkInvalid	-7881	The qLink field was not 0
scsiDeviceConflict	-7883	Attempt to register more than one driver to a device

SEE ALSO

See "Loading and Initializing a Driver," beginning on page 4-11, for more information about how device drivers are registered with the XPT.

SCSILookupRefNumXref

You can use the SCSILookupRefNumXref function to determine if a driver is installed for a SCSI device.

```
OSErr SCSIAction(SCSIDriverPB *scsiPB);
```

scsiPB   A pointer to a SCSI driver identification parameter block, which is described on page 4-35.

Parameter block

→	scsiPBLength	UInt16	The size of the parameter block.
→	scsiFunctionCode	UInt8	The SCSILookupRefNumXref function selector code (0x86).
←	scsiResult	OSErr	The returned result code.
→	scsiDevice	DeviceIdent	The device identification record.
→	scsiCompletion	CallbackProc	Unused. Must be set to nil.

←	scsiDriver	SInt16	The driver reference number.
←	scsiDriverFlags	UInt16	Optional driver flags.
←	scsiNextDevice	DeviceIdent	The device identification record of the next device in the driver registration table.

DESCRIPTION

The SCSILookupRefNumXref function returns the driver reference number for a device. You specify a device identification record in the scsiDevice field, and the function returns the driver reference number in the scsiDriver field. If no driver is registered for the device, the function returns nil in the scsiDriver field.

The scsiDriverFlags field returns the flags that were set when the driver was registered. The scsiNextDevice field returns the device identification record of the next device in the driver registration table. If this is the last device in the table, the function returns 0xFF in the scsiNextDevice.bus field.

To find all registered drivers you should first call this function with a value of 0xFF in the scsiDevice.bus field. The function returns the device identification record of the first device in the list in the scsiNextDevice field. You can then find other drivers by moving the scsiNextDevice value into the scsiDevice field and repeating the operation until the function returns 0xFF in the scsiNextDevice.bus field.

Because this function is always executed synchronously, the scsiCompletion field must be set to nil.

RESULT CODES

noErr	0	No error
scsiQLinkInvalid	-7881	The qLink field was not 0

SCSIRemoveRefNumXref

You use the SCSIRemoveRefNumXref function to deregister a device driver with the XPT.

```
OSErr SCSIAction(SCSIDriverPB *scsiPB);
```

scsiPB   A pointer to a SCSI driver identification parameter block, which is described on page 4-35.

Parameter block

→	scsiPBLength	UInt16	The size of the parameter block.
→	scsiFunctionCode	UInt8	The SCSIRemoveRefNumXref function selector code (0x87).
←	scsiResult	OSErr	The returned result code.
→	scsiDevice	DeviceIdent	The device identification record.
→	scsiCompletion	CallbackProc	Unused. Must be set to nil.

DESCRIPTION

The SCSIRemoveRefNumXref function removes a driver entry from the XPT's driver registration table. You specify the device identification record in the scsiDevice field.

Because this function is always executed synchronously, the scsiCompletion field must be set to nil.

SPECIAL CONSIDERATIONS

The SCSIRemoveRefNumXref function is executed synchronously, and may move memory; you should not call it at interrupt time.

RESULT CODES

noErr	0	No error
scsiQLinkInvalid	-7881	The qLink field was not 0
scsiNoSuchXref	-7882	No driver has been cross-referenced with this device

SEE ALSO

See "Loading and Initializing a Driver," beginning on page 4-11, for more information about how device drivers are registered with the XPT.

SIM Support Functions

This section describes the functions a SIM uses to register its bus and communicate with the XPT. If you are writing a SIM, you use these functions to

- register, deregister, or reregister your SIM with the XPT

- remove the existing XPT if you replace it

- inform the XPT when your code is running

- call a completion routine

SCSIRegisterBus

You use the SCSIRegisterBus function to register a SIM and HBA for use with the XPT.

OSErr SCSIRegisterBus(SIMInitInfo *SIMinfoPtr);

SIMinfoPtr   A pointer to a SIM initialization record, which is described on page 4-36.

Parameter block

←	SIMstaticPtr	UInt8 *	A pointer to the allocated static storage.
→	staticSize	SInt32	The amount of memory requested for static storage.

→	SIMInit	SIMInitProc	A pointer to the SIMInit function.
→	SIMAction	SIMActionProc	A pointer to the SIMAction function.
→	SIMInterruptPoll	InterruptPollProc	A pointer to the SIMInterruptPoll function.
→	NewOldCall	SIMActionProc	A pointer to the NewOldCall function.
→	ioPBSize	UInt16	The SCSI I/O parameter block size for this SIM.
→	oldCallCapable	Boolean	Set to true if the SIM emulates original SCSI Manager functions.
←	EnteringSIM	SCSIProc	A pointer to the EnteringSIM function.
←	ExitingSIM	SCSIProc	A pointer to the ExitingSIM function.
←	MakeCallback	MakeCallbackProc	A pointer to the MakeCallback function.
←	busID	UInt16	The bus number assigned to this SIM/HBA.

DESCRIPTION

You use the SIM initialization record to specify the characteristics of the HBA, the SIM's function entry points, and the number of bytes required for static data storage (global variables). The XPT returns a pointer to the allocated storage and a bus number that identifies the bus in all future transactions. In addition, the XPT returns pointers to the EnteringSIM, ExitingSIM, and MakeCallback functions.

Before assigning a bus number, the XPT calls the SIM's SIMInit function, which instructs the SIM to initialize itself. If the SIMInit function returns noErr, the XPT assigns a bus number and returns from the SCSIRegisterBus function. At this point the SIM is installed and should be ready to accept requests.

SPECIAL CONSIDERATIONS

The SCSIRegisterBus function may move memory; you should not call it at interrupt time.

RESULT CODES

noErr	0	No error
scsiTooManyBuses	-7888	SIM registration failed because the XPT registry is full

SEE ALSO

See "Writing a SCSI Interface Module," beginning on page 4-15, for more information about using this function.

SCSIDeregisterBus

You can use the `SCSIDeregisterBus` function to deregister a bus that is no longer available.

```
OSErr SCSIDeregisterBus(SCSI_PB *scsiPB);
```

`scsiPB`   A pointer to a SCSI Manager parameter block.

Parameter block

→	scsiPBLength	UInt16	The size of the parameter block.
←	scsiResult	OSErr	The returned result code.
→	scsiDevice	DeviceIdent	The device identification record. Only the bus number is required.
→	scsiCompletion	CallbackProc	Unused. Must be set to nil.

DESCRIPTION

The `SCSIDeregisterBus` function attempts to remove the SIM specified by the `scsiDevice.bus` field of the parameter block. The XPT marks the bus number as invalid and any subsequent requests to it are rejected. This function is not normally used by the Macintosh Operating System and may not be supported in all implementations.

Because this function is always executed synchronously, the `scsiCompletion` field must be set to `nil`.

SPECIAL CONSIDERATIONS

The `SCSIDeregisterBus` function may move memory; you should not call it at interrupt time.

RESULT CODES

noErr	0	No error
scsiBusInvalid	-7869	The bus ID is invalid
scsiFunctionNotAvailable	-7871	The function is not supported by this SIM

SCSIReregisterBus

You can use the `SCSIReregisterBus` function to reregister a bus if its entry points change or if the XPT is replaced.

```
OSErr SCSIReregisterBus(SIMInitInfo *SIMinfoPtr);
```

`SIMinfoPtr` A pointer to a SIM initialization record, which is described on page 4-36.

Parameter block

→	SIMstaticPtr	UInt8 *	A pointer to the SIM's existing static storage.
→	staticSize	SInt32	The size of the SIM's static storage.
→	SIMInit	SIMInitProc	A pointer to the SIMInit function.
→	SIMAction	SIMActionProc	A pointer to the SIMAction function.
→	SIMInterruptPoll	InterruptPollProc	A pointer to the SIMInterruptPoll function.
→	NewOldCall	SIMActionProc	A pointer to the NewOldCall function.
→	ioPBSize	UInt16	The SCSI I/O parameter block size for this SIM.
→	oldCallCapable	Boolean	Set to true if the SIM emulates original SCSI Manager functions.
←	EnteringSIM	SCSIProc	A pointer to the EnteringSIM function.
←	ExitingSIM	SCSIProc	A pointer to the ExitingSIM function.
←	MakeCallback	MakeCallbackProc	A pointer to the MakeCallback function.
→	busID	UInt16	The bus number requested.

DESCRIPTION

You normally call the SCSIReregisterBus function in response to a SCSIRegisterWithNewXPT request. This function is identical to SCSIRegisterBus except that the bus number and static storage pointer are passed *to* the XPT, rather than being returned by it. In addition, the XPT does not call the SIMInit function.

This function allows a SIM to retain its bus number and static storage if the XPT changes. It is also useful if you need to change the SIM's function entry points or other information.

SPECIAL CONSIDERATIONS

The SCSIReregisterBus function may move memory; you should not call it at interrupt time.

RESULT CODES

noErr	0	No error
scsiBusInvalid	-7869	The bus ID is invalid
scsiTooManyBuses	-7888	SIM registration failed because the XPT registry is full

SCSIKillXPT

You use the SCSIKillXPT function to remove an XPT that has been replaced.

```
OSErr SCSIKillXPT(void *);
```

DESCRIPTION

The SCSIKillXPT function forces the XPT to release any memory it allocated and remove any patches it may have installed. This function is typically called by a new XPT after it has installed itself and reregistered all existing SIMs.

SPECIAL CONSIDERATIONS

The SCSIKillXPT function may move memory; you should not call it at interrupt time.

RESULT CODES

noErr   0   No error

EnteringSIM

You use the EnteringSIM function to inform the XPT that your SIM code is running.

```
void EnteringSIM();
```

DESCRIPTION

The EnteringSIM function informs the XPT that subsequent code is not reentrant and instructs the Virtual Memory Manager to defer execution of VBL tasks, Time Manager tasks, completion routines, and any other code that could cause a page fault. A SIM must call this function whenever its code begins executing and call the corresponding ExitingSIM function on exit.

SPECIAL CONSIDERATIONS

You get the address of this function from the EnteringSIM field of the SIM initialization record.

SEE ALSO

See "Writing a SCSI Interface Module," beginning on page 4-15, for more information about using this function.

ExitingSIM

The `ExitingSIM` function is the counterpart to the `EnteringSIM` function.

```
void ExitingSIM();
```

DESCRIPTION

The `ExitingSIM` function informs the XPT that the SIM is about to pass control to an external routine that might cause a page fault. A SIM must call this function before returning to the XPT or calling a completion routine.

SPECIAL CONSIDERATIONS

You get the address of this function from the `ExitingSIM` field of the SIM initialization record.

SEE ALSO

See "Writing a SCSI Interface Module," beginning on page 4-15, for more information about using this function.

MakeCallback

You use the `MakeCallback` function to signal the XPT to call a completion routine.

```
void MakeCallback(SCSI_IO *scsiPB);
```

scsiPB   A pointer to a SCSI I/O parameter block, which is described on page 4-23.

Parameter block

→   scsiCompletion   CallbackProc   A pointer to a completion routine.

DESCRIPTION

The `MakeCallback` function instructs the XPT to execute the completion routine in the SCSI I/O parameter block. The XPT restores the client's A5 world and then calls the completion routine. A SIM should always use this function rather than calling completion routines directly because the XPT may chose to defer the actual execution of the routine until page faults are safe.

You should surround a call to `MakeCallback` with calls to `ExitingSIM` and `EnteringSIM` so that the Virtual Memory Manager can properly handle any page faults caused by the completion routine.

SPECIAL CONSIDERATIONS

You get the address of this function from the `MakeCallback` field of the SIM initialization record.

SEE ALSO

See "Writing a SCSI Interface Module," beginning on page 4-15, for more information about using this function.

SIM Internal Functions

This section describes the functions that a SIM must provide to be compatible with SCSI Manager 4.3 and the functions that a SIM must include if it supports original SCSI Manager emulation. These functions are called by the XPT to control or provide information to the SIM.

See "Writing a SCSI Interface Module," beginning on page 4-15, for more information about using these functions.

SIMInit

The XPT calls this function to initialize a SIM. The `SIMInit` function must conform to the following type definition:

```
typedef OSErr (*SIMInitProc) (Ptr SIMinfoPtr);
```

`SIMinfoPtr` A pointer to a SIM initialization record, which is described on page 4-36.

DESCRIPTION

The XPT calls this function after a SIM has called `SCSIRegisterBus`. Before returning from the `SCSIRegisterBus` function, the XPT calls this function to initialize the SIM. The SIM is responsible for initializing the HBA.

The XPT passes a pointer to the SIM initialization record, which contains pointers to the SIM's static data storage and the required XPT entry points (`EnteringSIM`, `ExitingSIM`, and `MakeCallback`).

RESULT CODES

noErr	0	No error
scsiNoHBA	-7884	No HBA detected

SIMAction

The XPT calls this function when a SCSIAction request is received that needs to be serviced by the SIM. The SIMAction function must conform to the following type definition:

```
typedef void (*SIMActionProc) (void * scsiPB, Ptr SIMGlobals);
```

scsiPB   A pointer to a SCSI Manager parameter block.

SIMGlobals A pointer to the SIM's static data storage.

DESCRIPTION

The SIMAction function is responsible for handling SCSIAction requests directed to the SIM's bus. The XPT passes the client's parameter block to the SIM, which should then queue the request, execute it, and call the completion routine. The SIM must conform to the behavior defined for the SCSIAction function.

In addition to supporting all client functions, the SIMAction function may optionally support two requests made by the XPT, SCSIOldCall and SCSIRegisterWithNewXPT.

RESULT CODES

The SIMAction function returns a result code in the scsiResult field of the parameter block. The code should be appropriate for the SCSIAction request being processed.

SIMInterruptPoll

The XPT calls this function when interrupts are disabled during a synchronous wait loop, to give the SIM an opportunity to handle interrupts from the HBA. The SIMAction function must conform to the following type definition:

```
typedef void (*InterruptPollProc) (Ptr SIMGlobals);
```

SIMGlobals A pointer to the SIM's static data storage.

DESCRIPTION

If the Device Manager is waiting for a synchronous request to complete, and processor interrupts are masked at level 2 (the level of NuBus interrupts) or higher, the XPT periodically calls the SIMInterruptPoll function for each SIM. The SIM can then check whether an interrupt is pending from the HBA, and execute its interrupt service routine if necessary.

SCSIOldCall

The XPT calls this function when a client calls the original SCSI Manager function
SCSISelect.

```
typedef void (*SIMActionProc) (void * scsiPB, Ptr SIMGlobals);
```

scsiPB   A pointer to a SCSI I/O parameter block, which is described on page 4-23.

SIMGlobals A pointer to the SIM's static data storage.

Parameter block

→	scsiPBLength	UInt16	The size of the parameter block.
→	scsiFunctionCode	UInt8	The SCSIOldCall function selector code (0x84).
→	scsiDevice	DeviceIdent	The device identification record.
→	scsiCompletion	CallbackProc	A pointer to a completion routine. If this field is set to nil, the function is executed synchronously.
→	scsiDriverStorage	UInt8 *	Optional pointer to the device driver's private storage.
←	scsiCurrentPhase	UInt16	The current SCSI bus phase.
→	scsiSelector	SInt16	The SCSISelect trap selector (0x02).
←	scsiOldCallResult	OSErr	The result code from SCSISelect.

DESCRIPTION

This function indicates the beginning of an original SCSI Manager transaction. A SIM
that supports original SCSI Manager emulation should attempt to select the device
described in the scsiDevice field. Because the entire SCSI transaction is not completed
by a call to SCSIOldCall, the result code for this function is returned in the
scsiOldCallResult field rather than the scsiResult field, as with other functions.
Subsequent original SCSI Manager function calls for this transaction are made through
the NewOldCall function.

If the SIM successfully selects the device, it should queue the parameter block like any
other SCSI I/O parameter block. The parameter block should not be removed until the
NewOldCall function completes a SCSIComplete command.

To provide full compatibility with the original SCSI Manager, a SIM must be able to
perform a SCSI arbitration and select process independent of a SCSI message-out or
command phase. If the SIM requires the CDB or message-out bytes it will not be able to
perform the select operation at the time of the SCSIOldCall request. The SIM should
return noErr in the scsiOldCallResult field and wait for a subsequent I/O request
before actually selecting the device.

RESULT CODES

The SCSIOldCall function returns an appropriate SCSISelect result code in the
scsiOldCallResult field of the parameter block.

NewOldCall

The XPT calls this function when a client calls any of the original SCSI Manager functions other than SCSISelect (which is handled by SCSIOldCall). The NewOldCall function must conform to the following type definition:

```
typedef void (*SIMActionProc) (void * scsiPB, Ptr SIMGlobals);
```

scsiPB   A pointer to a SCSI I/O parameter block, which is described on page 4-23.

SIMGlobals   A pointer to the SIM's static data storage.

Parameter block

→	scsiPBLength	UInt16	The size of the parameter block.
←	scsiResult	OSErr	The SCSIComplete result code.
→	scsiDevice	DeviceIdent	The device identification record.
→	scsiCompletion	CallbackProc	A pointer to a completion routine. If this field is set to nil, the function is executed synchronously.
→	scsiDriverStorage	UInt8 *	Optional pointer to the device driver's private storage.
←	scsiCurrentPhase	UInt16	The current SCSI bus phase.
→	scsiSelector	SInt16	The _SCSIDispatch trap selector.
←	scsiOldCallResult	OSErr	The function result code.
←	scsiSCSImessage	UInt8	The SCSIComplete message byte.

DESCRIPTION

After an original SCSI Manager transaction begins, the NewOldCall function receives all subsequent original SCSI Manager function requests until the transaction is completed. The XPT converts all original SCSI Manager function requests (except SCSIGet and SCSIStat) into SCSI Manager 4.3 parameter block requests and sends them to the appropriate SIM.

A SIM uses the scsiSelector field of the parameter block to determine which function to perform and should return the current bus phase and message byte in the appropriate fields after each request.

The XPT converts a SCSIReset request into a SCSIResetBus request and sends it to all SIMs that support original SCSI Manager emulation. The XPT handles SCSIStat requests itself, using the information returned in the scsiCurrentPhase field.

RESULT CODES

Result codes from all emulated functions except SCSIComplete are returned in the scsiOldCallResult field. The SCSIComplete result is returned in scsiResult. This indicates to the XPT that the transaction is complete and that the SIM is ready to start a new original SCSI Manager transaction. See the chapter "SCSI Manager" in this book for a list of original SCSI Manager result codes.

SCSIRegisterWithNewXPT

This function informs a SIM that a new XPT layer has been installed. The SIM should call the `SCSIReregisterBus` function to register itself with the new XPT.

```
typedef void (*SIMActionProc) (void * scsiPB, Ptr SIMGlobals);
```

scsiPB   A pointer to a SCSI Manager parameter block.

SIMGlobals A pointer to the SIM's static data storage.

Parameter block

→	scsiPBLength	UInt16	The size of the parameter block.
→	scsiFunctionCode	UInt8	The `SCSIRegisterWithNewXPT` function selector code (0x88).

DESCRIPTION

After a new XPT installs itself, and before it removes the old XPT, it sends the `SCSIRegisterWithNewXPT` request to all SIMs registered with the old XPT. Each SIM should then call the `SCSIReregisterBus` function to register with the new XPT. This allows SIMs to keep their existing bus number and static data storage when installing themselves in a new XPT.

RESULT CODES

noErr	0	No error
scsiQLinkInvalid	-7881	The qLink field was not 0

Summary of SCSI Manager 4.3

C Summary

Constants

```
enum {
    scsiVERSION = 43
};

/* SCSI Manager function codes */
enum {
    SCSINop                = 0x00,   /* no operation */
    SCSIExecIO             = 0x01,   /* execute a SCSI IO transaction */
    SCSIBusInquiry         = 0x03,   /* bus inquiry */
    SCSIReleaseQ           = 0x04,   /* release a frozen SIM queue */
    SCSIAbortCommand       = 0x10,   /* abort a SCSI command */
    SCSIResetBus           = 0x11,   /* reset the SCSI bus */
    SCSIResetDevice        = 0x12,   /* reset a SCSI device */
    SCSITerminateIO        = 0x13,   /* terminate I/O transaction */
    SCSIGetVirtualIDInfo   = 0x80,   /* return DeviceIdent of virtual ID */
    SCSILoadDriver         = 0x82,   /* load a driver from a SCSI device */
    SCSIOldCall            = 0x84,   /* begin old-API emulation */
    SCSICreateRefNumXref   = 0x85,   /* register a device driver */
    SCSILookupRefNumXref   = 0x86,   /* find a driver reference number */
    SCSIRemoveRefNumXref   = 0x87,   /* deregister a device driver */
    SCSIRegisterWithNewXPT = 0x88,   /* XPT replaced; SIM must reregister */
    vendorUnique           = 0xC0    /* 0xC0 through 0xFF */
};

/* allocation lengths for parameter block fields */
enum {
    handshakeDataLength    = 8,      /* handshake data length */
    maxCDBLength           = 16,     /* space for the CDB bytes/pointer */
    vendorIDLength         = 16      /* ASCII string length for vendor ID  */
};
```

```
/* types for the scsiTransferType field */
enum {
    scsiTransferBlind      = 0,          /* DMA if available, otherwise blind */
    scsiTransferPolled                   /* polled */
};

/* types for the scsiDataType field */
enum {
    scsiDataBuffer         = 0,          /* single contiguous buffer supplied */
    scsiDataTIB            = 1,          /* TIB supplied (ptr in scsiDataPtr) */
    scsiDataSG             = 2           /* scatter/gather list supplied */
};

/* flags for the scsiResultFlags field */
enum {
    scsiSIMQFrozen         = 0x0001,     /* the SIM queue is frozen */
    scsiAutosenseValid     = 0x0002,     /* autosense data valid for target */
    scsiBusNotFree         = 0x0004      /* SCSI bus is not free */
};

/* bit numbers of the scsiFlags field */
enum {
    kbSCSIDisableAutosense = 29,         /* disable autosense feature */
    kbSCSIFlagReservedA    = 28,
    kbSCSIFlagReserved0    = 27,
    kbSCSICDBLinked        = 26,         /* the PB contains a linked CDB */
    kbSCSIQEnable          = 25,         /* target queue actions are enabled */
    kbSCSICDBIsPointer     = 24,         /* the CDB field contains a pointer */
    kbSCSIFlagReserved1    = 23,
    kbSCSIInitiateSyncData = 22,         /* attempt sync data transfer and SDTR */
    kbSCSIDisableSyncData  = 21,         /* disable sync, go to async */
    kbSCSISIMQHead         = 20,         /* place PB at the head of SIM queue */
    kbSCSISIMQFreeze       = 19,         /* freeze the SIM queue */
    kbSCSISIMQNoFreeze     = 18,         /* disable SIM queue freezing */
    kbSCSIDoDisconnect     = 17,         /* definitely do disconnect */
    kbSCSIDontDisconnect   = 16,         /* definitely don't disconnect */
    kbSCSIDataReadyForDMA  = 15,         /* data buffer(s) are ready for DMA */
    kbSCSIFlagReserved3    = 14,
    kbSCSIDataPhysical     = 13,         /* S/G buffer data ptrs are physical */
    kbSCSISensePhysical    = 12,         /* autosense buffer ptr is physical */
    kbSCSIFlagReserved5    = 11,
    kbSCSIFlagReserved6    = 10,
    kbSCSIFlagReserved7    = 9,
    kbSCSIFlagReserved8    = 8,
```

```
    kbSCSIDataBufferValid   = 7,      /* data buffer valid */
    kbSCSIStatusBufferValid = 6,      /* status buffer valid */
    kbSCSIMessageBufferValid= 5,      /* message buffer valid */
    kbSCSIFlagReserved9     = 4
};

/* bit masks for the scsiFlags field */
enum {
    scsiDirectionMask       = 0xC0000000, /* data direction mask */
    scsiDirectionNone       = 0xC0000000, /* data direction (11: no data) */
    scsiDirectionReserved   = 0x00000000, /* data direction (00: reserved) */
    scsiDirectionOut        = 0x80000000, /* data direction (10: DATA OUT) */
    scsiDirectionIn         = 0x40000000, /* data direction (01: DATA IN) */
    scsiDisableAutosense    = 0x20000000, /* disable auto sense feature */
    scsiFlagReservedA       = 0x10000000,
    scsiFlagReserved0       = 0x08000000,
    scsiCDBLinked           = 0x04000000, /* the PB contains a linked CDB */
    scsiQEnable             = 0x02000000, /* target queue actions enabled */
    scsiCDBIsPointer        = 0x01000000, /* the CDB field is a pointer */
    scsiFlagReserved1       = 0x00800000,
    scsiInitiateSyncData    = 0x00400000, /* attempt sync data xfer & SDTR */
    scsiDisableSyncData     = 0x00200000, /* disable sync, go to async */
    scsiSIMQHead            = 0x00100000, /* place PB at the head of queue */
    scsiSIMQFreeze          = 0x00080000, /* freeze the SIM queue */
    scsiSIMQNoFreeze        = 0x00040000, /* disallow SIM Q freezing */
    scsiDoDisconnect        = 0x00020000, /* definitely do disconnect */
    scsiDontDisconnect      = 0x00010000, /* definitely don't disconnect */
    scsiDataReadyForDMA     = 0x00008000, /* buffer(s) are ready for DMA */
    scsiFlagReserved3       = 0x00004000,
    scsiDataPhysical        = 0x00002000, /* S/G buffer ptrs are physical */
    scsiSensePhysical       = 0x00001000, /* autosense ptr is physical */
    scsiFlagReserved5       = 0x00000800,
    scsiFlagReserved6       = 0x00000400,
    scsiFlagReserved7       = 0x00000200,
    scsiFlagReserved8       = 0x00000100
};

/* bit masks for the scsiIOFlags field */
enum {
    scsiNoParityCheck       = 0x0002,   /* disable parity checking */
    scsiDisableSelectWAtn   = 0x0004,   /* disable select w/Atn */
    scsiSavePtrOnDisconnect = 0x0008,   /* SaveDataPointer on disconnect */
    scsiNoBucketIn          = 0x0010,   /* don't bit-bucket on input */
    scsiNoBucketOut         = 0x0020,   /* don't bit-bucket on output */
```

```
   scsiDisableWide        = 0x0040,    /* disable wide negotiation */
   scsiInitiateWide       = 0x0080,    /* initiate wide negotiation */
   scsiRenegotiateSense   = 0x0100,    /* renegotiate sync/wide */
   scsiIOFlagReserved0080 = 0x0080,
   scsiIOFlagReserved8000 = 0x8000
};

/* SIM queue actions. */
enum {
   scsiSimpleQTag         = 0x20,      /* tag for a simple queue */
   scsiHeadQTag           = 0x21,      /* tag for head of queue  */
   scsiOrderedQTag        = 0x22       /* tag for ordered queue */
};

/* scsiHBAInquiry field bits */
enum {
   scsiBusMDP      = 0x80,    /* supports Modify Data Pointer message */
   scsiBusWide32   = 0x40,    /* supports 32-bit wide SCSI */
   scsiBusWide16   = 0x20,    /* supports 16-bit wide SCSI */
   scsiBusSDTR     = 0x10,    /* supports SDTR message */
   scsiBusLinkedCDB = 0x08,   /* supports linked CDBs */
   scsiBusTagQ     = 0x02,    /* supports tag queue message */
   scsiBusSoftReset = 0x01    /* supports soft reset */
};

/* scsiDataTypes field bits  */
/* bits 0-15 Apple-defined, 16-30 vendor unique, 31 = reserved */
enum {
   scsiBusDataBuffer      = (1<<scsiDataBuffer),  /* single buffer */
   scsiBusDataTIB         = (1<<scsiDataTIB), /* TIB (ptr in scsiDataPtr) */
   scsiBusDataSG          = (1<<scsiDataSG),      /* scatter/gather list */
   scsiBusDataReserved    = 0x80000000
};

/* scsiScanFlags field bits */
enum {
   scsiBusScansDevices    = 0x80, /* bus scans and maintains device list */
   scsiBusScansOnInit     = 0x40, /* bus scans at startup */
   scsiBusLoadsROMDrivers = 0x20  /* may load ROM drivers for targets */
};
```

```
/* scsiFeatureFlags field bits */
enum {
    scsiBusInternalExternalMask    = 0x000000C0, /* internal/external mask*/
    scsiBusInternalExternalUnknown = 0x00000000, /* unknown if in or out */
    scsiBusInternalExternal        = 0x000000C0, /* both inside and outside */
    scsiBusInternal                = 0x00000080, /* bus goes inside the box */
    scsiBusExternal                = 0x00000040, /* bus goes outside the box */
    scsiBusCacheCoherentDMA        = 0x00000020, /* DMA is cache coherent */
    scsiBusOldCallCapable          = 0x00000010, /* SIM supports old API */
    scsiBusDifferential            = 0x00000004, /* uses differential bus */
    scsiBusFastSCSI                = 0x00000002, /* HBA supports fast SCSI */
    scsiBusDMAavailable            = 0x00000001 /* DMA is available */
};


/* scsiWeirdStuff field bits */
enum {
    /* disconnects on odd byte boundries are unsafe with DMA or blind reads */
    scsiOddDisconnectUnsafeRead1  = 0x0001,
    /* disconnects on odd byte boundries unsafe with DMA or blind writes */
    scsiOddDisconnectUnsafeWrite1 = 0x0002,
    /* non-handshaked delays or disconnects on blind transfer may hang */
    scsiBusErrorsUnsafe           = 0x0004,
    /* non-handshaked delays or disconnects on blind transfer may corrupt */
    scsiRequiresHandshake         = 0x0008,
    /* targets that initiate synchronous negotiations are supported */
    scsiTargetDrivenSDTRSafe      = 0x0010
};


/* scsiHBAslotType values */
enum {
    scsiMotherboardBus            = 0x01,  /* a built-in Apple bus */
    scsiNuBus                     = 0x02,  /* a SIM on a NuBus card */
    scsiPDSBus                    = 0x03   /* a SIM on a PDS card  */
};


/* flags for the scsiDriverFlags field */
enum {
    scsiDeviceSensitive = 0x0001, /* only driver should access this device */
    scsiDeviceNoOldCallAccess = 0x0002 /* device does not support old API */
};
```

```
/* SCSI Phases (used by SIMs that support the original SCSI Manager) */
enum {
    kDataOutPhase,          /* encoded MSG, C/D, I/O bits */
    kDataInPhase,
    kCommandPhase,
    kStatusPhase,
    kPhaseIllegal0,
    kPhaseIllegal1,
    kMessageOutPhase,
    kMessageInPhase,
    kBusFreePhase,          /* additional phases */
    kArbitratePhase,
    kSelectPhase
};
```

Data Types

```
/* SCSI callback function prototypes */
typedef pascal void (*CallbackProc) (void * scsiPB);
typedef void    (*AENCallbackProc) (void);
typedef OSErr   (*SIMInitProc) (Ptr SIMinfoPtr);
typedef void    (*SIMActionProc) (void * scsiPB, Ptr SIMGlobals);
typedef void    (*SCSIProc) (void );
typedef void    (*MakeCallbackProc) (void * scsiPB);
typedef SInt32  (*InterruptPollProc) (Ptr SIMGlobals);

struct DeviceIdent
{
    UInt8 diReserved;               /* reserved */
    UInt8 bus;                      /* SCSI - bus number */
    UInt8 targetID;                 /* SCSI - target SCSI ID */
    UInt8 LUN;                      /* SCSI - logical unit number */
};
typedef struct DeviceIdent DeviceIdent;

union CDB
{
    UInt8 *cdbPtr;                  /* pointer to the CDB, or */
    UInt8 cdbBytes[maxCDBLength];   /* the actual CDB to send */
};
typedef union CDB CDB, *CDBPtr;
```

```
struct SGRecord
{
   Ptr        SGAddr;                /* scatter/gather buffer address */
   UInt32     SGCount;              /* buffer size */
};
typedef struct SGRecord SGRecord;

#define SCSIPBHdr \
   struct SCSIHdr *qLink;           /*    internal use, must be nil */      \
   SInt16     scsiReserved1;        /* -> reserved for input */            \
   UInt16     scsiPBLength;         /* -> length of the entire PB  */      \
   UInt8      scsiFunctionCode;     /* -> function selector */             \
   UInt8      scsiReserved2;        /* <- reserved for output*/            \
   OSErr      scsiResult;           /* <- returned result */               \
   DeviceIdent   scsiDevice;        /* -> device ID (bus+target+LUN) */    \
   CallbackProc scsiCompletion;     /* -> completion routine pointer */    \
   UInt32     scsiFlags;            /* -> assorted flags */                \
   UInt8      *scsiDriverStorage;   /* <> pointer for driver private use */ \
   Ptr        scsiXPTprivate;       /*    private field for XPT */         \
   SInt32     scsiReserved3;        /*    reserved */

struct SCSI_PB
{
   SCSIPBHdr
};
typedef struct SCSI_PB SCSI_PB;

#define SCSI_IO_Macro \
   SCSIPBHdr                        /*    header information fields */      \
   UInt16     scsiResultFlags;      /* <- flags that modify scsiResult */  \
   UInt16     scsiReserved12;       /* -> reserved */                      \
   UInt8      *scsiDataPtr;         /* -> data pointer */                  \
   UInt32     scsiDataLength;       /* -> data transfer length */          \
   UInt8      *scsiSensePtr;        /* -> autosense data buffer pointer */ \
   UInt8      scsiSenseLength;      /* -> size of the autosense buffer */  \
   UInt8      scsiCDBLength;        /* -> number of bytes for the CDB */   \
   UInt16     scsiSGListCount;      /* -> number of S/G list entries */    \
   UInt32     scsiReserved4;        /* <- reserved for output */           \
   UInt8      scsiSCSIstatus;       /* <- returned SCSI device status */   \
   SInt8      scsiSenseResidual;    /* <- autosense residual length */     \
   UInt16     scsiReserved5;        /* <- reserved for output */           \
   SInt32     scsiDataResidual;     /* <- data residual length */          \
   CDB        scsiCDB;              /* -> actual CDB or pointer to CDB */  \
   SInt32     scsiTimeout;          /* -> timeout value */                 \
```

```
    UInt8    *scsiReserved13;      /* -> reserved */                          \
    UInt16   scsiReserved14;       /* -> reserved */                          \
    UInt16   scsiIOFlags;          /* -> additional I/O flags */              \
    UInt8    scsiTagAction;        /* -> what to do for tag queuing */        \
    UInt8    scsiReserved6;        /* -> reserved for input */                \
    UInt16   scsiReserved7;        /* -> reserved for input */                \
    UInt16   scsiSelectTimeout;    /* -> select timeout value */              \
    UInt8    scsiDataType;         /* -> data description type */             \
    UInt8    scsiTransferType;     /* -> transfer type (blind/polled) */      \
    UInt32   scsiReserved8;        /* -> reserved for input */                \
    UInt32   scsiReserved9;        /* -> reserved for input */                \
    UInt16   scsiHandshake[handshakeDataLength]; /* -> handshake info */      \
    UInt32   scsiReserved10;       /* -> reserved for input */                \
    UInt32   scsiReserved11;       /* -> reserved for input */                \
    struct   SCSI_IO *scsiCommandLink; /* -> linked command pointer */        \
    UInt8    scsiSIMpublics[8];    /* -> reserved for SIM input */            \
    UInt8    scsiAppleReserved6[8];   /* -> reserved for input */             \
    /* XPT private fields for original SCSI Manager emulation */              \
    UInt16   scsiCurrentPhase;     /* <- bus phase after old call */          \
    SInt16   scsiSelector;         /* -> selector for old call */             \
    OSErr    scsiOldCallResult;    /* <- result of old call */                \
    UInt8    scsiSCSImessage;      /* <- SCSIComplete message byte */         \
    UInt8    XPTprivateFlags;      /* <> XPT private flags */                 \
    UInt8    XPTextras[12];        /*    reserved */

struct SCSI_IO
{
    SCSI_IO_Macro
};
typedef struct SCSI_IO SCSI_IO;
typedef SCSI_IO SCSIExecIOPB;

struct SCSIBusInquiryPB
{
    SCSIPBHdr                         /*    header information fields */
    UInt16   scsiEngineCount;         /* <- number of engines on HBA */
    UInt16   scsiMaxTransferType;     /* <- number of xfer types supported */
    UInt32   scsiDataTypes;           /* <- data types supported by this SIM */
    UInt16   scsiIOpbSize;            /* <- size of SCSI_IO PB for this SIM */
    UInt16   scsiMaxIOpbSize;         /* <- largest SCSI_IO PB for all SIMs */
    UInt32   scsiFeatureFlags;        /* <- supported features flags field */
    UInt8    scsiVersionNumber;       /* <- version number for the SIM/HBA */
    UInt8    scsiHBAInquiry;          /* <- mimic of INQ byte 7 for the HBA */
    UInt8    scsiTargetModeFlags;     /* <- flags for target mode support */
```

```
    UInt8    scsiScanFlags;           /* <- scan related feature flags */
    UInt32   scsiSIMPrivatesPtr;      /* <- pointer to SIM private data */
    UInt32   scsiSIMPrivatesSize;     /* <- size of SIM private data */
    UInt32   scsiAsyncFlags;          /* <- reserved for input */
    UInt8    scsiHiBusID;             /* <- highest path ID in the subsystem */
    UInt8    scsiInitiatorID;         /* <- ID of the HBA on the SCSI bus */
    UInt16   scsiBIReserved0;         /*    reserved */
    UInt32   scsiBIReserved1;         /*    reserved */
    UInt32   scsiFlagsSupported;      /* <- which scsiFlags are supported */
    UInt16   scsiIOFlagsSupported;    /* <- which scsiIOFlags are supported */
    UInt16   scsiWeirdStuff;          /* <- flags for strange behavior */
    UInt16   scsiMaxTarget;           /* <- maximum target ID supported */
    UInt16   scsiMaxLUN;              /* <- maximum LUN supported */
    SInt8 scsiSIMVendor[vendorIDLength]; /* <- vendor ID of the SIM */
    SInt8 scsiHBAVendor[vendorIDLength]; /* <- vendor ID of the HBA */
    SInt8 scsiControllerFamily[vendorIDLength]; /* <- controller family */
    SInt8 scsiControllerType[vendorIDLength];   /* <- controller model */
    SInt8 scsiXPTversion[4];          /* <- version number of XPT */
    SInt8 scsiSIMversion[4];          /* <- version number of SIM */
    SInt8 scsiHBAversion[4];          /* <- version number of HBA */
    UInt8    scsiHBAslotType;         /* <- type of slot this HBA is in */
    UInt8    scsiHBAslotNumber;       /* <- slot number of this HBA */
    UInt16   scsiSIMsRsrcID;          /* <- sResource ID of this SIM */
    UInt16   scsiBIReserved3;         /* <- reserved for input */
    UInt16   scsiAdditionalLength;    /* <- additional length of PB */
};
typedef struct SCSIBusInquiryPB SCSIBusInquiryPB;

struct SCSIAbortCommandPB
{
    SCSIPBHdr              /* header information fields */
    SCSI_IO  *scsiIOptr;   /* -> pointer to the PB to abort */
};
typedef struct SCSIAbortCommandPB SCSIAbortCommandPB;

struct SCSITerminateIOPB
{
    SCSIPBHdr              /* header information fields */
    SCSI_IO  *scsiIOptr;   /* -> pointer to the PB to terminate */
};
typedef struct SCSITerminateIOPB SCSITerminateIOPB;
```

```
struct SCSIGetVirtualIDInfoPB
{
    SCSIPBHdr                    /* header information fields */
    UInt16   scsiOldCallID; /* -> SCSI ID of device in question */
    Boolean  scsiExists;    /* <- true if device exists */
};
typedef struct SCSIGetVirtualIDInfoPB SCSIGetVirtualIDInfoPB;

struct SCSIDriverPB
{
    SCSIPBHdr                        /* header information fields */
    SInt16        scsiDriver;        /* -> driver refNum, for CreateRefNumXref */
                                     /* <- for LookupRefNumXref */
    UInt16        scsiDriverFlags;   /* <> details of driver/device */
    DeviceIdent   scsiNextDevice;    /* <- DeviceIdent of the next driver */
};
typedef struct SCSIDriverPB SCSIDriverPB;

struct SCSILoadDriverPB
{
    SCSIPBHdr                        /* header information fields */
    SInt16   scsiLoadedRefNum;    /* <- SIM returns driver reference number */
    Boolean  scsiDiskLoadFailed;  /* -> if true, previous call failed */
};
typedef struct SCSILoadDriverPB SCSILoadDriverPB;

struct SIMInitInfo
{
    UInt8           *SIMstaticPtr;  /* <- pointer to the SIM's static data */
    SInt32          staticSize;     /* -> size requested for SIM static data */
    SIMInitProc     SIMInit;        /* -> pointer to the SIMInit function */
    SIMActionProc   SIMAction;      /* -> pointer to the SIMAction function */
    SCSIProc        SIM_ISR;        /*    reserved */
    InterruptPollProc SIMInterruptPoll; /* -> pointer to SIMInterruptPoll */
    SIMActionProc   NewOldCall;     /* -> pointer to NewOldCall function */
    UInt16          ioPBSize;       /* -> size of SCSI_IO PB for this SIM */
    Boolean         oldCallCapable; /* -> true if SIM handles old-API calls */
    UInt8           simInfoUnused1; /*    reserved */
    SInt32          simInternalUse; /*    not affected or viewed by XPT */
    SCSIProc        XPT_ISR;        /*    reserved */
    SCSIProc        EnteringSIM;    /* <- pointer to EnteringSIM function */
    SCSIProc        ExitingSIM;     /* <- pointer to ExitingSIM function */
    MakeCallbackProc MakeCallback;  /* <- pointer to MakeCallback function */
    UInt16          busID;          /* <- bus number for the registered bus */
```

```
UInt16          simInfoUnused3; /* <- reserved */
SInt32          simInfoUnused4; /* <- reserved */
};
typedef struct SIMInitInfo SIMInitInfo;
```

Functions

```
OSErr SCSIAction        (SCSI_PB *scsiPB);
OSErr SCSIRegisterBus   (SIMInitInfo *SIMinfoPtr);
OSErr SCSIDeregisterBus (SCSI_PB *scsiPB);
OSErr SCSIReregisterBus (SIMInitInfo *SIMinfoPtr);
OSErr SCSIKillXPT       (void *);
```

Pascal Summary

Constants

```
CONST
    scsiVERSION    = 43;

    {SCSI Manager function codes}
    SCSINop                 = $00;    {no operation}
    SCSIExecIO              = $01;    {execute a SCSI IO transaction}
    SCSIBusInquiry          = $03;    {bus inquiry}
    SCSIReleaseQ            = $04;    {release a frozen SIM queue}
    SCSIAbortCommand        = $10;    {abort a SCSI command}
    SCSIResetBus            = $11;    {reset the SCSI bus}
    SCSIResetDevice         = $12;    {reset a SCSI device}
    SCSITerminateIO         = $13;    {terminate I/O transaction}
    SCSIGetVirtualIDInfo    = $80;    {return DeviceIdent of virtual ID}
    SCSILoadDriver          = $82;    {load a driver from a SCSI device}
    SCSIOldCall             = $84;    {begin old-API emulation}
    SCSICreateRefNumXref    = $85;    {register a device driver}
    SCSILookupRefNumXref    = $86;    {find a driver reference number}
    SCSIRemoveRefNumXref    = $87;    {deregister a device driver}
    SCSIRegisterWithNewXPT  = $88;    {XPT replaced; SIM must reregister}
    vendorUnique            = $C0;    {$C0 through $FF}
```

```
{allocation lengths for parameter block fields}
handshakeDataLength          = 8;       {handshake data length}
maxCDBLength                 = 16;      {space for the CDB bytes/pointer}
vendorIDLength               = 16;      {ASCII string length for Vendor ID}

{types for the scsiTransferType field}
scsiTransferBlind            = 0;       {DMA if available, otherwise blind}
scsiTransferPolled           = 1;       {polled}

{types for the scsiDataType field}
scsiDataBuffer               = 0;       {single contiguous buffer supplied}
scsiDataTIB                  = 1;       {TIB supplied (ptr in scsiDataPtr)}
scsiDataSG                   = 2;       {scatter/gather list supplied}

{flags for the scsiResultFlags field}
scsiSIMQFrozen               = $0001;   {the SIM queue is frozen}
scsiAutosenseValid           = $0002;   {autosense data valid for target}
scsiBusNotFree               = $0004;   {SCSI bus is not free}

{bit numbers in the scsiFlags field}
kbSCSIDisableAutosense       = 29;      {disable auto sense feature}
kbSCSIFlagReservedA          = 28;
kbSCSIFlagReserved0          = 27;
kbSCSICDBLinked              = 26;      {the PB contains a linked CDB}
kbSCSIQEnable                = 25;      {target queue actions are enabled}
kbSCSICDBIsPointer           = 24;      {the CDB field contains a pointer}
kbSCSIFlagReserved1          = 23;
kbSCSIInitiateSyncData       = 22;      {attempt sync data transfer and SDTR}
kbSCSIDisableSyncData        = 21;      {disable sync, go to async}
kbSCSISIMQHead               = 20;      {place PB at the head of SIM queue}
kbSCSISIMQFreeze             = 19;      {freeze the SIM queue}
kbSCSISIMQNoFreeze           = 18;      {disable SIM queue freezing}
kbSCSIDoDisconnect           = 17;      {definitely do disconnect}
kbSCSIDontDisconnect         = 16;      {definitely don't disconnect}
kbSCSIDataReadyForDMA        = 15;      {data buffer(s) are ready for DMA}
kbSCSIFlagReserved3          = 14;
kbSCSIDataPhysical           = 13;      {S/G buffer data ptrs are physical}
kbSCSISensePhysical          = 12;      {autosense buffer ptr is physical}
kbSCSIFlagReserved5          = 11;
kbSCSIFlagReserved6          = 10;
kbSCSIFlagReserved7          = 9;
kbSCSIFlagReserved8          = 8;
kbSCSIDataBufferValid        = 7;       {data buffer valid}
```

```
kbSCSIStatusBufferValid    = 6;        {status buffer valid}
kbSCSIMessageBufferValid   = 5;        {message buffer valid}
kbSCSIFlagReserved9        = 4;

{bit masks for the scsiFlags field}
scsiDirectionMask          = $C0000000;    {data direction mask}
scsiDirectionNone          = $C0000000;    {data direction (11: no data)}
scsiDirectionReserved      = $00000000;    {data direction (00: reserved)}
scsiDirectionOut           = $80000000;    {data direction (10: DATA OUT)}
scsiDirectionIn            = $40000000;    {data direction (01: DATA IN)}
scsiDisableAutosense       = $20000000;    {disable auto sense feature}
scsiFlagReservedA          = $10000000;
scsiFlagReserved0          = $08000000;
scsiCDBLinked              = $04000000;    {the PB contains a linked CDB}
scsiQEnable                = $02000000;    {target queue actions enabled}
scsiCDBIsPointer           = $01000000;    {the CDB field is a pointer}
scsiFlagReserved1          = $00800000;
scsiInitiateSyncData       = $00400000;    {attempt sync data xfer & SDTR}
scsiDisableSyncData        = $00200000;    {disable sync; go to async}
scsiSIMQHead               = $00100000;    {place PB at the head of queue}
scsiSIMQFreeze             = $00080000;    {freeze the SIM queue}
scsiSIMQNoFreeze           = $00040000;    {disallow SIM Q freezing}
scsiDoDisconnect           = $00020000;    {definitely do disconnect}
scsiDontDisconnect         = $00010000;    {definitely don't disconnect}
scsiDataReadyForDMA        = $00008000;    {buffer(s) are ready for DMA}
scsiFlagReserved3          = $00004000;
scsiDataPhysical           = $00002000;    {S/G buffer ptrs are physical}
scsiSensePhysical          = $00001000;    {autosense ptr is physical}
scsiFlagReserved5          = $00000800;
scsiFlagReserved6          = $00000400;
scsiFlagReserved7          = $00000200;
scsiFlagReserved8          = $00000100;

{bit masks for the scsiIOFlags field}
scsiNoParityCheck          = $0002;        {disable parity checking}
scsiDisableSelectWAtn      = $0004;        {disable select w/Atn}
scsiSavePtrOnDisconnect    = $0008;        {SaveDataPointer on disconnect}
scsiNoBucketIn             = $0010;        {don't bit-bucket on input}
scsiNoBucketOut            = $0020;        {don't bit-bucket on output}
scsiDisableWide            = $0040;        {disable wide negotiation}
scsiInitiateWide           = $0080;        {initiate wide negotiation}
scsiRenegotiateSense       = $0100;        {renegotiate sync/wide}
scsiIOFlagReserved0080     = $0080;
scsiIOFlagReserved8000     = $8000;
```

```
{SIM queue actions}
scsiSimpleQTag                    = $20;    {tag for a simple queue}
scsiHeadQTag                      = $21;    {tag for head of queue}
scsiOrderedQTag                   = $22;    {tag for ordered queue}

{scsiHBAInquiry field bits}
scsiBusMDP                        = $80;    {supports Modify Data Pointer message}
scsiBusWide32                     = $40;    {supports 32-bit wide SCSI}
scsiBusWide16                     = $20;    {supports 16-bit wide SCSI}
scsiBusSDTR                       = $10;    {supports SDTR message}
scsiBusLinkedCDB                  = $08;    {supports linked CDBs}
scsiBusTagQ                       = $02;    {supports tag queue message}
scsiBusSoftReset                  = $01;    {supports soft reset}

{scsiDataTypes field bits}
{bits 0-15 Apple-defined, 16-30 vendor unique, 31 = reserved}
scsiBusDataBuffer                 = $00000001; {single buffer}
scsiBusDataTIB                    = $00000002; {TIB (pointer in scsiDataPtr)}
scsiBusDataSG                     = $00000004; {scatter/gather list}
scsiBusDataReserved               = $80000000;

{scsiScanFlags field bits}
scsiBusScansDevices               = $80;    {bus scans and maintains device list}
scsiBusScansOnInit                = $40;    {bus scans at startup}
scsiBusLoadsROMDrivers            = $20;    {may load ROM drivers for targets}

{scsiFeatureFlags field bits}
scsiBusInternalExternalMask       = $000000C0; {internal/external mask}
scsiBusInternalExternalUnknown    = $00000000; {unknown if in or out}
scsiBusInternalExternal           = $000000C0; {both inside and outside}
scsiBusInternal                   = $00000080; {bus goes inside the box}
scsiBusExternal                   = $00000040; {bus goes outside the box}
scsiBusCacheCoherentDMA           = $00000020; {DMA is cache coherent}
scsiBusOldCallCapable             = $00000010; {SIM supports old-API}
scsiBusDifferential               = $00000004; {uses differential bus}
scsiBusFastSCSI                   = $00000002; {HBA supports fast SCSI}
scsiBusDMAavailable               = $00000001; {DMA is available}

{scsiWeirdStuff field bits}
scsiOddDisconnectUnsafeRead1      = $0001;  {odd byte disconnects unsafe}
scsiOddDisconnectUnsafeWrite1     = $0002;  {odd byte disconnects unsafe}
scsiBusErrorsUnsafe               = $0004;  {delays or disconnects may hang}
scsiRequiresHandshake             = $0008;  {delays/disconnects may corrupt}
scsiTargetDrivenSDTRSafe          = $0010;  {target-driven STDR supported}
```

```
{scsiHBAslotType values}
scsiMotherboardBus              = $01;    {a built-in Apple bus}
scsiNuBus                       = $02;    {a SIM on a NuBus card}
scsiPDSBus                      = $03;    {a SIM on a PDS card}

{flags for the scsiDriverFlags field}
scsiDeviceSensitive             = $0001; {only driver should access the device}
scsiDeviceNoOldCallAccess       = $0002; {device does not support old API}

{SCSI Phases (used by SIMs that support the original SCSI Manager)}
kDataOutPhase                   = $00;    {encoded MSG, C/D, I/O bits}
kDataInPhase                    = $01;
kCommandPhase                   = $02;
kStatusPhase                    = $03;
kPhaseIllegal0                  = $04;
kPhaseIllegal1                  = $05;
kMessageOutPhase                = $06;
kMessageInPhase                 = $07;
kBusFreePhase                   = $08;    {additional phases}
kArbitratePhase                 = $09;
kSelectPhase                    = $0A;
```

Data Types

```
TYPE
    {SCSI callback function prototypes}
    CallbackProc                = ProcPtr;
    AENCallbackProc             = ProcPtr;
    SIMInitProc                 = ProcPtr;
    SIMActionProc               = ProcPtr;
    SCSIProc                    = ProcPtr;
    MakeCallbackProc            = ProcPtr;
    InterruptPollProc           = ProcPtr;

TYPE
    DI =
    PACKED RECORD
        diReserved:             Byte;    {reserved}
        bus:                    Byte;    {SCSI - bus number}
        targetID:               Byte;    {SCSI - target SCSI ID}
        LUN:                    Byte;    {SCSI - logical unit number}
    END;
    DeviceIdent = DI;
```

```
CDBRec =
PACKED RECORD
CASE Integer OF
    0: cdbPtr:              ^Byte;                    {pointer to the CDB, or}
    1: cdbBytes:            ARRAY [0..15] OF Byte;    {the actual CDB to send}
END;
CDB = CDBRec;
CDBPtr = ^CDBRec;


SGR =
PACKED RECORD
    SGAddr:                 Ptr;            {scatter/gather buffer address}
    SGCount:                LongInt;        {buffer size}
END;
SGRecord = SGR;


SCSIHdr =
PACKED RECORD
    qLink:                  ^SCSIHdr;       {    internal use, must be NIL}
    scsiReserved1:          Integer;        {-> reserved for input}
    scsiPBLength:           Integer;        {-> length of the entire PB}
    scsiFunctionCode:       Byte;           {-> function selector}
    scsiReserved2:          Byte;           {<- reserved for output}
    scsiResult:             OSErr;          {<- returned result}
    scsiDevice:             DeviceIdent;    {-> device ID (bus+target+LUN)}
    scsiCompletion:         CallbackProc;   {-> completion routine pointer}
    scsiFlags:              LongInt;        {-> assorted flags}
    scsiDriverStorage:      ^Byte;          {<> pointer for driver private use}
    scsiXPTprivate:         Ptr;            {    private field for XPT}
    scsiReserved3:          LongInt;        {    reserved}
END;
SCSI_PB = SCSIHdr;


SCSI_IO =
PACKED RECORD
    qLink:                  ^SCSIHdr;       {    internal use, must be NIL}
    scsiReserved1:          Integer;        {-> reserved for input}
    scsiPBLength:           Integer;        {-> length of the entire PB}
    scsiFunctionCode:       Byte;           {-> function selector}
    scsiReserved2:          Byte;           {<- reserved for output}
    scsiResult:             OSErr;          {<- returned result}
    scsiDevice:             DeviceIdent;    {-> device ID (bus+target+LUN)}
    scsiCompletion:         CallbackProc;   {-> completion routine pointer}
    scsiFlags:              LongInt;        {-> assorted flags}
```

```
scsiDriverStorage:      ^Byte;          {<> pointer for driver private use}
scsiXPTprivate:         Ptr;            {   private field for XPT}
scsiReserved3:          LongInt;        {   reserved}
scsiResultFlags:        Integer;        {<- flags that modify scsiResult}
scsiReserved12:         Integer;        {-> reserved}
scsiDataPtr:            ^Byte;          {-> data pointer}
scsiDataLength:         LongInt;        {-> data transfer length}
scsiSensePtr:           ^Byte;          {-> autosense data buffer pointer}
scsiSenseLength:        Byte;           {-> size of the autosense buffer}
scsiCDBLength:          Byte;           {-> number of bytes for the CDB}
scsiSGListCount:        Integer;        {-> number of S/G list entries}
scsiReserved4:          LongInt;        {<- reserved for output}
scsiSCSIstatus:         Byte;           {<- returned SCSI device status}
scsiSenseResidual:      Char;           {<- autosense residual length}
scsiReserved5:          Integer;        {<- reserved for output}
scsiDataResidual:       LongInt;        {<- data residual length}
scsiCDB:                CDB;            {-> actual CDB or pointer to CDB}
scsiTimeout:            LongInt;        {-> timeout value}
scsiReserved13:         ^Byte;          {-> reserved}
scsiReserved14:         Integer;        {-> reserved}
scsiIOFlags:            Integer;        {-> additional I/O flags}
scsiTagAction:          Byte;           {-> what to do for tag queuing}
scsiReserved6:          Byte;           {-> reserved for input}
scsiReserved7:          Integer;        {-> reserved for input}
scsiSelectTimeout:      Integer;        {-> select timeout value}
scsiDataType:           Byte;           {-> data description type}
scsiTransferType:       Byte;           {-> transfer type (blind/polled)}
scsiReserved8:          LongInt;        {-> reserved for input}
scsiReserved9:          LongInt;        {-> reserved for input}
scsiHandshake:          ARRAY [0..7] OF Integer; {-> handshake info}
scsiReserved10:         LongInt;        {-> reserved for input}
scsiReserved11:         LongInt;        {-> reserved for input}
scsiCommandLink:        ^SCSI_IO;       {-> linked command pointer}
scsiSIMpublics:         ARRAY [0..7] OF Byte; {-> reserved for SIM input}
scsiAppleReserved6:     ARRAY [0..7] OF Byte; {-> reserved for input}
scsiCurrentPhase:       Integer;        {<- bus phase after old call}
scsiSelector:           Integer;        {-> selector for old call}
scsiOldCallResult:      OSErr;          {<- result of old call}
scsiSCSImessage:        Byte;           {<- SCSIComplete message byte}
XPTprivateFlags:        Byte;           {<> XPT private flags}
XPTextras:              ARRAY [0..11] OF Byte; {reserved}
END;
SCSIExecIOPB = SCSI_IO;
```

```
SCSIBusInquiryPB =
PACKED RECORD
    qLink:                  ^SCSIHdr;       {   internal use, must be NIL}
    scsiReserved1:          Integer;        {-> reserved for input}
    scsiPBLength:           Integer;        {-> length of the entire PB}
    scsiFunctionCode:       Byte;           {-> function selector}
    scsiReserved2:          Byte;           {<- reserved for output}
    scsiResult:             OSErr;          {<- returned result}
    scsiDevice:             DeviceIdent;    {-> device ID (bus+target+LUN)}
    scsiCompletion:         CallbackProc;   {-> completion routine pointer}
    scsiFlags:              LongInt;        {-> assorted flags}
    scsiDriverStorage:      ^Byte;          {<> pointer for driver private use}
    scsiXPTprivate:         Ptr;            {   private field for XPT}
    scsiReserved3:          LongInt;        {   reserved}
    scsiEngineCount:        Integer;        {<- number of engines on HBA}
    scsiMaxTransferType:    Integer;        {<- number of xfer types supported}
    scsiDataTypes:          LongInt;        {<- data types supported by SIM}
    scsiIOpbSize:           Integer;        {<- size of SCSI_IO PB for SIM}
    scsiMaxIOpbSize:        Integer;        {<- largest SCSI_IO PB registered}
    scsiFeatureFlags:       LongInt;        {<- supported features flags field}
    scsiVersionNumber:      Byte;           {<- version number for the SIM/HBA}
    scsiHBAInquiry:         Byte;           {<- mimic of INQ byte 7 for HBA}
    scsiTargetModeFlags:    Byte;           {<- flags for target mode support}
    scsiScanFlags:          Byte;           {<- scan related feature flags}
    scsiSIMPrivatesPtr:     LongInt;        {<- pointer to SIM private data}
    scsiSIMPrivatesSize:    LongInt;        {<- size of SIM private data}
    scsiAsyncFlags:         LongInt;        {<- reserved for input}
    scsiHiBusID:            Byte;           {<- highest bus ID registered}
    scsiInitiatorID:        Byte;           {<- ID of the HBA on the SCSI bus}
    scsiBIReserved0:        Integer;        {   reserved}
    scsiBIReserved1:        LongInt;        {   reserved}
    scsiFlagsSupported:     LongInt;        {<- which scsiFlags are supported}
    scsiIOFlagsSupported:   Integer;        {<- which scsiIOFlags supported}
    scsiWeirdStuff:         Integer;        {<- flags for strange behavior}
    scsiMaxTarget:          Integer;        {<- maximum target ID supported}
    scsiMaxLUN:             Integer;        {<- maximum LUN supported}
    scsiSIMVendor:          ARRAY [0..15] OF Char; {<- vendor ID of the SIM}
    scsiHBAVendor:          ARRAY [0..15] OF Char; {<- vendor ID of the HBA}
    scsiControllerFamily:   ARRAY [0..15] OF Char; {<- controller family}
    scsiControllerType:     ARRAY [0..15] OF Char; {<- controller model}
    scsiXPTversion:         ARRAY [0..3] OF Char; {<- version number of XPT}
    scsiSIMversion:         ARRAY [0..3] OF Char; {<- version number of SIM}
    scsiHBAversion:         ARRAY [0..3] OF Char; {<- version number of HBA}
```

```
    scsiHBAslotType:       Byte;         {<- type of slot this HBA is in}
    scsiHBAslotNumber:     Byte;         {<- slot number of this HBA}
    scsiSIMsRsrcID:        Integer;      {<- sResource ID of this SIM}
    scsiBIReserved3:       Integer;      {<- reserved for input}
    scsiAdditionalLength:  Integer;      {<- additional length of PB}
END;


SCSIAbortCommandPB =
PACKED RECORD
    qLink:                 ^SCSIHdr;     {    internal use, must be NIL}
    scsiReserved1:         Integer;      {-> reserved for input}
    scsiPBLength:          Integer;      {-> length of the entire PB}
    scsiFunctionCode:      Byte;         {-> function selector}
    scsiReserved2:         Byte;         {<- reserved for output}
    scsiResult:            OSErr;        {<- returned result}
    scsiDevice:            DeviceIdent;  {-> device ID (bus+target+LUN)}
    scsiCompletion:        CallbackProc; {-> completion routine pointer}
    scsiFlags:             LongInt;      {-> assorted flags}
    scsiDriverStorage:     ^Byte;        {<> pointer for driver private use}
    scsiXPTprivate:        Ptr;          {    private field for XPT}
    scsiReserved3:         LongInt;      {    reserved}
    scsiIOptr:             ^SCSI_IO;     {-> pointer to the PB to abort}
END;


SCSITerminateIOPB =
PACKED RECORD
    qLink:                 ^SCSIHdr;     {    internal use, must be NIL}
    scsiReserved1:         Integer;      {-> reserved for input}
    scsiPBLength:          Integer;      {-> length of the entire PB}
    scsiFunctionCode:      Byte;         {-> function selector}
    scsiReserved2:         Byte;         {<- reserved for output}
    scsiResult:            OSErr;        {<- returned result}
    scsiDevice:            DeviceIdent;  {-> device ID (bus+target+LUN)}
    scsiCompletion:        CallbackProc; {-> completion routine pointer}
    scsiFlags:             LongInt;      {-> assorted flags}
    scsiDriverStorage:     ^Byte;        {<> pointer for driver private use}
    scsiXPTprivate:        Ptr;          {    private field for XPT}
    scsiReserved3:         LongInt;      {    reserved}
    scsiIOptr:             ^SCSI_IO;     {-> pointer to the PB to terminate}
END;


SCSIGetVirtualIDInfoPB =
PACKED RECORD
    qLink:                 ^SCSIHdr;     {    internal use, must be NIL}
```

```
    scsiReserved1:        Integer;         {-> reserved for input}
    scsiPBLength:         Integer;         {-> length of the entire PB}
    scsiFunctionCode:     Byte;            {-> function selector}
    scsiReserved2:        Byte;            {<- reserved for output}
    scsiResult:           OSErr;           {<- returned result}
    scsiDevice:           DeviceIdent;     {-> device ID (bus+target+LUN)}
    scsiCompletion:       CallbackProc;    {-> completion routine pointer}
    scsiFlags:            LongInt;         {-> assorted flags}
    scsiDriverStorage:    ^Byte;           {<> pointer for driver private use}
    scsiXPTprivate:       Ptr;             {   private field for XPT}
    scsiReserved3:        LongInt;         {   reserved}
    scsiOldCallID:        Integer;         {-> SCSI ID of device in question}
    scsiExists:           Boolean;         {<- true if device exists}
END;


SCSIDriverPB =
PACKED RECORD
    qLink:                ^SCSIHdr;        {   internal use, must be NIL}
    scsiReserved1:        Integer;         {-> reserved for input}
    scsiPBLength:         Integer;         {-> length of the entire PB}
    scsiFunctionCode:     Byte;            {-> function selector}
    scsiReserved2:        Byte;            {<- reserved for output}
    scsiResult:           OSErr;           {<- returned result}
    scsiDevice:           DeviceIdent;     {-> device ID (bus+target+LUN)}
    scsiCompletion:       CallbackProc;    {-> completion routine pointer}
    scsiFlags:            LongInt;         {-> assorted flags}
    scsiDriverStorage:    ^Byte;           {<> pointer for driver private use}
    scsiXPTprivate:       Ptr;             {   private field for XPT}
    scsiReserved3:        LongInt;         {   reserved}
    scsiDriver:           Integer;         {<> driver reference number}
    scsiDriverFlags:      Integer;         {<> details of driver/device}
    scsiNextDevice:       DeviceIdent;     {<- DeviceIdent of the next driver}
END;


SCSILoadDriverPB =
PACKED RECORD
    qLink:                ^SCSIHdr;        {   internal use, must be NIL}
    scsiReserved1:        Integer;         {-> reserved for input}
    scsiPBLength:         Integer;         {-> length of the entire PB}
    scsiFunctionCode:     Byte;            {-> function selector}
    scsiReserved2:        Byte;            {<- reserved for output}
    scsiResult:           OSErr;           {<- returned result}
    scsiDevice:           DeviceIdent;     {-> device ID (bus+target+LUN)}
    scsiCompletion:       CallbackProc;    {-> completion routine pointer}
```

```
   scsiFlags:          LongInt;             {-> assorted flags}
   scsiDriverStorage:  ^Byte;               {<> pointer for driver private use}
   scsiXPTprivate:     Ptr;                 {   private field for XPT}
   scsiReserved3:      LongInt;             {   reserved}
   scsiLoadedRefNum:   Integer;             {<- SIM returns driver refNum}
   scsiDiskLoadFailed: Boolean;             {-> if true, previous call failed}
END;


SIMInitInfo =
PACKED RECORD
   SIMstaticPtr:       ^Byte;               {<- pointer to SIM's static data}
   staticSize:         LongInt;             {-> requested SIM static data size}
   SIMInit:            SIMInitProc;         {-> SIMInit function pointer}
   SIMAction:          SIMActionProc;       {-> SIMAction function pointer}
   SIM_ISR:            SCSIProc;            {   reserved}
   SIMInterruptPoll:   InterruptPollProc;   {-> SIMInterruptPoll function}
   NewOldCall:         SIMActionProc;       {-> NewOldCall function pointer}
   ioPBSize:           Integer;             {-> size of SCSI_IO PB for SIM}
   oldCallCapable:     Boolean;             {-> true if SIM supports old-API}
   simInfoUnused1:     Byte;                {   reserved}
   simInternalUse:     LongInt;             {   not affected or viewed by XPT}
   XPT_ISR:            SCSIProc;            {   reserved}
   EnteringSIM:        SCSIProc;            {<- EnteringSIM function pointer}
   ExitingSIM:         SCSIProc;            {<- ExitingSIM function pointer}
   MakeCallback:       MakeCallbackProc;    {<- MakeCallback function ptr}
   busID:              Integer;             {<- bus number assigned by XPT}
   simInfoUnused3:     Integer;             {<- reserved}
   simInfoUnused4:     LongInt;             {<- reserved}
END;
```

Routines

```
FUNCTION SCSIAction        (VAR ioPtr: SCSI_PB): OSErr;
FUNCTION SCSIRegisterBus   (VAR ioPtr: SIMInitInfo): OSErr;
FUNCTION SCSIDeregisterBus (VAR ioPtr: SIMInitInfo): OSErr;
FUNCTION SCSIReregisterBus (VAR ioPtr: SIMInitInfo): OSErr;
FUNCTION SCSIKillXPT       (VAR ioPtr: SIMInitInfo): OSErr;
```

Assembly-Language Summary

Data Structures

The Device Identification Record

0	diReserved	byte	reserved
1	bus	byte	bus number
2	targetID	byte	target SCSI ID
3	LUN	byte	logical unit number

The Command Descriptor Block Record

0	cdbPtr	long	CDB buffer pointer
4	cdbBytes	16 bytes	CDB buffer

The Scatter/Gather List Element

0	SGAddr	long	buffer pointer
4	SGCount	long	buffer size

The SCSI Manager Parameter Block Header

0	qLink	long	used internally by the SCSI Manager
4	scsiReserved	word	reserved
6	scsiPBLength	word	parameter block size
8	scsiFunctionCode	byte	function selector code
9	scsiReserved2	byte	reserved
10	scsiResult	word	result code
12	scsiDevice	4 bytes	device ID (bus number, target ID, LUN)
16	scsiCompletion	long	completion routine
20	scsiFlags	long	flags
24	scsiDriverStorage	long	driver private data
28	scsiXPTprivate	long	reserved
32	scsiReserved3	long	reserved

The SCSI I/O Parameter Block

0	SCSIPBHdr	36 bytes	parameter block header
36	scsiResultFlags	word	I/O result flags
38	scsiReserved12	word	reserved
40	scsiDataPtr	long	data buffer pointer
44	scsiDataLength	long	data buffer size
48	scsiSensePtr	long	autosense buffer pointer
52	scsiSenseLength	byte	autosense buffer size
53	scsiCDBLength	byte	CDB size
54	scsiSGListCount	word	number of scatter/gather list entries
56	scsiReserved4	long	reserved
60	scsiSCSIstatus	byte	SCSI device status

61	scsiSenseResidual	byte	autosense residual length
62	scsiReserved5	word	reserved
64	scsiDataResidual	long	data transfer residual length
68	scsiCDB	16 bytes	command descriptor block record
84	scsiTimeout	long	timeout value, in Time Manager format
88	scsiReserved13	long	reserved
92	scsiReserved14	long	reserved
94	scsiIOFlags	word	I/O flags
96	scsiTagAction	byte	reserved
97	scsiReserved6	byte	reserved
98	scsiReserved7	word	reserved
100	scsiSelectTimeout	word	selection timeout value, in milliseconds
102	scsiDataType	byte	data type of scsiDataPtr
103	scsiTransferType	byte	transfer mode (polled or blind)
104	scsiReserved8	long	reserved
108	scsiReserved9	long	reserved
112	scsiHandshake	16 bytes	handshaking instructions
128	scsiReserved10	long	reserved
132	scsiReserved1	long	reserved
136	scsiCommandLink	long	linked parameter block pointer
140	scsiSIMpublics	8 bytes	additional input to SIM
148	scsiAppleReserved6	8 bytes	reserved
156	scsiCurrentPhase	word	bus phase after original SCSI Manager function
158	scsiSelector	word	_SCSIDispatch selector for original function
160	scsiOldCallResult	word	result code of original function
162	scsiSCSImessage	byte	SCSIComplete message byte
163	XPTprivateFlags	byte	reserved
164	XPTextras	12 bytes	reserved

The SCSI Bus Inquiry Parameter Block

0	SCSIPBHdr	36 bytes	parameter block header
36	scsiEngineCount	word	number of engines on the HBA
38	scsiMaxTransferType	word	number of data transfer types supported
40	scsiDataTypes	long	bit map of supported data types
44	scsiIOpbSize	word	SCSI I/O parameter block size for this SIM
46	scsiMaxIOpbSize	word	largest parameter block for any registered SIM
48	scsiFeatureFlags	long	bus feature flags
52	scsiVersionNumber	byte	SIM/HBA version number
53	scsiHBAInquiry	byte	bus capability flags
54	scsiTargetModeFlags	byte	reserved
55	scsiScanFlags	byte	scan feature flags
56	scsiSIMPrivatesPtr	long	SIM private data pointer
60	scsiSIMPrivatesSize	long	SIM private data size
64	scsiAsyncFlags	long	reserved
68	scsiHiBusID	byte	highest registered bus number
69	scsiInitiatorID	byte	SCSI ID of the HBA
70	scsiBIReserved0	word	reserved
72	scsiBIReserved1	long	reserved
76	scsiFlagsSupported	long	bit map of supported scsiFlags

80	`scsiIOFlagsSupported`	word	bit map of supported `scsiIOFlags`
82	`scsiWeirdStuff`	word	miscellaneous flags
84	`scsiMaxTarget`	word	highest SCSI ID supported by the HBA
86	`scsiMaxLUN`	word	highest LUN supported by the HBA
88	`scsiSIMVendor`	16 bytes	SIM vendor string
104	`scsiHBAVendor`	16 bytes	HBA vendor string
120	`scsiControllerFamily`	16 bytes	SCSI controller family string
136	`scsiControllerType`	16 bytes	SCSI controller type string
152	`scsiXPTversion`	4 bytes	XPT version string
156	`scsiSIMversion`	4 bytes	SIM version string
160	`scsiHBAversion`	4 bytes	HBA version string
164	`scsiHBAslotType`	byte	HBA slot type
165	`scsiHBAslotNumber`	byte	HBA slot number
166	`scsiSIMsRsrcID`	word	SIM sResource ID
168	`scsiBIReserved3`	word	reserved
170	`scsiAdditionalLength`	word	additional size of the parameter block

The SCSI Abort Command Parameter Block

0	`SCSIPBHdr`	36 bytes	parameter block header
36	`scsiIOptr`	long	SCSI I/O parameter block pointer

The SCSI Terminate I/O Parameter Block

0	`SCSIPBHdr`	36 bytes	parameter block header
36	`scsiIOptr`	long	SCSI I/O parameter block pointer

The SCSI Virtual ID Information Parameter Block

0	`SCSIPBHdr`	36 bytes	parameter block header
36	`scsiOldCallID`	word	virtual SCSI ID of the device to search for
38	`scsiExists`	byte	Boolean (`true` if the device was found)

The SCSI Load Driver Parameter Block

0	`SCSIPBHdr`	36 bytes	parameter block header
36	`scsiLoadedRefNum`	word	driver reference number
38	`scsiDiskLoadFailed`	byte	Boolean (`true` if a driver could not be loaded)

The SCSI Driver Identification Parameter Block

0	`SCSIPBHdr`	36 bytes	parameter block header
36	`scsiDriver`	word	driver reference number
38	`scsiDriverFlags`	word	driver flags
40	`scsiNextDevice`	4 bytes	device ID of the next device in the list

The SIM Initialization Record

0	SIMstaticPtr	long	SIM private data pointer
4	staticSize	long	SIM private data size
8	SIMInit	long	SIMInit function pointer
12	SIMAction	long	SIMAction function pointer
16	SIM_ISR	long	reserved
20	SIMInterruptPoll	long	SIMInterruptPoll function pointer
24	NewOldCall	long	NewOldCall function pointer
28	ioPBSize	word	SCSI I/O parameter block size for this SIM
30	oldCallCapable	byte	Boolean (true if SIM accepts original functions)
31	simInfoUnused1	byte	reserved
32	simInternalUse	long	SIM private data
36	XPT_ISR	long	reserved
40	EnteringSIM	long	EnteringSIM function pointer
44	ExitingSIM	long	ExitingSIM function pointer
48	MakeCallback	long	MakeCallback function pointer
52	busID	word	bus number
54	simInfoUnused3	word	reserved
56	simInfoUnused4	long	reserved

Trap Macros

Trap Macros Requiring Routine Selectors

_SCSIAtomic

Selector	Routine
$0001	SCSIAction
$0002	SCSIRegisterBus
$0003	SCSIDeregisterBus
$0004	SCSIReregisterBus
$0005	SCSIKillXPT

Result Codes

`noErr`	0	No error
`scsiRequestInProgress`	1	Parameter block request is in progress
`scsiCDBLengthInvalid`	-7863	The CDB length supplied is not supported by this SIM; typically this means it was too big
`scsiTransferTypeInvalid`	-7864	The `scsiTransferType` is not supported by this SIM
`scsiDataTypeInvalid`	-7865	SIM does not support the requested `scsiDataType`
`scsiIDInvalid`	-7866	The initiator ID is invalid
`scsiLUNInvalid`	-7867	The logical unit number is invalid
`scsiTIDInvalid`	-7868	The target ID is invalid
`scsiBusInvalid`	-7869	The bus ID is invalid
`scsiRequestInvalid`	-7870	The parameter block request is invalid
`scsiFunctionNotAvailable`	-7871	The requested function is not supported by this SIM
`scsiPBLengthError`	-7872	The parameter block length is too small for this SIM
`scsiQLinkInvalid`	-7881	The `qLink` field was not 0
`scsiNoSuchXref`	-7882	No driver has been cross-referenced with this device
`scsiDeviceConflict`	-7883	Attempt to register more than one driver to a device
`scsiNoHBA`	-7884	No HBA detected
`scsiDeviceNotThere`	-7885	SCSI device not installed or available
`scsiProvideFail`	-7886	Unable to provide the requested service
`scsiBusy`	-7887	SCSI subsystem is busy
`scsiTooManyBuses`	-7888	SIM registration failed because the XPT registry is full
`scsiCDBReceived`	-7910	The SCSI CDB was received
`scsiNoNexus`	-7911	Nexus is not established
`scsiTerminated`	-7912	Parameter block request terminated by the host
`scsiBDRsent`	-7913	A SCSI bus device reset (BDR) message was sent to the target
`scsiWrongDirection`	-7915	Data phase was in an unexpected direction
`scsiSequenceFail`	-7916	Target bus phase sequence failure
`scsiUnexpectedBusFree`	-7917	Unexpected bus free phase
`scsiDataRunError`	-7918	Data overrun/underrun error
`scsiAutosenseFailed`	-7920	Automatic `REQUEST SENSE` command failed
`scsiParityError`	-7921	An uncorrectable parity error occurred
`scsiSCSIBusReset`	-7922	Execution of this parameter block was halted because of a SCSI bus reset
`scsiMessageRejectReceived`	-7923	`REJECT` message received
`scsiIdentifyMessageRejected`	-7924	The target issued a `REJECT` message in response to the `IDENTIFY` message; the LUN probably does not exist
`scsiCommandTimeout`	-7925	The timeout value for this parameter block was exceeded and the parameter block was aborted
`scsiSelectTimeout`	-7926	Target selection timeout
`scsiUnableToTerminate`	-7927	Unable to terminate I/O parameter block request
`scsiNonZeroStatus`	-7932	The target returned non-zero status upon completion of the request
`scsiUnableToAbort`	-7933	Unable to abort parameter block request
`scsiRequestAborted`	-7934	Parameter block request aborted by the host

ADB Manager

> "When I
> get a little
> money
> I buy
> books;
> and if any
> is left
> I buy food
> and
> clothes."
> -Erasmus

amazon.com

Contents

ADB Manager

This chapter describes the ADB Manager, the part of the Macintosh Operating System that allows you to get information about and communicate with hardware devices attached to the Apple Desktop Bus (ADB). On most Macintosh computers, the ADB is used to communicate with the keyboard, the mouse, and other user-input devices.

The Macintosh Operating System contains standard keyboard and mouse handling routines that automatically take care of all required ADB access operations. Applications typically receive keyboard and mouse input by calling the Event Manager, not by calling the ADB Manager. For complete information about receiving and interpreting keyboard and mouse input, see the chapter "Event Manager" in *Inside Macintosh: Macintosh Toolbox Essentials*.

This chapter begins with an overview of the Apple Desktop Bus and the ADB Manager. It also shows how to

■ get information about devices attached to the ADB

■ communicate with devices on the ADB at a very low level

■ write a device handler for a new user-input device that connects to the ADB

For detailed information about the ADB hardware, see *Guide to the Macintosh Family Hardware*, second edition.

About the Apple Desktop Bus

The **Apple Desktop Bus** is a low-speed serial bus that connects input devices, such as keyboards, mouse devices, and graphics tablets, to a Macintosh computer or to other hardware equipment. For information on the number of devices that you can connect to the ADB, see *Guide to the Macintosh Family Hardware*, second edition. Macintosh computers come equipped with one or two ADB connectors. Although a particular model might include two ADB connectors, all models come with only one Apple Desktop Bus.

The ADB is Apple Computer's standard interface for input devices such as keyboards and mouse devices. Apple provides a mouse with each Macintosh computer, except for models equipped with a trackball. Additionally, Apple provides various ADB keyboard options, such as the Apple Standard keyboard, the Apple Extended keyboard, and the Apple Adjustable keyboard.

Characteristics of ADB Devices

An **ADB device** is any input device that can connect to the ADB and meets the design requirements described in the *Apple Desktop Bus Specification*.

ADB Manager

IMPORTANT

Apple Computer, Inc. owns patents on the Apple Desktop Bus (ADB).
If you want to manufacture a device that works with the ADB
software, you must obtain a license and device handler ID
from Apple Computer, Inc. Write to this address:

Apple Software Licensing
Apple Computer, Inc.
1 Infinite Loop
Cupertino, CA 95014

A license includes a copy of the *Apple Desktop Bus Specification.* ▲

An ADB device generally communicates with the Macintosh Operating System through
a **device handler** —a set of low level routines designed to interact with a specific
ADB device. The Macintosh Operating System already includes device handlers
for Apple-supplied keyboards and mouse devices. You need to write your own device
handler and the code that installs it only if you are designing your own ADB device.
For more information on writing and installing an ADB device handler, see "Writing an
ADB Device Handler" on page 5-29.

A properly designed ADB device has the following features:

■ the memory in which to store data

■ a default ADB device address and device handler ID

■ the ability to detect and respond to bus collisions

■ the ability to assert a service request signal

Each ADB device may contain up to four device registers, which you can read from
or write to using certain ADB commands. One of these device registers stores the
device's default ADB device address and device handler ID, both provided by
Apple Software Licensing.

Each ADB device has a default address and initially responds to all ADB commands
at that address. A **default ADB device address** is a 4-bit bus address that uniquely
identifies the general type of device (such as a mouse or keyboard). An **ADB device
handler ID** (or device handler identification) is an 8-bit value that identifies a more
specific classification of the device type (such as the Apple Extended keyboard) or
specific mode of operation (such as whether the keyboard differentiates between the
Right and Left Shift keys). For more information on both these items, see "Default ADB
Device Address and Device Handler Identification" on page 5-11.

To avoid collision of multiple ADB devices over the bus, an ADB device must be able
to detect when another ADB device is transmitting data at the same time. For more
information on collision detection, see "Address Resolution," beginning on page
page 5-15.

An ADB device cannot initiate a data transaction. It must therefore be able to inform the
ADB Manager that it needs to transmit new data by asserting a service request signal. (In
addition, the ADB Manager continually queries ADB devices to see if they have data to

send.) For more details on service request signals, see "ADB Communication," beginning on page page 5-17.

About the ADB Manager

The ADB Manager is the part of the Macintosh Operating System that allows you to get information about and communicate with hardware devices attached to the Apple Desktop Bus. Most applications never need to interact with the ADB Manager, but can instead call the appropriate Event Manager routines for information about user actions on ADB devices such as keyboards or mouse devices. Also note that the ADB Manager does not interact with the Device Manager, but handles all ADB devices and ADB device handlers itself.

The ADB Manager handles three main tasks. First, at system startup, the ADB Manager builds the **ADB device table**, which contains the default ADB device address, device handler ID, and other identifying information for each ADB device. Whenever the ADB is reinitialized, the ADB Manager reinitializes the ADB device table. Second, if two or more ADB devices share the same default ADB device address when the ADB is building the ADB device table or when the ADB is reinitialized, the ADB Manager assigns each device a new ADB device address until no address conflict exists. This process is known as **address resolution** (see page 5-15 for more information). Third, the ADB Manager retrieves new data from the ADB devices and sends it to the appropriate device handler.

In general, ADB devices communicate with the Operating System only through the ADB Manager. The ADB Manager, in turn, calls a device handler to process data from the device. The device handler interprets data transmitted by the ADB device, and in some cases, passes this information to the Event Manager. A single device handler can manage more than one device of the same type (for example, the device handler for the Apple Extended keyboard can manage several keyboards). A single device handler can also manage more than one device type if the different device type emulates the device type associated with the particular device handler (for example, a mouse device handler can manage both a mouse and a graphics tablet emulating a mouse).

A device handler receives all data from its associated ADB device through the ADB Manager. The ADB Manager continually checks to see if ADB devices have new data to send. When the ADB Manager receives new data from an ADB device, it sends the data to the appropriate device handler. The device handler interprets the data and, if appropriate, places an event into the event queue using the `PostEvent` function. (For more information on `PostEvent`, see *Inside Macintosh: Macintosh Toolbox Essentials*.) For example, if the user types a key on the keyboard, the ADB Manager retrieves this data and sends the data to the device handler for the keyboard, which in turn places an event into the event queue. Figure 5-1 shows the relationship between the ADB Manager, device handlers, and the Event Manager.

Figure 5-1   The ADB Manager and device handlers

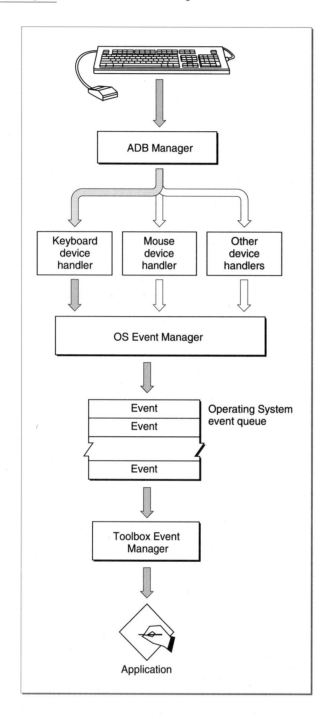

The ADB Manager retrieves data from an ADB device as a result of its normal polling process. The ADB Manager polls a device by sending it a command requesting it to return the contents of one of its registers. (Note that an ADB device should respond to the specific ADB command, Talk Register 0, only if the device has new data to send. See the next section, "ADB Commands," for more information.)

In general, the ADB Manager repeatedly polls the last ADB device that sent new data except under two circumstances: when it receives a service request signal, and when it builds the ADB device table. In these cases, the ADB Manager also polls other ADB devices. When responding to a service request signal, the ADB Manager polls all known addresses containing an ADB device until all pending data is transmitted and no device asserts a service request signal. When building the ADB device table, the ADB Manager polls each ADB device connected to the bus. For more information on the ADB device table, see "ADB Device Table" on page 5-13.

In general, only device handlers use the ADB Manager to communicate with devices. The normal polling of ADB devices performed by the ADB Manager retrieves data for the device handlers; your application should call the appropriate Event Manager routines for information about the user's input on ADB devices. If necessary, however, you can directly communicate with an ADB device using the ADBOp routine. You should use the ADBOp routine only for special purposes where you need to directly communicate with an ADB device (for example, to set the LED lights on an Apple Extended keyboard). Remember that in most circumstances, you do not need to call ADBOp.

ADB Commands

An **ADB command** is a 1-byte value that specifies the ADB device address of a device and encodes the desired action the target device should perform. In some cases, additional data may follow an ADB command. For example, the ADB Manager may transmit data to the device or the device may respond to a command by transmitting one or more bytes of data back to the ADB Manager. It's important to realize, however, that ADB devices never issue commands to the ADB Manager. At most, the device can assert a service request signal to request that the ADB Manager poll the bus for any devices wishing to transmit data. For more information on how ADB devices communicate with the ADB Manager, see "ADB Communication,"beginning on page page 5-17.

The ADB Manager can send any of four bus commands to an ADB device. Three of these commands, Talk, Listen, and Flush, are addressed to specific registers on a specific device. For more information on these registers, see "ADB Device Registers" on page 5-9. The fourth command, SendReset, applies to all ADB devices.

■ **Talk.** The ADB Manager sends a Talk command to a device to fetch user input (or other data) from the device. The Talk command requests that a specified device send the contents of a specified device register across the bus. After the device sends the data from the specified register, the ADB Manager places the data into a buffer in RAM, which the ADB Manager makes available for use by device handlers or (in rare cases) applications. In the case of a Talk Register 0 command, the ADB device should respond to the ADB Manager only if it has new data to send.

- **Listen.** The ADB Manager sends a Listen command to a device to instruct it to prepare to receive additional data. The Listen command indicates which data register is to receive the data. After sending a Listen command, the ADB Manager then transfers data from a buffer in RAM to the device. The device must overwrite the existing contents of the specified register with the new data.

- **Flush.** The ADB Manager sends a Flush command to a device to force it to flush any existing user-input data from a specified device register. The device should prepare itself to receive any further input from the user.

- **SendReset.** The ADB Manager uses a SendReset command to force all devices on the bus to reset themselves to their startup states. Each device should clear any of its pending device actions and prepare to accept new ADB commands and user input data immediately. Note that the ADB device does not actually receive the SendReset command but recognizes that it should reset itself when the bus is driven low by the 3 millisecond reset pulse. Your application should never send the SendReset command.

Figure 5-2 shows the command formats for the Talk, Listen, and Flush commands.

Figure 5-2   Command formats for Talk, Listen, and Flush

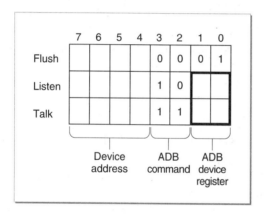

Bits 0 through 1 specify the ADB device register, bits 2 through 3 specify the command code, and bits 4 through 7 specify the device address.

Figure 5-3 shows the command format for the SendReset command.

Figure 5-3   Command format for SendReset

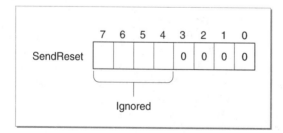

The first four bits of the SendReset command identify this command. Because the
SendReset command applies to all ADB devices, bits 4 through 7 do not specify the
address of a particular device. As previously described, an ADB device never receives
a SendReset command; instead, the device resets itself in response to the 3 millisecond
pulse.

ADB Transactions

An **ADB transaction** is a bus communication between the computer and an ADB device.
A transaction consists of a command sent by the computer, followed by a data packet of
several bytes sent either by the computer or a device. An ADB command consists of four
parts:

- an Attention signal

- a Sync signal

- one command byte

- one stop bit

Figure 5-4 shows a typical ADB transaction, consisting of a command followed by a data
packet.

Figure 5-4   A typical ADB transaction

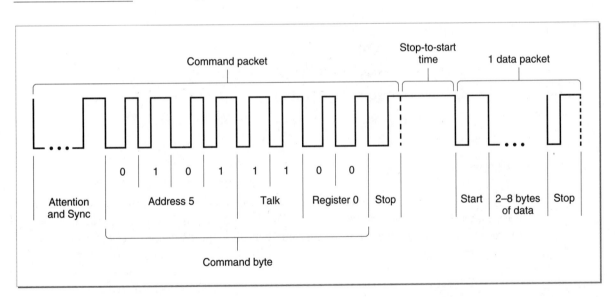

ADB Device Registers

Each device connected to the Apple Desktop Bus may provide up to four registers for
storing data. These registers are referred to as **ADB device registers**. An ADB device
can implement these registers as it chooses; that is, an ADB register does not have to
correspond to an actual hardware register on the ADB device. An ADB device is accessed

over the ADB by reading from or writing to these registers. Each ADB device register may store between 2 and 8 bytes of data.

The ADB device registers are numbered 0 through 3. Register 0 and register 3 are defined according to the specifications described in the next two sections. Register 1 and register 2 are device-dependent and can be defined by a device for any purpose.

Register 0

For most devices, register 0 is used to hold data that needs to be fetched by the Macintosh Operating System. For example, register 0 of the Apple Standard keyboard contains information about the key pressed by the user.

The ADB Manager polls all ADB devices to determine which one asserted a service request signal by sending a Talk Register 0 command to each device in turn. A device should respond to a Talk Register 0 command only if it has new data to send. For more information about polling, see "ADB Communication," beginning on page 5-17.

Table 5-1 shows the bits of register 0 as defined by the Apple Standard keyboard. Note that these bits represent key transition codes (also called raw key codes). For examples of the bits of register 0 used for the Apple standard mouse and the Apple Extended keyboard, see *Guide to the Macintosh Family Hardware*, second edition.

Table 5-1   Register 0 in the Apple Standard keyboard

Bit	Description
15	Key status for first key; 0 = down
14–8	Key transition code for first key; a 7-bit ASCII value
7	Key status for second key; 0 = down
6–0	Key transition code for second key; a 7-bit ASCII value

Register 3

The bits in register 3 are defined by the ADB Manager. Figure 5-5 shows the defined bits for register 3, which include the default ADB device address, the device handler ID, a service request enable field, an exceptional event field, and several reserved bits.

Figure 5-5   Format of device register 3

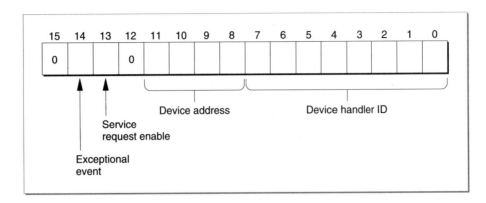

Table 5-2 provides a description of each bit in register 3.

Table 5-2   Bits in device register 3

Bit	Description
15	Reserved; must be 0
14	Exceptional event, device specific; always 1 if not used
13	Service request enable; 1 = enabled
12	Reserved; must be 0
11–8	ADB device address
7–0	Device handler ID

The functions of some of the bits in register 3 are discussed in detail in this chapter. For information on service request signals, "ADB Communication," beginning on page 5-17. For information on the default ADB device address and device handler ID, see the next section.

Default ADB Device Address and Device Handler Identification

As previously described, each ADB device has a default ADB device address and device handler identification (or device handler ID). Together, the default ADB device address and device handler ID identify the general type of device (such as a mouse or keyboard) as well as a more specific classification of the device type (such as the Apple Extended keyboard) or specific mode of operation (such as whether the keyboard differentiates between the Right and Left Shift keys).

A default ADB device address is a 4-bit bus address that uniquely identifies devices of the same type. The currently defined default ADB device addresses have values between 1 and 7. Table 5-3 shows the defined default ADB device addresses and their device type categories. Though it is not mandatory that an ADB device's default address define the device type, doing so significantly reduces the possibility of multiple devices on the ADB sharing the same default address. Most device default addresses are movable addresses, which means that they can be replaced with a new address. If two ADB devices have the same default address, the ADB Manager must move one of the devices to a new address. An example of this process is described in detail in "Address Resolution," beginning on page 5-15.

Table 5-3   Defined default ADB device addresses

Default address	Device type	Example
$1	Protection devices	Software execution control devices
$2	Encoded devices	Keyboards
$3	Relative-position devices	Mouse devices
$4	Absolute-position devices	Tablets
$5	Data transfer devices	Low-speed ADB modems
$6	Any other	Reserved
$7	Any other	Appliances/miscellaneous

Note

The default address $0 is reserved for the Macintosh computer. Addresses $8 through $E are reserved by the ADB Manager for dynamically relocating devices to resolve address collision. ◆

The ADB device handler ID is an 8-bit value that further identifies the specific device type or its mode of operation. For example, an Apple Standard keyboard has a device handler ID of 1, while an Apple Extended keyboard has a device handler ID of 2.

An ADB device can support several device handler IDs and change its mode of operation according to its current device handler ID. The Apple Extended keyboard, for example, supports two device handler IDs: $02 and $03. The Apple Extended keyboard uses $02 as a device handler ID by default. When its device handler ID is changed to $03, the Apple Extended keyboard sends separate key codes for the Left and Right Shift keys. A device handler, application, or the ADB Manager can request a device to change its device handler ID by sending it a Listen Register 3 command. If a device accepts a new device handler ID, it sends that device handler ID in response to any subsequent Listen Register 3 command. An ADB device should respond to a request to change its device handler ID only if it recognizes the device handler ID; otherwise, it should ignore the request and continue to send its default device handler ID in response to a Listen Register 3 command. For example, if the Apple Extended keyboard is requested to change its device handler ID to $52, the keyboard ignores this request. When an ADB device handler changes its device handler ID anytime after the ADB Manager sets initial values for that device in the ADB device table (that is, after initial address resolution is complete), the ADB Manager does not update the device's entry in the ADB device table.

Apple reserves certain device handler IDs for special purposes, as shown in Table 5-4. ADB devices must recognize and respond appropriately to these special device handler IDs. When a device receives a Listen Register 3 command containing a special device handler ID, the device should immediately perform the specified action. Note, however, that the device should not change its device handler ID to the special device handler ID specified by the Listen Register 3 command.

Table 5-4   Special device handler IDs

ID value	Description
$FF	Instructs the device to initiate a self-test.
$FE	Instructs the device to change its ADB device address (as stored in bits 8–11 of register 3) to the new address set in the command if no collision has been detected.
$FD	Instructs the device to change its ADB device address (as stored in bits 8–11 of register 3) to the new address set in the command if the activator is pressed. (See *Guide to the Macintosh Family Hardware,* second edition, for complete details on activators.)
$00	Instructs the device to change its ADB device address (as stored in bits 8–11 of register 3) and enable bit (bit 13) to the new values set in the command.

Note
The special device handler ID $00 can also be returned by a device that fails a self-test. ◆

ADB Device Table

The ADB Manager creates the ADB device table and places it in the system heap during system startup. The ADB Manager also reinitializes the ADB device table whenever the ADB is reinitialized (as a result of a call to the ADBReinit procedure, for example). For each ADB device, the ADB device table contains an **ADB device table entry**. The device table entry specifies the device's handler ID, default ADB device address and current ADB address, as well as the address of the device handler and the address of the area in RAM used for global storage by the handler. For information on the address ADB device and device handler ID, see "Default ADB Device Address and Device Handler Identification" on page 5-11. For information on device handlers, see "Writing an ADB Device Handler" on page 5-29.

Once the ADB Manager has set the initial values for an ADB device in the ADB device table, thereafter it updates the device table entry only to reflect changes to a device's device handler routine and data area pointer. If an ADB device changes its device handler ID, the ADB Manager does not update the ADB device table to reflect this change. To find out the new device handler ID for a device, you must send the device a Talk Register 3 command.

5

ADB Manager

ADB Manager

The ADB device table is accessible only through the ADB Manager routines GetIndADB, GetADBInfo, and SetADBInfo. The GetIndADB and GetADBInfo routines return information from the device table in an ADB data block, defined by the ADBDataBlock data type. These routines are described in detail later in this chapter.

At system startup, the ADB Manager sends a Talk Register 3 command to each device to retrieve its default ADB device address and device handler ID. For an Apple ADB device, the ADB Manager immediately places in the device table the address of the appropriate device handler provided by Apple for that device. Each nonstandard device, however, requires its own handler installation code to place the address of its device handler in the table. For information on installing a device handler, see "Installing an ADB Device Handler," beginning on page 5-30.

If more than one ADB device has the same default ADB device address, the ADB Manager performs address resolution. For more information, see "Address Resolution," beginning on page 5-15.

Table 5-5 shows an example of an ADB device table after all ADB devices have responded to polling and have been assigned unique ADB device addresses by the ADB Manager. This example shows just one way that address resolution might occur.

Table 5-5   Typical ADB device table at initialization

Index	Device handler ID	Current address	Default address	Address of device handler routine	Address of handler's data area
$1	$01	$2	$2 (keyboard)	$4080AB46	$5450
$2	$01	$3	$3 (mouse)	$4080AAE6	$0000
$3	$02	$E	$2 (keyboard)	$4080AB46	$548C
$4	$02	$D	$2 (keyboard)	$4080AB46	$548C
$5	$00	$0	$0	$0	$0
$6	$00	$0	$0	$0	$0
$F	$00	$0	$0	$0	$0

The leftmost column shows the device table index. In this example, four devices are connected to the ADB: three keyboards and a mouse. The keyboard at index $1 has a device handler ID of $01, specifying that it is an Apple Standard keyboard. The remaining two keyboards at index $3 and index $4 each have a device handler ID of $02, specifying that they are both Apple Extended keyboards. Because they are the same type of device, all three keyboards have a default ADB device address of $2. Each ADB device must have a unique ADB device address. The ADB Manager therefore performs address resolution by assigning each Apple Extended keyboard a new and unoccupied ADB address. See "Address Resolution," beginning on page 5-15, for complete details on address resolution.

Although the ADB Manager assigns each keyboard a unique current address, note that all three keyboards use the same device handler, which in this example is located at address $4080AB46. The device handler, however, stores data for the two keyboard types in different areas in RAM. In this example, the address of the data area for the two Apple Extended keyboards is at $548C, compared to the address of the data area for the Apple Standard keyboard located at $5450.

In contrast, the mouse at index $2 is the only ADB device of its type and therefore has the same default and current address. Also, the mouse uses a different device handler than the keyboards use, which in this example is located at address $4080AAE6. Finally, the mouse device handler does not need to use area in RAM for storage. As a result, the value for its data area is $0000.

Address Resolution

Each ADB device has a default ADB device address and initially responds to all ADB commands at that address. If two or more ADB devices respond to commands sent to a particular address, this is referred to as **address collision**. Due to the design of ADB devices and the ability of the ADB Manager to perform address resolution, most address collision occurs only at initial startup or when you reset the ADB. Furthermore, once the ADB Manager reassigns those addresses in conflict, subsequent address collision is quite rare.

Collision detection is the ability of an ADB device to detect that another ADB device is transmitting data at the same time. An ADB device should be able to detect a bus collision if it is bringing the bus high when another device is bringing the bus low. Whenever an ADB device attempts to bring the bus high, it should verify whether the bus actually goes high. If the bus instead goes low, this indicates that another device is also trying to send data. The device detecting the collision must immediately stop transmitting and save the data it was sending. Because the detecting device is no longer transmitting data, the device driving the bus low is not able to detect the other device. As a result, only one of the two colliding devices—the device driving the bus high—actually detects the collision.

When the ADB Manager performs address resolution, it reassigns default ADB device addresses so that all devices have a unique address. The new address locations are always between $8 through $E. Because these locations are dynamic, there is no way to predict the order in which the ADB Manager assigns new addresses to ADB devices or the exact address that it assigns to a given device. For the ADB Manager to accomplish address resolution, an ADB device must meet two design requirements: first, it must have collision detection, and second, it must always respond to a Talk Register 3 command by returning a random device address in bits 8 through 11.

A random device address is a four-bit value; an ADB device must return a random device address to the ADB Manager in response to a Talk Register 3 command. An ADB device is designed to respond only to a Talk Register 3 command that is specifically addressed to it. Because the address of an ADB device is already confirmed by its ability to respond to the Talk Register 3 command, the device does not need to provide its ADB device address to identify itself. The ability of devices to send random addresses plays a crucial role in collision detection.

At system startup, the ADB Manager polls all ADB devices at each ADB address and begins the process of building the ADB device table by sending a Talk Register 3 command to each device. Each ADB device at a specific address attempts to respond by sending a random device address. If more than one ADB device shares an address, however, each device that detects a collision immediately stops transmitting data. The device that has not detected the collision completes sending its random address across the bus.

In response, the ADB Manager sends to the original address a Listen Register 3 command that contains a new ADB device address and a device handler ID of $FE. A new ADB device address is always a value between $8 and $E. A device handler ID of $FE instructs a device to change to the new device address only if it does not detect a collision. Any detecting devices will therefore ignore the next Listen Register 3 command containing a new ADB device address. As a result, only the device that did not detect the collision moves to the new address; the detecting devices remain at the original address. The ADB Manager now sends another Talk Register 3 command to the new address to verify that the device moved to that location. In response, the moved device must once again return a random address.

The ADB Manager repeats this process until it receives no response when it sends a Talk Register 3 command to the shared address. This indicates that no devices reside at the address and that it is an available address location for a device. The ADB Manager then moves the first device it relocated to a new address back to its original address.

Figure 5-6 shows three keyboards, a mouse, and a graphics tablet. In this example, assume these ADB devices are all connected to an ADB. This example describes one possible order and method that the ADB Manager might use to relocate ADB devices. Remember, however, that the specific implementation of address resolution is private to the ADB Manager.

Figure 5-6　　Resolving address conflicts

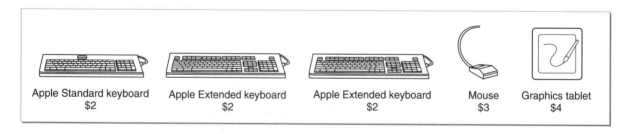

Apple Standard keyboard　　Apple Extended keyboard　　Apple Extended keyboard　　Mouse　　Graphics tablet
$2　　$2　　$2　　$3　　$4

In the example shown in Figure 5-6, all three keyboards are the same device type; thus, they share the same default ADB device address ($2). When the ADB Manager begins to build the device table by sending a Talk Register 3 command to address $2, all three keyboards attempt to respond and address collision occurs. The ADB Manager then begins the process of address resolution.

In this particular example, the ADB Manager first sends a Listen Register 3 command that specifies a device handler ID of $FE and a new device address of $E to the ADB device at address $2. Only the keyboard that did not detect the collision responds to this command and moves to address $E. Next, the ADB Manager sends a Talk Register 3 command to address $E to confirm that the keyboard has relocated there. Once the relocated keyboard responds with a random address, the ADB Manager again sends a Talk Register 3 command to address $2. Because two keyboards still remain at address $2, address collision occurs again. The ADB Manager therefore sends a Listen Register 3 command that specifies a device handler ID of $FE and a new device address of $D to the ADB device at address $2. Only the keyboard that did not detect the collision moves to address $D. There is now only one keyboard remaining at address $2. When the ADB Manager sends another Talk Register 3 command to address $2, the single keyboard does not detect a collision. It therefore accepts the next Listen Register 3 command from the ADB Manager that tells it to move to a new address ($C). Once more, the ADB Manager sends a Talk Register 3 command to address $2. When it receives no response from any devices, the ADB Manager moves the keyboard relocated to address $E back to address $2.

In contrast, the mouse and the graphics tablet are the only devices of their type connected to the ADB. As a result, neither device shares a default address with another device; the mouse is located at address $3 and the graphics tablet is located at address $4. When the ADB Manager builds the device table, no address collision occurs for either device and they remain at their original addresses.

For more information on the ADB device table, see "ADB Device Table" on page 5-13.

ADB Communication

ADB devices cannot issue commands to the ADB Manager. Communication is accomplished in two ways. First, the ADB Manager performs polling of the ADB devices, and second, each ADB device can assert a service request signal to inform the ADB Manager that it has data to send. The ADB Manager passes the data sent by each ADB device to the associated device handler. In general, the ADB Manager continuously polls the **active ADB device**, which is the last device that sent new data after requesting service with a service request signal. The default active device is located at address $3, which is usually the mouse.

Polling (or autopolling) is accomplished by the ADB Manager repeatedly sending Talk Register 0 commands to an ADB device to see if it has new data to return. Register 0 is therefore the primary register for transferring data for all ADB devices. For an example of the register 0 contents for the Apple Standard keyboard, see Table 5-1 on page 5-10.

Note

If the data that is significant to the ADB device resides in an ADB
register other than register 0, the device handler must directly retrieve
the data from that register. For example, the Apple Extended keyboard
contains data in both register 0 and register 2. The keyboard device
handler must therefore directly retrieve the register 2 contents. ◆

Figure 5-7 shows three ADB devices connected to the bus (a keyboard, a mouse, and
a graphics tablet) and the ADB Manager performing polling.

Figure 5-7   Polling the ADB

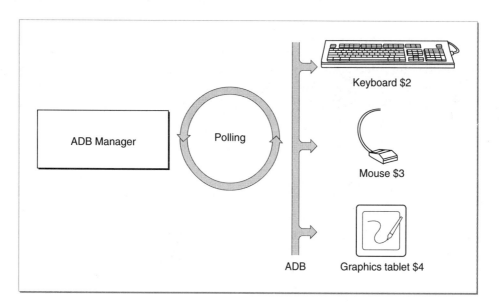

An ADB device should respond to a Talk Register 0 command only if it has new data to
send to the ADB Manager; that is, if the status of the device has changed since the last
Talk Register 0 command. For example, Figure 5-8 shows a situation where the mouse
is the active device. The ADB Manager polls the mouse, sending a Talk Register 0
command. If the mouse has new data to send, it should respond. Whenever the mouse
responds with new data to a Talk Register 0 command, the ADB Manager sends this new
data to the mouse handler, which uses the `PostEvent` function to place an event in the
event queue.

Figure 5-8 How an ADB device responds to a polling request by the ADB Manager

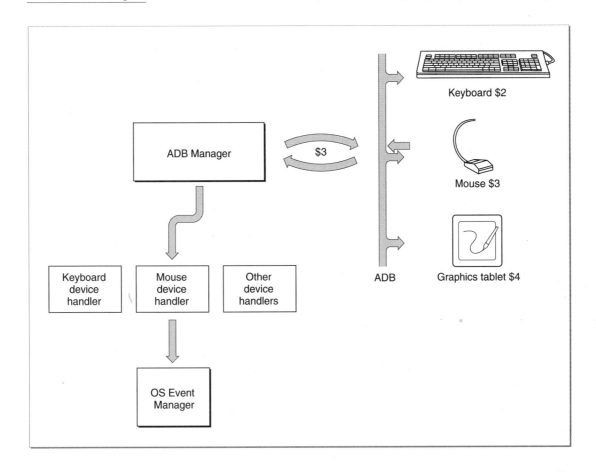

Note

Designing an ADB device to respond to a Talk Register 0 command only if it has new data to send can significantly optimize the performance of the Apple Desktop Bus. It reduces the effort required by the ADB Manager because it only has to call the device handler associated with a device when the device has actual data to send. It also avoids the endless polling cycles by the ADB Manager that can occur when an ADB device responds to a Talk Register 0 command with no new data. In an endless polling cycle, the ADB Manager continues to repeatedly poll the device not sending new data, rather than moving to the next ADB device that may have new data to send.

For further optimization, the ADB Manager automatically polls only those ADB devices that have an installed device handler. If an ADB device does not have a device handler installed, the ADB Manager skips that device during polling and instead polls an ADB device that has an installed device handler, even if the other device has not recently communicated with the ADB Manager. The ADB Manager may poll an ADB device that does not have an installed device handler, however, in response to a service request signal. ◆

ADB Manager

5

If a Talk Register 0 command is completing, the ADB device should assert a special signal, known as a **service request signal** (or **SRQ**), to inform the ADB Manager that it has data to send. As shown in Figure 5-9, an ADB device asserts an SRQ by holding the bus low during the low portion of the stop bit of any command or data transaction.

Figure 5-9   The ADB service request signal

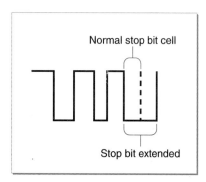

For information on the timing parameters for ADB signals, see *Guide to the Macintosh Family Hardware*, second edition.

To identify which device asserted the SRQ, the ADB Manager polls each address known to contain an ADB device, beginning with the active ADB device. That is, if the first device polled by the ADB Manager does not respond to the Talk Register 0 command, it polls the next device. When the ADB Manager polls the device that asserted the SRQ, that device responds with new data. If another device asserts an SRQ, the ADB Manager continues polling until it finds that device. If no SRQ is asserted, this indicates that all pending data has been fetched and that the ADB Manager can return to polling the active device. For example, Figure 5-10 shows three ADB devices, with the ADB Manager polling the active ADB device. One of the three ADB devices, a graphics tablet, sends an SRQ to the ADB Manager. In this particular example, the ADB Manager responds by polling the active ADB device (in this case, the keyboard) and then polling the remaining ADB devices. After receiving a Talk Register 0 command from the ADB Manager, the graphics tablet can send its new data.

ADB Manager

Figure 5-10   An ADB device asserts the service request signal

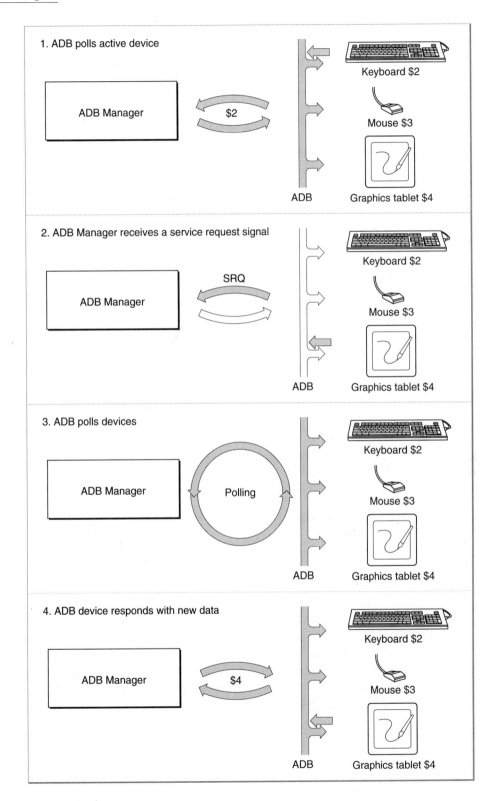

Using the ADB Manager

You can use the ADB Manager to communicate with and get information about devices attached to the Apple Desktop Bus. In general, applications interact with the ADB indirectly, by calling the Event Manager to retrieve information about user actions on the available input devices (keyboard, mouse, graphics tablet, and so forth). As a result, most applications do not need to know how to communicate directly with ADB devices, or even whether the ADB is present on the computer.

Some applications—such as diagnostic programs or other utilities—might want to report information about the ADB. Other software might even need to send commands directly to an ADB device (perhaps to query or modify device settings). This section shows how to

- determine whether the ADB Manager is present on the current computer

- get information about the devices attached to the ADB

- send commands to an ADB device in order to determine or modify device settings

For information on writing and installing ADB device handlers, see "Writing an ADB Device Handler" on page 5-29.

Checking for the ADB Manager

The Apple Desktop Bus was introduced on the Macintosh II and Macintosh SE computers. To test for the availability of the ADB Manager on your system, use the NGetTrapAddress function to see if the _CountADBs trap macro is available. See the chapter "Trap Manager" in *Inside Macintosh: Operating System Utilities* for information about the NGetTrapAddress function.

Getting Information About ADB Devices

You can use the ADB Manager to get several kinds of information about the ADB and about individual ADB devices on the bus. You can call CountADBs to determine how many devices are currently available on the Apple Desktop Bus. The CountADBs function simply counts the number of entries in the ADB device table.

You can call the GetIndADB function to get information about a device specified by its index in the ADB device table. The GetIndADB function returns as its function result the current ADB address of the device with the specified index and also returns additional information in a parameter block pointed to by one of its parameters. If you already know the address of an ADB device, you can call GetADBInfo to get that same information about the device.

Both GetIndADB and GetADBInfo return information about a particular device in an ADB data block, defined by the ADBDataBlock data type.

```
TYPE ADBDataBlock =
PACKED RECORD
    devType:            SignedByte;     {device handler ID}
    origADBAddr:        SignedByte;     {default ADB device address}
    dbServiceRtPtr:     Ptr;            {pointer to device handler}
    dbDataAreaAddr:     Ptr;            {pointer to data area}
END;
```

Note

The installation code for a device handler can set information
(specifically the address of its device handler and optional data area) in
its device's entry in the device table using the `SetADBInfo` function. ◆

You can examine the `devType` and `origADBAddr` fields of the `ADBData` block to
determine what kind of ADB device is located at a particular ADB address. (Remember
that once the ADB Manager has set the initial values for an ADB device in the ADB
device table, it updates the device table entry for the device to reflect changes only to
the address of the device handle routine and data area pointer. Thus, `GetIndADB` and
`GetADBInfo` return the device's original device handler ID and original (default) ADB
device address.) For example, the Apple Extended keyboard has a device handler ID of
$02 and a default address of $2. Listing 5-1 shows one way to determine whether an
ADB device is an Apple Extended keyboard.

Listing 5-1   Determining whether an ADB device is an Apple Extended keyboard

```
FUNCTION IsExtendedKeyboard (myAddress: ADBAddress): Boolean;
VAR
    myInfo:         ADBDataBlock;
    myCommand:      Integer;
    myErr:          OSErr;
CONST
    kExtKeyboardAddr = 2;
    kExtKeyboardOrigHandlerID = 2;
BEGIN
    myErr := GetADBInfo(myInfo, myAddress);
    IsExtendedKeyboard := (myInfo.origADBAddr = kExtKeyboardAddr)
                    AND (myInfo.devType = kExtKeyboardOrigHandlerID);
END;
```

The `IsExtendedKeyboard` function defined in Listing 5-1 is used later in this chapter,
in Listing 5-5 on page 5-28.

Communicating With ADB Devices

You can use the ADB Manager to communicate directly with ADB devices by sending ADB commands to those devices. In general, however, you don't need to do this, because the ADB Manager automatically polls for input from the connected ADB devices and passes any data received from a device to the device's device handler. Most applications should never interact directly with ADB devices, and even ADB device handlers need to do so only occasionally (for instance, to read or set device parameters stored in the device registers).

If you do need to send ADB commands directly to a device, you can do so using the ADBOp function. The ADBOp function transmits over the bus a command byte, whose structure is shown in Figure 5-2 on page 5-8 and Figure 5-3 on page 5-8. The command (Talk, Listen, Flush, and SendReset) and any register information are encoded into an integer that is passed to ADBOp. You also pass ADBOp three pointers:

■ A pointer to the optional data area used by the completion routine.

■ A pointer to a completion routine. This routine is executed once the command byte has been sent to the ADB device.

■ A pointer to a Pascal string (maximum 8 bytes data preceded by one length byte). The first byte specifies the length of the string and the remaining bytes (if any) contain data to be sent to the device or provide storage for the data to be received from the device.

The ADBOp function is always executed asynchronously. If the bus is busy, the ADB command passed to ADBOp is held in a command queue until the bus is free. If your application requires synchronous behavior, you'll need to use a completion routine to determine when the ADB command itself has completed. Figure 5-11 shows the relationships between the ADBOp routine, the device to which it is directly communicating, the ADB Manager, and an ADB completion routine.

Figure 5-11   The `ADBOp` routine and an ADB completion routine

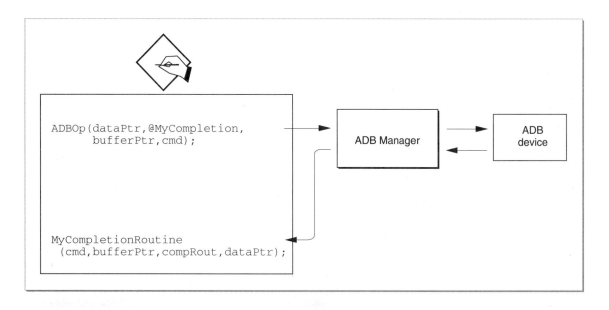

Listing 5-2 shows a way to send ADB commands synchronously.

Listing 5-2   Sending an ADB command synchronously

```
PROCEDURE MySetFlag;
{move a nonzero value into the word pointed to by register A2}
INLINE $34BC, $FFFF;        {MOVE.W #$FFFF, (A2)}

PROCEDURE MyCompletionRoutine;
BEGIN
   MySetFlag;               {set a flag to indicate done}
END;

FUNCTION MySendADBCommand (myBufferPtr: Ptr; myCommand: Integer): OSErr;
{send a command to an ADB device synchronously}
VAR
   myDone:     Integer;     {completion flag}
   myErr:      OSErr;
BEGIN
   myDone := 0;
   myErr := ADBOp(@myDone, @MyCompletionRoutine, myBufferPtr, myCommand);
   IF myErr = noErr THEN
      REPEAT
      UNTIL myDone <> 0;
```

```
        ELSE
            ; {ADB buffer overflowed -- retry command here}
        MySendADBCommand := myErr;
    END;
```

The `MySendADBCommand` function sets the completion flag `myDone` to zero and then calls `ADBOp`, passing the address of that completion flag and the address of a completion routine along with the two parameters passed to `MySendADBCommand`. The completion routine simply calls an inline assembly routine that moves a nonzero value into the word pointed to by register A2. (When the completion routine is called, register A2 points to the optional data area, in this case, to the `myDone` variable.) The `MySendADBCommand` function waits until the value of the `myDone` variable changes, and then returns.

Rather than provide a completion routine to verify that a Talk command has completed, you can initialize the first byte of the data buffer to 0 before sending the command. The first byte of the data buffer contains the length of the buffer (in the same manner that the first byte of a Pascal string contains the length of the string). The data buffer can include from 0 to 8 bytes of information. After sending the command with `ADBOp`, you can then test the first byte of the data buffer to determine whether the command has completed. Once the first byte of information contains a nonzero value, then the command has completed, and the first byte of the buffer indicates the number of bytes returned by the ADB device.

Listing 5-3, Listing 5-4, and Listing 5-5 illustrate how to use the `MySendADBCommand` function (defined in Listing 5-2) to blink the LED lights on the Apple Extended keyboard. The Apple Extended keyboard maintains the current setting of the LED lights in the lower 3 bits of device register 2. You can read the current light setting by issuing a Talk command to the keyboard, as shown in Listing 5-3.

Listing 5-3   Reading the current state of the LED lights

```
VAR
    gRegisterData:      PACKED ARRAY[0..8] of Byte;   {buffer for register data}
CONST
    kListenMask         = 8;       {masks for ADB commands}
    kTalkMask           = 12;
    kLEDRegister        = 2;       {register containing LED settings}
    kLEDValueMask       = 7;       {mask for bits containing current LED setting}

FUNCTION MyGetLEDValue (myAddress: ADBAddress; VAR myLEDValue: Integer)
                        : OSErr;
VAR
    myCommand:   Integer;
    myErr:       OSErr;
```

```
BEGIN
   {initialize length of buffer; on return, the ADB device sets }
   gRegisterData[0] := Byte(0);  { this byte to the number of bytes returned}
   {get existing register contents with a Talk command}
   myCommand := (myAddress * 16) + kTalkMask + kLEDRegister;
   myErr := MySendADBCommand(@gRegisterData, myCommand);
   IF myErr = noErr THEN              {make sure completed successfuly}
      {gRegisterData now contains the existing data in device register 2; }
      { the lower 3 bits of byte 2 contain the LED value}
      myLEDValue := Integer(BAND(gRegisterData[2], kLEDValueMask))
   ELSE
      myLEDValue := 0;
   MyGetLEDValue := myErr;
END;
```

The `MyGetLEDValue` function constructs a Talk Register 2 command by adding the address value to command and register masks defined by the application. Then it calls the `MySendADBCommand` function to communicate with the device at the specified address. If `MySendADBCommand` completes successfully, then the `gRegisterData` variable contains (in array elements 1 and 2) the two-byte value in device register 2. Only the lower 3 bits of that value are used for the LED settings. If one of those bits is set, the corresponding light is off. Note that if `MyGetLedValue` returns an error, this generally indicates that the `ADBOp` buffer overflowed.

The `MySetLEDValue` function defined in Listing 5-4 sets the LED lights to a specific pattern.

Listing 5-4   Setting the current state of the LED lights

```
FUNCTION MySetLEDValue (myAddress: ADBAddress; myValue: Integer): OSErr;
VAR
   myCommand:  Integer;
   myByte:     Byte;                   {existing byte 2 of device register 2}
   myErr:      OSErr;
BEGIN
   gRegisterData[0] := Byte(2);     {set length of buffer}
   {get existing register contents with a Talk command}
   myCommand := (myAddress * 16) + kTalkMask + kLEDRegister;
   myErr := MySendADBCommand(@gRegisterData, myCommand);
   MySetLEDValue := myErr;
   IF myErr <> noErr THEN              {make sure completed successfuly}
      EXIT(MySetLEDValue);
   {gRegisterData now contains the existing data in device register 2; }
   { reset the lower 3 bits of byte 2 to the desired value}
```

```
myByte := gRegisterData[2];
myByte := BAND(myByte, 255 - 7);          {mask off lower three bits}
myByte := BOR(myByte, Byte(myValue));     {install desired value}
gRegisterData[2] := myByte;
myCommand := (myAddress * 16) + kListenMask + kLEDRegister;
MySetLEDValue := MySendADBCommand(@gRegisterData, myCommand);
END;
```

Notice that the MySetLEDValue function first reads the current value in device register 2. This is necessary to preserve the bits in that register that do not encode the LED state. Register 2 contains sixteen bits; be sure to change only the three bits that represent the three LED lights.

Finally, the MyCountWithLEDs procedure shown in Listing 5-5 uses the MyGetLEDValue and MySetLEDValue routines to "count" in binary.

Listing 5-5   Counting in binary using a keyboard's LED lights

```
PROCEDURE MyCountWithLEDs;
VAR
    myValue:     Integer;
    myIndex:     Integer;
    myAddress:   ADBAddress;
    myOrigLED:   Integer;
    myInfo:      ADBDataBlock;       {needed for GetIndADB; ignored here}
    myDelay:     LongInt;            {needed for Delay; ignored here}
    myErr:       OSErr;
BEGIN
    FOR myIndex := 1 TO CountADBs DO
    BEGIN
        myAddress := GetIndADB(myInfo, myIndex);
        IF IsExtendedKeyboard(myAddress) THEN
        BEGIN
            {save original state of LED lights}
            myErr := MyGetLEDValue(myAddress, myOrigLED);
            myValue := 7;                        {turn all the lights OFF}
            WHILE myValue >= 0 DO
            BEGIN
                myErr := MySetLEDValue(myAddress, myValue);
                myValue := myValue - 1;
                Delay(30, myDelay);
            END;
            {restore original state of LED lights}
            myErr := MySetLEDValue(myAddress, myOrigLED);
```

```
        END; {IF}
    END; {FOR}
END;
```

The `MyCountWithLEDs` procedure looks for Apple Extended keyboards on the ADB and counts from 0 to 7, in binary, on the LED lights of any such keyboard it finds.

Note
The techniques shown in this section for reading and writing the LED state of an Apple Extended keyboard are provided for illustrative purposes only. Your application or other software should in general not modify the LED state of the user's keyboard. ◆

Writing an ADB Device Handler

The previous section, "Using the ADB Manager," illustrates how you can use the ADB Manager to communicate with and get information about devices attached to the ADB. This section describes how to write a device handler for an ADB device. You should write a device handler for a device only if you are the manufacturer of that device.

A device handler is a low-level routine that communicates with a particular ADB device. The device handler gathers data from an ADB device through the ADB Manager and interprets the data; depending on the device, the device handler might then post an event into the event queue using the `PostEvent` function.

A single device handler can manage more than one device; for example, the standard device handler for the Apple Extended keyboard can manage multiple extended keyboards. Also, in some cases the same handler can be used to manage two or more device types. For example, a relative-position graphics tablet could emulate a mouse, using the same default ADB device address and device handler ID as used by the mouse, and providing the same information in response to Talk commands. In this case, when both the mouse and tablet are connected to the ADB at the same time, the ADB Manager calls the mouse handler when either device requires it.

Each ADB device has a default ADB device address and default device handler ID. Some ADB devices support more than one device handler ID. In this case, the device handler manages the device based on the current device handler ID; this allows an ADB device to add or modify its performance or feature set. For more information about ADB addresses and device handler IDs, see "Default ADB Device Address and Device Handler Identification" on page 5-11.

In addition to writing a device handler for your device, you need to write the code that installs the device handler. The next few sections explain how to write a device handler and code to install the handler.

IMPORTANT

You need the information in this section only if you are writing a device handler for a new ADB device. The Macintosh Operating System includes device handlers for all Apple keyboards and Apple mouse devices. You do not need to write a device handler to receive input from these standard Apple devices; instead, your application should get information about mouse movements and key presses by calling the Event Manager. See the chapter "Event Manager" in *Inside Macintosh: Macintosh Toolbox Essentials* for complete information about how the Event Manager interacts with applications. ▲

Installing an ADB Device Handler

You install a device handler for an ADB device by placing the address of the device handler in the device's entry of the ADB device table. To do this, and to make your ADB device available to the user as soon as possible, Apple recommends that you provide users with a system extension that installs your device handler. Thus, your system extension should contain your device handler as well as the code that installs the device handler into the appropriate entry of the ADB device table. (See "ADB Device Table" on page 5-13 for a description of the structure of entries in the ADB device table.)

Your installation code should search the ADB device table for an entry whose default ADB device address and default device handler ID match the values assigned to your device. For example, if your ADB device has a default address of $7 and a default handler ID of 99, your installation code should search the ADB device table for entries matching these values. If your installation code finds any matching entries, it should install the address of your device handler into your device's entry in the ADB device table. The typical installation code for ADB devices other than a keyboard or mouse does this: calls the CountADBs function to determine the number of entries in the ADB device table; repeatedly calls the GetIndADB function to index through each device table entry and compares the default ADB device address and device handler ID with those of your device; for any matching entries, calls the SetADBInfo function to install the device handler for that device into the device's entry in the ADB device table. Note that before installing the address of your device handler into the ADB device table, your installation code must first allocate space in the system heap for your handler and copy your handler to this area; your installation code should also allocate space in the system heap for its optional data area.

If you provide a device handler for a mouse or keyboard you must consider whether your ADB device should use a standard device handler during initial startup (until your system extension has a chance to run and install the device's device handler) or whether your ADB device should use only its own device handler (which means your device will be unable to respond to the user until its handler is installed).

When the ADB Manager first builds the ADB device table, it associates with each device the device's default ADB address, the device's current ADB address, and the device's default device handler ID. In addition, for each device it initializes the field that contains the address of the device handler for the device and the field that contains a pointer to a data area used by the device handler. For Apple ADB devices, the ADB Manager installs the appropriate device handler provided by Apple. Thus, the device handler for an Apple keyboard or Apple mouse is available almost immediately after initial startup. For all other ADB devices, the device's device handler must be specifically installed by the device's installation code. For example, the ADB Manager does not install the Apple device handler for a keyboard with a default ADB device address of $2 and a default device handler ID of 99; instead, the device's system extension must install the device's device handler.

If your ADB device is a keyboard or mouse and you want it to function as soon as possible in the startup process and before system extensions are run, you can design your ADB device to emulate an Apple keyboard or mouse and use that device's device handler until its own device handler is installed. In this case, your ADB device's default ADB address and default device handler ID initially matches that of an Apple device. This causes the ADB Manager to install the address of an Apple device handler for your device's entry in the ADB device table. To install the actual device handler for your device, you can provide a system extension that

■ uses the `CountADBs` function to count the number of entries in the ADB device table.

■ repeatedly uses the `GetIndADB` function to examine each entry in the ADB device table for an entry with a default ADB device address and default device handler ID that matches that of a standard device.

■ upon finding a matching entry, uses the `ADBOp` function to send a Talk Register 3 command to the selected ADB device so that it sends its contents across the bus; uses the `ADBOp` function to send a Listen Register 3 command to the device to change its device handler ID from its default device handler ID to its actual device handler ID; and uses the `ADBOp` function to send another Talk Register 3 command to the device and examine the register contents to see whether the device returns the new device handler ID. If so, your extension has found the index entry for your device and can use the `SetADBInfo` function to install the appropriate device handler for your device. Note that when you request an ADB device to change to another device handler ID, the ADB Manager does not update the ADB device table entry to reflect the new device handler ID. You can find out the new handler ID for that device only by sending it a Talk Register 3 command.

Your installation code should also store a pointer to its reinitialization code in the system global variable `JADBProc` and should preserve the existing value of `JADBProc`, as illustrated in Listing 5-6 and Listing 5-7.

The next three listings, Listing 5-6, Listing 5-7, and Listing 5-8, show code that installs a device handler, handles reinitialization by appropriate use of the system global variable `JADBProc`, and performs the actual actions of the device handler.

Listing 5-6 shows an example of code that installs an ADB device handler. The code first defines some constants. It also defines a stack frame which includes storage for a variable called `myADBDB` that is used later as a parameter block for both `GetIndADB` and `SetADBInfo`. The installation code then jumps to the code starting at the label `MyInstallHandlers`; this code uses `CountADBs` and then `GetIndADB` to search all entries in the ADB device table for a matching default ADB device address and device handler ID. If it finds such an entry, it uses the code at the label `MySetDeviceInfo` to set up information for that device in the device's entry in the ADB device table.

Specifically, for each occurrence of a matching entry, the code at the label `MySetDeviceInfo` allocates space in the system heap for the data area used by the device handler for the ADB device at that address. (It does not need to allocate space for the handler itself at this time. This is because a resource containing the code shown in Listing 5-6 is marked to be loaded into the system heap; thus the system software loads the resource into the system heap when it executes this system extension.) The code then uses the `SetADBInfo` function to install into the ADB device table the address of the device's device handler as well as a pointer to the global data area used by the device handler.

Finally, the installation code stores in the `iNextProc` field the current value of the system global variable `JADBProc` and then sets `JADBProc` to contain a pointer to `myJADBProc`.

Listing 5-6   Installing an ADB device handler

```
;For installation to work, the resource containing this resource must be
;marked as sysHeap loaded. This way, you do not have to copy a version of it
;into the system heap prior to installing.
; MPW Build commands:
;    ASM 'ADBSample.a'
;    Link -t INIT -c WeSt -ra ADBSample=resSysHeap -rt INIT=128 -m MAIN -sg ∂
;        ADBSample 'ADBSample.a'.o -o ADBSample

myAddr          EQU       $xx                 ;default ADB device address
myADBType       EQU       $xx                 ;device handler ID definition


main            PROC      EXPORT


StackFrame      RECORD    {A6Link}, DECR      ;build a stack frame record
ParamBegin      EQU       *                   ;start parameters after this point
ParamSize       EQU       ParamBegin-*        ;size of all the passed parameters
RetAddr         DS.L      1                   ;place holder for return address
A6Link          DS.L      1                   ;place holder for A6 link
myADBDB         DS        ADBDataBlock        ;local handle to our ADB data block
LocalSize       EQU       *                   ;size of all the local variables
                ENDR

                WITH      StackFrame
                WITH      ADBDataBlock
                LINK      A6, #0              ;make a stack frame
                BSR       MyInstallHandlers  ;install handlers for our devices
                TST.W     D0                 ;D0 = number of old devices found
                BEQ.S     @exit              ;if none, exit
```

```
            LEA       main, A0        ;after installing, we need to
            _RecoverHandle, SYS       ; recover the handle and then
            MOVE.L    A0 -(SP)        ; detach this resource so it always
            _DetachResource           ; stays in memory

            LEA       iNextProc, A2   ;get pointer to old vector storage
            LEA       JADBProc, A3    ;make pointer to low memory vector
            MOVE.L    (A3), (A2)      ;save contents of vector for chaining

            LEA       myJADBProc, A2  ;get pointer to our jADBProc
            MOVE.L    A2, (A3)        ;install it in the low memory vector

@exit       UNLK      A6              ;dispose local variables
            RTS

;placeholder for MyADBHandler - see Listing 5-8 on page 5-37
;placeholder for myJADBProc - see Listing 5-7 on page 5-35


;MySetDeviceInfo routine (called by MyInstallHandlers)
; on entry: D0 = ADB address of our device
; does not preserve D4 or A1
MySetDeviceInfo
            LINK      A6, #LocalSize     ;make a stack frame
            LEA       myADBDB(A6), A1    ;pointer to stack-based param block
            LEA       MyADBHandler, A3   ;pointer to the handler routine
            MOVE.W    D0, D4             ;save the actual address
            MOVE.L    A3, (A1)           ;set up the handler address
            MOVE.L    #10, D0            ;data area for device is 10 bytes
            _NewPtr, SYS, CLEAR          ;allocate our data area
            TST.W     D0                 ;test for error
            BNE.S     @SDIExit           ;exit if error
            MOVE.L    A0, 4(A1)          ;put pointer to parameter data
                                         ; in data area
            MOVE.W    D4, D0             ;put actual address to set in D0
            MOVE.L    A1, A0             ;put parameter block pointer in A0
            _SetADBInfo                  ;set up info for this device
@SDIExit
            UNLK      A6                 ;dispose stack frame
            RTS                          ;exit this routine

iNextProc   DC.L      0                  ;store pointer to next jADBProc
```

```
;MyInstallHandlers routine (called by main)
; on exit: D0 = number of our device types found
; does not preserve D1, D2, D3, D4 or A1
MyInstallHandlers
                LINK     A6, #LocalSize      ;make a stack frame
                CLR.L    D3                  ;clear device counter
                _CountADBs                   ;get number of ADB devices
                MOVE.W   D0, D2              ;save this number in D2
                BEQ.S    @return             ;exit if none
                                                        ;put handler ID and
                MOVE.W   #(myADBType<<8)+myAddr, D1 ; default address into D1
@cntLoop
                MOVE.W   D2, D0              ;put device index in D0
                LEA      myADBDB(A6), A0     ;pointer to stack-based param block
                _GetINDADB                   ;get an ADB device table entry
                BMI.S    @nextRec            ;skip if invalid
                CMP.W    devType(A0), D1     ;is this one of our devices?
                BNE.S    @nextRec            ;skip if no match
                BSR.S    MySetDeviceInfo     ;set handler for this device
                ADDQ     #1, D3              ;found one of our devices, add to D3
@nextRec        SUBQ.W   #1, D2              ;try next index
                BNE.S    @cntLoop            ;loop if more
                MOVE.L   D3, D0              ;return number found in D0
@return         UNLK     A6
                RTS
                ENDP
                END
```

Note

In the past, Apple recommended that you install an ADB device handler
by placing the ADB device handler in an 'ADBS' resource in the System
file. In this case, the 'ADBS' resource ID corresponds to the ADB
device's default address. At system startup, the ADB Manager searches
the System file for 'ADBS' resources for only those ADB devices that
appear on the bus. The ADB Manager then loads these resources into
memory and executes them. The ADB Manager also reads register 3 for
each ADB device and places the device's default ADB device address
and device handler ID into the ADB device table. This method, however,
does not offer the same flexibility and scope as when you install a
handler with an extension. For example, because 'ADBS' resource IDs
are indexed only by their default addresses, you cannot install ADB
resources for two different devices at the same address using 'ADBS'
resources. Apple therefore recommends that you install all ADB device
handlers using a system extension. ◆

Your installation code should set up the value of JADBProc (by chaining) to point to a routine that you provide which appropriately handles the case when the ADB is reinitialized. When the ADB is reinitialized, the ADB Manager calls the routine pointed to by the system global variable JADBProc; it calls this routine twice: once before reinitializing the ADB, and once after reinitializing the ADB. When this routine is called, D0 contains the value 0 for preprocessing and 1 for postprocessing. Your routine must restore the value of D0 and branch to the original value of JADBProc on exit.

For preprocessing, your reinstallation routine should deallocate any storage. It must also take action for postprocessing. Because the ADB (and ADB device table) is reinitialized during postprocessing, the ADB Manager might need to perform address resolution. As a result, you cannot assume that your ADB device still resides at its default address after postprocessing occurs. Therefore, for postprocessing your reinstallation routine should search the ADB bus for a matching device (just as in its installation code) and install its entry into the ADB device table. Finally, the code jumps to the routine stored in iNextProc, and thus chains to the next routine that needs to perform postprocessing. Listing 5-7 shows an example of this entire process.

Listing 5-7 Installing a routine pointer into JADBProc

```
;main goes here, see Listing 5-6 on page 5-32
;handler code goes here, see Listing 5-8 on page 5-37
;NOTE: This routine must be installed as part of the handler.
myJADBProc
            LINK     A6, #LocalSize     ;make a stack frame
            MOVEM.L  D0-D2/A1, -(SP)    ;save registers for next procedure
            TST.B    D0                 ; D0 = 0 for pre-processing,
                                        ; D0 = 1 for post-processing
            BEQ.S    @preProc           ;if 0, pre-process data areas

@postProc
            BSR.S    MyInstallHandlers  ;install handlers (Listing 5-6)
            BRA.S    @JADBExit
@prePost
            LEA      myADBDB(A6), A1    ;pointer to stack-based param block
            LEA      MyADBHandler, A2   ;address of handler for comparison
            _CountADBs                  ;get the number of ADB devices
            MOVE.W   D0, D2             ;save this value in D2
            BEQ.S    @JADBExit          ;exit if none
                                                ;put handler ID and
            MOVE.W   #(myADBType<<8)+myAddr, D1 ; default address into D1
@preLoop
            MOVE.W   D2, D0             ;current index
            MOVE.L   A1, A0             ;address of data block
            _GetIndADB                 ;get ADB device table entry
```

5

ADB Manager

```
        BMI.S     @nextRec              ;skip if invalid
        CMP.W     devType(A0), D1       ;is this one of our devices?
        BNE.S     @nextRec              ;skip if no match
        CMPA.L    dbServiceRtPtr(A0), A2   ;compare with our handler ID
        BNE.S     @nextRec              ;if no match, don't delete pointer
        MOVE.L    dbDataAreaAddr(A0), A0  ;get the pointer to dispose
        _DisposePtr                     ;if matches, it's ours, so dispose
@nextRec
        SUBQ.W    #1, D2                ;get next index
        BNE.S     @preLoop              ;loop if more
@JADBExit
        MOVEM.L   (SP)+, D0-D2/A1       ;restore registers
        UNLK      A6                    ;dispose stack frame
        LEA       iNextProc, A0         ;get pointer to next procedure
        MOVE.L    (A0), A0
        JMP       (A0)                  ;jump to next procedure
```

Creating an ADB Device Handler

A device handler communicates with a particular ADB device by gathering data about the device it manages from the ADB Manager, and then interpreting that data. For example, the device handler for a particular device might then post an event into the event queue using PostEvent.

Whenever an ADB device sends data (by responding to a Talk Register 0 command), the ADB Manager calls the associated device handler. The ADB Manager passes these parameters to the device handler:

■ in register A0, a pointer to the ADB data sent by the ADB device

■ in register A1, a pointer to the device handler routine

■ in register A2, a pointer to the data area (if any) associated with the device handler

■ in register D0, the ADB command that resulted in the handler being called

Note
ADB device handlers are always called at interrupt time; they must follow all rules for interrupt-level processing as described in *Inside Macintosh: Processes*. ◆

Listing 5-8 gives an example of a simple device handler that handles data from an ADB device. (Listing 5-6 on page 5-32 shows code that installs the address of this handler into the ADB device table.) This device handler simply saves the data sent by the ADB device into the device handler's global data area. Note that you must include with your device handler code that handles reinitialization of the ADB (see Listing 5-7 on page 5-35 for details of reinitialization).

Listing 5-8   A sample device handler

```
MyADBHandler
        ANDI.B    #$0F, D0            ;check command
        CMPI.B    #$0C, D0            ;was it a talk R0 command?
        BNE.S     @exit              ; no, exit (something is wrong)
        MOVE.B    (A0)+, D0          ;get the count
        CMPI.B    #2, D0             ;this device only sends 2 bytes
        BNE.S     @exit              ;bad count, exit
        MOVE. B   (A0)+, HndlrData(A2) ;grab the 1st byte, save in global area
        MOVE.B    (A0)+, MoreData(A2)  ;grab the 2nd byte, save in global area
@exit           RTS
        ;code from Listing 5-7 goes here
```

ADB Manager Reference

This section describes the data structures and routines provided by the ADB Manager. See "Using the ADB Manager," beginning on page 5-22, and "Writing an ADB Device Handler" on page 5-29, for detailed instructions on using these routines.

Data Structures

This section describes the ADB data block, ADB information block, and ADB operation block.

ADB Data Block

You can get information about an ADB device by calling the functions GetIndADB and GetADBInfo. These functions return information from the ADB device table in an ADB data block, defined by the ADBDataBlock data type.

```
TYPE ADBDataBlock =
PACKED RECORD
    devType:        SignedByte;     {device handler ID}
    origADBAddr:    SignedByte;     {original ADB address}
    dbServiceRtPtr: Ptr;           {pointer to device handler}
    dbDataAreaAddr: Ptr;           {pointer to data area}
END;
ADBDBlkPtr = ^ADBDataBlock;
```

Field descriptions

devType   The device handler ID of the ADB device.

origADBAddr   The device's default ADB address.

dbServiceRtPtr

A pointer to the device's device handler.

dbDataAreaAddr

A pointer to the device handler's optional data area.

ADB Information Block

You can set a device's device handler routine and data area by calling the `SetADBInfo` function. You pass `SetADBInfo` an ADB information block, defined by the `ADBSetInfoBlock` data type.

```
TYPE ADBSetInfoBlock =
RECORD
    siServiceRtPtr:    Ptr;        {pointer to device handler}
    siDataAreaAddr:    Ptr;        {pointer to data area}
END;
ADBSInfoPtr = ^ADBSetInfoBlock;
```

Field descriptions

siServiceRtPtr

A pointer to the device handler.

siDataAreaAddr

A pointer to the device handler's optional data area.

Remember that once the ADB Manager has set the initial values for an ADB device in the ADB device table, it updates the device table entry for the device to reflect changes only to the address of the device handler routine and data area pointer.

ADB Operation Block

You use the ADB operation block to pass information to the `ADBOp` function if you call the function from assembly language. The ADB operation block is defined by the `ADBOpBlock` data type.

```
TYPE ADBOpBlock =
  RECORD
    dataBuffPtr:     Ptr;        {address of data buffer}
    opServiceRtPtr:  Ptr;        {pointer to device handler}
    opDataAreaPtr:   Ptr;        {pointer to optional data
                                  area}
  END;
  ADBOpBPtr = ^ADBOpBlock;
```

Field descriptions

dataBuffPtr   A pointer to a variable-length data buffer. The first byte of the buffer must contain the buffer's length.

opServiceRtPtr

A pointer to a completion routine.

opDataAreaPtr

A pointer to an optional data area.

ADB Manager Routines

The ADB Manager provides routines that you can use to initialize the ADB, communicate with ADB devices, and get or set ADB device information. In general, you need to use these routines only if you need to access devices on the ADB directly or communicate with a special device. You'll also need to use some of these routines to install an ADB device handler.

Initializing the ADB Manager

The ADB Manager provides the ADBReInit procedure to initialize the Apple Desktop Bus. As explained in the following paragraphs, however, you probably won't ever need to call ADBReInit.

ADBReInit

The Macintosh Operating System uses the ADBReInit procedure to reinitialize the Apple Desktop Bus.

```
PROCEDURE ADBReInit;
```

DESCRIPTION

The ADBReInit procedure reinitializes the Apple Desktop Bus to its original condition at system startup time. It clears the ADB device table and places a SendReset command on the bus to reset all devices to their original addresses. The ADB Manager resolves any address conflicts and rebuilds the device table.

IMPORTANT

In general, your application shouldn't call ADBReInit. If you need to assign a different device handler to a device, or activate a "virtual" device associated with some device that is already connected to the bus, you can use the SetADBInfo routine. ▲

The ADBReInit procedure also calls the routine pointed to by the system global variable JADBProc at the beginning and end of its execution. You can insert your own preprocessing and postprocessing routine by changing the value of JADBProc. When this routine is called, D0 contains the value 0 for preprocessing and 1 for postprocessing. Your routine must restore the value of D0 and branch to the original value of JADBProc on exit. Because the ADB is reinitialized during postprocessing, the ADB Manager might need to perform address resolution. As a result, you cannot assume that your ADB device still resides at its default address after postprocessing occurs.

SPECIAL CONSIDERATIONS

Calling ADBReInit on computers running system software versions earlier than 6.0.4 can cause incorrect keyboard layouts to be loaded.

The ADBReInit procedure does not deallocate memory that has been allocated by the device handler installation code.

If you provide a device handler that is installed by a system extension, you must reinstall the entry for your ADB device in the ADB device table. See "Installing an ADB Device Handler," beginning on page 5-30 for more information.

Communicating Through the ADB

You can use the ADBOp function to communicate with devices on the ADB. In general, however, you shouldn't need to call ADBOp. Applications should get information about the user's input on ADB devices by calling the appropriate Event Manager routines. In addition, the ADB Manager automatically polls device register 0 (the register that contains the data to be transmitted from the device to the ADB device handler) as part of its normal bus polling and service request handling. As a result, device handlers should need to call ADBOp only occasionally for special purposes, such as setting device modes or obtaining device status.

ADBOp

You can use the ADBOp function to send a command to an ADB device.

```
FUNCTION ADBOp (data: Ptr; compRout: ProcPtr; buffer: Ptr;
                commandNum: Integer): OSErr;
```

data   A pointer to an optional data area.

compRout   A pointer to a completion routine.

buffer   A pointer to a variable-length data buffer. The first byte of the buffer must contain the buffer's length.

commandNum

A command number. The command number is a 1-byte value that encodes the command to be performed, the register the command refers to, and the desired action the target device should perform.

DESCRIPTION

The ADBOp function transmits over the bus the command byte whose value is given by the commandNum parameter. See Figure 5-2 on page 5-8 for the structure of this command byte. For a Listen command, the ADB Manager also transmits the data pointed to by the buffer parameter. Upon completion of a Talk command, the area pointed to by the buffer parameter contains the data returned by the ADB device. The ADBOp function executes only when the ADB would otherwise be idle; if the bus is busy, the command byte is held in a command queue. If the command queue is full, the ADBOp function returns an error and the command is not placed in the queue.

The length of the data buffer pointed to by the buffer parameter must be contained in its first byte (in the same manner that the first byte of a Pascal string contains the length of the string). The data buffer can include from 0 to 8 bytes of information. For a Listen command, the data buffer should contain any data to be sent to the device. For a Talk command, the contents of the data buffer are valid only on completion of the command. To verify that the Talk command is completed, you should provide a completion routine when you send the command to an ADB device or simply test the value of the first byte of the data buffer (which contains the length of the buffer).

The optional data area to which the data parameter points is intended for storage used by the completion routine pointed to by the compRout parameter. When you use ADBOp to send a command, you can optionally supply a completion routine as a parameter. See "ADB Command Completion Routines," beginning on page 5-47 for details on completion routines.

SPECIAL CONSIDERATIONS

The ADBOp function is always executed asynchronously. The result code returned by ADBOp indicates only whether the ADB command was successfully placed into the ADB command queue, not whether the command itself was successful. A method for interacting with the ADB bus synchronously is illustrated in "Communicating With ADB Devices," beginning on page 5-24.

ASSEMBLY-LANGUAGE INFORMATION

The ADB operation block contains some of the information required by the ADBOp function. You'll need to set up an ADB operation block only if you call ADBOp from assembly-language. (In Pascal, the ADB operation block is defined by the ADBOpBlock data type.)

The registers on entry and exit for `ADBOp` are

Registers on entry

A0   Address of a parameter block of type `ADBOpBlock`

D0   A command number

Registers on exit

D0   Result code

The parameter block whose address is passed in register A0 has this structure

Parameter block:

→	`dataBuffPtr`	Ptr	A pointer to a variable-length data buffer. The first byte of the buffer must contain the buffer's length.
→	`opServiceRtPtr`	Ptr	A pointer to a completion routine.
→	`opDataAreaPtr`	Ptr	A pointer to an optional data area.

RESULT CODES

noErr	0	No error
errADBOp	–1	Command queue is full. Retry command.

SEE ALSO

See Listing 5-2 on page 5-25 for an example of using the `ADBOp` function.

Getting ADB Device Information

You can use the ADB Manager functions in this section to determine how many ADB devices are present and to get information about a specific ADB device, specified either by its ADB device address or by its index in the ADB device table.

CountADBs

You can use the `CountADBs` function to determine how many ADB devices are connected to the bus.

```
FUNCTION CountADBs: Integer;
```

DESCRIPTION

The `CountADBs` function returns a value representing the number of devices connected to the bus; it determines this information by counting the number of entries in the ADB device table.

GetIndADB

You can use the GetIndADB function to get information about an ADB device, specified by its index in the ADB device table.

```
FUNCTION GetIndADB (VAR info: ADBDataBlock;
                    devTableIndex: Integer): ADBAddress;
```

info   An ADB data block. On exit, the fields of this parameter block are filled with information about the specified ADB device.

devTableIndex
              An index into the ADB device table.

Parameter block

←	devType	SignedByte	The device handler ID.
←	origADBAddr	SignedByte	The device's default ADB address.
←	dbServiceRtPtr	Ptr	The address of the device's device handler routine.
←	dbDataAreaAddr	Ptr	The address of the device handler's data storage area.

DESCRIPTION

The GetIndADB function returns information from the ADB device table entry whose index number is specified by the devTableIndex parameter. The information is returned in an ADB data block, passed in the info parameter.

The GetIndADB function also returns the current ADB address of the specified device as its function result. If, however, GetIndADB is unable to find the specified entry in the ADB device table, it returns a negative value as its function result. In that case, the fields of the info data block are undefined.

SPECIAL CONSIDERATIONS

Once the ADB Manager has set the initial values for an ADB device in the ADB device table, it updates the device table entry for the device to reflect changes only to the address of the device handler routine and data area pointer.

GetADBInfo

You can use the GetADBInfo function to get information about an ADB device, specified by its ADB address.

```
FUNCTION GetADBInfo (VAR info: ADBDataBlock;
                     adbAddr: ADBAddress): OSErr;
```

info   An ADB data block. On exit, the fields of this parameter block are filled
            with information about the specified ADB device.

adbAddr   The ADB address of a device.

Parameter block

←	devType	SignedByte	The device handler ID.
←	origADBAddr	SignedByte	The device's default ADB address.
←	dbServiceRtPtr	Ptr	The address of the device's device handler.
←	dbDataAreaAddr	Ptr	The address of the device handler's data storage area.

DESCRIPTION

The GetADBInfo function returns, through the info parameter, information from the
ADB device table entry of the device whose ADB address is specified by the adbAddr
parameter.

SPECIAL CONSIDERATIONS

Once the ADB Manager has set the initial values for an ADB device in the ADB device
table, it updates the device table entry for the device to reflect changes only to the
address of the device handler routine and data area pointer.

RESULT CODES

noErr   0   No error

Setting ADB Device Information

You can call the ADB Manager function SetADBInfo to set or reset some of the
information in the ADB device table about an ADB device.

SetADBInfo

You can use the SetADBInfo function to set the address of the device handler routine
and data area address for a specified ADB device.

```
FUNCTION SetADBInfo (VAR info: ADBSetInfoBlock;
                    adbAddr: ADBAddress): OSErr;
```

info   An ADB information block. On entry, the fields of this parameter block
            should contain the desired address of the device handler routine and
            data area.

adbAddr   The ADB address of a device.

Parameter block

→	`siServiceRtPtr`	`Ptr`	The address of the device handler for this device.
→	`siDataAreaAddr`	`Ptr`	The address of the handler's data area for the device at the specified address.

DESCRIPTION

The `SetADBInfo` function sets the device handler address and the data area address in the ADB device table entry whose address is specified by the `adbAddr` parameter.

IMPORTANT

You should send a Flush command to the device after calling it with `SetADBInfo` to avoid sending old data to the new data area address. ▲

RESULT CODES

`noErr`   0   No error

SEE ALSO

See "ADB Information Block," beginning on page 5-38, for the structure of the ADB information block.

Application-Defined Routines

This section describes device handlers and ADB completion routines. A device handler is a low-level routine that communicates with a particular ADB device. An ADB completion routine is a routine that you can provide as a parameter to the `ADBOp` function.

ADB Device Handlers

The ADB Manager automatically polls for input from connected ADB devices and passes any data received from a device to the device's device handler. ADB device handlers are responsible for processing all input from ADB devices (except for commands sent to an ADB device using `ADBOp` or commands sent by the ADB Manager during address resolution).

MyDeviceHandler

Whenever an ADB device sends data (for example, in response to a Talk Register 0 command), the ADB Manager calls the device handler associated with that ADB device. You can provide a device handler to handle data from your ADB device.

```
PROCEDURE MyDeviceHandler;    {parameters passed in registers}
```

DESCRIPTION

When the ADB Manager calls a device handler, it passes parameters to the device handler in registers A0, A1, A2, and D0, as described next.

SPECIAL CONSIDERATIONS

ADB device handlers are always called at interrupt time; they must follow all rules for interrupt-level processing as described in *Inside Macintosh: Processes*.

ASSEMBLY-LANGUAGE INFORMATION

On entry to your device handler, the ADB Manager passes parameters in the following registers:

Register	Value
A0	A pointer to the data sent by the device. This area contains data stored as a Pascal string (maximum 8 bytes data preceded by one length byte).
A1	A pointer to the device handler routine.
A2	A pointer to the data area (if any) associated with the device handler.
D0	The ADB command number (byte) that resulted in the device handler being called.

A device handler should handle the data pointed to by register A0 in a manner appropriate to the device. For example, the mouse device handler interprets the data it receives in register A0 and posts an event to the event queue.

A device handler can use the area pointed to by register A2 to store global data as needed. (If a device handler needs a global data area, its installation code should allocate the needed memory at the same time it installs the device handler's address into the ADB device table.)

SEE ALSO

See "Writing an ADB Device Handler," beginning on page 5-29, for information on installing and creating an ADB device handler.

ADB Command Completion Routines

The `ADBOp` function is always executed asynchronously; if the bus is busy, the ADB command passed to `ADBOp` is held in a command queue until the bus is free. The result code returned by `ADBOp` indicates only whether the ADB command was successfully placed into the ADB command queue, not whether the command itself was successful.

Thus, when you use the `ADBOp` function to send a command to an ADB device, and your application requires synchronous behavior, you'll need to provide a completion routine to determine when the command has completed.

MyCompletionRoutine

When you use the `ADBOp` function to send a command to an ADB device, the ADB Manager calls your completion routine when the ADB device has completed the command.

```
PROCEDURE MyCompletionRoutine;    {parameters passed in registers}
```

DESCRIPTION

The ADB Manager passes parameters to a completion routine in registers A0, A1, A2, and D0, as described next.

ASSEMBLY-LANGUAGE INFORMATION

On entry to your completion routine, the ADB Manager sets the following registers:

Register	Value
A0	A pointer to the data area specified by the `buffer` parameter to the `ADBOp` function. This area contains data stored as a Pascal string (maximum 8 bytes of data preceded by one length byte). For example, data returned by an ADB device in response to a Talk command issued by a call to the `ADBOp` function can be accessed through this pointer.
A1	A pointer to the completion routine.
A2	A pointer to the data area that was specified by the `data` parameter to the `ADBOp` function. Your completion routine can use this area to store information; for example, to set a flag indicating that the command has completed.
D0	The ADB command number (byte) that resulted in the completion routine being called.

SEE ALSO

See Listing 5-2 on page 5-25 for an example of a completion routine.

5

ADB Manager

Summary of the ADB Manager

Pascal Summary

Data Types

```
TYPE ADBDataBlock =
    PACKED RECORD
        devType:          SignedByte;      {device handler ID}
        origADBAddr:      SignedByte;      {default ADB address}
        dbServiceRtPtr:   Ptr;             {pointer to device handler}
        dbDataAreaAddr:   Ptr;             {pointer to data area}
    END;
    ADBDBlkPtr = ^ADBDataBlock;

TYPE ADBSetInfoBlock =
    RECORD
        siServiceRtPtr:   Ptr;             {pointer to device handler}
        siDataAreaAddr:   Ptr;             {pointer to data area}
    END;
    ADBSInfoPtr = ^ADBSetInfoBlock;

TYPE ADBOpBlock =
    RECORD
        dataBuffPtr:      Ptr;             {address of data buffer}
        opServiceRtPtr:   Ptr;             {pointer to device handler}
        opDataAreaPtr:    Ptr;             {pointer to optional data area}
    END;
    ADBOpBPtr = ^ADBOpBlock;

    ADBAddress = SignedByte;
```

ADB Manager Routines

Initializing the ADB Manager

```
PROCEDURE ADBReInit;
```

Communicating Through the ADB

```
FUNCTION ADBOp                   (data: Ptr; compRout: ProcPtr; buffer: Ptr;
                                  commandNum: Integer): OSErr;
```

Getting ADB Device Information

```
FUNCTION CountADBs:              Integer;
FUNCTION GetIndADB               (VAR info: ADBDataBlock;
                                  devTableIndex: Integer): ADBAddress;
FUNCTION GetADBInfo              (VAR info: ADBDataBlock;
                                  adbAddr: ADBAddress): OSErr;
```

Setting ADB Device Information

```
FUNCTION SetADBInfo              (VAR info: ADBSetInfoBlock;
                                  adbAddr: ADBAddress): OSErr;
```

Application-Defined Routines

```
PROCEDURE MyDeviceHandler;

PROCEDURE MyCompletionRoutine;
```

C Summary

Data Types

```
typedef char ADBAddress;

struct ADBDataBlock {
    char        devType;               /*device type*/
    char        origADBAddr;           /*original ADB address*/
    Ptr         dbServiceRtPtr;        /*pointer to device handler*/
    Ptr         dbDataAreaAdd;         /*pointer to data area*/
};
typedef struct ADBDataBlock ADBDataBlock;
typedef ADBDataBlock *ADBDBlkPtr;

struct ADBSetInfoBlock {
    Ptr         siServiceRtPtr;        /*pointer to device handler*/
    Ptr         siDataAreaAddr;        /*pointer to data area*/
};
typedef struct ADBSetInfoBlock ADBSetInfoBlock;
```

```
typedef ADBSetInfoBlock *ADBSInfoPtr;

struct ADBOpBlock {
    Ptr             dataBuffPtr;            /*address of data buffer*/
    Ptr             opServiceRtPtr;         /*pointer to device handler*/
    Ptr             opDataAreaPtr;          /*pointer to optional data area*/
};
typedef struct ADBOpBlock ADBOpBlock;
typedef ADBOpBlock *ADBOpBPtr;
```

ADB Manager Functions

Initializing the ADB Manager

```
pascal void ADBReInit         (void);
```

Communicating Through the ADB

```
pascal OSErr ADBOp            (Ptr data, ProcPtr compRout, Ptr buffer,
                               short commandNum);
```

Getting ADB Device Information

```
pascal short CountADBs        (void);
pascal ADBAddress GetIndADB
                              (ADBDataBlock *info, short devTableIndex);
pascal OSErr GetADBInfo       (ADBDataBlock *info, ADBAddress adbAddr);
```

Setting ADB Device Information

```
pascal OSErr SetADBInfo       (ADBSetInfoBlock *info, ADBAddress adbAddr);
```

Application-Defined Functions

```
pascal void MyDeviceHandler (void);

pascal void MyCompletionRoutine (void);
```

Assembly-Language Summary

Data Structures

ADB Data Block

0	devType	byte	device type
1	origADBAddr	byte	original ADB address
2	dbServiceRtPtr	long	pointer to completion routine
6	dbDataAreaAddr	long	pointer to data area

ADB Information Block

0	siServiceRtPtr	long	pointer to completion routine
4	siDataAreaAddr	long	pointer to data area

ADB Operation Block

0	dataBuffPtr	long	address of data buffer
4	opServiceRtPtr	long	pointer to completion routine
8	opDataAreaPtr	long	pointer optional data area

Trap Macros

Trap Macro Names

Pascal name	Trap macro name
ADBReInit	_ADBReInit
ADBOp	_ADBOp
CountADBs	_CountADBs
GetIndADB	_GetIndADB
GetADBInfo	_GetADBInfo
SetADBInfo	_SetADBInfo

Global Variables

JADBProc	long	Pointer to ADBReInit preprocessing/postprocessing routine.
KbdLast	byte	ADB address of the keyboard last used.
KbdType	byte	Keyboard type of the keyboard last used.

Result Codes

noErr	0	No error
errADBop	−1	Unsuccessful completion

ADB Manager

Power Manager

Contents

Power Manager

This chapter describes the Power Manager, the part of the Macintosh Operating System that controls power to the internal hardware devices of battery-powered Macintosh computers (such as the Macintosh Portable, the Macintosh PowerBook computers, and the Macintosh Duo computers)

The Power Manager automatically shuts off power to internal devices to conserve power whenever the computer has not been used for a predetermined amount of time. In addition, the Power Manager allows your application or other software to

- install a procedure that is executed when power to internal devices is about to be shut off or when power has just been restored

- set a timer to wake up the computer at some time in the future

- set or disable the wakeup timer and read its current setting

- enable, disable, or delay the CPU idle feature

- read the current CPU clock speed

- control power to the internal modem and serial ports

- read the status of the internal modem

- read the state of the battery charge and the status of the battery charger

Most applications do not need to know whether they are executing on a battery-powered Macintosh computer because the transition between power states is largely invisible. As a result, most applications do not need to use Power Manager routines. You need the information in this chapter only if you are writing a program—such as a device driver— that must control power to some subsystem of a battery-powered Macintosh computer or that might be affected by the idle or sleep state. See "About the Power Manager," beginning on page 6-4, for a complete description of these power conservation states.

The Power Manager is available only in system software version 6.0.4 and later versions. You should use the `Gestalt` function to determine whether the Power Manager is available before calling it. See "Determining Whether the Power Manager Is Present," on page 6-14, for more information.

To use this chapter, you might need to be familiar with techniques for accessing information in your application's A5 world. The chapter "Introduction to Memory Management" in *Inside Macintosh: Memory* describes the A5 world and the routines you can use to manipulate the A5 register. This chapter provides complete code samples that illustrate how to access your application's A5 world in a sleep procedure. If you wish to display a dialog box from a sleep procedure, you also need to know about the Dialog Manager. See the chapter "Dialog Manager" in *Inside Macintosh: Macintosh Toolbox Essentials*.

This chapter begins with a preliminary description of the power conservation states controlled by the Power Manager and of the relationship between the power management hardware and software in portable Macintosh computers. It then discusses the power conservation states and the sleep queue in greater detail. The section "Using the Power Manager," beginning on page 6-13, describes how to use Power Manager routines to control the power conservation states and how to write and install sleep procedures.

The reference section is divided into three sections. The first section describes the data structures used by Power Manager routines. The second section, "Power Manager Routines," beginning on page 6-28, describes low-level Power Manager routines that you can use to control a variety of Power Manager functions. The third section, "Power Manager Dispatch Routines," beginning on page 6-40, describes high-level Power Manager routines that isolate you from the need to read or write directly to the Power Manager's private data structures and to parameter RAM. The Power Manager dispatch routines provide access to most of the Power Manager's internal parameters. Where a Power Manager dispatch routine duplicates the function of another Power Manager routine, the dispatch routine provides the preferred interface.

Whereas the Pascal programming language interface is used to describe the Power Manager routines in "Power Manager Routines," the C language interface is used for the newer routines described in "Power Manager Dispatch Routines." The section "Summary of the Power Manager," beginning on page 6-67, includes both Pascal and C interfaces for both sets of routines.

About the Power Manager

Battery-operated Macintosh computers (also known as **portable Macintosh computers**) draw power from a built-in battery that can be charged from a voltage converter plugged into an electric socket. In order to prolong the battery charge and thereby increase the amount of time the computer can be operated from the battery, portable Macintosh computers contain software and hardware components that can put the computer into various power conservation states, known as the *power-saver, idle,* and *sleep states.*

The software that controls power to the internal devices of portable Macintosh computers is the **Power Manager**. The Power Manager provides a software interface to the available power controlling hardware. On the Macintosh Portable computer, the power-management hardware is the 50753 microprocessor (known as the Power Manager integrated circuit or **Power Manager IC**). On other portable Macintosh computers, other hardware may be used.

The Power Manager also provides some services unique to portable Macintosh computers—such as reading the current clock speed—that are not directly related to power control. The power management circuits and the microcode in the on-chip ROM of the Power Manager IC are described in the *Guide to the Macintosh Family Hardware,* second edition. The Power Manager provides routines that your program can use to enable and disable the idle state, to control power to some of the subsystems of the computer, and to ensure that your program is not adversely affected when the Power Manager puts the computer into the sleep state.

The **power-saver state** is a low power-consumption state of several portable Macintosh computers in which the processor slows from its normal clock speed to some slower clock speed. On the PowerBook 170 computer, for example, the CPU clock speed can be reduced from 25 MHz to 16 MHz in order to conserve power.

In the **idle state,** the Power Manager slows the computer even further, from its current clock speed to a 1 MHz clock speed. The Power Manager puts a portable Macintosh computer in the idle state when the system has been inactive for 15 seconds. When the computer has been inactive for an additional period of time (the user can set the length of this period), the Power Manager and the various device drivers shut off power or remove clocks from the computer's various subsystems, including the CPU, RAM, ROM, and I/O ports. This condition is known as the **sleep state.**

No data is lost from RAM when a portable Macintosh computer is in the sleep state. Most applications can be interrupted by the idle and sleep states without any adverse effects. When the user resumes use of the computer (by pressing a key, for example), most of the applications that were running before the computer entered the sleep state are still loaded in memory and resume running as if nothing had happened. If your application or device driver cannot tolerate the sleep state, however, you can add an entry to an operating-system queue called the **sleep queue.** The Power Manager calls every sleep queue routine before the computer goes into the sleep state.

The user can also use the Battery desk accessory or a Finder menu item to cause a portable Macintosh computer to go into the sleep state immediately. If the user chooses Sleep from the Battery desk accessory (or from the Special menu in the Finder), the Power Manager checks to see if any network communications will be interrupted by going into the sleep state. If network communications will be affected, a built-in sleep procedure displays a dialog box (shown in Figure 6-1) giving the user the option of canceling the Sleep command.

Figure 6-1   A network driver's sleep dialog box

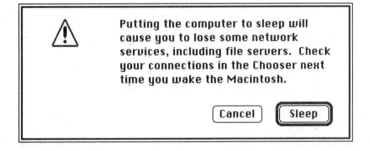

Note

Some portable Macintosh computers (for example, the Macintosh Portable) do not have a power switch. On these computers, if the user chooses Shut Down from Special menu in the Finder, the Power Manager puts the computer into the sleep state regardless of whether any network communication routines are running at the time. ◆

The power management circuits in portable Macintosh computers include a battery-voltage monitor, a voltage regulator and battery-charging circuit, and (on certain portable computers) the Power Manager IC. The Power Manager IC controls the clocks and power lines to the various internal components and external ports of the computer.

6

Power Manager

The microcode in the Power Manager IC implements many of the computer's power management features, such as power and clock control and the wakeup timer. A user or an application can set the **wakeup timer** to return the computer from the sleep state to the operating state at a specific time.

Note
The wakeup timer is not available on all portable Macintosh computers. ◆

The Power Manager firmware in the ROM of the computer provides an interface that allows your application to control some of the functions of the power control hardware. The power management hardware charges the battery, provides the voltages needed by the system, and automatically shuts down all power and clocks to the system if the battery voltage falls below a certain threshold. The automatic shutdown function helps to prevent possible damage to the battery resulting from low voltage.

At any given time, a portable Macintosh computer is in one of five power-consumption states:

- normal state
- power-saver state
- idle state
- sleep state
- shutdown state

When the computer is in its normal state, the CPU is running at its full clock speed and no measures are being taken to conserve power. The computer behaves exactly like any Macintosh computer that is not operated from a battery. Similarly, the shutdown state on a portable Macintosh computer is exactly like the shutdown state on any nonportable Macintosh computer, except that there is a very small drain on the battery to maintain the settings of the computer's parameter RAM.

The following sections provide more information about the three power conservation states (power-saver, idle, and sleep) managed by the Power Manager.

IMPORTANT
The exact implementation details—and indeed the very existence of one or more of the three power conservation states—is subject to variation across the entire line of portable Macintosh computers. In general, your application or other software should not be affected by any such variations. ▲

The Power-Saver State

The power-saver state, available on some portable Macintosh computers, is a power conservation state in which the processor slows from its normal clock speed to some slower clock speed. On the PowerBook 180 computer, for example, the user can use the PowerBook control panel to reduce the CPU clock speed from 33 MHz to 16 MHz.

Power Manager

There is currently no way for your application to put a portable Macintosh computer into the power-saver state or to return it to the normal (full-speed) state. Moreover, the power-saver state is not available on all portable Macintosh computers. If the operation of your application or other software component depends on the CPU clock speed, you can use the Power Manager's GetCPUSpeed function to determine the current speed. In general, of course, it's best to design your application so that it is unaffected by any changes in the clock speed of the CPU.

The Idle State

When a portable Macintosh computer has been inactive for some amount of time, the Power Manager causes the CPU to insert wait states into each RAM or ROM access. On the Macintosh Portable, for example, after 15 seconds of inactivity the Power Manager inserts 64 wait states, effectively changing the clock speed from 16 MHz to 1 MHz. This condition is referred to as the *idle state* or the *rest state*.

Note
The inactivity timeout interval, clock speed, and hardware implementation of the idle state are subject to variation across the entire line of portable Macintosh computers. ◆

For the purposes of determining whether to enter the idle state, inactivity is defined as the absence of any of the following:

- any execution of the PBRead or PBWrite function by the File Manager or Device Manager

- a call to the Event Manager's PostEvent or OSEventAvail function

- any access of the Apple Sound Chip (ASC) or other sound-producing hardware

- completion of an Apple Desktop Bus (ADB) transaction

- a call to the QuickDraw SetCursor procedure that changes the cursor

- the cursor displayed as the watch cursor

The Power Manager enters the idle state in one of two ways, depending on whether the computer supports a mode of idling called **power cycling.** If power cycling is available (for example, in the PowerBook 140 and later models), the CPU is turned off after two seconds of inactivity. After a short interval (on the order of one-half to three-fourths of a second), power is restored to the CPU. The Operating System then checks to see whether any relevant activity has occurred. If it has, the power cycling is stopped and the computer returns to the normal operating state. If, however, no activity has occurred, power cycling resumes with a slightly longer interval (up to several seconds). The CPU remains off for the duration of the cycling or until an interrupt occurs.

If power cycling is not available, the Power Manager uses an alternate method of entering the idle state. The Power Manager maintains an **activity timer** that measures the amount of time that has elapsed since the last relevant system activity. The activity timer is originally set to 15 seconds. When the timer counts down to 0, the Power Manager puts the computer into the idle state. Whenever the Power Manager detects one of the relevant forms of activity, it resets the activity timer to 15 seconds and, if the computer is in the idle state, returns the computer to the operating state.

Neither the user nor your application can change the activity timer to use a period other than 15 seconds. However, the user can disable the activity timer through the Portable or PowerBook control panel, and your application can reset, enable, and disable the activity timer by using the `IdleUpdate`, `EnableIdle`, and `DisableIdle` routines. Your application can also use the `GetCPUSpeed` function to determine whether the computer is currently in the idle state. See "Enabling or Disabling the Idle State," beginning on page 6-15, for a further discussion of these routines.

The Sleep State

The Operating System sends a sleep command to the power management hardware when the user requests it (through the Battery desk accessory or the Finder), when the battery voltage falls below a preset level, or when the system has remained inactive for an amount of time that the user sets through the Portable or PowerBook control panel.

The Operating System uses the power management hardware to shut down power to the CPU, the ROM, and some of the control logic. Sufficient power is maintained to the RAM so that no data is lost. Before the Operating System sends the sleep command to the power management hardware, it performs the following tasks:

■ It pushes the contents of all of the CPU's internal registers onto the stack.

■ It calls all sleep procedures listed in the sleep queue to inform them that the system is about to be put into the sleep state. These procedures include the device drivers for the serial ports and floppy disk drives. Each device driver must call the power management hardware to stop power or clocks to the peripheral device controlled by that driver. If the device contains any internal registers, the device driver must save their contents before turning off power to the device. The sleep queue is described in the following section, "The Sleep Queue."

■ It pushes onto the stack the Reset vector, the contents of the versatile interface adapter (VIA) chip, and the contents of the Apple Sound Chip (ASC) control registers.

■ It saves the stack pointer in memory.

While a portable Macintosh computer is in the sleep state, the clock to the power management hardware (for example, the Power Manager IC) is off so that the hardware does no processing. On each rising edge of the 60 Hz clock signal (from one of the computer's logic chips), a hardware circuit restores the clock signal to the power management hardware, which updates the time in the real-time clock and checks the status of the system to determine whether to return the computer to its operating state. The power management hardware checks for the existence of the following conditions:

■ A key on the keyboard has been pressed.

■ The wakeup timer is enabled and the time to which the wakeup timer is set equals the time in the real-time clock.

■ An internal modem is installed, the user has activated the ring-detect feature, and the modem has detected a ring (that is, someone has called the modem).

Note that use of the mouse or trackball cannot be detected by the power management hardware.

If the power management hardware does not detect any of these conditions, it deactivates its own clock until the next rising edge of the 60 Hz clock signal. If the power management hardware does detect one of these conditions, it restores power to the CPU, ROM, and any other hardware that was running when the computer entered the sleep state. Then the Power Manager's wakeup procedure reverses the procedure that put the computer into the sleep state, including calling each routine listed in the sleep queue to allow it to restore power to any subsystems it controls.

The Sleep Queue

The Power Manager maintains an operating-system queue called the *sleep queue*. The sleep queue contains pointers to all of the routines—called **sleep procedures**—that the Power Manager must call before it puts the computer into the sleep state or returns it to the operating state. Each device driver, for example, can place in the sleep queue a pointer to a routine that controls power to the subsystem that the driver controls. When the Power Manager is ready to put the computer into the sleep state, it calls each of the sleep procedures listed in the sleep queue. Each procedure performs whatever tasks are necessary to prepare for the sleep state, including calling Power Manager routines, and then returns control to the Power Manager. Similarly, the Power Manager calls each sleep procedure when it is returning the computer to the operating state.

If you are writing a device driver or if you want your program to be informed before the computer enters the sleep state, you can place an entry for your sleep procedure in the sleep queue. If you do place an entry in the sleep queue, remember to remove it before your device driver or application terminates. You use the `SleepQInstall` and `SleepQRemove` procedures to install and remove sleep queue entries, as described in "Installing a Sleep Procedure," beginning on page 6-18.

Your sleep procedure can be called at any of four different times, namely

- when the Power Manager wants to know whether it may put the computer into the sleep state (a sleep request)

- when the Power Manager is about to put the computer into the sleep state (a sleep demand)

- when the Power Manager has just returned the computer to the normal operating state (a wakeup demand)

- when the Power Manager has decided not to put the computer into the sleep state but has already issued a sleep request (a sleep-request revocation)

Your sleep procedure will need to respond differently, depending on the reason it is being called. The following four sections describe these cases.

Sleep Requests

The Power Manager sends your sleep procedure a **sleep request** when it would like to put the computer into the sleep state. Your sleep procedure then has the option of denying the sleep request. If any procedure in the sleep queue denies the sleep request, the Power Manager sends a sleep-request revocation to each routine that it has already called with a sleep request, and the computer does not enter the sleep state. If, on the other hand, every sleep procedure in the sleep queue accepts the sleep request, then the Power Manager sends a sleep demand to each sleep procedure in the sleep queue. After every sleep procedure has processed the sleep demand, the Power Manager puts the computer into the sleep state.

Before sending a sleep request to any of the sleep procedures in the sleep queue, the Power Manager calls a built-in sleep procedure that checks the status of certain network services, as summarized in Table 6-1. Only if all of the network services permit sleep does the Power Manager continue by sending sleep requests to the routines in the sleep queue. The network services in Table 6-1 are described in *Inside Macintosh: Networking*.

The Power Manager issues a sleep request when a sleep timeout occurs (that is, when the period of inactivity set by the user in the Portable or PowerBook control panel has expired).

Table 6-1   Response of network services to sleep requests and sleep demands

Network service in use	Response to sleep request	Response to conditional sleep demand	Response to unconditional sleep demand
.MPP low-level protocol (DDP, NBP, RTMP, AEP)	Close driver if computer is on battery; else deny request	Close driver if user gives okay; else deny request	Close driver
.XPP extended protocol (ASP, AFP); no server volume mounted	Close driver if computer is on battery; else deny request	Close driver if user gives okay; else deny request	Close driver
.XPP; server volume mounted	Deny request	Close server sessions and close driver if user gives okay; else deny request	Close server sessions and close driver
An application is currently using AppleTalk	Deny request	Close server sessions and close driver if user gives okay; else deny request	Close server sessions and close driver

Sleep Demands

The Power Manager sends your sleep procedure a **sleep demand** when it is about to put the portable Macintosh computer into the sleep state. When a procedure in the sleep queue receives a sleep demand, it must prepare for the sleep state as quickly as possible and return control to the Power Manager.

From the point of view of the Power Manager, there are two types of sleep demands—conditional and unconditional. The Power Manager might cancel a conditional sleep demand if certain network services are in use; an unconditional sleep demand cannot be canceled. When your sleep procedure receives a sleep demand, however, your procedure has no way to determine whether it originated as a conditional sleep demand or an unconditional sleep demand. Your device driver or application must prepare for the sleep state and return control promptly to the Power Manager when it receives a sleep demand.

The Power Manager processes a conditional sleep demand when the user chooses Sleep from the Battery desk accessory or from the Special menu in the Finder. When the Power Manager processes a conditional sleep demand, it first sends a sleep request to the network driver's sleep procedure (see Table 6-1). Whenever one of the network services is in use, the sleep procedure displays a dialog box requesting the user's permission to put the computer into the sleep state. The wording of the message in the dialog box depends on the nature of the network service in use. For example, if an .XPP driver protocol is in use, has opened a server, and has mounted a volume, then the message warns the user that the volume will be closed when the computer is put into the sleep state.

If the user denies permission to close the driver, the Power Manager does not send sleep demands to the routines in the sleep queue. If the user does give permission to close the driver, the Power Manager sends a sleep demand to the network driver's sleep procedure and then to every other sleep procedure in the sleep queue.

The Power Manager issues an unconditional sleep demand when the battery voltage falls below a preset level or when the user chooses Shut Down from the Special menu in the Finder. In this case, the Power Manager sends a sleep demand to the network driver's sleep procedure, which closes all network drivers. Then the Power Manager sends a sleep demand to every other sleep procedure in the sleep queue. As always for a sleep demand, each sleep procedure must prepare for the sleep state and return control to the Power Manager as quickly as possible. In this case, the Power Manager does not display any warnings or dialog boxes; neither the network services, the user, nor any application can deny the sleep demand.

Wakeup Demands

After restoring full power to the CPU, RAM, and ROM, the Power Manager's wakeup procedure calls each sleep procedure in the sleep queue with a wakeup demand. A **wakeup demand** informs your sleep procedure that it must reverse whatever steps it followed when it prepared for the sleep state. For example, a database application might reestablish communications with a remote database.

Sleep-Request Revocations

If any sleep procedure in the sleep queue denies a sleep request, the Power Manager sends a **sleep-request revocation** to every sleep procedure that it has already called with a sleep request. Your sleep procedure must reverse whatever steps it followed when it prepared to receive a sleep demand. A communications application that prevents users from opening new sessions while it is waiting to receive a sleep demand, for example, might once again allow users to open new sessions.

Power Manager Dispatch

Software that reads and writes directly to the Power Manager's private data structures and parameter RAM must be updated any time Apple Computer, Inc. makes a change to the internal operation of the Power Manager. The Power Manager for some versions of the Macintosh Operating System includes routines—referred to as the *Power Manager dispatch routines*—that eliminate the need for applications to deal directly with the Power Manager's data structures. These routines provide access to most of the Power Manager's internal parameters. The interface is extensible, and may grow over time to accommodate new kinds of functions.

You can use the routines described in "Power Manager Dispatch Routines," beginning on page 6-40, to isolate your application from future changes to the internal operation of the Power Manager software.

IMPORTANT

Apple Computer, Inc. reserves the right to change the internal operation of the Power Manager software. Applications should not depend on the Power Manager's internal data structures or parameter RAM. ▲

You should not depend on the Power Manager's internal data structures staying the same in future versions of system software. In particular, do not assume that

■ timeout values such as the hard disk spindown time reside at the same locations in parameter RAM

■ the power cycling process works the same way or uses the same parameters

■ direct commands to the Power Manager microcontroller are supported in all models

Note

Whereas the Pascal programming language interface is used to describe the Power Manager routines in "Power Manager Routines," beginning on page 6-28, the C language interface is used for the newer routines described in "Power Manager Dispatch Routines," beginning on page 6-40. The section "Summary of the Power Manager," beginning on page 6-67, includes both Pascal and C interfaces for both sets of routines. ◆

Using the Power Manager

You can use the Power Manager to install a sleep procedure that is executed when power to internal devices is about to be shut off or after power has just been restored. Most applications or other software components that are sensitive to the power-consumption state of the computer can use sleep procedures to perform any necessary processing at those times. See "Writing a Sleep Procedure," beginning on page 6-20, and "Installing a Sleep Procedure," beginning on page 6-18, for complete details on how to write and install sleep procedures.

The Power Manager provides routines that you can use to monitor the state of the battery charge and the status of the battery charger. See "Monitoring the Battery and Battery Charger," beginning on page 6-26, for details. In all likelihood, only utility programs will need to use these routines.

If you are writing an application that is sensitive to the clock speed of the computer, you can use the Power Manager to disable the CPU idle state when necessary.

IMPORTANT

Do not disable the idle state except when executing a routine that must run at full speed. Disabling the idle state shortens the amount of time the user can operate the computer from a battery. ▲

If you want to ensure that a portable Macintosh computer is in the operating state at a particular time in the future, you can use the SetWUTime function to set the wakeup timer. You can use the wakeup timer in conjunction with the Time Manager, for example, when you want to use the computer to perform tasks that must be done at a specific time, like printing a large file in the middle of the night.

If you are writing a device driver for a portable Macintosh computer, you might need to use the Power Manager to control power to the subsystem that your driver controls. See "Switching Serial Power On and Off," on page 6-25, for a discussion of power control for the serial communications subsystem. For power control for other devices, consult Apple Developer Technical Support. The Power Manager cannot control power to external peripheral devices such as hard disks and CD-ROM drives because such devices have their own power supplies.

IMPORTANT

Because the Power Manager saves the contents of all of the CPU registers, including the stack pointer, before putting the computer into the sleep state, and because the contents of RAM are preserved while the computer is in the sleep state, most applications are not adversely affected by the sleep state. Because a portable Macintosh computer does not enter the idle state when almost any sort of activity is going on (or even when the watch cursor is being displayed), few programs are adversely affected by the idle state. Therefore, it is likely that your application will not have to make calls to the Power Manager. ▲

Determining Whether the Power Manager Is Present

You can use the Gestalt function with the gestaltPowerMgrAttr selector to determine whether the Power Manager is available on a particular computer and whether certain other devices in the computer can be put into the idle or sleep state. The Gestalt function returns in the response parameter a 32-bit value that may have some or all of the following bits set:

```
CONST
    gestaltPMgrExists         = 0;  {Power Manager is present}
    gestaltPMgrCPUIdle        = 1;  {CPU can idle}
    gestaltPMgrSCC            = 2;  {can stop SCC clock}
    gestaltPMgrSound          = 3;  {can shut off sound circuits}
    gestaltPMgrDispatchExists = 4;  {dispatch routines are present}
```

If the gestaltPMgrExists bit is set, the Power Manager is present. If the gestaltPMgrCPUIdle bit is set, the CPU is capable of going into a state of low power consumption. If the gestaltPMgrSCC bit is set, it is possible to stop the SCC clock, thus effectively turning off the serial ports. If the gestaltPMgrSound bit is set, it is possible to turn off power to the sound circuits. If the gestaltPMgrDispatchExists bit is set, the Power Manager dispatch routines are available; see the next section for more information.

Note

For complete details on using the Gestalt function, see the chapter "Gestalt Manager" in *Inside Macintosh: Operating System Utilities.* ◆

Determining Whether the Power Manager Dispatch Routines are Present

You can use the Gestalt function with the gestaltPowerMgrAttr selector to determine whether the Power Manager dispatch routines are available on a particular computer. If the gestaltPMgrDispatchExists bit is set in the response parameter, the Power Manager dispatch routines are available.

Because more routines may be added in the future, the PMSelectorCount function (described on page 6-41) returns the number of dispatch routines that are implemented. The sample code in Listing 6-1 shows how you can use the Gestalt function to determine whether the Power Manager dispatch routines are present, and then use the PMSelectorCount function to find out which routines are supported. In this case, the sample code tests for the existence of the hard disk spindown routine (selector $07).

Listing 6-1   Determining which Power Manager dispatch routines exist

```
long pmgrAttributes;
Boolean routinesExist;

routinesExist = false;
if (! Gestalt(gestaltPowerMgrAttr, &pmgrAttributes))
if (pmgrAttributes & (1<<gestaltPMgrDispatchExists))
if (PMSelectorCount() >= 7) /* do the first 8 routines exist? */
    routinesExist = true;
```

▲ **WARNING**
If you call a routine that does not exist, the call to the public Power
Manager trap (if the trap exists) will return an error code, which your
program could misinterpret as data. ▲

Enabling or Disabling the Idle State

You can reset the activity timer to 15 seconds, disable or enable the idle state, and read
the current CPU clock speed by using Power Manager routines.

IMPORTANT
Keep in mind that it is almost always better to design your code so
that it is not affected by the idle state. If you do so, the computer can
conserve power whenever possible. Note also that disabling the idle
state does not disable the sleep state. To prevent your program from
being adversely affected by the sleep state, you need to place a sleep
procedure in the sleep queue, as described in "Installing a Sleep
Procedure," beginning on page 6-18. ▲

To reset the activity timer to count down another 15 seconds before the Power Manager
puts the computer into the idle state, use the `IdleUpdate` function. The `IdleUpdate`
function takes no parameters and returns the value in the `Ticks` global variable at the
time the function was called.

If you want to disable the idle state—that is, prevent the computer from entering the idle
state—for more than 15 seconds, use the `DisableIdle` procedure. If your application
cannot tolerate the idle state at all, you can call the `DisableIdle` procedure when your
application starts up and then call the `EnableIdle` procedure when your application
terminates.

The `EnableIdle` procedure cancels the last call to the `DisableIdle` procedure. Note
that canceling the last call to the `DisableIdle` procedure is not always the same thing
as enabling the idle state. For example, if the user has used the Portable control panel to
disable the idle state, then a call to the `EnableIdle` procedure does not enable the idle
state. Similarly, if your routine called the `DisableIdle` procedure more than once or if
another routine has called the `DisableIdle` procedure, then a call to the `EnableIdle`
procedure cancels only the last call to the `DisableIdle` procedure; it does not enable
the idle state.

The Power Manager does not actually reenable the idle state until every call to the `DisableIdle` procedure has been matched by a call to the `EnableIdle` procedure, and then only if the user has not disabled the idle state through the Portable (or PowerBook) control panel. For this reason, you must be very careful to match each call to the `DisableIdle` procedure with a single call to the `EnableIdle` procedure. Be careful to avoid making extra calls to the `EnableIdle` procedure so that you do not inadvertently reenable the idle state while another application needs it to remain disabled.

Calls to the `EnableIdle` procedure are not cumulative; that is, after you make several calls to the `EnableIdle` procedure, a single call to the `DisableIdle` procedure still disables the idle state. Disabling the idle state always takes precedence over enabling the idle state. A call to the `DisableIdle` procedure disables the idle state no matter how many times the `EnableIdle` procedure has been called and whether or not the user has enabled the idle state through the Portable or PowerBook control panel.

The following examples should help to clarify the use of `EnableIdle` and `DisableIdle`:

- If an application calls the `EnableIdle` routine but the user disables or has disabled the idle state, the idle state is disabled.

- If an application calls the `DisableIdle` routine and the user enables or has enabled the idle state, the idle state is disabled.

- If an application calls the `DisableIdle` routine twice in a row and then calls the `EnableIdle` routine once, the idle state is disabled.

- If an application calls the `EnableIdle` routine twice in a row and then calls the `DisableIdle` routine once, the idle state is disabled.

- If the idle state is initially enabled and if an application calls the `DisableIdle` routine twice in a row and then calls the `EnableIdle` routine twice, the Power Manager first disables and then reenables the idle state.

To determine whether a portable Macintosh computer is currently in the idle state, read the current clock speed with the `GetCPUSpeed` function. If the value returned by the `GetCPUSpeed` function is 1, the computer is in the idle state.

Setting, Disabling, and Reading the Wakeup Timer

When a portable Macintosh computer is in the sleep state, the power management hardware updates the real-time clock and compares it to the wakeup timer once each second. When the real-time clock and the wakeup timer have the same setting, the power management circuits return the computer to the operating state. The Power Manager provides functions that you can use to set the wakeup timer, disable the wakeup timer, and read the wakeup timer's current setting.

IMPORTANT

In some portable Macintosh computers, the power management hardware does not receive this periodic "tickle." As a result, the wakeup timer cannot be used on those machines. To determine whether a particular portable Macintosh computer supports the use of the wakeup timer, call the GetWUTime function. An error is returned if the timer is not available. ▲

Use the SetWUTime function to set the wakeup timer. You pass one parameter to the SetWUTime function, an unsigned long word specifying the number of seconds since midnight, January 1, 1904. Setting the wakeup timer automatically enables it. Listing 6-2 illustrates how to call the SetWUTime function.

Listing 6-2   Setting the wakeup timer

```
FUNCTION WakeMeUp (when: LongInt): OSErr;
VAR
    myTime:  LongInt;
BEGIN
    GetDateTime(myTime);                    {get the current time}
    myTime := myTime + when;                {add desired delay}
    WakeMeUp := SetWUTime(LongInt(@myTime));
END;
```

The when parameter passed to the WakeMeUp function defined in Listing 6-2 specifies how long from the current time the wakeup timer should go off. The WakeMeUp function determines the current time by calling GetDateTime and then passes the appropriate value to SetWUTime. Note that the parameter passed to SetWUTime is the *address* of the desired wakeup time, not the wakeup time itself.

To disable the wakeup timer, you can set the wakeup timer to any time earlier than the current setting of the real-time clock (that is, to some time in the past), or you can use the DisableWUTime function. To reenable the wakeup timer, you must use the SetWUTime function to set the timer to a new time in the future.

To get the current setting of the wakeup timer, use the GetWUTime function. This function returns two parameters: the time to which the wakeup timer is set (in seconds since midnight, January 1, 1904) and a flag indicating whether the wakeup timer is enabled.

If the computer is already in the operating state when the real-time clock reaches the setting in the wakeup timer, nothing happens.

Note

The power management circuits do not return the computer to the operating state while battery voltage is low, even if the wakeup timer and real-time clock settings coincide. ◆

Installing a Sleep Procedure

If you want your program to be notified before the Power Manager puts a portable Macintosh computer into the sleep state or returns it to the operating state, you can put an entry in the sleep queue. If you do place an entry in the sleep queue, remember to remove it before your device driver or application terminates.

The sleep queue is a standard operating-system queue, as described in *Inside Macintosh: Operating System Utilities*. The `SleepQRec` data type defines a **sleep queue record** as follows:

```
TYPE SleepQRec =                          {sleep queue record}
   RECORD
      sleepQLink:    SleepQRecPtr;  {next queue element}
      sleepQType:    Integer;       {queue type = 16}
      sleepQProc:    ProcPtr;       {pointer to sleep procedure}
      sleepQFlags:   Integer;       {reserved}
   END;
```

To add an entry to the sleep queue, fill in the `sleepQType` and `sleepQProc` fields of a sleep queue record. The `sleepQLink` and `sleepQFlags` fields are maintained privately by the Power Manager; your application should not modify these fields, except to initialize them before it calls the `SleepQInstall` procedure. `SleepQInstall` takes one parameter, a pointer to your sleep queue record. Listing 6-3 shows how to add an entry to the sleep queue.

Listing 6-3   Adding an entry to the sleep queue

```
VAR
   gSleepRec:     SleepQRec;         {a sleep queue record}

PROCEDURE MyInstallSleepProcedure;
BEGIN
   {Set up the record before installing it into the sleep queue.}
   WITH gSleepRec DO
   BEGIN
      sleepQLink := NIL;             {initialize reserved field}
      sleepQType := slpQType;        {set sleep queue type}
      sleepQProc := @MySleepProc;    {set address of sleep proc}
      sleepQFlags := 0;              {initialize reserved field}
   END;
   SleepQInstall(@gSleepRec);        {install the record}
END;
```

To remove your routine from the sleep queue, use the `SleepQRemove` procedure. This procedure also takes as its one parameter a pointer to your sleep queue record.

Using Application Global Variables in Sleep Procedures

When a sleep procedure installed by an application is called, the A5 world of that application might not be valid. That is to say, the A5 register might not point to the boundary between the application's global variables and its application parameters. When this happens, any attempt by the sleep procedure to read the application's global variables or to access any other information in the application's A5 world is likely to return erroneous information.

As a result, if you use an application to install a sleep procedure and your sleep procedure accesses any information in your application's A5 world, you'll need to make sure that, at the time you access that information, the A5 register points to your application's global variables. Your sleep procedure must also restore the A5 register to its previous value before exiting. This saving and restoring of the A5 register is necessary whenever your sleep procedure uses any information in your application's A5 world, such as your application global variables or any of your application's QuickDraw global variables.

Note

The techniques described in this section are relevant only to sleep procedures installed by applications. Sleep procedures installed from other kinds of code (for example, from system extensions) do not need to worry about saving and restoring the A5 register. ◆

It's easy enough to use the `SetA5` function to read the value of the A5 register when your sleep procedure begins executing and to restore the register immediately before your procedure exits. (See Listing 6-6 on page 6-21.) It's a bit harder to pass your application's A5 value to the sleep procedure. A standard way to do this in a high-level language like Pascal is to define a new data structure that contains both a sleep queue record and room for the A5 value. For example, you can define a structure of type `SleepInfoRec`, as follows:

```
TYPE SleepInfoRec =                 {sleep information record}
   RECORD
      mySleepQRec:   SleepQRec;     {a sleep queue record}
      mySlpRefCon:   LongInt;       {address of app's A5 world}
   END;
   SleepInfoRecPtr = ^SleepInfoRec;
```

Then, you simply need to call the `SetCurrentA5` function at a time that your application is the current application and pass the result of that function to your sleep procedure (via the `mySlpRefCon` field of the sleep information record). Listing 6-4 shows how to do this.

Listing 6-4   Installing a sleep procedure that uses application global variables

```
VAR
    gSleepInfoRec:    SleepInfoRec;  {a sleep information record}

PROCEDURE MyInstallSleepProc;
BEGIN
   {Set up the record before installing it into the sleep queue.}
   WITH gSleepInfoRec.mySleepQRec DO
   BEGIN
      sleepQLink := NIL;            {initialize reserved field}
      sleepQType := slpQType;       {set sleep queue type}
      sleepQProc := @MySleepProc;   {set address of sleep proc}
      sleepQFlags := 0;             {initialize reserved field}
   END;

   {Install app's A5 value into expanded sleep record.}
   gSleepInfoRec.mySlpRefCon := SetCurrentA5;

   SleepQInstall(@gSleepInfoRec));  {install the record}
END;
```

The Power Manager puts the address you pass to `SleepQInstall` into register A0 when your sleep procedure is called. Thus, the sleep procedure simply needs to retrieve the `SleepInfoRec` record and extract the appropriate value of the application's A5 world. See the next section, "Writing a Sleep Procedure," for a sample sleep procedure that does this.

Note

For more information about your application's A5 world and routines you can use to manipulate the A5 register, see the chapter "Introduction to Memory Management" in *Inside Macintosh: Memory.* ◆

Writing a Sleep Procedure

After you've added an entry to the sleep queue, the Power Manager calls your sleep procedure when the Power Manager issues a sleep request, a sleep demand, a wakeup demand, or a sleep-request revocation. Whenever the Power Manager calls your routine, the A0 register contains a pointer to your sleep queue record and the D0 register contains a **sleep procedure selector code** indicating the reason your routine is being called. One of four selector codes will be in the D0 register:

```
CONST
    sleepRequest    = 1;    {sleep request}
    sleepDemand     = 2;    {sleep demand}
    sleepWakeUp     = 3;    {wakeup demand}
    sleepRevoke     = 4;    {sleep-request revocation}
```

When your routine receives a sleep request, it must either allow or deny the request and place its response in the D0 register. To allow the sleep request, clear the D0 register to 0 before returning control to the Power Manager. To deny the sleep request, return a nonzero value in the D0 register. (Note that you cannot deny a sleep demand.) Listing 6-5 defines two assembly-language glue routines that you can use to accept or deny the request from a high-level language.

Listing 6-5   Accepting and denying a sleep request

```
PROCEDURE MyAllowSleepRequest;
INLINE
    $7000;        {MOVEQ #0, D0}


PROCEDURE MyDenySleepRequest;
INLINE
    $7001;        {MOVEQ #1, D0}
```

If your routine or any other routine in the sleep queue denies the sleep request, the Power Manager sends a sleep-request revocation to each routine that it has already called with a sleep request. If none of the routines denies the sleep request, the Power Manager sends a sleep demand to each routine in the sleep queue. Because your routine will be called a second time in any case, it is not necessary to prepare for sleep in response to a sleep request; your routine need only allow or deny the sleep request by returning a result in the D0 register. Listing 6-6 shows a sample sleep procedure.

Listing 6-6   A sleep procedure

```
PROCEDURE MySleepProc;
VAR
    mySleepInfoPtr:    SleepInfoRecPtr;
    mySleepCommand:    LongInt;
    myOldA5:           LongInt;          {A5 upon entry to procedure}
    myCurA5:           LongInt;
```

```
BEGIN
   mySleepInfoPtr := MyGetSleepInfoPtr; {get the address of the sleep record}
   mySleepCommand := MyGetSleepCommand; {get the task we are to perform}

   {Set A5 register to app's A5 value, and save the original A5 value.}
   myOldA5 := SetA5(mySleepInfoPtr^.mySlpRefCon);

   CASE mySleepCommand OF                    {do the right thing}
      sleepRequest:
         MySleepRequest;
      sleepDemand:
         MySleepDemand;
      sleepWakeUp:
         MyWakeupDemand;
      sleepRevoke:
         MySleepRevoke;
      OTHERWISE
         ;
   END; {CASE}

   myOldA5 := SetA5(myOldA5);                {restore original A5}
END;
```

The `MySleepProc` sleep procedure defined in Listing 6-6 retrieves the address of the sleep queue record contained in register A0 and the selector code contained in register D0. Then it calls the appropriate application-defined routine to handle the selector code. `MySleepProc` uses two assembly-language glue routines, defined in Listing 6-7, to get those values from the appropriate registers.

Listing 6-7   Retrieving the sleep queue record and the selector code

```
{Retrieve the address of our sleep info record from A0.}
FUNCTION MyGetSleepInfoPtr: SleepInfoRecPtr;
INLINE
    $2E88;        {MOVE.L A0, (A7)}

{Retrieve the command code for the sleep procedure from D0.}
FUNCTION MyGetSleepCommand: LongInt;
INLINE
    $2E80;        {MOVE.L D0, (A7)}
```

When your sleep procedure receives a sleep demand, it must prepare for the sleep state and return control to the Power Manager as quickly as possible. Because sleep demands are never sent by an interrupt handler, your sleep procedure can perform whatever tasks

Power Manager

are necessary to prepare for sleep, including making calls to the Memory Manager. You can, for example, display an alert box to inform the user of potential problems, or you can even display a dialog box that requires the user to specify the action to be performed. However, if several applications display alert or dialog boxes, the user might become confused or alarmed. More important, if the user is not present to answer the alert box or dialog box, control is never returned to the Power Manager and the computer does not go to sleep. Listing 6-8 defines a procedure that displays a dialog box whenever a sleep demand is received.

Listing 6-8   Displaying a dialog box in response to a sleep demand

```
PROCEDURE MySleepDemand;
VAR
    myItem:        Integer;        {item number for ModalDialog}
    myRect:        Rect;           {rectangle for NewDialog}
    myOrigPort:    GrafPtr;        {original graphics port}
BEGIN
    myItem := 0;
    gOrigTime := TickCount;        {initialize timer}

    IF gDialog = NIL THEN          {create a dialog window}
    BEGIN
       SetRect(myRect, 50, 50, 400, 150);
       gDialog := NewDialog(NIL, myRect, '', FALSE, dBoxProc,
                            WindowPtr(-1), FALSE, 0, gItemHandle);
    END;

    IF gDialog <> NIL THEN
    BEGIN
       GetPort(myOrigPort);        {remember current port}
       ShowWindow(gDialog);        {make dialog visible}
       SelectWindow(gDialog);
       SetPort(gDialog);
       REPEAT
          ModalDialog(@MyTimeOutFilter, myItem);
       UNTIL myItem = 1;

       HideWindow(gDialog);
       SetPort(myOrigPort);        {restore original port}
    END;
END;
```

To display a dialog box, you need to build the dialog box from within the sleep procedure itself to ensure that the newly created dialog box appears frontmost on the screen. You can facilitate this process by passing a handle to the dialog item list to your sleep procedure. In Listing 6-8, the global variable `gItemHandle` is assumed to contain a handle to the dialog item list. You can execute the following line of code early in your application's execution to set `gItemHandle` to the correct value:

```
gItemHandle := Get1Resource('DITL', kAlertDITL);
```

▲ **WARNING**
If your sleep procedure displays an alert box or modal dialog box, the computer does not enter the sleep state until the user responds. If the computer remains in the operating state until the battery voltage drops below a preset value, the power management hardware automatically shuts off all power to the system, without preserving the state of open applications or data that has not been saved to disk. To prevent this from happening, you should automatically remove your dialog box after several minutes have elapsed. ▲

An easy way to implement this time-out feature is to pass the `ModalDialog` procedure the address of a modal dialog filter function that intercepts null events until the desired amount of time has elapsed. Listing 6-9 illustrates such a filter function.

Listing 6-9   A modal dialog filter function that times out

```
FUNCTION MyTimeOutFilter (myDialog: DialogPtr;
                          VAR myEvent: EventRecord;
                          VAR myItem: Integer): Boolean;
CONST
   kTimeOutMax = 18000;    {remove dialog box after 5 minutes}
BEGIN
   MyTimeOutFilter := FALSE;

   CASE myEvent.what OF
      nullEvent:
         BEGIN
            IF (TickCount - gOrigTime) >= kTimeOutMax THEN
            BEGIN
               myItem := 1;
               MyTimeOutFilter := TRUE;
            END;
         END;
      {handle other relevant events here}
      OTHERWISE
         ;
   END; {CASE}
END;
```

The global variable `gOrigTime` is initialized in the `MySleepDemand` procedure; the modal dialog filter function defined in Listing 6-9 simply waits until the appropriate number of ticks (sixtieths of a second) have elapsed before simulating a click on the OK button (assumed to be dialog item number 1).

When your routine receives a wakeup demand, it must prepare for the operating state and return control to the Power Manager as quickly as possible.

When your routine receives a sleep-request revocation, it must reverse any changes it made in response to the sleep request that preceded it and return control to the Power Manager.

Switching Serial Power On and Off

The serial I/O subsystem of a portable Macintosh computer includes the following components:

- the Serial Communications Controller (SCC) chip
- the serial driver chips
- the –5 volt supply
- the internal modem (if installed)

Because serial drivers always use these components in certain combinations, the Power Manager provides five serial power procedures that perform the following tasks:

- The `AOn` procedure switches on power to serial port A and switches on power to the internal modem if it is installed.
- The `AOnIgnoreModem` procedure switches on power to serial port A (the modem port) but does not switch on power to the internal modem.
- The `BOn` procedure switches on power to serial port B.
- The `AOff` procedure switches off power to serial port A and to the internal modem if it is in use.
- The `BOff` procedure switches off power to serial port B.

If no internal modem is installed, then calling any of the power-on routines switches on power to the SCC, the serial driver chips, and the –5 volt supply.

To switch power on for port B whether or not there is an internal modem installed, use the `BOn` procedure. This procedure switches on power to the SCC, the serial driver chips, and the –5 volt supply.

If the internal modem is installed, then you can use the `AOn` procedure to switch on the modem. In this case, this procedure switches on power to the SCC, the –5 volt supply, and the modem; the internal modem does not use the serial driver chips.

If the internal modem is installed but you do not want to use it (whether or not the user has used the Portable control panel to disconnect the modem), then use the `AOnIgnoreModem` procedure to switch on power to the SCC, the serial driver chips, and the –5 volt supply.

Note

You can use the Power Manager's ModemStatus function to determine whether an internal modem is turned on or off. For details, see the description of ModemStatus beginning on page 6-36. ◆

Monitoring the Battery and Battery Charger

You can use the Power Manager to monitor the status of the battery and battery charger. To do so, use the BatteryStatus function to determine the current voltage in the battery.

For most accurate results, you might want to average the voltage over some extended period of time (anywhere from 30 seconds to several minutes). The power load within a portable Macintosh computer varies dynamically, and the current draw of the various subsystems affects the voltage read at any one moment.

Power Manager Reference

This section describes the data structures and routines provided by the Power Manager. See "Using the Power Manager," beginning on page 6-13, for detailed instructions on using these routines.

Data Structures

This section describes the data structures used by the Power Manager. The sleep queue record is shown in Pascal. The other data structures, which are used by the functions described in "Power Manager Dispatch Routines," beginning on page 6-40, are shown in C.

Sleep Queue Record

The SleepQInstall and SleepQRemove procedures take as a parameter the address of a sleep queue record, which is defined by the SleepQRec data type.

```
TYPE SleepQRec =
   RECORD
      sleepQLink:     SleepQRecPtr;    {next queue element}
      sleepQType:     Integer;         {queue type = 16}
      sleepQProc:     ProcPtr;         {pointer to sleep procedure}
      sleepQFlags:    Integer;         {reserved}
   END;
   SleepQRecPtr = ^SleepQRec;
```

Field descriptions

sleepQLink	A pointer to the next element in the queue. This pointer is maintained internally by the Power Manager; your application should not modify this field.
sleepQType	The type of the queue, which must be the constant slpQType (16).
sleepQProc	A pointer to your sleep procedure. See "Sleep Procedures," on page 6-65, for details on this routine.
sleepQFlags	Reserved for use by Apple Computer, Inc.

Hard Disk Queue Structure

The HardDiskQInstall and HardDiskQRemove functions take as a parameter the address of a hard disk queue structure, which is defined by the HDQueueElement data type.

```
struct HDQueueElement {
    Ptr                 hdQLink;        /* pointer to next queue element */
    short               hdQType;        /* queue type (must be HDPwrQType) */
    short               hdFlags;        /* reserved */
    HDSpindownProc      hdProc;         /* pointer to routine to call */
    long                hdUser;         /* user-defined private storage */
} HDQueueElement;
```

Wakeup Time Structure

The wakeup time structure used by the GetWakeupTimer and SetWakeupTimer functions is defined by the WakeupTime data type.

```
typedef struct WakeupTime {
 unsigned long wakeTime;    /* wakeup time as number of seconds since
                                  midnight, January 1, 1904 */
 char wakeEnabled;          /* 1 = enable timer, 0=disable timer */
} WakeupTime;
```

Battery Information Structure

The GetScaledBatteryInfo function returns information about the battery in a data structure of type BatteryInfo.

```
typedef struct BatteryInfo {
    unsigned char       flags;          /* misc flags (see below) */
    unsigned char       warningLevel;   /* scaled warning level (0-255) */
```

```
char            reserved;        /* reserved for internal use */
unsigned char   batteryLevel;    /* scaled battery level (0-255) */
} BatteryInfo;
```

The values of the bits in the flags field are as follows:

Bit name	Bit number	Description
batteryInstalled	7	A battery is installed.
batteryCharging	6	The battery is charging.
chargerConnected	5	The charger is connected.

Battery Time Structure

The GetBatteryTimes function returns information about the time remaining on the computer's battery or batteries in a data structure of type BatteryTimeRec.

```
typedef struct BatteryTimeRec {
    unsigned long expectedBatteryTime;  /* estimated time remaining */
    unsigned long minimumBatteryTime;   /* minimum time remaining */
    unsigned long maximumBatteryTime;   /* maximum time remaining */
    unsigned long timeUntilCharged;     /* time until full charge */
} BatteryTimeRec;
```

Power Manager Routines

This section describes the routines provided by the Power Manager. You can use these routines to

- enable, disable, and read the idle state
- control and read the wakeup timer
- add and remove elements from the sleep queue
- control power to the serial ports
- read the status of the internal modem
- read the status of the battery and battery charger

Controlling the Idle State

The Power Manager provides routines that you can use to modify and control the idle state. See "The Idle State," on page 6-7, for a complete description of a computer's idle state and activity timer.

IdleUpdate

You can use the `IdleUpdate` function to reset the Power Manager's activity timer.

```
FUNCTION IdleUpdate: LongInt;
```

DESCRIPTION

The `IdleUpdate` function resets the activity timer. It takes no parameters and returns the value in the `Ticks` global variable at the time the function was called.

EnableIdle

You can use the `EnableIdle` procedure to enable the idle state.

```
PROCEDURE EnableIdle;
```

DESCRIPTION

The `EnableIdle` procedure cancels the effect of a call to the `DisableIdle` procedure. A call to the `EnableIdle` procedure enables the idle state only if the user has not used the Portable or PowerBook control panel to disable the idle state and if every call to the `DisableIdle` procedure has been balanced by a call to the `EnableIdle` procedure.

ASSEMBLY-LANGUAGE INFORMATION

The MPW development system provides an assembly-language macro to execute the `EnableIdle` routine. That macro calls the `_IdleState` trap. To call the `_IdleState` trap directly, you must first put a longword routine selector in the D0 register. For `EnableIdle`, the routine selector is 0.

SEE ALSO

See "Enabling or Disabling the Idle State," beginning on page 6-15, for more discussion of `EnableIdle`.

DisableIdle

You can use the `DisableIdle` procedure to disable the idle state.

```
PROCEDURE DisableIdle;
```

DESCRIPTION

The DisableIdle procedure disables the idle state, even if the user has used the Portable or PowerBook control panel to enable the idle state. Every call to the DisableIdle procedure must be balanced by a call to the EnableIdle procedure before the idle state is reenabled.

ASSEMBLY-LANGUAGE INFORMATION

The MPW development system provides an assembly-language macro to execute the DisableIdle routine. That macro calls the _IdleState trap. To call the _IdleState trap directly, you must first put a longword routine selector in the D0 register. For DisableIdle, the routine selector can be any value that is greater than 0.

SEE ALSO

See "Enabling or Disabling the Idle State," beginning on page 6-15, for more discussion of DisableIdle.

GetCPUSpeed

You can use the GetCPUSpeed function to read the current CPU clock speed.

```
FUNCTION GetCPUSpeed: LongInt;
```

DESCRIPTION

The GetCPUSpeed function returns the current effective clock speed (in megahertz) of the CPU.

ASSEMBLY-LANGUAGE INFORMATION

The MPW development system provides an assembly-language macro to execute the GetCPUSpeed routine. That macro calls the _IdleState trap. To call the _IdleState trap directly, you must first put a longword routine selector in the D0 register. For GetCPUSpeed, the routine selector can be any value that is less than 0. The CPU speed is returned as a single byte in register D0.

Controlling and Reading the Wakeup Timer

The Power Manager provides functions to set the wakeup timer, disable the wakeup timer, and read the current setting of the wakeup timer.

IMPORTANT

Some portable Macintosh computers do not support the wakeup timer. There is currently no direct way to determine whether a particular portable computer supports the wakeup timer. You can, however, inspect the result code from the GetWUTime function to see whether the call executed successfully. ▲

SetWUTime

You can use the SetWUTime function to set the wakeup timer.

```
FUNCTION SetWUTime (WUTime: LongInt): OSErr;
```

WUTime   The time at which the wakeup timer is to wake up, specified as a number of seconds since midnight, January 1, 1904.

DESCRIPTION

The SetWUTime function sets and enables the wakeup timer. When a portable Macintosh computer is in the sleep state, the power management hardware updates the real-time clock and compares it to the wakeup timer once each second. When the real-time clock and the wakeup timer have the same setting, the power management hardware returns the computer to the operating state.

The WUTime parameter specifies the time at which the power management hardware will return the computer to the operating state. You specify the time as the number of seconds since midnight, January 1, 1904.

If the computer is not in the sleep state when the wakeup timer and the real-time clock settings coincide, nothing happens. If you set the wakeup timer to a time earlier than the current setting of the real-time clock, you effectively disable the wakeup timer.

RESULT CODES

noErr   0   No error

SEE ALSO

See "Setting, Disabling, and Reading the Wakeup Timer," beginning on page 6-16, for an example of calling SetWUTime.

You can use the SetWakeupTimer function (page 6-45) to explicitly enable and disable the wakeup timer.

DisableWUTime

You can use the DisableWUTime function to disable the wakeup timer.

```
FUNCTION DisableWUTime: OSErr;
```

DESCRIPTION

The DisableWUTime function disables the wakeup timer. You must set a new wakeup time to reenable the wakeup timer.

RESULT CODES

noErr   0   No error

GetWUTime

You can use the GetWUTime function to read the current setting of the wakeup timer.

```
FUNCTION GetWUTime (VAR WUTime: LongInt; VAR WUFlag: Byte): OSErr;
```

WUTime   On exit, the current setting of the wakeup timer, specified as the number of seconds since midnight, January 1, 1904.

WUFlag   On exit, a bit field encoding the state of the wakeup timer.

DESCRIPTION

The GetWUTime function returns the current setting of the wakeup timer and indicates whether the wakeup timer is enabled. The value returned in the WUTime parameter is the current setting of the wakeup timer, specified as the number of seconds since midnight, January 1, 1904. If the low-order bit (bit 0) of the WUFlag parameter is set to 1, the wakeup timer is enabled. The other bits in the WUFlag parameter are reserved.

SPECIAL CONSIDERATIONS

The GetWUTime function returns an error on machines that do not support the wakeup timer.

RESULT CODES

noErr   0   No error
pmBusyErr   –13001   Wakeup timer is not available on this machine

Controlling the Sleep Queue

The Power Manager allows you to install a sleep procedure that is executed whenever the machine is about to go into the sleep state or just after the machine returns from the sleep state.

SleepQInstall

You can use the SleepQInstall procedure to add an entry to the sleep queue.

```
PROCEDURE SleepQInstall (qRecPtr: SleepQRecPtr);
```

qRecPtr   A pointer to a sleep queue record.

DESCRIPTION

The SleepQInstall procedure adds the specified sleep queue record to the sleep queue. The qRecPtr parameter is a pointer to a sleep queue record.

SPECIAL CONSIDERATIONS

You should make sure to remove any elements you installed in the sleep queue before your application or other software exits.

SEE ALSO

See "Sleep Queue Record," on page 6-26, for the structure of a sleep queue record. See "Sleep Procedures," beginning on page 6-65, for information about sleep procedures.

SleepQRemove

You can use the SleepQRemove procedure to remove an entry from the sleep queue.

```
PROCEDURE SleepQRemove (qRecPtr: SleepQRecPtr);
```

qRecPtr   A pointer to a sleep queue record, which is described on page 6-26.

DESCRIPTION

The SleepQRemove procedure removes the specified sleep queue record from the sleep queue. The qRecPtr parameter is a pointer to the sleep queue record that you provided when you added your routine to the sleep queue.

Controlling Serial Power

The Power Manager provides five procedures that you can use to control power to the serial ports and internal modem.

Assembly-Language Note

Although MPW provides assembly-language macros to execute these routines, each of these macros calls the _SerialPower trap macro. To call the _SerialPower trap macro directly, you must first put a routine selector in the D0 register, setting the bits of the selector as follows:

Bit	Use
0	Set to 0 to use internal modem; set to 1 to ignore modem.
2	Set to 0 for port B; set to 1 for port A.
7	Set to 0 to switch on power; set to 1 to switch off power. ◆

AOn

You can use the AOn procedure to turn on the power to serial port A.

```
PROCEDURE AOn;
```

DESCRIPTION

The AOn procedure switches on power to the SCC and the –5 volt supply. If the internal modem is installed and is connected to port A, the AOn procedure also switches on power to the modem. If either of these conditions is not met, the AOn procedure switches on power to the serial driver chips.

ASSEMBLY-LANGUAGE INFORMATION

The MPW development system provides an assembly-language macro to execute the AOn routine. That macro calls the _SerialPower trap. To call the _SerialPower trap directly, you must first put a longword routine selector in the D0 register. For AOn, the routine selector is $4.

AOnIgnoreModem

You can use the AOnIgnoreModem procedure to turn on the power to serial port A but not to the internal modem.

```
PROCEDURE AOnIgnoreModem;
```

DESCRIPTION

The AOnIgnoreModem procedure switches on power to the SCC, the –5 volt supply, and the serial driver chips. This procedure does not switch on power to the internal modem, even if the user has used the Portable or PowerBook control panel to select the modem.

ASSEMBLY-LANGUAGE INFORMATION

The MPW development system provides an assembly-language macro to execute the AOnIgnoreModem routine. That macro calls the _SerialPower trap. To call the _SerialPower trap directly, you must first put a longword routine selector in the D0 register. For AOnIgnoreModem, the routine selector is $5.

BOn

You can use the BOn procedure to turn on the power to serial port B.

PROCEDURE BOn;

DESCRIPTION

The BOn procedure switches on power to the SCC, the –5 volt supply, and the serial driver chips.

ASSEMBLY-LANGUAGE INFORMATION

The MPW development system provides an assembly-language macro to execute the BOn routine. That macro calls the _SerialPower trap. To call the _SerialPower trap directly, you must first put a longword routine selector in the D0 register. For BOn, the routine selector is $0.

AOff

You can use the AOff procedure to turn off the power to serial port A and to the internal modem.

PROCEDURE AOff;

DESCRIPTION

The AOff procedure always switches off power to the SCC and the –5 volt supply if serial port B is not in use. If the internal modem is installed, connected to port A, and switched on, this procedure switches off power to the modem. If any of these conditions are not met, it switches off power to the serial driver chips, unless they are being used by port B.

ASSEMBLY-LANGUAGE INFORMATION

The MPW development system provides an assembly-language macro to execute the AOff routine. That macro calls the _SerialPower trap. To call the _SerialPower trap directly, you must first put a longword routine selector in the D0 register. For AOff, the routine selector is $84.

BOff

You can use the BOff procedure to turn off the power to serial port B and to the internal modem.

```
PROCEDURE BOff;
```

DESCRIPTION

The BOff procedure switches off power to the SCC and the –5 volt supply if serial port A is not in use. If the internal modem is installed, connected to port B, and switched on, this procedure switches off power to the modem. Otherwise, the BOff procedure switches off power to the serial driver chips, unless they are being used by port A.

ASSEMBLY-LANGUAGE INFORMATION

The MPW development system provides an assembly-language macro to execute the BOff routine. That macro calls the _SerialPower trap. To call the _SerialPower trap directly, you must first put a longword routine selector in the D0 register. For BOff, the routine selector is $80.

Reading the Status of the Internal Modem

The Power Manager provides a function that allows you to determine the status of the internal modem.

ModemStatus

You can use the ModemStatus function to get information about the state of the internal modem.

```
FUNCTION ModemStatus (VAR Status: Byte): OSErr;
```

Status   On exit, a byte value whose bits encode information about the current state of the internal modem. See the description below for the meaning of each bit.

DESCRIPTION

The ModemStatus function returns information about the internal modem in a portable Macintosh computer. Bits 0 and 2 through 5 of the Status parameter encode information about the state of the internal modem. (Currently, bits 6 and 7 are reserved; in addition, bit 1 is reserved and is always set.) The Power Manager recognizes the following constants for specifying bits in the Status parameter.

```
CONST
    modemOnBit          = 0;    {1 if modem is on}
    ringWakeUpBit       = 2;    {1 if ring wakeup is enabled}
    modemInstalledBit   = 3;    {1 if internal modem is installed}
    ringDetectBit       = 4;    {1 if incoming call is detected}
    modemOnHookBit      = 5;    {1 if modem is off hook}
```

Constant descriptions

modemOnBit   The modem's power is on or off. If this bit is set, the modem is switched on. You can use the serial power control functions to control power to the modem. See "Switching Serial Power On and Off," beginning on page 6-25, for information about these functions.

ringWakeUpBit   The state of the ring-wakeup feature. If this bit is set, the ring-wakeup feature is enabled.

modemInstalledBit
                      The modem is or is not installed. If this bit is set, an internal modem is installed.

ringDetectBit   The ring-detect state. If this bit is set, the modem has detected an incoming call.

modemOnHookBit   The modem is on or off hook. If this bit is set, the modem is off hook. The modem indicates that it is off hook whenever it is busy sending or receiving data or processing commands. The modem cannot receive an incoming call when it is off hook.

The Power Manager also defines these bit masks:

```
CONST
    modemOnMask         = $1;    {modem on}
    ringWakeUpMask      = $4;    {ring wakeup enabled}
    modemInstalledMask  = $8;    {internal modem installed}
    ringDetectMask      = $10;   {incoming call detected}
    modemOnHookMask     = $20;   {modem off hook}
```

The user can use the Portable or PowerBook control panel to enable or disable the ring-wakeup feature. When the ring-wakeup feature is enabled and the computer is in the sleep state, the Power Manager returns the computer to the operating state when the modem receives an incoming call.

RESULT CODES

noErr   0   No error

Reading the Status of the Battery and the Battery Charger

The Power Manager monitors the voltage level of the internal battery and warns the user when the voltage drops below a threshold value stored in parameter RAM. If the voltage continues to drop and falls below another, lower value stored in parameter RAM, the Power Manager puts the computer into the sleep state. The Power Manager provides a function that allows you to read the state of charge of the battery and the status of the battery charger.

BatteryStatus

You can use the BatteryStatus function to get information about the state of the internal battery.

```
FUNCTION BatteryStatus (VAR Status: Byte; VAR Power: Byte): OSErr;
```

Status   On exit, a byte value whose bits encode information about the current state of the battery charger. See the description below for the meaning of each bit.

Power   On exit, a byte whose value indicates the current level of the battery voltage. See the description below for a method of calculating the voltage from this value.

DESCRIPTION

The BatteryStatus function returns the status of the battery charger (in the Status parameter) and the voltage level of the battery (in the Power parameter).

Bits 0 through 5 of the Status parameter encode information about the state of the battery charger. (Currently, bits 6 and 7 are reserved.) The Power Manager recognizes the following constants for specifying bits in the Status parameter.

```
CONST
    chargerConnBit          = 0;      {1 if charger is connected}
    hiChargeBit             = 1;      {1 if charging at hicharge rate}
    chargeOverFlowBit       = 2;      {1 if hicharge counter has overflowed}
```

```
batteryDeadBit            = 3;      {always 0}
batteryLowBit             = 4;      {1 if battery is low}
connChangedBit            = 5;      {1 if charger connection has changed}
```

Constant descriptions

chargerConnBit   The charger is or is not connected. If this bit is set, the battery charger is connected to the computer.

hiChargeBit   The charge rate. If this bit is set, the battery is charging at the hicharge rate.

chargeOverFlowBit

The hicharge counter overflow. If this bit is set, the hicharge counter has overflowed. When the hicharge counter has overflowed, it indicates that the charging circuit is having trouble charging the battery.

batteryDeadBit

The dead battery indicator. This bit is always 0, because the Power Manager automatically shuts the system down when the battery voltage drops below a preset level.

batteryLowBit   The battery warning. If this bit is set, the battery voltage has dropped below the value set in parameter RAM. The power management hardware sends an interrupt to the CPU once every second when battery voltage is low.

connChangedBit

The charger connection has or has not changed state. If this bit is set, the charger has been recently connected or disconnected.

The Power Manager also defines these bit masks:

```
CONST
    chargerConnMask       = $1;      {charger is connected}
    hiChargeMask          = $2;      {charging at hicharge rate}
    chargeOverFlowMask    = $4;      {hicharge counter has overflowed}
    batteryDeadMask       = $8;      {battery is dead}
    batteryLowMask        = $10;     {battery is low}
    connChangedMask       = $20;     {connection has changed}
```

Due to the nature of lead-acid batteries, the battery power remaining is difficult to measure accurately. Temperature, load, and other factors can alter the measured voltage by 30 percent or more. The Power Manager takes as many of these factors into account as possible, but the voltage measurement can still be in error by up to 10 percent. The measurement is most accurate when the computer has been in the sleep state for at least 30 minutes.

When the battery charger is connected to a portable Macintosh computer with a low battery, the battery is charged at the hicharge rate (1.5 amps) until battery voltage reaches its full charge (7.2 volts on most portable Macintosh computers). The Power Manager has a counter (the **hicharge counter**) that measures the time required to raise the battery voltage to this level.

6

Power Manager

After the full charge level is reached, the power management circuits maintain the hicharge connection until the hicharge counter counts down to 0. This ensures that the battery is fully charged. At the end of that time, the power management circuits supply the battery with just enough current to replace the voltage lost through self-discharge.

RESULT CODES

noErr   0   No error

SEE ALSO

For more functions for determining the status of the battery and battery charger, see "Getting Information About the Internal Batteries," beginning on page 6-54.

Power Manager Dispatch Routines

This section describes the Power Manager dispatch routines. You can use these routines to

- determine what Power Manager features are available
- set and read the sleep and wakeup timers and disable or disable the sleep timer
- set, read, enable, and disable the timer that dims the screen
- control the hard disk
- get information about the battery
- get and set the state of the internal modem
- control the processing speed of the processor and processor cycling
- get and set the SCSI ID the computer uses in SCSI disk mode

Note
The functions in this section are described using the C language interface. The section "Summary of the Power Manager," beginning on page 6-67, includes both Pascal and C interfaces. ◆

Assembly-language note:
All the functions in this section share a single trap, _PowerMgrDispatch ($A09E). The trap is register based: parameters are passed in register D0 and sometimes also in A0. A routine selector value passed in the low word of register D0 determines which routine is executed. ◆

Determining the Power Manager Features Available

The functions in this section return the number of Power Manager dispatch functions available and return information about the Power Manager features available.

PMSelectorCount

You can use the `PMSelectorCount` function to determine which Power Manager dispatch functions are implemented.

```
short PMSelectorCount();
```

DESCRIPTION

The `PMSelectorCount` function returns the number of routine selectors present. Any function whose selector value is greater than the returned value is not implemented.

ASSEMBLY-LANGUAGE INFORMATION

The trap is `_PowerMgrDispatch` ($A09E). The selector value for `PMSelectorCount` is 0 ($00) in the low word of register D0. The number of selectors is returned in the low word of register D0.

PMFeatures

You can use the `PMFeatures` function to find out which features of the Power Manager are implemented.

```
unsigned long PMFeatures();
```

DESCRIPTION

The `PMFeatures` function returns a 32-bit field describing hardware and software features associated with the Power Manager on a particular machine. If a bit value is 1, that feature is supported or available; if the bit value is 0, that feature is not available. Unused bits are reserved by Apple for future expansion.

Bit name	Bit number	Description
`hasWakeupTimer`	0	The wakeup timer is supported.
`hasSharedModemPort`	1	The hardware forces exclusive access to either SCC port A or the internal modem. (If this bit is not set, port A and the internal modem can be used simultaneously by means of the Communications Toolbox.)
`hasProcessorCycling`	2	Processor cycling is supported; that is, when the computer is idle, the processor power will be cycled to reduce power use.
`mustProcessorCycle`	3	The processor cycling feature must be left on (turn it off at your own risk).

6

Power Manager

Bit name	Bit number	Description
hasReducedSpeed	4	Processor can be started up at a reduced speed in order to extend battery life.
dynamicSpeedChange	5	Processor speed can be switched dynamically between its full and reduced speed at any time, rather than only at startup time.
hasSCSIDiskMode	6	The SCSI disk mode is supported.
canGetBatteryTime	7	The computer can provide an estimate of the battery time remaining.
canWakeupOnRing	8	The computer supports waking up from the sleep state when an internal modem is installed and the modem detects a ring.
hasDimmingSupport	9	The computer has dimming support built into the ROM.

ASSEMBLY-LANGUAGE INFORMATION

The trap is _PowerMgrDispatch ($A09E). The selector value for PMFeatures is 1 ($01) in the low word of register D0. The 32-bit field of supported features is returned in register D0.

Controlling the Sleep and Wakeup Timers

The functions in this section read and set the sleep and wakeup timers and enable or disable the automatic sleep feature.

GetSleepTimeout

You can use the GetSleepTimeout function to find out how long the computer will wait before going to sleep.

```
unsigned char GetSleepTimeout();
```

DESCRIPTION

The GetSleepTimeout function returns the amount of time that the computer will wait after the last user activity before going to sleep. The value of GetSleepTimeout is expressed as the number of 15-second intervals that the computer will wait before going to sleep.

The trap is _PowerMgrDispatch ($A09E). The selector value for GetSleepTimeout is 2 ($02) in the low word of register D0. The sleep timeout value is returned in the low word of register D0.

SetSleepTimeout

You can use the SetSleepTimeout function to set how long the computer will wait before going to sleep.

```
void SetSleepTimeout(unsigned char timeout);
```

timeout   The amount of time that the computer will wait after the last user activity before going to sleep expressed as a number of 15-second intervals.

DESCRIPTION

The SetSleepTimeout function sets the amount of time the computer will wait after the last user activity before going to sleep. The value of SetSleepTimeout is expressed as the number of 15-second intervals making up the desired time. If a value of 0 is passed in, the function sets the timeout value to the default value (currently equivalent to 8 minutes).

ASSEMBLY-LANGUAGE INFORMATION

The trap is _PowerMgrDispatch ($A09E). The selector value for SetSleepTimeout is 3 ($03) in the low word of register D0. The sleep timeout value to set is passed in the high word of register D0.

AutoSleepControl

You can use the AutoSleepControl function to turn the automatic sleep feature on and off.

```
void AutoSleepControl(Boolean enableSleep);
```

enableSleep
            A Boolean that specifies whether to enable the automatic sleep feature. Set this parameter to true to enable automatic sleep.

DESCRIPTION

The `AutoSleepControl` function enables or disables the automatic sleep feature that causes the computer to go into sleep mode after a preset period of time. When `enableSleep` is set to `true`, the automatic sleep feature is enabled (this is the normal state). When `enableSleep` is set to `false`, the computer will not go into the sleep mode unless it is forced to either by some user action—for example, by the user's selecting Sleep from the Special menu of the Finder—or in a low battery situation.

SPECIAL CONSIDERATIONS

Calling `AutoSleepControl` with `enableSleep` set to `false` multiple times increments the auto sleep disable level so that it requires the same number of calls to `AutoSleepControl` with `enableSleep` set to `true` to reenable the auto sleep feature. If more than one piece of software makes this call, auto sleep may not be reenabled when you think it should be.

ASSEMBLY-LANGUAGE INFORMATION

The trap is `_PowerMgrDispatch` ($A09E). The selector value for `AutoSleepControl` is 13 ($0D) in the low word of register D0. The Boolean value is passed in the high word of register D0.

IsAutoSlpControlDisabled

You can use the `IsAutoSlpControlDisabled` function to find out whether automatic sleep control is enabled.

```
Boolean IsAutoSlpControlDisabled();
```

DESCRIPTION

The `IsAutoSlpControlDisabled` function returns a Boolean `true` if automatic sleep control is disabled, or `false` if automatic sleep control is enabled.

ASSEMBLY-LANGUAGE INFORMATION

The trap is `_PowerMgrDispatch` ($A09E). The selector value for `IsAutoSlpControlDisabled` is 33 ($21) in the low word of register D0. The Boolean result is passed in the low byte of register D0.

GetWakeupTimer

You can use the `GetWakeupTimer` function to find out when the computer will wake up from sleep mode.

```
void GetWakeupTimer(WakeupTime *theTime);
```

theTime   A pointer to a `WakeupTime` structure, which specifies whether the timer is enabled or disabled and the time at which the wakeup timer is set to wake the computer.

DESCRIPTION

The `GetWakeupTimer` function returns the time when the computer will wake up from sleep mode.

If the PowerBook model doesn't support the wakeup timer, `GetWakeupTimer` returns a value of 0.

ASSEMBLY-LANGUAGE INFORMATION

The trap is `_PowerMgrDispatch` ($A09E). The selector value for `GetWakeupTimer` is 22 ($16) in the low word of register D0. The pointer to `WakeupTime` is passed in register A0.

SEE ALSO

The `WakeupTime` structure is described in "Wakeup Time Structure," on page 6-27.

SetWakeupTimer

You can use the `SetWakeupTimer` function to set the time when the computer will wake up from sleep mode.

```
void SetWakeupTimer(WakeupTime *theTime);
```

theTime   A pointer to a WakeupTime structure, which specifies whether to enable or disable the timer and the time at which the wakeup timer is to wake the computer.

DESCRIPTION

The `SetWakeupTimer` function sets the time when the computer will wake up from sleep mode and enables or disables the timer. On a PowerBook model that doesn't support the wakeup timer, `SetWakeupTimer` does nothing.

ASSEMBLY-LANGUAGE INFORMATION

The trap is _PowerMgrDispatch ($A09E). The selector value for SetWakeupTimer is 23 ($17) in the low word of register D0. The pointer to WakeupTime is passed in register A0.

SEE ALSO

The WakeupTime structure is described in "Wakeup Time Structure," on page 6-27.

Controlling the Dimming Timer

The functions in this section read and set the dimming timer and enable or disable the automatic screen-dimming feature. The dimmer acts as a screen saver, dimming the screen after a preset time of user inactivity.

GetDimmingTimeout

You can use the GetDimmingTimeout function to find out how long the computer will wait before dimming the screen.

```
unsigned char GetDimmingTimeout();
```

DESCRIPTION

The GetDimmingTimeout function returns the amount of time that the computer will wait after the last user activity before dimming the screen. The value of GetDimmingTimeout is expressed as the number of 15-second intervals that the computer will wait before dimming the screen.

ASSEMBLY-LANGUAGE INFORMATION

The trap is _PowerMgrDispatch ($A09E). The selector value for GetDimmingTimeout is 29 ($1D) in the low word of register D0. The dimming timeout value is returned in the low word of register D0.

SetDimmingTimeout

You can use the SetDimmingTimeout function to set how long the computer will wait before dimming the screen.

```
void SetDimmingTimeout(unsigned char timeout);
```

timeout   The amount of time that the computer will wait after the last user activity before dimming the screen expressed as a number of 15-second intervals. Specify 0 to cause the screen to dim immediately.

DESCRIPTION

The SetDimmingTimeout function sets the amount of time the computer will wait after the last user activity before dimming the screen. The value of SetDimmingTimeout is expressed as the number of 15-second intervals making up the desired time.

ASSEMBLY-LANGUAGE INFORMATION

The trap is _PowerMgrDispatch ($A09E). The selector value for SetDimmingTimeout is 30 ($1E) in the low word of register D0. The dimming timeout value to set is passed in the high word of register D0.

SEE ALSO

You can use the PMFeatures function (page 6-41) to determine whether the computer supports automatic dimming.

DimmingControl

You can use the DimmingControl function to turn the automatic dimming feature on and off.

```
void DimmingControl(Boolean enableDimming);
```

enableDimming
        A Boolean that specifies whether to enable the automatic dimming feature. Set this parameter to true to enable automatic dimming.

DESCRIPTION

The DimmingControl function enables or disables the automatic dimming feature that causes the computer to dim the screen after a preset period of time. When enableDimming is set to true, the automatic dimming feature is enabled (this is the normal state). When enableDimming is set to false, the computer will not dim the screen.

SPECIAL CONSIDERATIONS

Calling DimmingControl with enableDimming set to false multiple times increments the auto dimming disable level so that it requires the same number of calls to DimmingControl with enableDimming set to true to reenable the auto dimming

6

Power Manager

feature. If more than one piece of software makes this call, auto dimming may not be reenabled when you think it should be.

ASSEMBLY-LANGUAGE INFORMATION

The trap is _PowerMgrDispatch ($A09E). The selector value for DimmingControl is 31 ($1F) in the low word of register D0. The Boolean value is passed in the high word of register D0.

SEE ALSO

You can use the PMFeatures function (page 6-41) to determine whether the computer supports automatic dimming.

IsDimmingControlDisabled

You can use the IsDimmingControlDisabled function to find out whether automatic dimming is enabled.

```
Boolean IsDimmingControlDisabled();
```

DESCRIPTION

The IsDimmingControlDisabled function returns a Boolean true if automatic dimming is disabled, or false if dimming is enabled.

ASSEMBLY-LANGUAGE INFORMATION

The trap is _PowerMgrDispatch ($A09E). The selector value for IsDimmingControlDisabled is 32 ($20) in the low word of register D0. The Boolean result is passed in the low byte of register D0.

SEE ALSO

You can use the PMFeatures function (page 6-41) to determine whether the computer supports automatic dimming.

Controlling the Hard Disk

The functions in this section return information about the hard disk timer and the state of the hard disk, and allow you to control the spin down of the hard disk. You can also use functions in this section to install and remove hard disk queue elements. The hard disk queue notifies your software when power to the internal hard disk is about to be turned off.

GetHardDiskTimeout

You can use the `GetHardDiskTimeout` function to find out how long the computer will wait before turning off power to the internal hard disk.

```
unsigned char GetHardDiskTimeout();
```

DESCRIPTION

The `GetHardDiskTimeout` function returns the amount of time the computer will wait after the last use of a SCSI device before turning off power to the internal hard disk. The value of `GetHardDiskTimeout` is expressed as the number of 15-second intervals the computer will wait before turning off power to the internal hard disk.

ASSEMBLY-LANGUAGE INFORMATION

The trap is `_PowerMgrDispatch` ($A09E). The selector value for `GetHardDiskTimeout` is 4 ($04) in the low word of register D0. The hard disk timeout value is returned in the low word of register D0.

SetHardDiskTimeout

You can use the `SetHardDiskTimeout` function to set how long the computer will wait before turning off power to the internal hard disk.

```
void SetHardDiskTimeout(unsigned char timeout);
```

timeout   The amount of time that the computer will wait after the last user activity before turning off the hard disk, expressed as a number of 15-second intervals.

DESCRIPTION

The `SetHardDiskTimeout` function sets how long the computer will wait after the last use of a SCSI device before turning off power to the internal hard disk. The value of `SetHardDiskTimeout` is expressed as the number of 15-second intervals the computer will wait before turning off power to the internal hard disk. If a value of 0 is passed in, the function sets the `timeout` value to the default value (currently equivalent to 4 minutes).

The trap is _PowerMgrDispatch ($A09E). The selector value for
SetHardDiskTimeout is 5 ($05) in the low word of register D0. The hard disk timeout
value to set is passed in the high word of register D0.

HardDiskPowered

You can use the HardDiskPowered function to find out whether the internal hard disk
is on.

```
Boolean HardDiskPowered();
```

DESCRIPTION

The HardDiskPowered function returns a Boolean value indicating whether or not the
internal hard disk is powered up. A value of true means that the hard disk is on, and a
value of false means that the hard disk is off.

ASSEMBLY-LANGUAGE INFORMATION

The trap is _PowerMgrDispatch ($A09E). The selector value for HardDiskPowered
is 6 ($06) in the low word of register D0. The Boolean result is returned in the low word
of register D0.

SpinDownHardDisk

You can use the SpinDownHardDisk function to force the hard disk to spin down.

```
void SpinDownHardDisk();
```

DESCRIPTION

The SpinDownHardDisk function immediately forces the hard disk to spin down and
power off if it was previously spinning. Calling SpinDownHardDisk will not spin
down the hard disk if spindown is disabled by calling the SetSpindownDisable
function.

ASSEMBLY-LANGUAGE INFORMATION

The trap is _PowerMgrDispatch ($A09E). The selector value for SpinDownHardDisk
is 7 ($07) in the low word of register D0.

IsSpindownDisabled

You can use the `IsSpindownDisabled` function to find out whether automatic hard disk spindown is enabled.

```
Boolean IsSpindownDisabled();
```

DESCRIPTION

The `IsSpindownDisabled` function returns a Boolean `true` if automatic hard disk spindown is disabled, or `false` if spindown is enabled.

ASSEMBLY-LANGUAGE INFORMATION

The trap is `_PowerMgrDispatch` ($A09E). The selector value for `IsSpindownDisabled` is 8 ($08) in the low word of register D0. The Boolean result is passed in the low byte of register D0.

SetSpindownDisable

You can use the `SetSpindownDisable` function to disable hard disk spindown.

```
void SetSpindownDisable(Boolean setDisable);
```

setDisable   A Boolean that specifies whether the spindown feature is enabled (`false`) or disabled (`true`).

DESCRIPTION

The `SetSpindownDisable` function enables or disables hard disk spindown, depending on the value of `setDisable`. If the value of `setDisable` is `true`, hard disk spindown is disabled; if the value is `false`, spindown is enabled.

Disabling hard disk spindown affects the `SpinDownHardDisk` function, as well as the normal spindown that occurs after a period of hard disk inactivity.

ASSEMBLY-LANGUAGE INFORMATION

The trap is `_PowerMgrDispatch` ($A09E). The selector value for `SetSpindownDisable` is 9 ($09) in the low word of register D0. The Boolean value to set is passed in the high word of register D0.

SEE ALSO

The `SpinDownHardDisk` function is described on page 6-50.

HardDiskQInstall

You can use the `HardDiskQInstall` function to notify your software when power to the internal hard disk is about to be turned off.

```
OSErr HardDiskQInstall(HDQueueElement *theElement);
```

theElement A pointer to an element for the hard disk power down queue.

DESCRIPTION

The `HardDiskQInstall` function installs an element into the hard disk power down queue to provide notification to your software when the internal hard disk is about to be powered off. For example, this feature might be used by the driver for an external battery-powered hard disk. When power to the internal hard disk is turned off, the external hard disk could be turned off as well.

When power to the internal hard disk is about to be turned off, the software calls the routine pointed to by the `hdProc` field so that it can do any special processing. The routine is passed a pointer to its queue element so that, for example, the routine can reference its variables.

Before calling `HardDiskQInstall`, the calling program must set the `hdQType` field to `HDPwrQType` or the queue element won't be added to the queue and `HardDiskQInstall` will return an error.

ASSEMBLY-LANGUAGE INFORMATION

The trap is `_PowerMgrDispatch` ($A09E). The selector value for `HardDiskQInstall` is 10 ($0A) in the low word of register D0. The pointer to the `HDQueue` element is passed in register A0. The result code is returned in the low word of register D0.

RESULT CODES

noErr   0   No error

SEE ALSO

The `HDQueueElement` structure is defined in "Hard Disk Queue Structure," on page 6-27.

The application-defined hard disk spindown function is described in "Hard Disk Spindown Function," on page 6-66.

HardDiskQRemove

You can use the `HardDiskQRemove` function to discontinue notification of your software when power to the internal hard disk is about to be turned off.

```
OSErr HardDiskQRemove(HDQueueElement *theElement);
```

theElement A pointer to the element for the hard disk power down queue that you wish to remove.

DESCRIPTION

The `HardDiskQRemove` function removes a queue element installed by `HardDiskQInstall`. If the `hdQType` field of the queue element is not set to `HDPwrQType`, `HardDiskQRemove` simply returns an error.

ASSEMBLY-LANGUAGE INFORMATION

The trap is `_PowerMgrDispatch` ($A09E). The selector value for `HardDiskQRemove` is 11 ($0B) in the low word of register D0. The pointer to the `HDQueue` element is passed in register A0. The result code is returned in the low word of register D0.

RESULT CODES

noErr   0   No error

SEE ALSO

The `HDQueueElement` structure is defined in "Hard Disk Queue Structure," on page 6-27.

The application-defined hard disk spindown function is described in "Hard Disk Spindown Function," on page 6-66.

6

Power Manager

Getting Information About the Internal Batteries

The functions in this section return information about the battery or batteries in the computer.

GetScaledBatteryInfo

You can use the GetScaledBatteryInfo function to find out the condition of the battery or batteries.

```
void GetScaledBatteryInfo(short whichBattery,
                          BatteryInfo *theInfo);
```

whichBattery
　　　　　The battery for which you want information. Set this parameter to 0 to receive combined information about all the batteries in the computer.

theInfo　　A pointer to a BatteryInfo data structure, which returns information about the specified battery.

DESCRIPTION

The GetScaledBatteryInfo function provides a generic means of returning information about the battery or batteries in the system. Instead of returning a voltage value, the function returns the battery level as a fraction of the total possible voltage.

Note
Battery technologies such as nickel cadmium (NiCad) and nickel metal hydride (NiMH) have replaced sealed lead acid batteries in portable Macintosh computers. There is no single algorithm for determining the battery voltage that is correct for all portable Macintosh computers. ◆

The value of whichBattery determines whether GetScaledBatteryInfo returns information about a particular battery or about the total battery level. The value of GetScaledBatteryInfo should be in the range of 0 to BatteryCount(). If the value of whichBattery is 0, GetScaledBatteryInfo returns a summation of all the batteries, that is, the effective battery level of the whole system. If the value of whichBattery is out of range, or the selected battery is not installed, GetScaledBatteryInfo will return a result of 0 in all fields. Here is a summary of the effects of the whichBattery parameter:

Value of whichBattery	Information returned
0	Total battery level for all batteries
From 1 to BatteryCount()	Battery level for the selected battery
Less than 0 or greater than BatteryCount()	0 in all fields of theInfo

The `flags` character contains several bits that describe the battery and charger state. If a bit value is 1, that feature is available or is operating; if the bit value is 0, that feature is not operating. Unused bits are reserved by Apple for future expansion.

Bit name	Bit number	Description
`batteryInstalled`	7	A battery is installed.
`batteryCharging`	6	The battery is charging.
`chargerConnected`	5	The charger is connected.

The value of `warningLevel` is the battery level at which the first low battery warning message will appear. The function returns a value of 0 in some cases when it's not appropriate to return the warning level.

The value of `batteryLevel` is the current level of the battery. A value of 0 represents the voltage at which the Power Manager will force the computer into sleep mode; a value of 255 represents the highest possible voltage.

ASSEMBLY-LANGUAGE INFORMATION

The trap is `_PowerMgrDispatch` ($A09E). The selector value for `GetScaledBatteryInfo` is 12 ($0C) in the low word of register D0. The `BatteryInfo` data are returned in the low word of register D0 as follows:

Bits	Contents
31–24	Flags
23–16	Warning level
15–8	Reserved
7–0	Battery level

SEE ALSO

The `BatteryInfo` data type is described in "Battery Information Structure," on page 6-27.

BatteryCount

You can use the `BatteryCount` function to find out how many batteries the computer supports.

```
short BatteryCount();
```

DESCRIPTION

The `BatteryCount` function returns the number of batteries that are supported internally by the computer. The value of `BatteryCount` returned may not be the same as the number of batteries currently installed.

ASSEMBLY-LANGUAGE INFORMATION

The trap is `_PowerMgrDispatch` ($A09E). The selector value for `BatteryCount` is 26 ($1A) in the low word of register D0. The number of batteries supported is returned in the low word of register D0.

GetBatteryVoltage

You can use the `GetBatteryVoltage` function to find out the battery voltage.

```
Fixed GetBatteryVoltage(short whichBattery);
```

`whichBattery`
> The battery for which you want a voltage reading.

DESCRIPTION

The `GetBatteryVoltage` function returns the battery voltage as a fixed-point number.

The value of `whichBattery` should be in the range 0 to `BatteryCount()`–1. If the value of `whichBattery` is out of range, or the selected battery is not installed, `GetBatteryVoltage` will return a result of 0.0 volts.

ASSEMBLY-LANGUAGE INFORMATION

The trap is `_PowerMgrDispatch` ($A09E). The selector value for `GetBatteryVoltage` is 27 ($1B) in the low word of register D0. The battery number is passed in the high word of register D0. The 32-bit value of the battery voltage is returned in register D0.

GetBatteryTimes

You can use the `GetBatteryTimes` function to find out about how much battery time remains.

```
void GetBatteryTimes (short whichBattery,
                      BatteryTimeRec *theTimes);
```

whichBattery
: The battery for which you want to know the time remaining. Specify 0 to get combined information about all the batteries.

theTimes
: A pointer to a battery time structure, which contains information about the time remaining for the batteries. The `BatteryTimeRec` data type is described on page 6-28.

DESCRIPTION

The `GetBatteryTimes` function returns information about the time remaining on the computer's battery or batteries. The time values are in seconds. The value of `theTimes.expectedBatteryTime` is the estimated time remaining based on current use patterns. The values of `theTimes.minimumBatteryTime` and `theTimes.maximumBatteryTime` are worst-case and best-case estimates, respectively. The value of `theTimes.timeUntilCharged` is the time that remains until the battery or batteries are fully charged.

The value of `whichBattery` determines whether `GetBatteryTimes` returns the time information about a particular battery or the total time for all batteries. The value of `GetScaledBatteryInfo` should be in the range of 0 to `BatteryCount()`. If the value of `whichBattery` is 0, `GetBatteryTimes` returns a total time for all the batteries, that is, the effective battery time for the whole system. If the value of `whichBattery` is out of range, or the selected battery is not installed, `GetBatteryTimes` will return a result of 0 in all fields. Here is a summary of the effects of the `whichBattery` parameter:

Value of `whichBattery`	Information returned
0	Total battery time for all batteries
From 1 to `BatteryCount()`	Battery time for the selected battery
Less than 0 or greater than `BatteryCount()`	0 in all fields of `theTimes`

ASSEMBLY-LANGUAGE INFORMATION

The trap is `_PowerMgrDispatch` ($A09E). The selector value for `GetBatteryTimes` is 28 ($1C) in the low word of register D0. The pointer to `BatteryTimeRec` is passed in register A0.

Controlling the Internal Modem

The functions in this section return information about the internal modem and configure the internal modem's state information.

GetIntModemInfo

You can use the GetIntModemInfo function to find out information about the internal modem.

```
unsigned long GetIntModemInfo();
```

DESCRIPTION

The GetIntModemInfo function returns a 32-bit field containing information that describes the features and state of the internal modem. It can be called whether or not a modem is installed and will return the correct information.

If a bit is set, that feature or state is supported or selected; if the bit is cleared, that feature is not supported or selected. Undefined bits are reserved by Apple for future expansion.

Bit name	Bit number	Description
hasInternalModem	0	An internal modem is installed.
intModemRingDetect	1	The modem has detected a ring on the telephone line.
intModemOffHook	2	The internal modem has taken the telephone line off hook (that is, you can hear the dial tone or modem carrier).
intModemRingWakeEnb	3	The computer will come out of sleep mode if the modem detects a ring on the telephone line and the computer supports this feature (see the canWakeupOnRing bit in PMFeatures).
extModemSelected	4	The external modem is selected (if this bit is set, then the modem port will be connected to port A of the SCC; if the modem port is not shared by the internal modem and the SCC, then this bit can be ignored).

Bits 15–31 contain the modem type, which can have one of the following values:

Value	Meaning
–1	Modem is installed but type not recognized.
0	No modem is installed.
1	Modem is a serial modem.
2	Modem is a PowerBook Duo–style Express Modem.
3	Modem is a PowerBook 160/180–style Express Modem.

ASSEMBLY-LANGUAGE INFORMATION

The trap is `_PowerMgrDispatch` ($A09E). The selector value for `GetIntModemInfo` is 14 ($0E) in the low word of register D0. The bit field to set is passed in the high word of register D0.

SetIntModemState

You can use the `SetIntModemState` function to set some parts of the state of the internal modem.

```
void SetIntModemState(short theState);
```

`theState`   A set of bits you can use to set the modem state. Set bit 15 of this parameter to 1 to set bits in the modem state. Clear bit 15 to 0 to clear bits in the modem state. The modem state bits are described in the preceding function description.

DESCRIPTION

The `SetIntModemState` function configures some of the internal modem's state information. Currently the only items that can be changed are the internal/external modem selection and the wakeup-on-ring feature.

To change an item of state information, the calling program sets the corresponding bit in the parameter `theState`. For example, to select the external modem, set bit 4 of `theState` to 1 and set bit 15 to 1. To select the internal modem, set bit 4 to 1 but set bit 15 to 0.

SPECIAL CONSIDERATIONS

In some PowerBook computers, there is a hardware switch to connect either port A of the SCC or the internal modem to the modem port. The two are physically separated, but software emulates the serial port interface for those applications that don't use the Communications Toolbox. You can check the `hasSharedModemPort` bit returned by `PMFeatures` to determine which way the computer is set up.

6

Power Manager

The trap is _PowerMgrDispatch ($A09E). The selector value for SetIntModemState is 15 ($0F) in the low word of register D0. The bit field is returned in register D0.

Controlling the Processor

The functions in this section return information about the processor speed and processor cycling, set the processor speed, and enable or disable processor cycling.

MaximumProcessorSpeed

You can use the MaximumProcessorSpeed function to find out the maximum speed of the computer's microprocessor.

```
short MaximumProcessorSpeed();
```

DESCRIPTION

The MaximumProcessorSpeed function returns the maximum clock speed of the computer's microprocessor, in MHz.

ASSEMBLY-LANGUAGE INFORMATION

The trap is _PowerMgrDispatch ($A09E). The selector value for MaximumProcessorSpeed is 16 ($10) in the low word of register D0. The processor speed value is returned in the low word of register D0.

CurrentProcessorSpeed

You can use the CurrentProcessorSpeed function to find out the current clock speed of the microprocessor.

```
short CurrentProcessorSpeed();
```

DESCRIPTION

The CurrentProcessorSpeed function returns the current clock speed of the computer's microprocessor, in MHz. The value returned will be different from the maximum processor speed if the computer has been configured to run with a reduced processor speed to conserve power.

ASSEMBLY-LANGUAGE INFORMATION

The trap is _PowerMgrDispatch ($A09E). The selector value for
CurrentProcessorSpeed is 17 ($11) in the low word of register D0. The processor
speed value is returned in the low word of register D0.

FullProcessorSpeed

You can use the FullProcessorSpeed function to find out whether the computer will
run at full speed the next time it restarts.

```
Boolean FullProcessorSpeed();
```

DESCRIPTION

The FullProcessorSpeed function returns a Boolean value of true if, on the next
restart, the computer will start up at its maximum processor speed; it returns false if
the computer will start up at its reduced processor speed.

ASSEMBLY-LANGUAGE INFORMATION

The trap is _PowerMgrDispatch ($A09E). The selector value for
FullProcessorSpeed is 18 ($12) in the low word of register D0. The Boolean result is
returned in the low byte of register D0.

SetProcessorSpeed

You can use the SetProcessorSpeed function to set the clock speed the
microprocessor will use the next time it is restarted.

```
Boolean SetProcessorSpeed(Boolean fullSpeed);
```

fullSpeed   A Boolean that sets the processor speed to full speed (true) or reduced
             speed (false).

DESCRIPTION

The SetProcessorSpeed function sets the processor speed that the computer will use
the next time it is restarted. If the value of fullSpeed is set to true, the processor will
start up at its full speed (the speed returned by MaximumProcessorSpeed, described
on page 6-60). If the value of fullSpeed is set to false, the processor will start up at
its reduced speed.

SPECIAL CONSIDERATIONS

For PowerBook models that support changing the processor speed dynamically, the current processor speed is also changed. If the speed is actually changed, `SetProcessorSpeed` returns `true`; if the speed is not changed, it returns `false`.

ASSEMBLY-LANGUAGE INFORMATION

The trap is `_PowerMgrDispatch` ($A09E). The selector value for `SetProcessorSpeed` is 19 ($13) in the low word of register D0. The Boolean value to set is passed in the high word of register D0. The Boolean result is returned in register D0.

SEE ALSO

You can use the `PMFeatures` function (page 6-41) to determine whether the computer supports changing the processor speed dynamically.

IsProcessorCyclingEnabled

You can use the `IsProcessorCyclingEnabled` function to find out whether processor cycling is enabled.

```
Boolean IsProcessorCyclingEnabled();
```

DESCRIPTION

The `IsProcessorCyclingEnabled` function returns a Boolean value of `true` if processor cycling is currently enabled, or `false` if it is disabled.

ASSEMBLY-LANGUAGE INFORMATION

The trap is `_PowerMgrDispatch` ($A09E). The selector value for `IsProcessorCyclingEnabled` is 24 ($18) in the low word of register D0. The Boolean result is returned in register D0.

EnableProcessorCycling

You can use the `EnableProcessorCycling` function to turn the processor cycling feature on and off.

```
void EnableProcessorCycling(Boolean enable);
```

enable   A Boolean that specifies whether to enable processor cycling.

DESCRIPTION

The EnableProcessorCycling function enables processor cycling if a value of true is passed in, and disables it if false is passed.

▲ **WARNING**

You should follow the advice of the mustProcessorCycle bit in the feature flags when turning processor cycling off. Turning processor cycling off when it's not recommended can result in hardware failures due to overheating. ▲

ASSEMBLY-LANGUAGE INFORMATION

The trap is _PowerMgrDispatch ($A09E). The selector value for EnableProcessorCycling is 25 ($19) in the low word of register D0. The Boolean value to set is passed in the high word of register D0.

SEE ALSO

You can use the PMFeatures function (page 6-41) to determine whether the computer supports processor cycling.

Getting and Setting the SCSI ID

The functions in this section return and set the SCSI ID the computer uses in SCSI disk mode.

GetSCSIDiskModeAddress

You can use the GetSCSIDiskModeAddress function to find out the SCSI ID the computer uses in SCSI disk mode.

```
short GetSCSIDiskModeAddress();
```

DESCRIPTION

The GetSCSIDiskModeAddress function returns the SCSI ID that the computer uses when it is started up in SCSI disk mode. The returned value is in the range 1 to 6.

Note

When the computer is in SCSI disk mode, the computer appears as a hard disk to another computer. ◆

Power Manager

ASSEMBLY-LANGUAGE INFORMATION

The trap is `_PowerMgrDispatch` ($A09E). The selector value for
`GetSCSIDiskModeAddress` is 20 ($14) in the low word of register D0. The SCSI ID
is returned in the low word of register D0.

SEE ALSO

You can use the `PMFeatures` function (page 6-41) to determine whether the computer
supports SCSI disk mode.

SetSCSIDiskModeAddress

You can use the `SetSCSIDiskModeAddress` function to set the SCSI ID for the
computer to use in SCSI disk mode.

```
void SetSCSIDiskModeAddress(short scsiAddress);
```

`scsiAddress`
> The SCSI ID that the computer uses if it is started up in SCSI disk mode.
> You must specify a value in the range of 1 to 6.

DESCRIPTION

The `SetSCSIDiskModeAddress` function sets the SCSI ID that the computer will use if
it is started up in SCSI disk mode.

The value of `scsiAddress` must be in the range of 1 to 6. If any other value is given, the
software sets the SCSI ID for SCSI disk mode to 2.

ASSEMBLY-LANGUAGE INFORMATION

The trap is `_PowerMgrDispatch` ($A09E). The selector value for
`SetSCSIDiskModeAddress` is 21 ($15) in the low word of register D0. The SCSI ID
to set is passed in the high word of register D0.

SEE ALSO

You can use the `PMFeatures` function (page 6-41) to determine whether the computer
supports SCSI disk mode.

Application-Defined Routines

The Power Manager allows you to define a sleep procedure that is called at various stages of the sleep and wakeup processes. You install a sleep procedure by calling the `SleepQInstall` procedure.

Sleep Procedures

You pass the address of a sleep procedure in the `sleepQProc` field of a sleep queue record.

MySleepProc

A sleep procedure can perform any operations required to prepare your application (or other software) for the sleep state. Your sleep procedure is also called when the computer reawakens.

DESCRIPTION

Your sleep procedure is called at various stages in the Power Manager's sleep and wakeup processes. It is called in response to a sleep request, a sleep demand, a wakeup demand, and a sleep-request revocation. You can determine which of these messages the Power Manager is sending by inspecting the sleep procedure selector code passed in register D0. This code is one of four values:

```
enum {
    /* sleep procedure selector codes */
    sleepRequest            = 1,     /* sleep request */
    sleepDemand             = 2,     /* sleep demand */
    sleepWakeUp             = 3,     /* wakeup demand */
    sleepRevoke             = 4      /* sleep-request revocation */
};
```

When called in response to a sleep request, your procedure must either accept or deny the request by either clearing register D0 or leaving it alone. When passed any other selector code, your sleep procedure should take any appropriate actions.

SPECIAL CONSIDERATIONS

A sleep procedure is never executed at interrupt time. As a result, you can, if necessary, call Memory Manager routines or other routines that allocate memory. You can also interact with the user by displaying dialog or alert boxes.

If your sleep procedure displays a dialog or alert box, you should make sure to remove the box after a reasonable amount of time. Failure to do so will prevent the computer from going to sleep and may permanently damage the screen.

ASSEMBLY-LANGUAGE INFORMATION

When your sleep procedure is called, register A0 contains the address of the sleep queue record associated with that procedure and the D0 register contains a sleep procedure selector code.

SEE ALSO

See "Writing a Sleep Procedure," beginning on page 6-20, for instructions on writing a sleep procedure, and see "Installing a Sleep Procedure," beginning on page 6-18, for instructions on installing a sleep procedure.

Hard Disk Spindown Function

You pass the address of a hard disk spindown function in the `hdProc` field of a hard disk queue structure.

MyHDSpindownProc

A hard disk spindown function can perform any operations you require to prepare for the hard disk to spin down.

```
pascal void MyHDSpindownProc(HDQueueElement *theElement);
```

`theElement`   A pointer to the element in the hard disk power down queue that was used to install this function.

DESCRIPTION

The `HardDiskQInstall` function installs an element into the hard disk power down queue to provide notification to your software when the internal hard disk is about to be powered off. For example, this feature might be used by the driver for an external battery-powered hard disk. When power to the internal hard disk is turned off, the external hard disk could be turned off as well.

When power to the internal hard disk is about to be turned off, the software calls the routine pointed to by the `hdProc` field so that it can do any special processing. The routine will be passed a pointer to its queue element so that, for example, the routine can reference its variables.

SEE ALSO

The hard disk power down queue elements are defined in "Hard Disk Queue Structure," on page 6-27.

The `HardDiskQInstall` function is described on page 6-52. The `HardDiskQRemove` function is described on page 6-53.

Summary of the Power Manager

Pascal Summary

Constants

```
CONST
    {Power Manager Gestalt selector}
    gestaltPowerMgrAttr            = 'powr';    {Power Manager attributes selector}

    {bit values in Gestalt response parameter}
    gestaltPMgrExists             = 0;         {Power Manager is present}
    gestaltPMgrCPUIdle            = 1;         {CPU can idle}
    gestaltPMgrSCC               = 2;         {can stop SCC clock}
    gestaltPMgrSound             = 3;         {can shut off sound circuits}
    gestaltPMgrDispatchExists    = 4;         {Power Manager dispatch exists }

    slpQType                     = 16;        {sleep queue type}
    sleepQType                   = 16;        {sleep queue type}

    {bit positions for ModemStatus}
    modemOnBit                   = 0;         {1 if modem is on}
    ringWakeUpBit                = 2;         {1 if ring wakeup is enabled}
    modemInstalledBit            = 3;         {1 if internal modem is installed}
    ringDetectBit                = 4;         {1 if incoming call is detected}
    modemOnHookBit               = 5;         {1 if modem is off hook}

    {masks for ModemStatus}
    modemOnMask                  = $1;        {modem on}
    ringWakeUpMask               = $4;        {ring wakeup enabled}
    modemInstalledMask           = $8;        {internal modem installed}
    ringDetectMask               = $10;       {incoming call detected}
    modemOnHookMask              = $20;       {modem off hook}

    {bit positions for BatteryStatus}
    chargerConnBit               = 0;         {1 if charger is connected}
    hiChargeBit                  = 1;         {1 if charging at hicharge rate}
    chargeOverFlowBit            = 2;         {1 if hicharge counter has overflowed}
    batteryDeadBit               = 3;         {always 0}
    batteryLowBit                = 4;         {1 if battery is low}
    connChangedBit               = 5;         {1 if charger connection has changed}
```

```
{masks for BatteryStatus}
chargerConnMask      = $1;     {charger is connected}
hiChargeMask         = $2;     {charging at hicharge rate}
chargeOverFlowMask   = $4;     {hicharge counter has overflowed}
batteryDeadMask      = $8;     {battery is dead}
batteryLowMask       = $10;    {battery is low}
connChangedMask      = $20;    {connection has changed}

{sleep procedure selector codes}
sleepRequest         = 1;      {sleep request}
sleepDemand          = 2;      {sleep demand}
sleepWakeUp          = 3;      {wakeup demand}
sleepRevoke          = 4;      {sleep-request revocation}

{bits in bitfield returned by PMFeatures}
hasWakeupTimer       = 0;      {1 = wakeup timer is supported}
hasSharedModemPort   = 1;      {1 = modem port shared by SCC and internal modem}
hasProcessorCycling  = 2;      {1 = processor cycling is supported}
mustProcessorCycle   = 3;      {1 = processor cycling should not be turned off}
hasReducedSpeed      = 4;      {1 = processor can be started up at reduced speed}
dynamicSpeedChange   = 5;      {1 = processor speed can be switched dynamically}
hasSCSIDiskMode      = 6;      {1 = SCSI Disk Mode is supported}
canGetBatteryTime    = 7;      {1 = battery time can be calculated}
canWakeupOnRing      = 8;      {1 = can wakeup when the modem detects a ring}
hasDimmingSupport    = 9;      {1 = has dimming support built into the ROM}

{bits in BatteryInfo.flags}
batteryInstalled     = 7;      {1 = battery is currently connected}
batteryCharging      = 6;      {1 = battery is being charged}
chargerConnected     = 5;      {1 = charger is connected to the PowerBook }
                               { (this does not mean the charger is plugged in)}

{bits in bitfield returned by GetIntModemInfo}
hasInternalModem     = 0;      {1 = internal modem installed}
intModemRingDetect   = 1;      {1 = internal modem has detected a ring}
intModemOffHook      = 2;      {1 = internal modem is off hook}
intModemRingWakeEnb  = 3;      {1 = wakeup on ring is enabled}
extModemSelected     = 4;      {1 = external modem selected}


modemSetBit          = 15; {1 = set bit, 0=clear bit}


HDPwrQType           ='HD';{hard disk notification queue element type}
```

Data Types

```
TYPE SleepQRec =
   RECORD
      sleepQLink:     SleepQRecPtr;   {next queue element}
      sleepQType:     Integer;        {queue type = 16}
      sleepQProc:     ProcPtr;        {pointer to sleep procedure}
      sleepQFlags:    Integer;        {reserved}
   END;
   SleepQRecPtr = ^SleepQRec;

TYPE HDQueueElement =
   RECORD
      hdQLink:        Ptr;            {pointer to next queue element}
      hdQType:        Integer;        {queue element type (must be HDQType)}
      hdFlags:        Integer;        {miscellaneous flags}
      hdProc:         ProcPtr;        {pointer to routine to call}
      hdUser:         LongInt;        {user-defined (variable storage, etc.)}
   END;

TYPE WakeupTime =
   PACKED RECORD
      wakeTime:       LongInt;        {wakeup time (same format as time)}
      wakeEnabled:    Byte;           {1 = enable, 0=disable wakeup timer}
   END;

TYPE BatteryInfo =
   PACKED RECORD
      flags:          Byte;           {misc flags (see above)}
      warningLevel:   Byte;           {scaled warning level (0-255)}
      reserved:       Byte;           {reserved for internal use}
      batteryLevel:   Byte;           {scaled battery level (0-255)}
   END;

TYPE BatteryTimeRec =
   RECORD

      expectedBatteryTime: LongInt;   {estimated battery time remaining}
      minimumBatteryTime:  LongInt;   {minimum battery time remaining}
      maximumBatteryTime:  LongInt;   {maximum battery time remaining}
      timeUntilCharged:    LongInt;   {time until battery is fully charged}
   END;
```

Power Manager Routines

Controlling the Idle State

```
FUNCTION IdleUpdate        : LongInt;
PROCEDURE EnableIdle;
PROCEDURE DisableIdle;
FUNCTION GetCPUSpeed       : LongInt;
```

Controlling and Reading the Wakeup Timer

```
FUNCTION SetWUTime         (WUTime: LongInt): OSErr;
FUNCTION DisableWUTime     : OSErr;
FUNCTION GetWUTime         (VAR WUTime: LongInt; VAR WUFlag: Byte): OSErr;
```

Controlling the Sleep Queue

```
PROCEDURE SleepQInstall    (qRecPtr: SleepQRecPtr);
PROCEDURE SleepQRemove     (qRecPtr: SleepQRecPtr);
```

Controlling Serial Power

```
PROCEDURE AOn;
PROCEDURE AOnIgnoreModem;
PROCEDURE BOn;
PROCEDURE AOff;
PROCEDURE BOff;
```

Reading the Status of the Internal Modem

```
FUNCTION ModemStatus       (VAR Status: Byte): OSErr;
```

Reading the Status of the Battery and the Battery Charger

```
FUNCTION BatteryStatus     (VAR Status: Byte; VAR Power: Byte): OSErr;
```

Power Manager Dispatch Routines

Determining the Power Manager Features Available

```
FUNCTION PMSelectorCount   : Integer;
FUNCTION PMFeatures        : LongInt;
```

Controlling the Sleep and Wakeup Timers

```
FUNCTION GetSleepTimeout : Byte;

PROCEDURE SetSleepTimeout(timeout : Byte);

PROCEDURE AutoSleepControl(enableSleep : Boolean);

FUNCTION IsAutoSlpControlDisabled() : Boolean;

PROCEDURE GetWakeupTimer(VAR theTime : WakeupTime);

PROCEDURE SetWakeupTimer(theTime : WakeupTime);
```

Controlling the Dimming Timer

```
FUNCTION GetDimmingTimeout() : Byte;

PROCEDURE SetDimmingTimeout(timeout : Byte);

PROCEDURE DimmingControl(enableDimming : Boolean);

FUNCTION IsDimmingControlDisabled() : Boolean;
```

Controlling the Hard Disk

```
FUNCTION GetHardDiskTimeout : Byte;

PROCEDURE SetHardDiskTimeout(timeout : Byte);

FUNCTION HardDiskPowered : Boolean;

PROCEDURE SpinDownHardDisk;

FUNCTION IsSpindownDisabled : Boolean;

PROCEDURE SetSpindownDisable(setDisable : BOOLEAN);

FUNCTION HardDiskQInstall(VAR theElement : HDQueueElement) : OSErr;

FUNCTION HardDiskQRemove(VAR theElement : HDQueueElement) : OSErr;
```

Getting Information About the Battery

```
PROCEDURE GetScaledBatteryInfo(whichBattery : Integer; VAR theInfo :
                              BatteryInfo);

FUNCTION BatteryCount : Integer;

FUNCTION GetBatteryVoltage(whichBattery : Integer) : Fixed;

PROCEDURE GetBatteryTimes(whichBattery : INTEGER; VAR theTimes :
                              BatteryTimeRec);
```

Controlling the Internal Modem

```
FUNCTION GetIntModemInfo : LongInt;

PROCEDURE SetIntModemState(theState : Integer);
```

Controlling the Processor

```
FUNCTION MaximumProcessorSpeed : Integer;
```

```
FUNCTION CurrentProcessorSpeed : Integer;

FUNCTION FullProcessorSpeed : Boolean;

FUNCTION SetProcessorSpeed(fullSpeed : Boolean) : Boolean;

FUNCTION IsProcessorCyclingEnabled : Boolean;

PROCEDURE EnableProcessorCycling(enable : Boolean);
```

Getting and Setting the SCSI ID

```
FUNCTION GetSCSIDiskModeAddress : Integer;

PROCEDURE SetSCSIDiskModeAddress(scsiAddress : Integer);
```

Application-Defined Routines

```
PROCEDURE MySleepProc;

PROCEDURE MyHDSpindownProc(theElement : HDQueueElement);
```

C Summary

Constants and Data Types

```
/* Power Manager Gestalt selector */
#define gestaltPowerMgrAttr 'powr'  /* Power Manager attributes selector */

/* bit values in Gestalt response parameter */
enum {
    gestaltPMgrExists           = 0,     /* Power Manager is present */
    gestaltPMgrCPUIdle          = 1,     /* CPU can idle */
    gestaltPMgrSCC              = 2,     /* can stop SCC clock */
    gestaltPMgrSound            = 3,     /* can shut off sound circuits */
    gestaltPMgrDispatchExists   = 4      /* Power Manager dispatch exists */
};

enum {
    slpQType                    = 16,    /* sleep queue type */
    sleepQType                  = 16     /* sleep queue type */
};

enum {
    /* bit positions for ModemStatus */
    modemOnBit                  = 0,     /* 1 if modem is on */
    ringWakeUpBit               = 2,     /* 1 if ring wakeup is enabled */
```

```
modemInstalledBit          = 3,     /* 1 if internal modem is installed */
ringDetectBit              = 4,     /* 1 if incoming call is detected */
modemOnHookBit             = 5,     /* 1 if modem is off hook */

/* masks for ModemStatus */
modemOnMask                = 0x1,   /* modem on */
ringWakeUpMask             = 0x4,   /* ring wakeup enabled */
modemInstalledMask         = 0x8,   /* internal modem installed */
ringDetectMask             = 0x10,  /* incoming call detected */
modemOnHookMask            = 0x20,  /* modem off hook */

/* bit positions for BatteryStatus */
chargerConnBit             = 0,     /* 1 if charger is connected */
hiChargeBit                = 1,     /* 1 if charging at hicharge rate */
chargeOverFlowBit          = 2,     /* 1 if hicharge counter has overflowed */
batteryDeadBit             = 3,     /* always 0 */
batteryLowBit              = 4,     /* 1 if battery is low */
connChangedBit             = 5,     /* 1 if charger connection has changed */

/* masks for BatteryStatus */
chargerConnMask            = 0x1,   /* charger is connected */
hiChargeMask               = 0x2,   /* charging at hicharge rate */
chargeOverFlowMask         = 0x4,   /* hicharge counter has overflowed */
batteryDeadMask            = 0x8,   /* battery is dead */
batteryLowMask             = 0x10,  /* battery is low */
connChangedMask            = 0x20,  /* connection has changed */

/* sleep procedure selector codes */
sleepRequest               = 1,     /* sleep request */
sleepDemand                = 2,     /* sleep demand */
sleepWakeUp                = 3,     /* wakeup demand */
sleepRevoke                = 4      /* sleep-request revocation */
};

/* bits in bitfield returned by PMFeatures */
#define hasWakeupTimer 0            /* 1 = wakeup timer is supported */
#define hasSharedModemPort 1        /* 1 = modem port shared by SCC and */
                                    /*   internal modem */
#define hasProcessorCycling 2       /* 1 = processor cycling is supported */
#define mustProcessorCycle 3        /* 1 = processor cycling should not be */
                                    /*   turned off */
#define hasReducedSpeed 4           /* 1 = processor can be started up at */
                                    /*   reduced speed */
#define dynamicSpeedChange 5        /* 1 = processor speed can be */
                                    /*   switched dynamically */
```

```
#define hasSCSIDiskMode 6        /* 1 = SCSI Disk Mode is supported */
#define canGetBatteryTime 7      /* 1 = battery time can be calculated */
#define canWakeupOnRing 8        /* 1 = can wakeup when the modem detects */
                                 /*  a ring */
#define hasDimmingSupport 9      /* 1 = has dimming support built into the ROM */

/* bits in bitfield returned by GetIntModemInfo and set by SetIntModemState */
#define hasInternalModem 0       /* 1 = internal modem installed */
#define intModemRingDetect 1     /* 1 = internal modem has detected a ring */
#define intModemOffHook 2        /* 1 = internal modem is off hook */
#define intModemRingWakeEnb 3    /* 1 = wakeup on ring is enabled */
#define extModemSelected 4       /* 1 = external modem selected */

#define modemSetBit 15           /* 1 = set bit, 0=clear bit (SetIntModemState) */

/* bits in BatteryInfo.flags */
#define batteryInstalled 7       /* 1 = battery is currently connected */
#define batteryCharging 6        /* 1 = battery is being charged */
#define chargerConnected 5       /* 1 = charger is connected to the PowerBook */
                                 /*  (this does not mean the charger is */
                                 /*  plugged in) */

struct SleepQRec {
    struct SleepQRec  *sleepQLink;   /* next queue element */
    short             sleepQType;    /* queue type = 16 */
    ProcPtr           sleepQProc;    /* pointer to sleep procedure */
    short             sleepQFlags;   /* reserved */
};
typedef struct SleepQRec SleepQRec;
typedef SleepQRec *SleepQRecPtr;

/* hard disk spindown notification queue element */
typedef struct HDQueueElement HDQueueElement;

typedef pascal void (*HDSpindownProc)(HDQueueElement *theElement);

struct HDQueueElement {
    Ptr hdQLink;                /* pointer to next queue element */
    short hdQType;              /* queue element type (must be HDQType) */
    short hdFlags;              /* miscellaneous flags */
    HDSpindownProc hdProc;      /* pointer to routine to call */
    long hdUser;                /* user-defined private storage */
};

#define HDPwrQType 'HD'      /* queue element type */
```

```
/* wakeup time record */
typedef struct WakeupTime {
    unsigned long wakeTime;      /* wakeup time (same format as current time) */
    char wakeEnabled;            /* 1 = enable wakeup timer, 0=disable */
} WakeupTime;

/* battery time information (in seconds) */
typedef struct BatteryTimeRec {
    unsigned long expectedBatteryTime; /* estimated battery time remaining */
    unsigned long inimumBatteryTime;   /* minimum battery time remaining */
    unsigned long maximumBatteryTime;  /* maximum battery time remaining */
    unsigned long timeUntilCharged;    /* time until battery is fully charged */
} BatteryTimeRec;
```

Power Manager Functions

Controlling the Idle State

```
pascal long IdleUpdate        (void);
pascal void EnableIdle        (void);
pascal void DisableIdle       (void);
pascal long GetCPUSpeed       (void);
```

Controlling and Reading the Wakeup Timer

```
pascal OSErr SetWUTime        (long WUTime);
pascal OSErr DisableWUTime    (void);
pascal OSErr GetWUTime        (long *WUTime, Byte *WUFlag);
```

Controlling the Sleep Queue

```
pascal void SleepQInstall     (SleepQRecPtr qRecPtr);
pascal void SleepQRemove      (SleepQRecPtr qRecPtr);
```

Controlling Serial Power

```
pascal void AOn               (void);
pascal void AOnIgnoreModem    (void);
pascal void BOn               (void);
pascal void AOff              (void);
pascal void BOff              (void);
```

Reading the Status of the Internal Modem

```
pascal OSErr ModemStatus      (Byte *Status);
```

Reading the Status of the Battery and the Battery Charger

```
pascal OSErr BatteryStatus  (Byte *Status, Byte *Power);
```

Power Manager Dispatch Functions

Determining the Power Manager Features Available

```
short PMSelectorCount       (void);
unsigned long PMFeatures    (void);
```

Controlling the Sleep and Wakeup Timers

```
unsigned char GetSleepTimeout(void);
void SetSleepTimeout        (unsigned char timeout);
void AutoSleepControl       (Boolean enableSleep);
Boolean IsAutoSlpControlDisabled(void);
void GetWakeupTimer         (WakeupTime *theTime);
void SetWakeupTimer         (WakeupTime *theTime);
```

Controlling the Dimming Timer

```
unsigned char GetDimmingTimeout(void);
void SetDimmingTimeout      (unsigned char timeout);
void DimmingControl         (Boolean enableDimming);
Boolean IsDimmingControlDisabled(void);
```

Controlling the Hard Disk

```
unsigned char GetHardDiskTimeout(void);
void SetHardDiskTimeout     (unsigned char timeout);
Boolean HardDiskPowered     (void);
void SpinDownHardDisk        (void);
Boolean IsSpindownDisabled  (void);
void SetSpindownDisable     (Boolean setDisable);
OSErr HardDiskQInstall      (HDQueueElement *theElement);
OSErr HardDiskQRemove       (HDQueueElement *theElement);
```

Getting Information About the Battery

```
void GetScaledBatteryInfo    (short whichBattery, BatteryInfo *theInfo);
short BatteryCount           (void);
Fixed GetBatteryVoltage      (short whichBattery);
void GetBatteryTimes         (short whichBattery, BatteryTimeRec *theTimes);
```

Controlling the Internal Modem

```
unsigned long GetIntModemInfo(void);
void SetIntModemState        (short theState);
```

Controlling the Processor

```
short MaximumProcessorSpeed (void);
short CurrentProcessorSpeed (void);
Boolean FullProcessorSpeed  (void);
Boolean SetProcessorSpeed    (Boolean fullSpeed);
Boolean IsProcessorCyclingEnabled(void);
void EnableProcessorCycling (Boolean enable);
```

Getting and Setting the SCSI ID

```
short GetSCSIDiskModeAddress (void);
void SetSCSIDiskModeAddress (short scsiAddress);
```

Application-Defined Functions

```
void MySleepProc            (void);
void (*HDSpindownProc)(HDQueueElement *theElement);
```

Assembly-Language Summary

Data Structures

Sleep Queue Data Structure

0	sleepQLink	long	pointer to next element in the queue
4	sleepQType	word	queue type (should be 16)
6	sleepQProc	long	pointer to a sleep procedure
10	sleepQFlags	word	reserved

Hard Disk Queue Structure

0	hdQLink	long	pointer to next element in the queue
4	hdQType	word	queue type (should be HDPwrQType)
6	hdFlags	word	reserved
8	hdProc	long	pointer to a hard disk power-down procedure
12	hdUser	long	user defined

Wakeup Time Structure

0	wakeTime	long	wakeup time in seconds since 00:00:00, 1/1/1904
4	wakeEnabled	byte	1 = enable wakeup timer, 0 = disable timer

Battery Information Structure

0	flags	byte	flags
1	warningLevel	byte	scaled warning level (0—255)
2	reserved	byte	reserved
3	batteryLevel	byte	scaled battery level (0—255)

Battery Time Structure

0	expectedBatteryTime	long	estimated battery time remaining in seconds
4	minimumBatteryTime	long	minimum battery time remaining
8	maximumBatteryTime	long	maximum battery time remaining
12	timeUntilCharged	long	time remaining until battery is fully charged

Trap Macros

Trap Macros Requiring Routine Selectors

_IdleState

Selector	Routine
0	EnableIdle
Any positive number	DisableIdle
Any negative number	GetCPUSpeed

_SerialPower

Selector	Routine
$04	AOn
$05	AOnIgnoreModem
$00	BOn
$84	AOff
$80	BOff

`_PowerMgrDispatch`

Selector	Routine
$00	PMSelectorCount
$01	PMFeatures
$02	GetSleepTimeout
$03	SetSleepTimeout
$04	GetHardDiskTimeout
$05	SetHardDiskTimeout
$06	HardDiskPowered
$07	SpinDownHardDisk
$08	IsSpindownDisabled
$09	SetSpindownDisable
$0A	HardDiskQInstall
$0B	HardDiskQRemove
$0C	GetScaledBatteryInfo
$0D	AutoSleepControl
$0E	GetIntModemInfo
$0F	SetIntModemState
$10	MaximumProcessorSpeed
$11	CurrentProcessorSpeed
$12	FullProcessorSpeed
$13	SetProcessorSpeed
$14	GetSCSIDiskModeAddress
$15	SetSCSIDiskModeAddress
$16	GetWakeupTimer
$17	SetWakeupTimer
$18	IsProcessorCyclingEnabled
$19	EnableProcessorCycling
$1A	BatteryCount
$1B	GetBatteryVoltage
$1C	GetBatteryTimes
$1D	GetDimmingTimeout
$1E	SetDimmingTimeout
$1F	DimmingControl
$20	IsDimmingControlDisabled
$21	IsAutoSlpControlDisabled

Result Codes

noErr	0	No error
pmBusyErr	−13000	Power Manager IC stuck busy
pmReplyTOErr	−13001	Timed out waiting to begin reply handshake
pmSendStartErr	−13002	Power Manager IC did not start handshake
pmSendEndErr	−13003	During send, Power Manager did not finish handshake
pmRecvStartErr	−13004	During receive, Power Manager did not start handshake
pmRecvEndErr	−13005	During receive, Power Manager did not finish handshake

Serial Driver

Contents

This chapter describes how you can use the Serial Driver to transfer data to a device connected to a Macintosh modem or printer port. The **Serial Driver** supports asynchronous serial data communication between applications and serial devices through these ports.

The Serial Driver provides low-level support for communicating with serial devices that cannot be accessed through the Communications Toolbox or Printing Manager. For example, a scientific instrument or a printer that does not support QuickDraw. Before you decide to use the Serial Driver, you should determine whether it is the appropriate solution for your communication needs.

The Communications Toolbox is the recommended method for integrating modems and other telecommunications devices into the Macintosh environment. The Communications Toolbox provides hardware-independent services and a standard interface that offers compatibility with all Macintosh models. To find out more about the Communications Toolbox, see *Inside the Macintosh Communications Toolbox*.

Likewise, the Printing Manager is the recommended interface for printers and similar output devices. Using the Printing Manager makes your hardware or software product compatible with every other device or application that supports this standard interface. Refer to *Inside Macintosh: Imaging With QuickDraw* for more information.

To use the Serial Driver, you should understand how to open, close, and communicate with device drivers using the Device Manager. You can find this information in the chapter "Device Manager" in this book. For information about the Macintosh serial port hardware, including circuit diagrams and signal descriptions, see *Guide to the Macintosh Family Hardware*, second edition.

This chapter begins with a brief summary of key concepts in serial data communication, then describes how you can use the Serial Driver to

- configure a Macintosh serial port
- specify a data transfer buffer
- send and receive data through a serial port
- interpret serial communication errors

Introduction to Serial Communication

Serial Communication, like any data transfer, requires coordination between the sender and receiver. For example, when to start the transmission and when to end it, when one particular bit or byte ends and another begins, when the receiver's capacity has been exceeded, and so on. A **protocol** defines the specific methods of coordinating transmission between a sender and receiver.

The scope of serial data transmission protocols is large and complex, encompassing everything from electrical connections to data encoding methods. This section summarizes the most important protocols and standards related to using the Serial Driver.

Asynchronous and Synchronous Communication

Serial data transfers depend on accurate timing in order to differentiate bits in the data stream. This timing can be handled in one of two ways: asynchronously or synchronously. In asynchronous communication, the scope of the timing is a single byte. In synchronous communication, the timing scope comprises one or more blocks of bytes. The terms asynchronous and synchronous are slightly misleading, because both kinds of communication require synchronization between the sender and receiver.

Asynchronous communication is the prevailing standard in the personal computer industry, both because it is easier to implement and because it has the unique advantage that bytes can be sent whenever they are ready, as opposed to waiting for blocks of data to accumulate.

IMPORTANT

Do not confuse asynchronous communication with asynchronous execution. Asynchronous communication is a protocol for coordinating serial data transfers. Asynchronous execution refers to the capability of a device driver to carry out background processing. The Serial Driver supports both asynchronous communication and asynchronous execution. ▲

The Serial Driver does not support synchronous communication protocols. However, it does support synchronous clocking supplied by an external device.

Duplex Communication

Another important characteristic of digital communication is the extent to which simultaneous two-way transfers of data can be achieved.

In a simple connection, the hardware configuration is such that only one-way communication is possible (for example, from a computer to a printer that cannot send status signals back to the computer). In a half-duplex connection, two-way transfer of data is possible, but only in one direction at a time. That is, the two parties to the connection take turns transmitting and receiving data. In a full-duplex connection, both parties can send and receive data simultaneously. The Serial Driver supports full-duplex operation.

Flow Control Methods

Because a sender and receiver can't always process data at the same rate, some method of negotiating when to start and stop transmission is required. The Serial Driver supports two methods of controlling serial data flow. One method relies on the serial port hardware, the other is implemented in software.

Hardware flow control uses two of the serial port signal lines to control data transmission. When the Serial Driver is ready to accept data from an external device, it asserts the Data Terminal Ready (DTR) signal on pin 1 of the serial port, which the external device receives through its Clear to Send (CTS) input. Likewise, the Macintosh receives the external device's DTR signal through the CTS input on pin 2 of the serial port. When either the Macintosh or the external device is unable to receive data, it negates its DTR signal and the sender suspends transmission until the signal is asserted again.

Flow control can also be handled in software by using an agreed-upon set of characters as start and stop signals. The Serial Driver supports XON/XOFF flow control, which typically assigns the ASCII DC1 character (also known as control-Q) as the start signal and the DC3 character (control-S) as the stop signal, although you can choose different characters.

Asynchronous Serial Communication Protocol

This section provides an overview of the protocol that governs the lowest level of data transmission—how serialized bits are sent over a single electrical line. This standard rests on more than a century of evolution in teleprinter technology.

When a sender is connected to a receiver over an electrical connecting line, there is an initial state in which communication has not yet begun, called the idle or mark state. Because older electromechanical devices operate more reliably with current continually passing through them, the mark state employs a positive voltage level. Changing the state of the line by shifting the voltage to a negative value is called a space. Once this change has occurred, the receiver interprets a negative voltage level as a 0 bit, and a positive voltage level as a 1 bit. These transitions are shown in Figure 7-1.

The change from mark to space is known as the start bit, and this triggers the synchronization necessary for asynchronous serial transmission. The start bit delineates the beginning of the transmission unit defined as a character frame. The receiver then samples the voltage level at periodic intervals known as the bit time, to determine whether a 0-bit or a 1-bit is present on the line.

Figure 7-1   The format of serialized bits

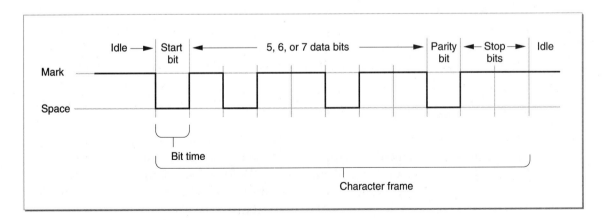

The bit time is expressed in samples per second, known as **baud** (in honor of telecommunication pioneer Emile Baudot). This sampling rate must be agreed upon by sender and receiver prior to start of transmission in order for a successful transfer to occur. Common values for the sampling rate are 1200 baud and 2400 baud. In the case where one sampling interval can signal a single bit, a baud rate of 1200 results in a transfer rate of 1200 bits per second (bps). Note that because modern protocols can express more than one bit value within the sampling interval, the baud rate and the data rate (bps) are not always identical.

Prior to transmission, the sender and receiver agree on a serial data format; that is, how many bits of data constitute a character frame, and what happens after those bits are sent. The Serial Driver supports frames of 5, 6, 7, or 8 bits in length. Character frames of 7 or 8 data bits are commonly used for transmitting ASCII characters.

After the data bits in the frame are sent, the sender can optionally transmit a parity bit for error-checking. There are various parity schemes, which the sender and receiver must agree upon prior to transmission. In odd parity, a bit is sent so that the entire frame always contains an odd number of 1 bits. Conversely, in even parity, the parity bit results in an even number of 1 bits. No parity means that no additional bit is sent. Other less-used parity schemes include mark parity, in which the extra bit is always 1, and space parity, in which its value is always 0. Using parity bits for error checking, regardless of the scheme, is now considered a rudimentary approach to error detection. Most communication systems employ more reliable techniques for error detection and correction.

To signify the end of the character frame, the sender places the line back to the mark state (positive voltage) for a minimum specified time interval. This interval has one of several possible values: 1 bit time, 2 bit times, or 1-1/2 bit times. This signal is known as the stop bit, and returns the transmission line back to idle status.

Electrical lines are always subject to environmental perturbations known as noise. This noise can cause errors in transmission, by altering voltage levels so that a bit is reversed (flipped), shortened (dropped), or lengthened (added). When this occurs, the ability of the receiver to distinguish a character frame may be affected, resulting in a framing error.

The break signal is a special signal that falls outside the character frame. The break signal occurs when the line is switched from mark (positive voltage) to space (negative voltage) and held there for longer than a character frame. The break signal resembles an ASCII NUL character (a string of 0-bits), but exists at a lower level than the ASCII encoding scheme (which governs the encoding of information *within* the character frame).

The RS-422 Serial Interface

The electrical characteristics of a serial communication connection are specified by various interfacing standards, one of which is the RS-422 standard used in all Macintosh computers. This standard is an enhancement of the RS-232 standard, with electrical characteristics modified to allow higher transmission rates over longer lines. Although the electrical voltage differences can be critical at times and should therefore not be ignored, most of the terminology and concepts remain the same across these two standards. For purposes of this discussion, it is convenient to treat these two standards as a single entity.

The specifications of the RS-422 and RS-232 interfacing standards are contained in documents available from the Electronic Industries Associations (EIA). The specifications cover several aspects of the connection between data terminal equipment and data communication equipment. These aspects include the electrical signal characteristics, the mechanical description of the interface circuits, and the functional description of the circuits.

The principal interface signals specified by the EIA are described in the following list. The term **data terminal equipment** (DTE) is used to describe the initiator or controller of the serial connection, typically the computer. The term **data communication equipment** (DCE) describes the device that is connected to the DTE, such as a modem or printer.

The RS-422/RS-232 signals are described below. For specific information about how these signals are used in Macintosh computers, see *Guide to the Macintosh Family Hardware*, second edition.

■ *Data Terminal Ready* (DTR). The DTR signal indicates that the DTE (that is, your computer) is ready to communicate. Deasserting this signal causes the DCE to suspend transmission. The DTR signal is the most important control line for a modem, because when it is deasserted, most modem functions cease and the modem disconnects from the telephone line. In Macintosh computers, the DTR signal is connected to the CTS signal, discussed next.

■ *Request to Send* (RTS) and *Clear to Send* (CTS). The RTS signal was originally intended to switch a half-duplex modem from transmit to receive mode. The computer would send an RTS signal to the modem and wait for the modem to respond by asserting CTS. Since most communications between microcomputers are full-duplex nowadays, RTS/CTS handshaking is not often used in its original form. Rather, in most full-duplex modems, the CTS signal is permanently asserted, and the RTS signal is not used. In Macintosh computers, the CTS signal is connected to the DTR signal.

■ *Data Set Ready* (DSR). The DSR signal is not used by Macintosh computers and is usually permanently asserted on microcomputer modems. It was intended to signal the computer that the modem had made a proper connection to the telephone line and received an answer tone from the modem on the other end. Modern modems communicate this information by sending messages to the computer.

■ *Transmitted Data* (TD). The TD signal carries the serial data stream from the DTE to the DCE. The EIA specifications dictate that the DTR, RTS, CTS, and DSR signals must be asserted before data can be transmitted, but this requirement is not strictly followed in the computer industry.

■ *Received Data* (RD). The RD signal is the counterpart of the TD signal, and carries data from the DCE to the DTE. Although the EIA specifies that this signal be in the mark state when no carrier is present, this requirement is rarely adhered to.

■ *Data Carrier Detect* (DCD). The DCD signal is not used by Macintosh computers. In systems that use the signal, it is asserted by the DCE when a carrier signal is received.

■ *Ring Indicator* (RI). The RI signal is not used by Macintosh computers. In systems that use the signal, it is asserted by the DCE when the telephone line is ringing.

As you can see, implementations of the RS-422/RS-232 interface do not always correspond to the specifications set forth by the EIA. This is especially true when the DCE is not a modem.

About the Serial Driver

The Serial Driver is a part of the Macintosh Operating System that provides low-level support for asynchronous, interrupt-driven serial data transfers through the modem and printer ports.

The Serial Driver provides routines that allow you to

- initialize and terminate communication
- transmit and receive data
- examine and change communication settings

You access the Serial Driver routines using standard Device Manager functions such as open, close, read, write, control, and status. The Serial Driver also includes some convenience routines that you can call from Pascal or C.

The Serial Driver supports the following communication settings

- 5, 6, 7, or 8 data bits per character
- odd, even, or no parity
- 1, 1.5, or 2 stop bits
- 300 to 57600 baud transmission rates (depending on hardware capability)
- hardware or software flow control

The Serial Driver default settings are 9600 baud, 8 data bits per character, no parity, and 2 stop bits. Hardware handshaking is the default under System 7, although some earlier versions of the Serial Driver defaulted to software handshaking.

Additional control and status functions allow you to

- determine the version number of the Serial Driver
- change the input buffer from the default buffer to one that you specify
- obtain information about transmission errors such as overrun, framing, parity, and break signals.
- enable the automatic replacement of characters that have parity errors
- use an external timing signal for synchronous clocking

Macintosh Serial Architecture

The Serial Driver consists of a set of four Macintosh device drivers and assorted convenience routines that interface to the Device Manager. Within the overall Macintosh software architecture, the location and boundaries of the Serial Driver are not sharply defined. This is because its role as mediator between applications and devices is supplemented by routines belonging to the Device Manager.

Although the hardware architecture of the serial ports varies, the Serial Driver provides a universal interface for applications. For example, some Macintosh computers use the

Zilog Z8530 Serial Communications Controller (SCC) microchip, while others use custom devices. By using the Serial Driver rather than relying on a particular hardware configuration, your application is compatible with all Macintosh computers.

Figure 7-2 shows the Serial Driver and its relation to the Macintosh serial architecture. Conceptually, there are three functional layers: the application layer, the system software layer, and the hardware layer. The Serial Driver, the Device Manager, and the four serial device drivers all exist within the system software layer. Although you normally access the Serial Driver through Device Manager routines, the Serial Driver interface includes a set of convenience routines such as `SerStatus` that provide a high-level interface to some functions.

Figure 7-2   The role of the Serial Driver

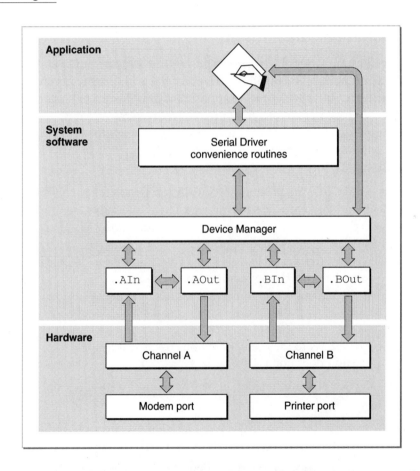

The four device drivers that control the serial ports differ from other Macintosh device drivers in that they share common internal routines and data structures, as illustrated by the horizontal interconnecting arrows in Figure 7-2. Each driver is associated with a communication channel, either Channel A or Channel B, and each channel is associated with a serial port. Channel A controls the modem port, and Channel B controls the printer port. Each channel has both an input driver and an output driver associated with it. The drivers for the modem port are named .AIn and .AOut, and those for the printer port are named .BIn and .BOut.

Each input driver receives data from a serial port and transfers it to the application. Each output driver takes data from the application and sends it out its serial port. Although the input and output drivers for a port are closely related and share some of the same routines, each driver has its own device control entry data structure. This means that read and write operations can be processed simultaneously, which allows the Serial Driver to support full-duplex communication.

Because the input and output drivers are not completely distinct entities, some functions (for example, the SerReset function) only need to be invoked on the output driver—the desired operation occurs on the input side as well. Note, however, that you must always explicitly open and close both the input and output drivers.

Serial Communication Errors

Data received from the serial port passes through a hardware buffer and then into a software buffer managed by the input driver for the port. Characters are removed from the input driver's buffer each time an application calls the driver's read routine. Each input driver's buffer can initially hold up to 64 characters, but you can specify a larger buffer using the SerSetBuf function. You need to increase the input buffer size if the buffer fills up faster than your application can read from it, as indicated by overrun errors and lost data.

Because the serial hardware in some Macintosh computers relies on processor interrupts during I/O operations, overrun errors are possible if interrupts are disabled while data is being received at the serial port. To prevent such errors, the Disk Driver and other system software components are designed to store any data received by the modem port while they have interrupts disabled, and then pass this data to the port's input driver. Because the system software only monitors the modem port, the printer port is not recommended for two-way communication at data rates above 300 baud.

Note
AppleTalk is not subject to the same limitations because it is not interrupt-driven and does not use the Serial Driver. ◆

You can use the SerStatus function to detect the most common serial communication errors:

- Hardware overrun errors occur when the serial hardware input buffer overflows, usually because the input driver doesn't read it often enough.

- Software overrun errors occur when an input driver's buffer overflows, usually because the application doesn't issue read calls to the driver often enough.

- Parity errors occur when the serial hardware detects an incorrect parity bit.

- Framing errors occur when the serial hardware detects an error in the stop bits.

- Break errors occur when a break signal is received.

Overrun, parity, and framing errors are usually handled by requesting that the sender retransmit the affected data. Break errors are typically initiated by the user and handled as appropriate for the particular application. When an input driver receives a break signal, it terminates any pending read requests. You can terminate pending write requests by sending a `KillIO` request to the output driver.

Using the Serial Driver

The basic steps in using the Serial Driver are

1. Open the output device driver for the serial port, then open the input device driver. Always open both drivers, even if you only need one.

2. Optionally, allocate a buffer that is larger than the default 64-byte input buffer, and then use the `SerSetBuf` function to select the alternate buffer.

3. Set the handshaking mode.

4. Set the baud rate and data format.

5. Read or write the desired data.

6. When you are finished using the Serial Driver, terminate any pending I/O with the Device Manager `KillIO` function.

7. Restore the default input buffer.

8. Close the input and output drivers. Always close the input driver first.

The program shown in Listing 7-1 illustrates these steps. The following sections describe each step in more detail.

Listing 7-1   Using the Serial Driver

```
PROGRAM UsingTheSerialDriver;
{An example of the basic steps required to set up and use the Serial Driver.}
{ Note that all function calls demonstrated here are synchronous and thus   }
{ should not be called at interrupt time.                                   }
USES
   Serial;

VAR
   gOutputRefNum:    Integer;    {output driver reference number}
   gInputRefNum:     Integer;    {input driver reference number}
   gInputBufHandle:  Handle;     {handle to my input buffer}
   gOSErr:           OSErr;      {function results}
```

```
PROCEDURE MyOpenSerialDriver;
{Use the Device Manager OpenDriver function to open the drivers.}
BEGIN
    gOSErr := OpenDriver('.AOut', gOutputRefNum); {always open output first}
    IF gOSErr = noErr THEN
        gOSErr := OpenDriver('.AIn', gInputRefNum); {then open the input driver}
END;


PROCEDURE MyChangeInputBuffer;
{Replace the default input buffer with a larger buffer.}
CONST
    kInputBufSize = 1024; {size of my input buffer in bytes}
BEGIN
    gInputBufHandle := NewHandle(kInputBufSize); {allocate storage}
    HLock(gInputBufHandle); {lock it}
    SerSetBuf(gInputRefNum, gInputBufHandle^, kInputBufSize); {set the buffer}
END;


PROCEDURE MySetHandshakeOptions;
{Set flow control method and other options. Note that you only need to set}
{ the output driver; the settings are reflected on the input side.}
VAR
    mySerShkRec: SerShk; {serial handshake record}
BEGIN
    WITH mySerShkRec DO
        BEGIN
            fXOn := 0;      {turn off XON/XOFF output flow control}
            fCTS := 0;      {turn off CTS/DTR flow control}
            errs := 0;      {clear error mask}
            evts := 0;      {clear event mask}
            fInX := 0;      {turn off XON/XOFF input flow control}
            fDTR := 0;      {turn off DTR input flow control}
        END;
    {Use control call 14 instead of the SerHShake function}
    { because it allows control over DTR handshaking.}
    gOSErr := Control(gOutputRefNum, 14, @mySerShkRec); {csCode = 14}
END;


PROCEDURE MyConfigureThePort;
{Set baud rate and data format.  Note that you only need to set the}
{ output driver; the settings are reflected on the input side.}
CONST
    kConfigParam = baud2400+data8+noParity+stop10; {create bit field}
```

```
BEGIN
    gOSErr := SerReset(gOutputRefNum, kConfigParam); {configure the port}
END;


PROCEDURE MySendMessage;
{Use the Device Manager PBWrite function to send data to the output driver.}
VAR
    myMessage:        Str255;        {the data to send}
    myMsgLen:         LongInt;       {number of bytes to send}
    myParamBlock:     ParamBlockRec; {parameter block for the PBWrite function}
    myPBPtr:          ParmBlkPtr;    {pointer to the parameter block}
BEGIN
    myMessage := 'The Eagle has landed.';
    myMsgLen := Length(myMessage);    {get the size of the message string}
    WITH myParamBlock DO {fill in required fields of the parameter block}
        BEGIN
            ioRefNum := gOutputRefNum;     {write to the output driver}
            ioBuffer := @myMessage[1];     {pointer to the data}
            ioReqCount := myMsgLen;        {number of bytes to send}
            ioCompletion := NIL;           {no completion routine specified}
            ioVRefNum := 0;                {not used by the Serial Driver}
            ioPosMode := 0;                {not used by the Serial Driver}
        END;
    myPBPtr := @myParamBlock
    gOSErr := PBWrite(myPBPtr, FALSE);  {synchronous Device Manager request}
END;


PROCEDURE MyReceiveMessage;
{Use the Device Manager PBRead function to read data from the input driver.}
VAR
    myBuffer:         Str255;        {a buffer to receive the data}
    myReadCount:      LongInt;       {number of bytes to read}
    myParamBlock:     ParamBlockRec; {parameter block for the PBRead function}
    myPBPtr:          ParmBlkPtr;    {pointer to the parameter block}
BEGIN
    myBuffer := '';
    myReadCount := 0;
    gOSErr := SerGetBuf(gInputRefNum, myReadCount); {determine how many bytes}
                                                    { are in the input buffer}

    IF myReadCount > 0 THEN
        BEGIN
            WITH myParamBlock DO {fill in required fields of the parameter block}
                BEGIN
```

```
                  ioRefNum := gInputRefNum;   {read from the input driver}
                  ioBuffer := @myBuffer[1];   {pointer to my data buffer}
                  ioReqCount := myReadCount;   {number of bytes to read}
                  ioCompletion := NIL;         {no completion routine specified}
                  ioVRefNum := 0;              {not used by the Serial Driver}
                  ioPosMode := 0;              {not used by the Serial Driver}
               END;
            myPBPtr := @myParamBlock;
            gOSErr := PBRead(myPBPtr, FALSE);{synchronous Device Manager request}
         END;
   END;


PROCEDURE MyRestoreInputBuffer;
{Restore the default input buffer.}
BEGIN
   SerSetBuf(gInputRefNum, gInputBufHandle^, 0); {0 means restore default}
   HUnlock(gInputBufHandle); {release my old buffer}
END;


PROCEDURE MyCloseSerialDriver;
{Use the Device Manager KillIO function to terminate all current and pending}
{ operations, then close the drivers. Note that you only need to call KillIO}
{ on the output driver to terminate both input and output operations.}
BEGIN
   gOSErr := KillIO(gOutputRefNum); {terminate all pending I/O operations}
   IF gOSErr = noErr THEN
      gOSErr := CloseDriver(gInputRefNum); {close the input driver first}
   IF gOSErr = noErr THEN
      gOSErr := CloseDriver(gOutputRefNum); {then close the output driver}
END;


BEGIN {UsingTheSerialDriver}
   MyOpenSerialDriver;                {open the output and input drivers}
   MyChangeInputBuffer;               {replace the default input buffer}
   MySetHandshakeOptions;             {select flow control method}
   MyConfigureThePort;                {set baud rate and data format}
   MySendMessage;                     {send some bytes to the output driver}
   MyReceiveMessage;                  {read some bytes from the input driver}
   MyRestoreInputBuffer;              {restore the default input buffer}
   MyCloseSerialDriver;               {terminate I/O and close the drivers}
END.
```

Opening the Serial Driver

Because the Serial Driver uses separate device drivers for the input and output functions, you need to open both drivers for two-way communication. On Macintosh computers with two serial ports, you access the modem port through the `.AIn` and `.AOut` drivers, and the printer port through the `.BIn` and `.BOut` drivers.

On computers with a single serial port, such as the Macintosh PowerBook Duo models, the serial port can be used for either modem or printer connections. There is only one serial channel on these models, which you access through the `.AIn` and `.AOut` drivers.

You open the serial port drivers using the Device Manager `OpenDriver` or `PBOpen` functions. You should always open the output driver first because the Serial Driver initializes its local variables for both the input and output drivers when you open the output driver. Opening the output driver also installs interrupt handlers and allocates and locks buffer storage for both input and output.

When the Serial Driver receives an open request it first verifies that the serial port is available and correctly configured. If the port is unavailable or not configured, the Serial Driver returns the result code `portInUse` or `portNotCf`. Any other errors, such as attempting to open the `.BIn` or `.BOut` driver on a Macintosh with only one serial port, return the `openErr` result code.

When a device driver is opened successfully, the Device Manager returns a driver reference number, which you use to identify the driver in subsequent I/O requests. Although the reference numbers of the serial input and output drivers have remained constant for some time, you should not assume these values are fixed. Because future versions of the Operating System may assign other reference numbers to these drivers, your application should always use the reference numbers returned by the Device Manager.

Because of hardware differences between the serial ports in some Macintosh models, you should use the printer port for output-only connections to devices such as printers, at a maximum data rate of 9600 baud. The printer port is not recommended for two-way communication at data rates above 300 baud.

Note
If AppleTalk is active you cannot open the printer port for serial communication unless AppleTalk is using an alternate connection, such as EtherTalk or TokenTalk. ◆

Specifying an Alternate Input Buffer

An optional but recommended practice is to increase the size of the input driver's buffer. The default buffer size, 64 bytes, is not always sufficient for sustained transfers at data rates above 300 baud. A larger buffer will help avoid buffer overruns and consequent loss of data. You can specify a buffer size of up to 32 KB, but 1 to 2 KB is usually sufficient.

You use the `SerSetBuf` function to specify an alternate input buffer, and also to reset the default buffer. To ensure compatibility and avoid heap fragmentation you must reset the default buffer before closing the input driver.

Setting the Handshaking Options

The recommended method of setting handshaking options is to send a control request to the output driver, with a `csCode` value of 14. This is equivalent to using the `SerHShake` function, but allows you to select DTR handshaking. To specify the desired options, you pass the following data structure to the driver:

```
TYPE SerShk =
    PACKED RECORD
        fXOn: Byte;  {XON/XOFF output flow control enabled flag}
        fCTS: Byte;  {CTS hardware handshake enabled flag}
        xOn:  Char;  {XON character}
        xOff: Char;  (XOFF character}
        errs: Byte;  {error mask for input errs that cause abort}
        evts: Byte;  {mask for status changes that cause events}
        fInX: Byte;  {XON/XOFF input flow control flag}
        fDTR: Byte;  {DTR input flow control (for csCode=14 only)}
    END;
```

The Data Terminal Ready (DTR) signal is normally asserted when the Serial Driver is opened and negated when it is closed. You can change this behavior using one of several control routines described in the section "Low-Level Routines," beginning on page 7-27.

The fields of the `SerShk` data structure are described in the section "Serial Driver Reference," beginning on page 7-18.

Setting the Baud Rate and Data Format

When you open the Serial Driver it configures the selected port with default settings of 9600 baud, 8 data bits, no parity bit, and 2 stop bits. You can change these settings using the `SerReset` function, described on page 7-19.

Reading and Writing to the Serial Ports

Once you have configured the serial port, you can read and write data using the Device Manager `PBRead` and `PBWrite` functions. These functions can be called either synchronously or asynchronously, as described in the chapter "Device Manager" in this book.

Synchronous I/O Requests

When you make a synchronous request to a device driver, the Device Manager places your request at the end of the driver's I/O queue and does not return control to your application until the request completes. To avoid hanging, your application needs to take steps to ensure that a request will complete properly before calling the Device Manager.

For example, because the PBRead function requires you to specify the number of bytes to be read, you need to determine how many bytes are in the input driver's buffer before you call PBRead. You can use the SerGetBuf function to determine how many characters are in the input buffer, as shown in Listing 7-1.

If you try to read more bytes than are available in the input buffer, the driver waits until it receives enough characters to satisfy your request. If the external serial device does not send the required number of bytes, there is no way for your application regain control of the processor or terminate the read request.

Similarly, the PBWrite function will not complete until the specified number of bytes have been transmitted to the external serial device. If the external device is holding off transfers through hardware or software handshaking, the Device Manager will never return control to your application. You can use the SerStatus function, described on page 7-25, to query the status of the output driver and determine if output is suspended by handshaking.

For more information about how synchronous I/O requests are processed, see the chapter "Device Manager" in this book.

Asynchronous I/O Requests

Asynchronous execution allows your application to continue to process user input or perform other tasks while waiting for serial I/O requests to complete. To take full advantage of asynchronous operation you should supply a completion routine for the Device Manager to call when an asynchronous request completes. You should also implement a timer function to notify your application if a request is not satisfied within a reasonable period.

See the chapter "Device Manager" in this book for information about how asynchronous I/O requests are processed.

Closing the Serial Driver

Before closing the Serial Driver you must restore the default input buffer using the SerSetBuf function. After restoring the default buffer, you can terminate any pending I/O using the Device Manager KillIO function. Finally, you should close the input and output drivers using the Device Manager CloseDriver or PBClose functions.

Synchronous Clocking

Although the Serial Driver does not support synchronous communication protocols, it does allow you to select an external timing signal for synchronous clocking between the sender and receiver. You connect the external timing signal to the handshake input (HSKi) signal on pin 2 of the serial port, and select external clocking by sending a control request to the output driver with a `csCode` value of 16 and bit 6 set in the `csParam` field. See the section "Low-Level Routines," beginning on page 7-27, for more information.

Serial Driver Reference

This section describes the programming interface to the Serial Driver. This interface consists of the Serial Driver routines and the Device Manager functions for accessing them. The Serial Driver defines two data structures, the serial handshake record and the serial status record, which are described along with the routines that use these structures (the `SerHShake` and `SerStatus` functions, respectively).

Serial Driver Routines

You can use the Serial Driver routines to

- reset and configure the serial port device drivers
- set the size of the serial input buffer
- set handshaking options
- set or clear a break signal
- determine the number of characters in the input buffer
- get status information for a serial port

This section describes the control and status routines unique to the Serial Driver, as well the convenience routines for accessing them. Other Serial Driver functions, such as reading and writing, are accessed through the Device Manager. For information about the Device Manager functions for opening, closing, and communicating with device drivers, see the chapter "Device Manager" in this book.

IMPORTANT

The Serial Driver convenience routines described in this section are always executed synchronously when called using the high-level interface. To execute these functions asynchronously you must use the equivalent low-level Device Manager control or status call (`PBControlAsync` or `PBStatusAsync`). The `csCode` value for each routine is listed in the assembly-language information section of the routine description. ▲

SerReset

You can use the SerReset function to reset the serial port drivers and configure the port for a specified transmission rate and character frame.

```
FUNCTION SerReset (refNum: Integer; serConfig: Integer): OSErr;
```

refNum   The driver reference number of the serial output driver.

serConfig   A 16-bit value that specifies the configuration information.

DESCRIPTION

The SerReset function resets the output and input device drivers for the serial port, and also configures the port according to the format of the serConfig parameter shown in Figure 7-3.

Figure 7-3   The serConfig parameter format

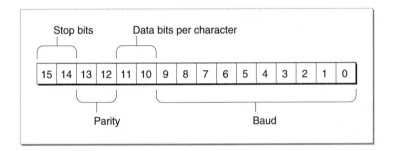

You can use the following constants to set the values of the bit fields in the serConfig parameter:

```
CONST
     baud300      = 380;     {300 baud}
     baud600      = 189;     {600 baud}
     baud1200     = 94;      {1200 baud}
     baud1800     = 62;      {1800 baud}
     baud2400     = 46;      {2400 baud}
     baud3600     = 30;      {3600 baud}
     baud4800     = 22;      {4800 baud}
     baud7200     = 14;      {9600 baud}
     baud9600     = 10;      {3600 baud}
     baud14400    = 6;       {14400 baud}
     baud19200    = 4;       {19200 baud}
```

```
baud28800    = 2;         {28800 baud}
baud38400    = 1;         {38400 baud}
baud57600    = 0;         {57600 baud}
stop10       = 16384;     {1 stop bit}
stop15       = -32768;    {1.5 stop bits}
stop20       = -16384;    {2 stop bits}
noParity     = 0;         {no parity}
oddParity    = 4096;      {odd parity}
evenParity   = 12288;     {even parity}
data5        = 0;         {5 data bits}
data6        = 2048;      {6 data bits}
data7        = 1024;      {7 data bits}
data8        = 3072;      {8 data bits}
```

For example, the default setting of 9600 baud, eight data bits, two stop bits, and no parity bit is equivalent to passing the following value in the serConfig parameter:

```
baud9600 + data8 + stop20 + noParity.
```

This value has a binary representation of 1100110000001010 and a hexadecimal representation of $CC0A.

ASSEMBLY-LANGUAGE INFORMATION

The SerReset function is equivalent to a Device Manager control request with a csCode value of 8. You pass the serConfig parameter in the csParam field (csParam[0] = serConfig).

RESULT CODES

noErr   0   No error

SerSetBuf

You can use the SerSetBuf function to increase the size of the serial input buffer, or to restore the driver's default buffer.

```
FUNCTION SerSetBuf (refNum: Integer; serBPtr: Ptr;
                    serBLen: Integer): OSErr
```

refNum   The driver reference number of the serial input driver.

serBPtr   A pointer to the new input buffer.

serBLen   The size of the new input buffer, or 0 to restore the default buffer.

DESCRIPTION

The `SerSetBuf` function replaces the input buffer for the specified input driver. The `serBPtr` parameter points to the buffer, and the `serBLen` parameter specifies the number of bytes in the buffer. The buffer must be locked while in use. Before closing the driver you must restore the default buffer by calling `SerSetBuf` with the `serBLen` parameter equal to 0.

ASSEMBLY-LANGUAGE INFORMATION

The `SerSetBuf` function is equivalent to a Device Manager control request with a `csCode` value of 9. You pass the `serBPtr` and `serBLen` parameters in the `csParam` field (`csParam[0] = serBPtr; csParam[4] = serBLen`).

RESULT CODE

noErr   0   No error

SerHShake

You can use the `SerHShake` function to set software handshaking options and other control information.

```
FUNCTION SerHShake (refNum: Integer; flags: SerShk): OSErr;
```

refNum   The driver reference number of the serial output driver.

flags   A pointer to a serial handshake record.

DESCRIPTION

The `SerHShake` function enables flow control, sets flow control characters, and specifies which conditions will cause input requests to be aborted.

Note that the `SerHShake` function has been superseded by a newer function that allows control over DTR handshaking. There is no high-level interface to the new function, you access it using a Device Manager control request with a `csCode` value of 14. This function uses the same `SerShk` data structure, but adds an additional field for DTR hardware flow control. See the section "Low-Level Routines," beginning on page 7-27, for a description of control routine 14.

The serial handshake record is defined by the `SerShk` data type:

```
TYPE SerShk =
PACKED RECORD
    fXOn:    Byte;      {XON/XOFF output flow control flag}
    fCTS:    Byte;      {CTS output flow control flag}
    xOn:     Char;      {XON character}
```

```
    xOff:      Char;      {XOFF character}
    errs:      Byte;      {mask for errors that will terminate input}
    evts:      Byte;      {mask for status changes that cause events}
    fInX:      Byte;      {XON/XOFF input flow control flag}
    fDTR:      Byte;      {DTR input flow control flag (csCode 14 only)}
END;
```

Field descriptions

fXOn   Set this byte to a non-zero value to enable XON/XOFF output flow
                control.

fCTS   Set this byte to a non-zero value to enable CTS output flow control.

xOn   If XON/OFF flow control is enabled, this field specifies the
                character to use for XON.

xOff   If XON/XOFF flow control is enabled, this field specifies the
                character to use for XOFF.

errs   Indicates which errors will cause input requests to be terminated,
                using the bit mask constants shown below.

evts   Indicates whether changes in the CTS signal or the break signal will
                cause the Serial Driver to post device driver events, using the bit
                mask constants shown below.

fInX   Set this byte to a non-zero value to enable XON/XOFF input flow
                control.

fDTR   Set this byte to a non-zero value to enable DTR input flow control.
                This field is only used by control function 14; it is ignored by the
                SerHShake function.

You can use the following constants as bit mask values for the errs field, to specify
which errors will cause input requests to be aborted. Because these are bit mask values,
you can sum them to specify more than one error condition.

```
CONST
    parityErr      = 16; {parity error}
    hwOverrunErr   = 32; {hardware overrun error}
    framingErr     = 64; {framing error}
```

You can use the following constants as bit mask values for the evts field, to specify
which status changes will cause the Serial Driver to post device driver events. Because
these are bit mask values, you can sum them to specify more than one event.

```
CONST
    ctsEvent    = 32;     {change in CTS signal}
    breakEvent  = 128;    {change in break signal}
```

▲ **WARNING**
Using device driver events is discouraged because interrupts are disabled during the event posting process, which may cause serial data to be lost or other events to be missed. Instead, you should use the `SerStatus` function to check the value of the `ctsHold` or `breakErr` flags in the serial status record. ▲

ASSEMBLY-LANGUAGE INFORMATION

The `SerHShake` function is equivalent to a Device Manager control request with a `csCode` value of 10. To specify DTR flow control, use a `csCode` value of 14 and set the `fDTR` flag to a non-zero value. You pass the `flags` parameter in the `csParam` field (`csParam[0] = flags`).

RESULT CODES

noErr   0   No error

SerSetBrk

You can use the `SerSetBrk` function to assert a break signal.

```
FUNCTION SerSetBrk (refNum: Integer): OSErr;
```

refNum   The driver reference number of the serial output driver.

DESCRIPTION

The `SerSetBrk` function forces the output data line into the space state. To form a break signal, the line must be left in this state longer than a character frame.

ASSEMBLY-LANGUAGE INFORMATION

The `SerSetBrk` function is equivalent to a Device Manager control request with a `csCode` value of 12.

RESULT CODES

noErr   0   No error

SerClrBrk

You can use the `SerClrBrk` function to deassert the break signal.

```
FUNCTION SerClrBrk (refNum: Integer): OSErr;
```

refNum   The driver reference number of the serial output driver.

DESCRIPTION

The `SerClrBrk` function restores the output driver to normal operation after asserting a break signal with the `SerSetBrk` function.

ASSEMBLY-LANGUAGE INFORMATION

The `SerClrBrk` function is equivalent to a Device Manager control request with a `csCode` value of 11.

RESULT CODES

noErr   0   No error

SerGetBuf

You can use the `SerGetBuf` function to determine the number of characters available in the driver's input buffer.

```
FUNCTION SerGetBuf (refNum: Integer; VAR count: LongInt): OSErr;
```

refNum   The driver reference number of the serial input driver.
count   On exit, the number of characters in the input buffer.

DESCRIPTION

The `SerGetBuf` function returns, in the `count` parameter, the number of characters present in the input buffer.

ASSEMBLY-LANGUAGE INFORMATION

The `SerGetBuf` function is equivalent to a Device Manager status request with a `csCode` value of 2. The `count` value is returned in `csParam` as a long word (`csParam[0]` = count).

RESULT CODES

noErr   0   No error

SerStatus

You can use the SerStatus function to obtain status information from the Serial Driver.

```
FUNCTION SerStatus (refNum: Integer; VAR serSta: SerStaRec):OSErr;
```

refNum   The driver reference number of the serial input or output driver.

serSta   A pointer to a serial status record.

DESCRIPTION

The SerStatus function returns status information for the specified input or output driver. This information includes error conditions, flow control status, and whether there are read or write operations pending. Because the serial status record is shared, the SerStatus function returns the same information whether you reference the input or output driver. The serial status record is defined by the SerStaRec data type:

```
TYPE SerStaRec =
PACKED RECORD
    cumErrs:    Byte;        {cumulative errors}
    xOffSent:   Byte;        {XOFF sent as input flow control}
    rdPend:     Byte;        {read pending flag}
    wrPend:     Byte;        {write pending flag}
    ctsHold:    Byte;        {CTS flow control hold flag}
    xOffHold:   Byte;        {XOFF flow control hold flag}
END;
```

Field descriptions

cumErrs   A bit field that indicates what errors have occurred since the last time the SerStatus function was called. You can use the bit mask constants shown below to test for particular errors. Errors detected include software overrun, break asserted, parity error, hardware overrun, and framing error.

xOffSent   A bit field that indicates if the driver has initiated input flow control by sending an XOFF character or negating the DTR signal. You can use the bit mask constants shown below to test for these conditions.

rdPend   This field contains a non-zero value if the driver has a read operation pending.

wrPend   This field contains a non-zero value if the driver has a write operation pending.

ctsHold   This field contains a non-zero value if the driver has suspended output due to the CTS handshake signal.

xOffHold   This field contains a non-zero value if the driver has suspended output due to receiving an XOFF character.

Serial Driver

You can use the following constants as bit mask values for the cumErrs field, to detect which errors have occurred since the last time the SerStatus function was called. Because these are bit mask values, you can sum them to specify more than one error condition. The remaining bit values in the cumErrs field are reserved.

```
CONST
    swOverrunErr    = 1;        {software overrun error}
    breakErr        = 8;        {break signal asserted}
    parityErr       = 16;       {parity error}
    hwOverrunErr    = 32;       {hardware overrun error}
    framingErr      = 64;       {framing error}
```

You can use the following constants as bit mask values to test the xOffSent field for the specified conditions. The remaining bit values in the xOffSent field are reserved.

```
CONST
    dtrNegated      = 64;       {DTR signal was negated}
    xOffWasSent     = 128;      {XOFF character was sent}
```

IMPORTANT

Calling SerStatus resets cumErrs and other fields of the serial status record, so repeated calls to SerStatus may not return identical results. ▲

ASSEMBLY-LANGUAGE INFORMATION

The SerStatus function is equivalent to a Device Manager status request with a csCode value of 8; the serial status record is returned in the first 6 bytes of the csParam field (csParam[0] = SerStaRec).

You can execute the status request immediately, bypassing the I/O queue, by setting bit 9 of the trap word. You can set this bit by appending the word IMMED as the second argument to the trap macro. For example:

```
_Status, IMMED
```

This technique is recommended when you need to determine the current status of a port before issuing a subsequent I/O request.

RESULT CODES

noErr   0   No error

Low-Level Routines

This section describes the low-level Serial Driver routines that you can call using the Device Manager control and status functions. These calls should be made to the output device driver—they affect the input driver as well.

Serial Driver Version   [status code 9]

csCode = 9   csParam = word

This status routine returns the version number of the Serial Driver in the `csParam` field. The version number is an integer value.

Set Baud Rate   [control code 13]

csCode = 13   csParam = word

This control routine provides an additional method (besides the `SerReset` function) of setting the baud rate. You specify the baud rate value as an integer in the `csParam` field (for example, 9600). The Serial Driver attempts to set the serial port to the specified baud rate, or the closest baud rate supported by the hardware. The actual baud rate selected is returned in the `csParam` field.

Set Handshaking Options   [control code 14]

csCode = 14   csParam = SerShk record

This control routine is identical to the `SerHShake` function (control code 10) with the additional specification of the `fDTR` flag in the eighth byte of the `SerShk` record. You enable DTR input flow control by setting this flag to a non-zero value. See the description of the `SerHShake` function on page 7-21 for information about the other fields of the `SerShk` record.

Set Miscellaneous Options   [control code 16]

csCode = 16   csParam = byte

This control routine sets miscellaneous control options. Bits 0-5 are reserved and should be set to 0 for compatibility with future options. Bit 6 enables external clocking through the CTS handshake line (the HSKi signal on pin 2 of the serial port). Set bit 6 to 1 to allow an external device to drive the serial data clock. Set bit 6 to 0 to restore internal clocking. Bit 7 controls the state of the DTR signal when the driver is closed. When bit 7 is 0 (the default) the DTR signal is automatically negated when the driver closes. Set bit 7 to 1 if you want the DTR signal to be left unchanged when the driver is closed. This can be used to prevent a modem from hanging up or a printer from going offline when the driver closes.

Assert DTR   [control code 17]

csCode = 17

This control routine asserts the DTR signal.

Negate DTR [control code 18]

csCode = 18

This control routine negates the DTR signal.

Simple Parity Error Replacement [control code 19]

csCode = 19   csParam = char

This control routine enables simple parity error replacement, in which incoming characters with parity errors are replaced by the ASCII character specified in csParam (for example, $FF). If a valid incoming character matches the replacement character, the most significant bit of the character is cleared. Therefore, if it is possible for your replacement character to appear in the data stream, you should use control code 20 instead. Set csParam to 0 to disable parity error replacement.

Extended Parity Error Replacement [control code 20]

csCode = 20   csParam[0] = char   csParam[1] = char

This control routine enables extended parity error replacement. Incoming characters with parity errors are replaced by the ASCII character specified in csParam[0]. The difference between this routine and the simple version (control code 19) is that if a valid incoming character matches the parity replacement character, it is replaced by the alternate character specified in csParam[1]. Set csParam[0] to 0 to disable parity error replacement.

Note
The ASCII NUL character ($00) can be used as the alternate character but not as the parity replacement. ◆

Set XOFF State [control code 21]

csCode = 21

This control routine unconditionally sets the xOffHold flag, which is equivalent to receiving an XOFF character. If software handshaking is enabled, data transmission is halted until an XON character is received, or until you clear the XOFF state using control code 22.

Clear XOFF State [control code 22]

csCode = 22

This control routine unconditionally clears the xOffHold flag, which is equivalent to receiving an XON character. If software handshaking is enabled, data transmission is resumed.

Send XON Conditional   [control code 23]

csCode = 23

This control routine sends an XON character for input flow control if the last input flow control character sent was XOFF.

Send XON Unconditional   [control code 24]

csCode = 24

This control routine unconditionally sends an XON character for input flow control, regardless of the current state of input flow control.

Send XOFF Conditional   [control code 25]

csCode = 25

This control routine sends an XOFF character for input flow control if the last input flow control character sent was XON.

Send XOFF Unconditional   [control code 26]

csCode = 26

This control routine unconditionally sends an XOFF character for input flow control, regardless of the current state of input flow control.

Serial Hardware Reset   [control code 27]

csCode = 27

This control routine resets the serial port hardware for a channel. Because this routine may leave the serial port in an unknown state, you must call the SerReset function before you use the port.

Summary of the Serial Driver

Pascal Summary

Constants

```
CONST
    {values for the transmission rate in the SerConfig parameter}
    baud300        = 380;        {300 baud}
    baud600        = 189;        {600 baud}
    baud1200       = 94;         {1200 baud}
    baud1800       = 62;         {1800 baud}
    baud2400       = 46;         {2400 baud}
    baud3600       = 30;         {3600 baud}
    baud4800       = 22;         {4800 baud}
    baud7200       = 14;         {7200 baud}
    baud9600       = 10;         {9600 baud}
    baud14400      = 6;          {14400 baud}
    baud19200      = 4;          {19200 baud}
    baud28800      = 2;          {28800 baud}
    baud38400      = 1;          {38400 baud}
    baud57600      = 0;          {57600 baud}

    {values for the number of stop bits in the SerConfig parameter}
    stop10         = 16384;      {1 stop bit}
    stop15         = -32768;     {1.5 stop bits}
    stop20         = -16384;     {2 stop bits}

    {values for the parity in the SerConfig parameter}
    noParity       = 0;          {no parity}
    oddParity      = 4096;       {odd parity}
    evenParity     = 12288;      {even parity}

    {values for the number of data bits in the SerConfig parameter}
    data5          = 0;          {5 data bits}
    data6          = 2048;       {6 data bits}
    data7          = 1024;       {7 data bits}
    data8          = 3072;       {8 data bits}
```

```
{bit mask values to test for indicated errors}
swOverrunErr   = 1;               {software overrun error}
breakErr       = 8;               {break occurred}
parityErr      = 16;              {parity error}
hwOverrunErr   = 32;              {hardware overrun error}
framingErr     = 64;              {framing error}

{bit mask values for the evts field in the SerShk record}
ctsEvent       = 32;              {CTS change}
breakEvent     = 128;             {break status change}

{bit mask value for the xOffHold field of the SerStaRec record}
dtrNegated     = 64;              {DTR signal was negated}
xOffWasSent    = 128;             {XOFF character was sent}
```

Data Types

```
TYPE
   SerShk =
   PACKED RECORD
      fXOn:    Byte;     {XON/XOFF output flow control flag}
      fCTS:    Byte;     {CTS output flow control flag}
      xOn:     Char;     {XON character}
      xOff:    Char;     {XOFF character}
      errs:    Byte;     {mask for errors that will terminate input}
      evts:    Byte;     {mask for status changes that cause events}
      fInX:    Byte;     {XON/XOFF input flow control flag}
      fDTR:    Byte;     {DTR input flow control flag (csCode 14 only)}
   END;

   SerStaRec =
   PACKED RECORD
      cumErrs:    Byte;     {cumulative errors}
      xOffSent:   Byte;     {XOFF sent as input flow control}
      rdPend:     Byte;     {read pending flag}
      wrPend:     Byte;     {write pending flag}
      ctsHold:    Byte;     {CTS flow control hold flag}
      xOffHold:   Byte;     {XOFF flow control hold flag}
   END;
```

Routines

```
FUNCTION SerReset            (refNum: Integer; serConfig: Integer): OSErr;
FUNCTION SerSetBuf           (refNum: Integer; serBPtr: Ptr;
                              serBLen: Integer): OSErr;
FUNCTION SerHShake           (refNum: Integer; flags: SerShk): OSErr;
FUNCTION SerSetBrk           (refNum: Integer): OSErr;
FUNCTION SerClrBrk           (refNum: Integer): OSErr;
FUNCTION SerGetBuf           (refNum: Integer; VAR count: LongInt): OSErr;
FUNCTION SerStatus           (refNum: Integer; VAR serSta: SerStaRec): OSErr;
```

C Summary

Constants

```
enum {
  /*values for the transmission rate in the SerConfig parameter*/
  baud300       = 380,      /*300 baud*/
  baud600       = 189,      /*600 baud*/
  baud1200      = 94,       /*1200 baud*/
  baud1800      = 62,       /*1800 baud*/
  baud2400      = 46,       /*2400 baud*/
  baud3600      = 30,       /*3600 baud*/
  baud4800      = 22,       /*4800 baud*/
  baud7200      = 14,       /*7200 baud*/
  baud9600      = 10,       /*9600 baud*/
  baud14400     = 6,        /*14400 baud*/
  baud19200     = 4,        /*19200 baud*/
  baud28800     = 2,        /*28800 baud*/
  baud38400     = 1,        /*38400 baud*/
  baud57600     = 0,        /*57600 baud*/

  /*values for the number of stop bits in the SerConfig parameter*/
  stop10        = 16384,    /*1 stop bit*/
  stop15        = -32768,   /*1.5 stop bits*/
  stop20        = -16384,   /*2 stop bits*/

  /*values for the parity in the SerConfig parameter*/
  noParity      = 0,        /*no parity*/
  oddParity     = 4096,     /*odd parity*/
  evenParity    = 12288,    /*even parity*/
```

```
/*values for the number of data bits in the SerConfig parameter*/
data5        = 0,          /*5 data bits*/
data6        = 2048,       /*6 data bits*/
data7        = 1024,       /*7 data bits*/
data8        = 3072,       /*8 data bits*/

/*bit mask values to test for indicated errors*/
swOverrunErr = 1,          /*software overrun error*/
breakErr     = 8,          /*break occurred*/
parityErr    = 16,         /*parity error*/
hwOverrunErr = 32,         /*hardware overrun error*/
framingErr   = 64,         /*framing error*/

/*bit mask values for the evts field in the SerShk record*/
ctsEvent     = 32,         /*CTS change*/
breakEvent   = 128,        /*break status change*/

/*bit mask value for the xOffHold field of the SerStaRec record*/
dtrNegated   = 64,         /*DTR signal was negated*/
xOffWasSent  = 128         /*XOFF character was sent*/
};
```

Data Types

```
struct SerShk {
    char          fXOn;    /*XON/XOFF output flow control flag*/
    char          fCTS;    /*CTS output flow control flag*/
    unsigned char xOn;     /*XON character*/
    unsigned char xOff;    /*XOFF character*/
    char          errs;    /*mask for errors that will terminate input*/
    char          evts;    /*mask for status changes that cause events*/
    char          fInX;    /*XON/XOFF input flow control flag*/
    char          fDTR;    /*DTR input flow control flag (csCode 14 only)*/
};
typedef struct SerShk SerShk;

struct SerStaRec {
    char    cumErrs;       /*cumulative errors*/
    char    xOffSent;      /*XOFF sent as input flow control*/
    char    rdPend;        /*read pending flag*/
    char    wrPend;        /*write pending flag*/
    char    ctsHold;       /*CTS flow control hold flag*/
```

```
    char     xOffHold;        /*XOFF flow control hold flag*/
};
typedef struct SerStaRec SerStaRec;
```

Functions

```
pascal OSErr SerReset        (short refNum, short serConfig);
pascal OSErr SerSetBuf       (short refNum, Ptr serBPtr, short serBLen);
pascal OSErr SerHShake       (short refNum, const SerShk *flags);
pascal OSErr SerSetBrk       (short refNum);
pascal OSErr SerClrBrk       (short refNum);
pascal OSErr SerGetBuf       (short refNum, long *count);
pascal OSErr SerStatus       (short refNum, SerStaRec *serSta);
```

Assembly-Language Summary

Data Structures

Serial Handshake Record

0	fXOn	byte	XON/XOFF output flow control flag
1	fCTS	byte	CTS output flow control flag
2	xOn	byte	XOn character
3	xOff	byte	XOff character
4	errs	byte	mask for errors that will terminate input
5	evts	byte	mask for status changes that cause events
6	fInX	byte	XON/XOFF input flow control flag
7	fDTR	byte	DTR input flow control flag (csCode 14 only)

Serial Status Record

0	cumErrs	byte	cumulative errors
1	xOffSent	byte	XOFF sent as input flow control
2	rdPend	byte	read pending flag
3	wrPend	byte	write pending flag
4	ctsHold	byte	CTS flow control hold flag
5	xOffHold	byte	XOFF flow control hold flag

Device Manager Interface

Status Routines

Code	Parameters	Function
2	long	Return the number of bytes currently in the input data buffer (SerGetBuf).
8	6 bytes	Return status information (SerStatus).
9	word	Return driver version number.

Control Routines

Code	Parameters	Function
8	word	Set data rate and character frame (SerReset).
9	long, word	Specify either a new input buffer or the default buffer (SerSetBuf).
10	8 bytes	Set software handshaking and other control information (SerHShake).
11		Deassert the break signal (SerClrBrk).
12		Assert the break signal (SerSetBrk).
13	word	Set baud rate.
14	8 bytes	Equivalent to control code 10, plus DTR handshaking.
16	byte	Set miscellaneous control options.
17		Assert DTR.
18		Negate DTR.
19	byte	Simple parity error replacement.
20	2 bytes	Extended parity error replacement.
21		Set XOFF state.
22		Clear XOFF state.
23		Send XON for input flow control if XOFF was sent last.
24		Unconditionally send XON for input flow control.
25		Send XOFF for input flow control if XON was sent last.
26		Unconditionally send XOFF for input flow control.
27		Reset serial hardware channel.

Result Codes

noErr	0	No error
openErr	−23	Unable to open device driver
portInUse	−97	Port is in use
portNotCf	−98	Port is not configured

Glossary

active ADB device The last ADB device to have sent data to the ADB Manager.

activity timer A timer maintained by the Power Manager that measures the time that has elapsed since the last relevant system activity.

ADB See **Apple Desktop Bus**.

ADB command A 1-byte value sent by the ADB Manager to devices on the ADB. The ADB command encodes the register the command refers to and the desired action the target device should perform.

ADB device Any input device connected to the ADB that conforms to requirements described in the *Apple Desktop Bus Specification*.

ADB device handler ID An 8-bit value that further identifies a specific ADB device type (such as the Apple Extended Keyboard) or its mode of operation (such as whether the keyboard differentiates between the right and left shift keys).

ADB device register One of four locations, identified as registers 0 through 3, that an ADB device uses to store data.

ADB device table A structure, located in the system heap, that contains information about all ADB devices attached to the computer.

ADB device table entry The part of the ADB device table that specifies for an ADB device its device handler ID, its default ADB address, its current ADB address, the address of its device handler, and the address of the area in RAM used for storage by the handler.

ADB Manager The part of the Macintosh Operating System that allows you to communicate with and get information about hardware devices attached to the Apple Desktop Bus (ADB).

ADB transaction A communication between the computer and an ADB device, consisting of a command sent by the computer, followed by a data packet sent either by the computer or the device.

address collision When more than one ADB device responds to commands sent to a particular address. See also **address resolution**.

address mapping The assignment of portions of the address space of the computer to specific devices.

address resolution When the ADB Manager reassigns addresses for ADB devices until they are all unique. See also **default ADB device address**.

address space A range of accessible memory. See also **address mapping**.

A5 world An area of memory in an application's partition that contains the QuickDraw global variables, the application global variables, the application parameters, and the jump table—all of which are accessed through the A5 register.

Apple Desktop Bus (ADB) A low-speed serial bus that connects input hardware devices to Macintosh computers and other equipment.

application program interface (API) The set of routines that applications and device drivers use to access services provided by system software.

arbitration phase The phase in which an initiator attempts to gain control of the SCSI bus.

asynchronous communication A method of data transmission in which the receiving and sending devices don't share a common timer and no timing data is transmitted.

asynchronous device driver A device driver that can begin processing a request and return control to the Device Manager before the request is complete. This type of driver typically uses hardware interrupts and callback routines to carry out background processing.

autosense A feature of SCSI Manager 4.3 that automatically sends a REQUEST SENSE command in response to a CHECK CONDITION status, and retrieves the sense data.

baud   A measure of the bit sampling rate of a serial communication device.

bit-bucketing   The practice of throwing away excess data when a SCSI target tries to supply more data than the initiator expects. Also includes sending meaningless data when a target requests more data than the initiator is prepared to supply. Both of these situations are abnormal and cause the SCSI Manager to return an error result code.

blind transfer   A Macintosh-specific method of transferring data between memory and the SCSI controller hardware, in which the SCSI Manager assumes that the SCSI controller (and the target device) can keep up with a specified transfer rate. Compare **polled transfer**.

block device   A device that reads or writes blocks of bytes as a group. Disk drives, for example, can read and write blocks of 512 bytes or more. See also **character device**.

board sResource   A unique sResource in an expansion card's declaration ROM that describes the card so that the Slot Manager can identify it. An expansion card can have only one board sResource. The board sResource entries include the card's identification number, board flags, vendor information, initialization code, and so on.

bus   A path along which information is transmitted electronically within a computer. Buses connect computer devices, such as processors, expansion cards, and memory.

bus free phase   The phase in which no device is actively using the SCSI bus.

bus interface   The electronics connecting the processor bus to the NuBus expansion interface in Macintosh computers.

byte lane   Any of 4 bytes that make up the 32-bit NuBus data width. NuBus expansion cards may use any or all of the byte lanes to communicate with each other or with the Macintosh computer.

card   See **expansion card**.

character device   A device that reads or writes a stream of characters, or bytes, one at a time. The keyboard and the serial ports are examples of character devices. See also **block device**.

close routine   A device driver routine that deactivates the driver and usually deallocates memory. All device drivers must implement a close routine.

collision detection   The ability of an ADB device to detect that another ADB device is transmitting data at the same time.

command descriptor block (CDB)   A data structure defined by the SCSI specification for communicating commands from an initiator to a target.

command phase   The phase in which a SCSI target requests a command from the initiator.

configuration ROM   See **declaration ROM**.

control routine   A device driver routine used to send control information. The function of the control routine is driver-specific. This routine is optional and need not be implemented.

data communication equipment (DCE)   Any device connected to the serial port, such as a modem or printer.

data phase   The phase in which data transfer takes place between a SCSI initiator and target.

data terminal equipment (DTE)   The initiator or controller of a serial data connection, typically the computer.

declaration ROM   A ROM on a NuBus expansion card that contains information identifying the card and its functions, and that may also contain code or other data. Proper configuration of the declaration ROM firmware will allow the card to communicate with the computer through the Slot Manager routines.

default ADB device address   A 4-bit bus address between $0 and $E that uniquely identifies the general type of ADB device (such as a mouse or keyboard).

device   A physical part of the Macintosh, or a piece of external equipment, that can exchange information with applications or with the Macintosh Operating System. Input devices transfer information into the Macintosh, while output devices receive information from the Macintosh. An I/O device can transfer information in either direction.

device control entry (DCE) A Device Manager data structure containing information about a device driver.

device driver A program that controls devices.

device handler A low-level routine that communicates with a particular ADB device.

Device Manager The part of the Macintosh Operating System that controls the exchange of information between applications and device drivers.

device package A type of code resource that responds to Chooser messages. The device package is responsible for communicating the user's choices to a device driver.

driver reference number A number that identifies each installed device driver. It is the one's complement of the driver's unit number.

expansion card A removable printed circuit card that plugs into a connector (slot) in the computer's expansion interface. Macintosh computers can use expansion cards designed for the NuBus expansion interface or for the processor-direct slot expansion interface. Expansion cards are also referred to as slot cards or simply as cards.

firmware Programs or data permanently stored in ROM.

Flush An ADB command to a device that forces it to remove any existing user-input data from the appropriate device register. See also **Listen**, **SendReset**, and **Talk**.

format block An element in the firmware structure of a declaration ROM that provides a standard entry point for other elements in the structure. The format block allows the Slot Manager to find the declaration ROM and validate it.

functional sResource An sResource in an expansion card's declaration ROM that describes a specific function of the card. For example, a video card may have separate functional sResources for all of the display modes it supports.

hicharge counter A counter in portable Macintosh computers that measures the time required to raise the battery voltage to 7.2 volts.

host bus adapter (HBA) The hardware that controls a SCSI bus.

idle state A power conservation state of portable Macintosh computers in which the processor slows from its normal clock speed to a 1 MHz clock speed. Also called the rest state. See also **power-saver state** and **sleep state**.

initiator device A device capable of initiating SCSI transactions.

interrupt service routine (ISR) A routine that processes interrupts generated by the processor, expansion cards, or external devices.

Listen An ADB command to a device that instructs it to prepare to receive additional data. See also **Flush**, **SendReset**, and **Talk**.

logical block An abstract location on a storage device, defined by software and independent of the physical characteristics of the device. See also **physical block**.

message phase The phase in which SCSI devices exchange message information.

minor slot space An Apple-specific term that describes the first megabyte of the 16 MB standard slot space.

NuBus expansion interface A 32-bit-wide synchronous, multislot expansion bus used for interfacing expansion cards to some Macintosh computers. See also **bus interface**, **NuBus slot**.

NuBus slot A connector on the NuBus expansion interface in a Macintosh computer, into which an expansion card can be installed.

open routine A device driver routine that allocates memory and initializes the driver's data structures. It may also initialize a hardware device or perform any other tasks necessary to make the driver operational. All drivers must implement an open routine.

partition A series of contiguous logical blocks on a storage device that have been allocated to a particular operating system, file system, or device driver.

physical block A fixed location on a storage device that is defined by the physical characteristics of the device. See also **logical block**.

polled transfer   A Macintosh-specific method of transferring data between memory and the SCSI controller hardware, in which the SCSI Manager senses the state of the internal registers of the SCSI controller to determine when the controller is ready to transfer another byte. Compare **blind transfer**.

polling   When the ADB Manager repeatedly sends each ADB device a Talk Register 0 command to see if it has new data to return.

portable Macintosh computer   Any Macintosh computer that can be battery powered.

power cycling   A method of entering the idle state in which power to the CPU is cycled on and off for increasing intervals, until some relevant system activity is detected.

Power Manager   The part of the Macintosh Operating System that controls power to the internal hardware devices of battery-powered Macintosh computers. The Power Manager also provides some service unique to portable Macintosh computers—such as reading the current CPU clock speed—that are not directly related to power control.

Power Manager IC   The 50753 microprocessor in the Macintosh Portable computer and some other portable Macintosh computers. The Power Manager IC (along with other circuits) controls power to the various subsystems of the computer. The power control functions may be handled by different hardware on other portable Macintosh computers.

power-saver state   A power conservation state of portable Macintosh computers in which the processor slows from its normal clock speed to some slower clock speed. On the PowerBook 180 computer, for example, the CPU clock speed can be reduced from 33 MHz to 16 MHz in order to conserve power. See also **idle state** and **sleep state**.

prime routine   A device driver routine that implements the input and output functions of the driver. This routine is optional and need not be implemented.

processor-direct slot (PDS)   An Apple-specific expansion interface architecture included in some Macintosh computers. It uses a single connector that allows an expansion card direct access to all of the microprocessor signals.

protocol   A standard set of rules for coordinating transmission between a sender and receiver.

reentrant device driver   A device driver that is capable of handling multiple requests simultaneously.

reselection phase   An optional phase in which a SCSI target device reconnects to the initiator.

rest state   See **idle state**.

scatter/gather list   A SCSI Manager 4.3 data type consisting of one or more elements, each of which describes the location and size of one data buffer.

SCSI (Small Computer System Interface)   An industry standard parallel data bus that provides a consistent method of connecting computers and peripheral devices.

SCSI bus   A bus that conforms to the physical and electrical specifications of the SCSI standard.

SCSI command   An instruction from an initiator to a target to conduct an operation, such as reading or writing a block of data. See also **command descriptor block, command phase**.

SCSI device   A device connected to the SCSI bus, either a peripheral device or a computer.

SCSI ID   An integer value from 0 to 7 that uniquely identifies a device during SCSI transactions.

SCSI interface module (SIM)   A software module between the transport (XPT) and the host bus adapter (HBA) in SCSI Manager 4.3. The SIM processes and executes SCSI requests, and provides a hardware-independent interface to the HBA.

SCSI Manager   The part of the Macintosh Operating System that controls the exchange of information between a Macintosh computer and peripheral devices connected through the Small Computer System Interface (SCSI).

SCSI message   Information exchanged by the target and initiator at the completion of a SCSI transaction. See also **message phase**.

selection phase   The phase in which a SCSI initiator selects the target device for a transaction.

SendReset   An ADB command that instructs all ADB devices to reset themselves to their startup states. See also **Flush**, **Listen**, and **Talk**.

Serial Driver   The part of the Macintosh Operating System that provides low-level support for asynchronous, interrupt-driven serial data transfers through the modem and printer ports.

service request signal (SRQ)   A signal sent by an ADB device to inform the ADB Manager that it has data to send.

sleep demand   A message from the Power Manager that informs a sleep procedure that the Power Manager is about to put the computer into the sleep state.

sleep procedure   A procedure that the Power Manager calls before it puts a portable Macintosh computer into the sleep state or returns it to the operating state. Sleep procedures are maintained in the sleep queue.

sleep procedure selector code   An integer passed (in register D0) to a sleep procedure that specifies whether the procedure is being called with a sleep request, a sleep demand, a wakeup demand, or a sleep-request revocation.

sleep queue   An operating-system queue that contains pointers to all currently installed sleep procedures.

sleep queue record   A data structure that contains information about a sleep procedure. Defined by the `SleepQRec` data type.

sleep request   A message from the Power Manager that informs a sleep procedure that the Power Manager would like to put the computer into the sleep state. The sleep procedure has the option of denying this request.

sleep-request revocation   A message from the Power Manager that informs a sleep procedure that the Power Manager has canceled a sleep request. The procedure can then reverse any changes it made in response to the sleep request.

sleep state   A power conservation state of portable Macintosh computers in which the Power Manager and the various device drivers shut off power or remove clocks from the computer's various subsystems, including the CPU, RAM, ROM, and I/O ports. See also **idle state** and **power-saver state**.

slot   1. A connector attached to the processor bus or the NuBus expansion interface. 2. A region in address space allocated to a physical slot.

slot ID   The hexadecimal digit corresponding to each card slot. For Macintosh computers with the NuBus expansion interface, each slot ID number is established by the main logic board of the computer and communicated to the card through the /IDx signals.

slot information record   A Slot Manager data structure containing information about a slot. If a card is installed, the slot information record contains the card's initialization status, a pointer to the sResource directory, and other information.

Slot Manager   The set of Macintosh Operating System routines that communicate with an expansion card's declaration ROM and allow applications to access expansion cards.

slot resource   See **sResource**.

slot resource table (SRT)   A private Slot Manager data structure that lists all of the sResource data structures currently available to the system. Applications and device drivers use Slot Manager routines to get information from the slot resource table.

slot space   The address space assigned to expansion cards in Macintosh computers. See also **standard slot space**, **super slot space**.

sResource   A data structure in the firmware of an expansion card's declaration ROM that defines a function or capability of the card. An sResource is also called a *slot resource*; the small *s* indicates a slot resource as opposed to the type of resource associated with the Resource Manager. There is one board sResource that identifies the card, and a functional sResource for each function a card can perform.

sResource directory   An element in a card's declaration ROM that lists all the sResources and provides an offset to each one.

sResource ID   A field in the sResource directory that identifies the type of sResource contained in or pointed to by the offset field.

SRQ   See **service request signal**.

standard device drivers   The device drivers built into the Macintosh ROM or Operating System.

standard slot space   The upper one-sixteenth of the total address space. These addresses are in the form $Fsxx xxxx, where s is a slot ID and x is any hexadecimal digit. This address space is geographically divided among the NuBus slots according to slot ID number. Compare **super slot space**.

status phase   The phase in which a SCSI target sends 1 byte of status information to the initiator.

status routine   A device driver routine used to return status information from a driver. The function of the status routine is driver-specific. This routine is optional and need not be implemented.

super slot space   The portion of memory in the range $9000 0000 through $EFFF FFFF. NuBus addresses of the form $sxxx xxxx address the super slot space that belongs to the card in slot s, where s is a slot ID and x is any hexadecimal digit. Compare **standard slot space**.

synchronous device driver   A device driver that completes each request before returning control to the Device Manager. This type of device driver has no provision for background processing.

Talk   An ADB command that requests a specific device to send the contents of a specific device register across the bus. See also **Flush**, **Listen**, and **SendReset**.

target device   A SCSI device that responds to commands from an initiator.

TIB instructions   Commands that control the SCSI Manager data transfer routines.

TIB pseudoprogram   A sequence of TIB instructions.

transfer instruction block (TIB)   A data structure used to pass instructions to the SCSI Manager data transfer routines.

transport (XPT)   The part of SCSI Manager 4.3 that accepts I/O requests and passes them to the appropriate SCSI interface module (SIM).

unit number   The position of a device driver's entry in the unit table. It is the one's complement of the driver reference number.

unit table   A Device Manager data structure containing an array of handles to the device control entries of all installed device drivers.

virtual bus   The grouping of SCSI devices on different buses into a single logical bus for compatibility with software that cannot address multiple buses.

virtual ID   The SCSI ID of a device on the virtual bus.

wakeup demand   A message from the Power Manager that informs a sleep procedure that it must reverse whatever steps it followed when it prepared for the sleep state.

wakeup timer   A timer that the Power Manager uses to return a portable Macintosh computer from the sleep state to the operating state at a specific time.

Index

This Apple manual was written, edited, and composed on a desktop publishing system using Apple Macintosh computers and FrameMaker software. Proof pages were created on an Apple LaserWriter Pro printer. Final page negatives were output directly from text files on an Optrotech SPrint 220 imagesetter. Line art was created using Adobe Illustrator™ and Adobe Photoshop™. PostScript™, the page-description language for the LaserWriter, was developed by Adobe Systems Incorporated.

Text type is Palatino® and display type is Helvetica®. Bullets are ITC Zapf Dingbats®. Some elements, such as program listings, are set in Apple Courier.

WRITERS
Mark Turner, Daphne Steck, Tim Monroe

LEAD WRITERS
Sharon Everson, Tony Francis

EDITORS
Wendy Krafft, Antonio Padial, George Truett

ART DIRECTOR
Bruce Lee

ILLUSTRATOR
Shawn Morningstar

PRODUCTION EDITOR
Gerri Gray

PROJECT LEADER
Patricia Eastman

COVER DESIGNER
Barbara Smyth

Special thanks to Clinton Bauder, Mark Baumwell, Cameron Birse, Paul Black, Lorraine Findlay, Jerry Katzung, Jim Mensch, Martin Minow, Craig Prouse, Mike Puckett, Gary Rensberger, Eric Shapiro, Paul Wolf, Bill Worzel, Colleen Zuffoletto

Acknowledgments to Marq Laube, Ray Valdès, Allen Watson

About Inside Macintosh

Inside Macintosh is a collection of books, organized by topic, that describe the system software of Macintosh computers. Together, these books provide the essential reference for programmers, designers, and engineers creating applications for the Macintosh family of computers.

Inside Macintosh: Overview

This book provides a general introduction to the Macintosh Operating System, the Macintosh Toolbox, and other system software services. It illustrates how to write a Macintosh application by gradually dissecting the source code of a sample application. The book also provides guidelines for writing software that is compatible with all supported Macintosh computers.

272 pages, ISBN 0-201-63247-0

Inside Macintosh: Macintosh Toolbox Essentials

This book describes how to implement essential user interface components in a Macintosh application. The Macintosh Toolbox is at the heart of the Macintosh, and every programmer creating a Macintosh application needs to be familiar with the material in this book. This book explains how to create menus; create windows, dialog boxes, and alerts boxes; create controls such as buttons and scroll bars; and create icons for an application and its documents. This book provides a complete technical reference for the Event Manager, Menu Manager, Window Manager, Control Manager, and Dialog Manager.

928 pages, ISBN 0-201-63243-8

Inside Macintosh: More Macintosh Toolbox

A companion to *Inside Macintosh: Macintosh Toolbox Essentials*, this book describes important features such as how to support copy and paste, provide Balloon Help, and create control panels. This book provides a complete technical reference to the Resource Manager, Scrap Manager, Help Manager, List Manager, Component Manager, Translation Manager, and Desktop Manager.

928 pages, ISBN 0-201-63299-3

Inside Macintosh: Imaging With QuickDraw

This book describes QuickDraw, the part of the Macintosh Toolbox that performs graphics operations, and the Printing Manager, which allows applications to print the images created with QuickDraw. This book explains how to create images, display them in black and white or color, and print them.

832 pages , ISBN 0-201-63242-X

Inside Macintosh: Text

This book describes how to create applications that can perform all kinds of text handling—from simple character display to complex, multi-language text processing. It provides a brief introduction to the unique Macintosh approach to text handling and shows how to draw characters, strings, and lines of text; how to work with fonts in any size, style, and language; how to use utility routines to format numbers, dates, and times; and how to use the WorldScript technology to design an application that handles text in any language.

1120 pages, ISBN 0-201-63298-5

Inside Macintosh: Files

This book describes the parts of the Macintosh Operating System that allow you to manage files and other objects in the file system. It describes how to create an application that can handle the commands typically found in the File menu. This books also provides a complete technical reference for the File Manager, the Standard File Package, the Alias Manager, the Disk Initialization Manager, and other file-related services provided by the system software.

544 pages, ISBN 0-201-63244-6

Inside Macintosh: Memory

This book describes the parts of the Macintosh Operating System that allow you to directly allocate, release, or otherwise manipulate memory. It shows how an application can manage the memory partition that it is allocated and perform other memory-related operations. This book also provides a complete technical reference for the Memory Manager, the Virtual Memory Manager, and other memory-related utilities provided by the system software.

312 pages, ISBN 0-201-63240-3

Inside Macintosh: Processes

This book describes the parts of the Macintosh Operating System that allow you to manage processes and tasks. It shows in detail how an application can manage processes and tasks and provides a complete technical reference for the Process Manager, the Notification Manager, the Time Manager, the Deferred Task Manager, and other task-related services provided by the system software.

208 pages, ISBN 0-201-63241-1

Inside Macintosh: Operating System Utilities

This book describes the parts of the Macintosh Operating System that allow you to manage low-level aspects of the Operating System. It describes how you can get information about the available software features, how to manage operating-system queues, get information about parameter RAM settings, and manipulate the trap dispatch tables. It also describes other utilities, such as mathematical and logical utilities; date, time, and measurement utilities; and the System Error Handler. This book provides a complete technical reference to the Gestalt Manager, Trap Manager, Start Manager, and Package Manager.

400 pages , ISBN 0-201-62270-X

Inside Macintosh: Devices

This book is a companion volume to both *Guide to Macintosh Family Hardware* and *Designing Cards and Drivers for the Macintosh Family*. It is written for anyone writing software that interacts with built-in and peripheral hardware devices and covers critical hardware and device programming topics including the Device Manager, SCSI Manager, Power Manager, ADB Manager, Serial Driver, and Slot Manager.

560 pages , ISBN 0-201-62271-8

Inside Macintosh: Interapplication Communication

This book explains how to create applications that work with other applications to give users even greater power and flexibility in accomplishing their tasks. It provides an introduction to how applications work together in a cooperative environment and discusses how they can share data with other applications, request information or services from other applications, and respond to scripts written in a scripting language. This book provides a complete technical reference to the Apple Event Manager, the AppleScript component, the Program-to-Program Communications Toolbox, and the Data Access Manager.

1008 pages, ISBN 0-201-62200-9

Inside Macintosh: Networking

This book describes key concepts of networking the Macintosh with other computers. It describes in detail the components and organization of AppleTalk, how to select an AppleTalk protocol, and how to write software that uses AppleTalk networking protocols.

592 pages, ISBN 0-201-62269-6

Inside Macintosh: QuickTime

This book describes how to create applications that can use QuickTime, Apple's system software extension that supports time-based data in the Macintosh desktop environment. Time-based data is any information that changes over time, such as sound, video, or animation. *Inside Macintosh: QuickTime* discusses how to manipulate time-based data in the same way that you work with text and graphic elements, and it describes how to use the Movie Toolbox to load, play, create, edit, and store objects that contain time-based data. It also explains how to use image compression and decompression to enhance the performance of QuickTime movies in an application.

736 pages, ISBN 0-201-62201-7

Inside Macintosh: QuickTime Components

This book is a companion to *Inside Macintosh: QuickTime*. It describes how you can use or develop QuickTime components such as clock components, image compressors, movie controllers, sequence grabbers, and video digitizers.

848 pages, ISBN 0-201-62202-5

Inside Macintosh: Sound

This book describes the parts of the Macintosh Toolbox that allow you to manipulate sound and speech. It shows how to use the Sound Manager, the Sound Input Manager, and the Speech Manager to create and record sounds, and to convert written text to speech.

432 pages , ISBN 0-201-62272-6

Inside Macintosh: AOCE Application Interfaces

This book describes the application interfaces to the Apple Open Collaboration Environment (AOCE), the technology behind the PowerTalk system software. This book is intended for anyone who wants to add mail services, messaging services, catalog services, digital signatures, or authentication services to their application. It also shows how to write templates that extend the Finder ability of display information in PowerTalk catalogs.

1,232 pages , ISBN 0-201-40848-1

Inside Macintosh: AOCE Service Access Modules

A companion book to *Inside Macintosh: AOCE Application Interfaces*, this book is required reading for anyone developing software modules that give users and PowerTalk-enabled applications access to a new or existing mail and messaging service or catalog service. It also describes how to provide an interface that lets a user install and set up the service.

400 pages , ISBN 0-201-40846-5

Inside Macintosh: PowerPC System Software

This book describes the new process execution environment and system software services provided with the first release of PowerPC processor-based Macintosh computers. It describes the 68LC040 Emulator, which allows existing 680x0 applications to execute unchanged on PowerPC processor-based Macintosh computers, as well as the Mixed Mode Manager, which handles switching between the PowerPC and 680x0 environments. It also documents the Code Fragment Manager and the Exception Manager.

224 pages, ISBN 0-201-40727-2

Inside Macintosh: PowerPC Numerics

This book describes the floating-point numerics provided with the first release of PowerPC processor-based Macintosh computers. It provides a description of the IEEE Standard 754 for floating-point arithmetic and shows how PowerPC Numerics complies with it. This book also shows how to create floating-point values and how to perform operations on floating-point values in high-level languages such as C and in PowerPC assembly language.

352 pages, ISBN 0-201-40728-0

Inside Macintosh QuickDraw GX Library

QuickDraw GX is the powerful new graphics architecture for the Macintosh that provides a unified approach to graphics and typography, and that gives programmers unprecedented flexibility and power in drawing and printing all kinds of shapes, images, and text. This extension to Macintosh system software is documented in a suite of books that are themselves an extension to the Inside Macintosh series. The Inside Macintosh QuickDraw GX Library contains volumes that are clear, concise, and organized by topic. They contain detailed explanations and abundant programming examples.

QuickDraw GX Programmer's Overview

This book provides an introduction to the QuickDraw GX development environment. It begins with an overview of QuickDraw GX and the key elements of QuickDraw GX programs and then moves on to illustrate these features using practical programming examples.

304 pages, ISBN 0-201-40847-3

Inside Macintosh: QuickDraw GX Objects

This book gets you started in understanding how to work with QuickDraw GX and how to create the objects that underlie all of its capabilities. It focuses on the object architecture as a whole, and how to use the objects that make up a QuickDraw GX shape: the shape object, the style object, the ink object, and the transform object.

656 pages, ISBN 0-201-40675-6

Inside Macintosh: QuickDraw GX Graphics

This book shows you how to create and manipulate the fundamental geometric shapes of QuickDraw GX to generate a vast range of graphic entities. It also shows you how to work with bitmaps and pictures, specialized QuickDraw GX graphic shapes.

672 pages, ISBN 0-201-40673-X

Inside Macintosh: QuickDraw GX Typography

This books shows you how to create and manipulate the three different types of text shapes supported by QuickDraw GX, and how to support sophisticated text layout, including text with mixed directions and multiple language text.

608 pages, ISBN 0-201-40679-9

Inside Macintosh: QuickDraw GX Printing

This book shows you how to support basic printing features including desktop printers, and how to use QuickDraw GX printing objects to customize printing and perform advanced printing-related tasks.

416 pages, ISBN 0-201-40677-2

Inside Macintosh: QuickDraw GX Printing Extensions and Drivers

This book shows you how to extend the printing capabilities of QuickDraw GX by creating a printing extension that can work with any application and any kind of printer. It also shows how to create a QuickDraw GX printer driver.

512 pages, ISBN 0-201-40678-0

Inside Macintosh: QuickDraw GX Environment and Utilities

This book shows you how to set up your program to use QuickDraw GX, how QuickDraw GX relates to the rest of the Macintosh environment, and how to handle errors and debug your code. It also describes a public data format for objects, and documents several managers that extend the object architecture and provide utility functions.

624 pages, ISBN 0-201-40676-4

Inside Macintosh

Book title	Information on
Inside Macintosh: Macintosh Toolbox Essentials	Control Manager; Dialog Manager; Event Manager; Finder Interface; Menu Manager; Window Manager
Inside Macintosh: More Macintosh Toolbox	Component Manager; Control Panels; Desktop Manager; Help Manager; Icon Utilities; List Manager; Resource Manager; Scrap Manager; Translation Manager
Inside Macintosh: Imaging With QuickDraw	Color QuickDraw; Cursor Utilities; Graphics Devices; Offscreen Graphics Worlds; Printing Manager; QuickDraw
Inside Macintosh: Text	Dictionary Manager; Font Manager; International Resources; Keyboard Resources; QuickDraw Text; Script Manager; TextEdit; Text Services Manager; Text Utilities; WorldScript Extensions
Inside Macintosh: Files	Alias Manager; Disk Initialization Manager; File Manager; Standard File Package
Inside Macintosh: Memory	Memory Management Utilities; Memory Manager; Virtual Memory Manager
Inside Macintosh: Processes	Deferred Task Manager; Notification Manager; Process Manager; Segment Manager; Shutdown Manager; Time Manager; Vertical Retrace Manager
Inside Macintosh: Operating System Utilities	Control Panel Extensions; Date, Time, and Measurement Utilities; Gestalt Manager; Mathematical and Logical Utilities; Package Manager; PRAM Utilities; Queue Utilities; Start Manager; System Error Handler; Trap Manager
Inside Macintosh: Devices	Apple Desktop Bus Manager; Device Manager; Power Manager; SCSI Manager; Serial Driver; Slot Manager
Inside Macintosh: Interapplication Communication	Apple Event Manager; AppleScript Component; Data Access Manager; Edition Manager; Program-to-Program Communications Toolbox
Inside Macintosh: Networking	AppleTalk Data Stream Protocol (ADSP); AppleTalk Filing Protocol (AFP); AppleTalk Session Protocol (ASP); AppleTalk Transaction Protocol (ATP); AppleTalk Utilities; Datagram Delivery Protocol (DDP); Ethernet, Token Ring, and FDDI Drivers; Link-Access Protocol (LAP) Manager; Name-Binding Protocol (NBP); Zone Information Protocol (ZIP)

Inside Macintosh (continued)

Book title	Information on
Inside Macintosh: QuickTime	Image Compression Manager; Movie Toolbox
Inside Macintosh: QuickTime Components	Clock Components; Derived Media Handler Components; Image Compressor Components; Movie Controller Components; Movie Data Exchange Components; Preview Components; Sequence Grabber Components; Standard Image-Compressor Dialog Components; Video Digitizer Components
Inside Macintosh: Sound	Sound Input Manager; Sound Manager; Speech Manager
Inside Macintosh: AOCE Application Interfaces	AOCE Utilities; Authentication Manager; Catalog Manager; Digital Signature Manager; Interprogram Messaging Manager; Standard Catalog Package; Standard Mail Package
Inside Macintosh: AOCE Service Access Modules	Catalog Service Access Modules; Messaging Service Access Modules
Inside Macintosh: QuickDraw GX Objects	Color Objects; Ink Objects; Shape Objects; Style Objects; Tag Objects; Transform Objects; View Objects
Inside Macintosh: QuickDraw GX Graphics	Bitmap Shapes; Geometric Operations; Geometric Shapes; Geometric Styles; Picture Shapes
Inside Macintosh: QuickDraw GX Typography	Fonts; Glyph Shapes; Layout Shapes; Text Shapes; Typographic Shapes; Typographic Styles
Inside Macintosh: QuickDraw GX Printing	Dialog Box Customization; Page Formatting; Printing
Inside Macintosh: QuickDraw GX Printing Extensions and Drivers	Printer Drivers; Printing Extensions; Printing Functions; Printing Messages; Printing Resources
Inside Macintosh: QuickDraw GX Environment and Utilities	Collection Manager; Debugging; Mathematical Functions; Memory Management; Message Manager; Stream Format
Inside Macintosh: PowerPC System Software	Code Fragment Manager; Exception Manager; Mixed Mode Manager
Inside Macintosh: PowerPC Numerics	Conversions; Environmental Controls; Numeric Operations and Functions